Clinton's
Grand Strategy

Clinton's Grand Strategy

US foreign policy in a post-Cold War world

JAMES D. BOYS

Bloomsbury Academic
An imprint of Bloomsbury Publishing Plc

B L O O M S B U R Y
LONDON • NEW DELHI • NEW YORK • SYDNEY

Bloomsbury Academic

An imprint of Bloomsbury Publishing Plc

50 Bedford Square
London
WC1B 3DP
UK

1385 Broadway
New York
NY 10018
USA

www.bloomsbury.com

**BLOOMSBURY and the Diana logo are trademarks of
Bloomsbury Publishing Plc**

First published 2015

British Library Cataloguing-in-Publication Data
A catalogue record for this book is available from the British Library.

ISBN: PB: 978-1-4725-2427-0
HB: 978-1-4725-3322-7
ePDF: 978-1-4725-2970-1
ePub: 978-1-4725-3130-8

Library of Congress Cataloging-in-Publication Data
A catalog record for this book is available from the Library of Congress.

Typeset by Newgen Knowledge Works (P) Ltd., Chennai, India
Printed and bound in Great Britain

For my wife and inspiration,
Dr Carly Beckerman-Boys

CONTENTS

ACKNOWLEDGMENTS

This work is part of an ongoing research project into the Clinton administration that has so far spanned over two decades. My continuing work has brought me into contact with many former members of the Clinton administration, including the former president and vice president, providing insights and perspectives that have contributed directly to my writings and which continue to drive me into new areas of research. Several members of the Clinton administration were very generous with their time, and contributed greatly to this project; for this, they have my sincere thanks. This is particularly true in regard to Anthony Lake, Nancy Soderberg, Morton Halperin, Charles A. Kupchan, Leon Fuerth, as well as Robert Reich and Sidney Blumenthal. Thanks also to Stephen A. Smith, Clinton's Chief of Staff from his days as Governor of Arkansas, and his wife Lindsley, who provided a fascinating insight into President Clinton's formative years.

I am grateful for the assistance this project has received from so many in the international academic community: Thanks to my mentors on the journey to this point: Professor Scott Lucas of the University of Birmingham, Professor Robert McGeehan of the Institute of United States Studies, and David Waller of the University of Northampton. Thanks also to Dr Ian Jackson, formerly of De Montfort University, Professor Rob Singh of Birkbeck College, Professor Bruce Hoffman of Georgetown University, and Professor Gregory S. Gordon of the University of North Dakota for arranging my Visiting Fellowship in 2010. Thanks also to Professor John Dumbrell and Professor Philip Davies for their early career encouragement that led to teaching at the University of Leicester and De Montfort University, respectively. I particularly appreciate the assistance this project received from Richmond, The American International University in London.

I am very grateful for the many wonderful students that I have encountered over the years at a host of universities, particularly in my US Grand Strategy class, whose enthusiasm for this project has been most heartfelt. Seeing many of them graduate and achieve their ambitions, including working on Capitol Hill and at the White House, has been particularly gratifying. I am also most grateful to Professor Rory Miller for the pivotal role he played in securing my Visiting Senior Research Fellowship at King's College, London.

I am grateful to the editors of several journals who have been supportive of my work and have seen fit to publish my research, much of which has fed directly or indirectly into this publication. Thanks in particular to Dr Jenel Virden, co-editor of the *European Journal of American Studies*, Professor Brian Gaines, editor of *American Politics Research*, and Dr Oz Hassan and Professor Jason Ralph, guest editors of the *International Journal of Human Rights*.

I am indebted to the kind support shown for this project by Sir Malcolm Rifkind, MP, who took time from his busy schedule as Chairman of the Intelligence and Security Committee to share his recollections of the Clinton administration from his time as UK Foreign Secretary and Defence Secretary under Prime Minister John Major. Thanks also to the members of the House of Commons' Foreign Affairs Committee, particularly its Chairman, Sir Richard Ottaway MP, Rory Stewart MP, and Frank Roy MP for inviting me before their 2013 hearings on UK Government Foreign Policy Towards the United States, and for incorporating my findings into their final report.

Thanks also to the Cambridge Union and to Chatham House for their gracious invitations to speak on my research and related material. My thanks also for the support and encouragement this project has received from my friends and contacts at Sky News, the BBC, Al Jazeera English, and Monocle 24. I am particularly grateful to J. F. O. McAllister for his recollections as White House Correspondent at *Time*.

At Bloomsbury, my great thanks to Caroline Wintersgill for her faith in this project and for shepherding it through all stages of its development, as well as to her colleagues, Mark Richardson and Jyoti Basuita.

On a personal note, many thanks for the help, encouragement, and support I have received from my many friends, particularly Robert and Nicki Bannister, Chris Capece, Stuart, and Jayne Bannister and Rob Jones. I am particularly grateful to my parents, Roger and Pauleen, without whose initial support none of this would have been possible. Thanks also to lifelong family friends Chris and Liz Roper and to my in-laws, Jonathon and Carol, for their support and encouragement these years.

Finally, and most importantly, thanks to my wonderful wife, Carly, whose devotion and support were instrumental in ensuring that this project not only saw the light of day, but was also able to be completed on schedule. She has my eternal thanks and I gladly dedicate this endeavor to her.

ABBREVIATIONS

NSSUS91:	The National Security Strategy of the United States (1991)
NSSR94:	A National Security Strategy of Engagement and Enlargement (1994)
NSSR95:	A National Security Strategy of Engagement and Enlargement (1995)
NSSR96:	A National Security Strategy of Engagement and Enlargement (1996)
NSSR97:	A National Security Strategy For A New Century (1997)
NSSR98:	A National Security Strategy For A New Century (1998)
NSSR99:	A National Security Strategy For A New Century (1999)
NSSR2000:	A National Security Strategy For A Global Age (2000)
PDD:	Presidential Decision Directive
PRD:	Presidential Review Directive
PPPGB:	Public Papers of the President of the United States, George Bush
PPPGWB:	Public Papers of the President of the United States, George W. Bush
PPPJFK:	Public Papers of the President of the United States, John F. Kennedy
PPPRR:	Public Papers of the President of the United States, Ronald Reagan
PPPWJC:	Public Papers of the President of the United States, William J. Clinton
USGPO:	United States Government Printing Office

INTRODUCTION

The view from
the twenty-first century

Why study the Clinton administration and its grand strategy initiative? In the years since it left office, tumultuous events have occurred that suggest its time in power belongs in a previous era. The attacks of September 11 (9/11), wars in Iraq and Afghanistan, as well as domestic clashes over healthcare and the economy raise doubts about the continued relevance of Clinton's time in office and imply that if the end of the Cold War marked *The End of History*, then perhaps 9/11 constituted its recommencement. Those who lament President Clinton's apparent disengagement with foreign affairs and the supposed absence of a discernable Clinton Doctrine exacerbate this sentiment. In their view, there is all too little to study and too few reasons to do so, except perhaps as a cautionary tale. Such views, however, are fundamentally flawed.

Bill Clinton had a natural inclination toward domestic politics, but this did not mean he was disinterested in world affairs. He attended Georgetown University's School of Foreign Service, served on the staff of Senator Fulbright, Chair of the Senate Foreign Relations Committee, and studied at Oxford University as a Rhodes Scholar. These are not the actions of someone disinterested in the outside world. However, notwithstanding his education, Bill Clinton's tenure as governor of Arkansas and requisite focus on domestic affairs left him vulnerable to the charge of being unqualified to preside over a challenging period in global history following the end of the Cold War.

The Clinton administration came to power as the global environment became less stable and more dangerous and was forced to address a new geopolitical environment "with no rules and no patterns."[1] Communism's collapse heralded not an era of peace, but a time of uncertainty, as President

Clinton sought to "find a role for an America that [could] neither dominate nor retreat."[2] The administration's external challenges were compounded by internal struggles, as its efforts to devise a grand strategy were hindered by bureaucratic sensibilities, personal rivalries, and intense partisanship in Washington, DC. Despite these difficulties, the Clinton administration produced a series of strategic documents in line with congressional requirements that revealed the continuing intent behind its grand strategy. Issues of globalization, international trade, the rise of China, and the emergence of the European Union were all addressed as the administration recalibrated the US global role in the aftermath of the Cold War.

This book considers the development of policy on the Clinton presidential campaign and the manner in which this was enacted in office as US Grand Strategy between January 1993 and January 2001. It addresses the development of Clinton's Grand Strategy and the manner in which this was influenced by the individuals who devised it and the events that helped to shape it. This, therefore, is not a book driven by events, or an attempt to chronicle every foreign policy decision taken by the Clinton administration; those seeking a strict chronological account of Clinton's foreign policy initiatives must look elsewhere. Neither is this an attempt to contort the administration's policies into an abstract theoretical framework, nor arcane conceptual constructs. It is, instead, a political history of the effort to devise and implement US Grand Strategy in the post-Cold War world and of the individuals responsible for this. This book provides an insight into the previously underappreciated coherence that underpinned US Grand Strategy in the 1990s; what it was, how it worked, what and who drove it, and what it sought to achieve. This book addresses a number of key areas: first, the administration's commitment to a series of key principles that were extolled on the campaign trail and implemented in office; secondly, the importance of personality and bureaucratic sensibilities in the formulation of policy; finally, it notes that regardless of well-intended ideas, global events have a habit of making a mockery of well-laid plans.

This book draws extensively on primary material, including speeches by the principals, National Security Strategy Reports, documentation from the National Security Council, Presidential Decision Directives, Presidential Review Documents, as well as newly declassified materials from the Clinton Presidential Library. Interviews with senior members of the administration have been conducted, revealing the development and implementation of policy from deep within the West Wing of the Clinton White House. These new commentaries provide an insight into the nature of the interpersonal politics of the Clinton White House, as former members of the administration reflect not only on the policy they devised, but also on the reaction to it and the manner in which it was implemented.

This book focuses on "declaratory" grand strategy, using the National Security Strategy documents as both a guide to analyze policy, and a structural device through which to consider the emerging policies. At the heart of this book is President Clinton's replacement of Containment with the grand strategy of Engagement and Enlargement. This was based on three elements first espoused on the campaign trail in December 1991, which sought to "tear down the wall in . . . thinking between domestic and foreign policy."[3] These were enhanced security, prosperity promotion, and democracy promotion. There was an important and overlooked link between these elements that remained in place throughout Clinton's presidency: by stressing the need to enhance US national security, the administration sought to prove that Democrats could be trusted with security issues, reduce global tensions and as a result, cut the defense budget; the promotion of prosperity sought increased exports to new overseas markets, higher wages, lower unemployment, and rising confidence on Wall Street, all vital for a successful 1996 reelection campaign; finally, democracy promotion ensured the United States would "stand up for democracy," promised open markets, and reduced global tension, building on the benefits of the first two initiatives.[4] This trinity embraced and advanced American values and deliberately combined foreign and domestic initiatives to utilize the strengths and reduce the perceived weakness of President Clinton in the international arena.

These issues will be examined sequentially in the following chapters. Chapter one addresses the tensions between the development of foreign and domestic policy on Clinton's 1992 campaign and the challenges that this caused once in office. The chapter addresses the process of developing strategy in a campaign setting and the role it played during the debates. The chapter analyzes the individuals who advised Governor Clinton during the campaign and the role they played in preparing him for power. The chapter examines Clinton's campaign speeches on foreign affairs and dissects their importance and meaning, both domestically and internationally, as foreign governments began to take note of what the candidate said on the future direction of US Grand Strategy.

Having considered the development of policy on the campaign trail, chapter two addresses the first months of the Clinton administration as it came to power, sought to adjust to its newfound role, and was seen to flounder in its initial steps on the world stage. President George H. W. Bush had spoken of a New World Order; however, the world he bequeathed Bill Clinton was best characterized by its total lack of order, as the authority of the United States was tested in ways that could not have been imagined only 4 years previously. The chapter analyzes President Clinton's first foreign policy speeches to discern the new directions to be adopted and the structural alterations that the Clinton administration introduced.

Chapter three considers the various approaches to grand strategy that emerged during 1993 and 1994. The chapter considers the individuals responsible for their development, their personal focus, and the speeches that shaped policy. The eventual grand strategy of Engagement and Enlargement was drawn from Bill Clinton's campaign speeches, the ambitions of his advisers, and done so, partly, to maximize Clinton's economic interests and reduce focus on his lack of foreign policy experience. The chapter considers the extent to which the Clinton administration redefined US Grand Strategy in a manner that recognized that a new era was beginning, just as an old one was ending.

With a new grand strategy having been devised, the following three chapters assess its core pillars and consider their implementation: chapter four addresses the national security component of grand strategy and the extent to which events in Somalia and Rwanda impacted the administration as the realities of power encroached upon the theoretical construct of policy. The chapter also addresses the decision to expand NATO and the importance of this to Clinton's Grand Strategy.

Chapter five considers the decision to place prosperity promotion at the heart of grand strategy. The chapter addresses the concept's implications as the administration steered the nation out of recession and into the longest period of sustained growth in the twentieth century. The policy depended, in part, on access to sensitive data and, therefore, the chapter addresses the use of the CIA to assist American business and thereby bolster the economy. The chapter addresses the decision to support Mexico during the Peso crisis and the administration's structural alterations to the executive branch, including the creation of the National Economic Council (NEC). The chapter demonstrates the domestic implications of policy, as efforts to open foreign markets to US goods and services led to a need for more American jobs to feed the growing international appetite, resulting in a decline in unemployment figures and a booming economy.

Chapter six addresses the most contentious element of Clinton's Grand Strategy: democracy promotion. The chapter examines the administration's dedication to the policy, the bureaucratic clashes that threatened its implementation, and the degree to which it was accomplished. The chapter considers the extent to which this policy was a step too far for key members of the administration and how this influenced the degree to which it was implemented. The chapter addresses the implications of this policy on global regions and how the war in Bosnia became a focal point for US diplomatic efforts.

Having addressed the evolution and execution of Clinton's Grand Strategy, chapter seven considers its overall impact and implications. The chapter considers the fact that while America was certainly engaged abroad, few Americans had any idea with whom the nation was engaged, nor why it was so engaged, with the world apparently at peace. The chapter notes that the Clinton administration brought 8 years of stability and economic growth that was accompanied by a lack of clear sense of mission or national reason. At the time this seemed unimportant, but in retrospect it is clear that it was a harbinger for tough times ahead and that perhaps too little was done to prepare a populace for the brewing storms that waited in the twenty-first century.

This book directly challenges the claim by John Lewis Gaddis that there was "an absence of any grand design," or that there was "a kind of incrementalism and *ad-hocism* to things" and, instead, reveals a hitherto unexplored continuity of core policies from October 1991 to January 2001.[5] These policies must be examined, and the relationship between them understood, to appreciate the true nature of US Grand Strategy in the 1990s. Too little consideration has so far been paid to the interconnectivity of Clinton's policy initiatives, which redefined the direction of US Grand Strategy in the 1990s. Instead, critics have lamented a decade of lost opportunities and confused initiatives, during which the United States allegedly lacked purpose and direction.[6] This has been exacerbated by an inability of former administration officials to explain their grand strategy initiative adequately in their memoirs. Accordingly, studies of the Clinton administration to date have failed to consider the evolution of policy and the impact of events on its formulation, ensuring that Clinton's efforts remain misunderstood and their lasting impact underappreciated.[7]

By covering the entire duration of Clinton's presidential odyssey, from his 1991 Announcement Speech to his final day in office, this work covers the evolution of policy on the 1992 campaign, the staffing of foreign policy posts during the transition, and the manner in which events influenced the evolution of policy and how the evolution of policy impacted events. Through it all, the roles played by key individuals are considered to provide a telling insight into the implementation of US Grand Strategy under President Clinton.

The Clinton administration devised US Grand Strategy for the post-Cold War world that moved beyond a preponderance of power, to embrace ideas that were both radical and yet quintessentially American; that ethics should count in foreign policy; and that how other nations ruled their own people should matter to the United States. It placed the free movement of people, capital, and ideas at the heart of foreign policy and sought to lock the United States into an ever-increasing number of global entities. The Clinton administration's grand strategy was the tale of years of toil and planning that did not necessarily develop as expected, but which made for a fascinating spectacle, whose legacy continues to impact the world many years after leaving office.

Notes

1 Author's interview with Leon Fuerth (National Security Adviser to Vice-President Gore, 1993–2001), George Washington University, Washington, DC, June 8, 2004.

2 Henry Kissinger, "Clinton and the World," *Newsweek* 121, no. 5 (February 1, 1993), p. 45.

3 William J. Clinton, "A New Covenant for American Security," speech at Georgetown University, Washington, DC, December 12, 1991, in Stephen A. Smith (ed.), *Preface to the Presidency: Selected Speeches of Bill Clinton 1974–1992* (Fayetteville, AR: University of Arkansas Press, 1996), p. 113.

4 William J. Clinton, "Strategic Security in a Changing World," speech at the Los Angeles World Affairs Council, California, August 13, 1992, in Smith (ed.), *Preface to the Presidency*, p. 271.

5 John Lewis Gaddis, quoted in John F. Harris, "Despite 'Lessons,' Clinton Still Seen Lacking Strategy," *Washington Post*, March 27, 1999, p. A15.

6 For critical analysis of the Clinton administration's foreign policy initiatives, see William G. Hyland, *Clinton's World: Remaking American Foreign Policy* (Westport, CT: Praeger Publishers, 1999); Linda B. Miller, "The Clinton Years: Reinventing Foreign Policy," *International Affairs* 70 (October 1994), pp. 621–634; Michael Mandelbaum, "Foreign Policy as Social Work," *Foreign Affairs* 75, no. 1 (January–February 1996), pp. 16–32; Joshua Muravchik, "Carrying a Small Stick," *National Review* (September 2, 1996), pp. 57–62; William G. Hyland, "A Mediocre Record," *Foreign Policy* 101 (Winter 1995–1996), pp. 69–74; Richard H. Ullman, "A Late Recovery," *Foreign Policy* 101 (Winter 1995–1996), pp. 75–79.

7 All too few scholars have attempted to address a broad analysis of the Clinton administration's foreign engagements to date. Rare exceptions include John Dumbrell, *Clinton's Foreign Policy: Between the Bushes, 1992–2000* (Abingdon, Oxon: Routledge, 2009) and Richard Sale, *Clinton's Secret Wars: The Evolution of a Commander in Chief* (New York: St. Martin's Press, 2009).

CHAPTER ONE

The long road from Little Rock

Before he could enact US Grand Strategy for the post-Cold War world, Bill Clinton had to win the presidency, a tall order considering his background as the governor of a poor state and George Bush's historic approval ratings following the Gulf War. Clinton secured victory, in part, by turning the 1992 election into a referendum on the state of the US economy, with his campaign being remembered for the expression, "It's the economy, stupid," which captured the importance of economic issues for the candidate.[1] However, while Clinton focused on domestic issues, international considerations were addressed on the campaign as a series of foreign policy positions were developed that both helped and hindered Bill Clinton following his election as president. The challenge for the Clinton team was how to address global issues on a domestically focused campaign, and prepare their candidate to serve as commander-in-chief. The 1992 campaign served as a training ground for power, during which Bill Clinton developed the skills and accrued much of the knowledge required to serve as president. The campaign revealed much about Bill Clinton's ability to withstand media attention, his decision-making processes, his choice of advisers, and the issues he chose to address. Through a consideration of campaign speeches and the contribution of key advisers, it is possible to discern the evolution of the candidate and his grand strategy on the long road from Little Rock to the White House.

Grand strategy in principle and history

Bill Clinton's presidential campaign team members were not the first to consider concepts of grand strategy, nor were they the first to struggle with its definitions or implementation. Indeed, the very expression is open to varying interpretation, causing Sir Lawrence Freedman to refer to the "developing muddle in use of this fundamental term."[2] Concepts of strategy, grand or otherwise, have evolved over the millennia from a deliberation of military might to a wide-ranging consideration of national power and its use to advance national interests. From Sun Tzu and Clausewitz to Gaddis and Kennedy, grand strategy has been considered and differing elements emphasized, as strategists sought to define the term for their times.[3] As Freedman cautions, the word "strategy" originates from the Greek word *strategos*, translated as "the art of the general."[4] It is apt, therefore, that a seemingly problematic contradiction must be addressed—grand strategies must be specific enough to identify a series of criteria, yet be fluid enough to adapt to changing circumstances as well as interpretation. The production of a grand strategy document poses several challenges, not least of which is the fact that it may quickly be rendered irrelevant by global events.

Today's approach to grand strategy, indeed its very definition, has evolved from a narrow focus on military methodology and now seeks to chart the manner in which the full resources of a nation (economic, diplomatic, social, political, military, even cultural) may be operationalized to advance the national interest. This is a profound shift from Sun Tzu's focus on the military and use of "extraordinary and the normal forces," or Clausewitz's attention to "the use of engagements for the object of war."[5] Reflecting on the career of General Grant, J. F. C. Fuller used the term in a broader context, defining it as "the national fabric upon which the war picture . . . is woven [which necessitated] directing all warlike resources towards the winning of the war."[6] Given the times during which these definitions were devised, it is perhaps unsurprising that many adopt a militaristic nature, a practice that continued throughout much of the twentieth century.

The total mobilization required during the Second World War and the accompanying writings of Edward Mead Earle and Sir Basil Liddell Hart both broadened the meaning of grand strategy and took the concept to a broader audience. Writing in 1943, Earle argued that drawing together aspects of national power to achieve an important objective was no less imperative in peacetime than in war.[7] In *Strategy*, Liddell Hart established a definition of grand strategy as a mechanism to "co-ordinate and direct all the resources of a nation, or band of nations, towards the attainment of the political object of the war." Liddell Hart's definition of grand strategy as being "the art of distributing and applying military means to fulfil ends of policy" may have been apt for the interwar period, but became less relevant with the end of the Cold War. His distinction between nations at war and those that were not, as well as the state-centric focus of his work also reduce its relevance in the current era of multipolarity and non-state actors. He did, however, warn of the potential costs of victory, in a message that predated President Eisenhower's renowned Farewell Address by several years: Grand strategy, he warned, "should not only combine the various instruments [of statecraft], but also regulate their use as to avoid damage to the future state of peace."[8] Liddell Hart also offered a glimpse of a more Clintonesque approach, suggesting that grand strategy should "calculate and develop the economic resources and manpower of nations in order to sustain the fighting services."[9] The blending of national security with economics was of particular interest to Governor Clinton and found its way into administration policy in the 1990s.

As the Cold War ended, Paul Kennedy observed that "the crux of grand strategy lies therefore in policy, that is, in the capacity of the nation's leaders to bring together all of the elements, both military and non-military, for the preservation and enhancement of the nation's long-term (i.e., in wartime and peacetime) best interests."[10] Kennedy's prescription, of military and nonmilitary elements, was seized upon by the Clinton campaign as it sought to erase distinctions between foreign and domestic policy in the post-Cold War era.

Following the attacks of September 2001, former presidential candidate Senator Gary Hart defined grand strategy as being, "a coherent framework of purpose and direction in which random and not so random events can be interpreted, given meaning and then responded to as required."[11] More recently, Stephen D. Krasner defined grand strategy as "a conceptual framing that describes how the world is, envisions how it ought to be, and specifies a set of policies that can achieve that ordering." Unsurprisingly, perhaps, given the complexities involved, Krasner concedes that such efforts rarely succeed, since "it is hard to align vision, policies, and resources."[12] Clearly, therefore, the concept of grand strategy has developed to a point where it must now accommodate the modern era's geopolitical reality; that nations remain on high alert without being at war and utilize all resources to advance their national interest.

The current requirement for a US Grand Strategy document has its origins in the 1986 Goldwater-Nichols Department of Defense Reorganization Act (codified in 50 USC 404a), which mandated that administrations provide an annual account of foreign policies and ambitions. The congressionally mandated report is designed to reveal the approach adopted by an administration in pursuit of its broader aspirations. However, the necessity to commit grand strategy to paper has several drawbacks: first, it sets strategy in stone, despite the need to react rapidly in a highly fluid international system.[13] Secondly, it telegraphs national intent that may be undermined by international rivals. This ensures that grand strategy is positively reactive; designed to address a dynamic international system, within which competitors (and allies) are constantly seeking to advance their own national interests. However, partly because of this legislation, modern definitions of grand strategy may now legitimately consider the role of presidential doctrines and national security strategies, a central element of this book.[14]

John Lewis Gaddis insists that the production of grand strategy documents is "an ecological discipline, in that it requires the ability to see how all of the parts of a problem relate to one another and therefore to the whole thing."[15] Amy Zegart developed upon this, noting that grand strategy "is a multi-player game with powerful adversaries who are seeking their own future state of the world to serve their own interests." To be relevant, they depend "on knowing the number and identities of these key adversaries, what they want, how they operate and what damage they can inflict." As the Clinton administration discovered, the writing of such documents is part intellectual puzzle and part political maneuvering—a process imbued with inherent risks. Grand strategy documents must, by definition, be horizon-scanning reports that necessarily require an investment of time and energy. They must also avoid sounding too prophetic, or risk descending into the fanciful and the idealistic (or alternatively, the pessimistic and the apocryphal). As Zegart has noted, grand strategy "has always been seductive because it promises policy coherence in the face of complexity." However, they are "usually alluring but elusive."[16]

Such a conclusion has been borne out by events, as debate over the composition of grand strategy has occurred throughout the history of the United States. The 1990s were no different, with serious debate being conducted regarding the direction of US Grand Strategy due to the end of the Cold War, continuing a historical debate that predates the foundation of the Republic.

Writing in 1776, Thomas Paine sowed the seeds of a nascent isolationist approach to grand strategy initiatives, declaring "It is in the interest of America to steer clear of Europe."[17] This was a view echoed subsequently by George Washington, whose 1796 Farewell Address warned of the "insidious wiles of foreign influence," since "tis folly in one nation to look for disinterested favours from another," and by Thomas Jefferson, who promised "peace, commerce, and honest friendship with all nations, entangling alliances with none," in his 1801 Inaugural Address.[18] Despite these repeated commitments to avoid alliances, the United States took an early interest in the Western hemisphere, issuing what may be its first grand strategy document in 1823, the Monroe Doctrine.

An apparent turning point in US Grand Strategy came with the 1912 election of Woodrow Wilson. A sense of idealism has had a pronounced impact on the United States and her role in the world ever since, as Wilson ensured the application of morality to foreign diplomacy. Henry Kissinger noted, "it is above all to the drumbeat of Wilsonian idealism that American foreign policy has marched since his watershed presidency and continues to march to this day."[19] However, after the First World War, America saw a return to Warren Harding's "normalcy" and for many years this was the status of America's place in the world: neutral, disarmed, unready, and unable to adequately lead the world.

The outbreak of the Second World War, however, established the United States as a true global power, exacerbated by its participation in the United Nations, due in part to the efforts of Secretary of State Cordell Hull, whose

Trade, Prosperity, and Peace concept later exerted a strong influence on the Clinton administration. In the ensuing decades, America's place in the world and its accompanying grand strategy was defined by its response to the Soviet threat that came to overshadow the remainder of the twentieth century. Those decades witnessed the globalization of American power as it sought to defend freedom, not only on its own shores, but also far from home.

As Bill Clinton prepared to challenge for the presidency, the end of the Cold War offered a rare opportunity to reevaluate the direction of US Grand Strategy and to reflect on the last such demarcation point: the presidency of Harry Truman at the dawn of the Cold War. In retrospect, the era was viewed as the high point of US Grand Strategy, during which time NATO, the CIA, the NSC, the Department of Defense, and the United Nations were established; the Marshall Plan and the Truman Doctrine were announced; NSC-68 was drafted; and the National Security Act of 1947 was implemented to contain the growing Soviet threat. Leslie Gelb has suggested that the Truman administration "marked the golden age of US foreign policy . . . as glorious in our history as the founding fathers' creation of the Constitution."[20] Like Truman, Clinton was a Democrat with little foreign policy experience, at the dawn of a new international era, required to redefine grand strategy. To Clinton, however, fell the unenviable task of replacing the much-lauded grand strategy of Containment, credited as having been responsible for winning the Cold War.

However, Containment had not been a static policy. As Gaddis relates in *Strategies of Containment*, it necessarily took into account changes in circumstances and evolved according to the undulating nature of global politics.[21] This most revered of grand strategies, therefore, was one that "had to be developed, refined, and adjusted amid a seemingly ceaseless flow of events."[22] As the father of Containment, George Kennan observed "any policy must rest on principles . . . but its application must be in a constant state of flux."[23] Kennan's Long Telegram of 1946 and subsequent article in *Foreign Affairs* "helped define American views of the Soviet threat, and they laid out the intellectual premises for a strong but measured response," ensuring that Kennan "came as close to authoring the diplomatic doctrine of his era as any diplomat in our history."[24]

Although revered in hindsight, however, the Truman administration was simply reacting to events and situations as best it could. Kennan's recommendations, "to be of good heart, to look to our own social and economic health, to present a good face to the world," were described by Dean Acheson as being "of no help." Acheson conceded that Kennan's "historical analysis might or might not have been sound" but recognized that "his predictions and warnings could not have been better." Despite this, Washington "responded to them slowly."[25] While being viewed with reverence retrospectively, James Forrestal declared at the time, "there has been a notable lack of any central planning on American policy."[26]

The internal divisions and evolving international environment that contributed to the evolution of grand strategy under Truman was evident in the shift away from Kennan as the architect of policy. Having been named director of the newly established Policy Planning Staff from 1947 to 1949, Kennan's thinking was overtaken by events. By 1950, following the loss of China and the US nuclear monopoly, Truman ordered a review of national security that resulted in the production of NSC-68 under Kennan's replacement, Paul Nitze. The report incorporated existing concepts, including those expressed by Kennan, and also incorporated a new commitment to prevent further Soviet advances in peripheral areas, if necessary through the use of proxy wars.[27]

The drafting of NSC-68 was driven in part by the evolving international system, and also by the domestic impact of McCarthyism, which had a devastating impact on the Truman administration and helped solidify Cold War sentiment. The impact of domestic politics on the implementation of grand strategy likewise became a challenge for President Clinton, particularly after 1994. This highlights the fact that the American system of government, with its 2-year electoral cycle, rarely rewards long-term, horizon-scanning policies. The failure to deliver rapid solutions with demonstrable results may result in foreign policy falling prey to partisan attacks, ensuring that the very system of government that grand strategy is in part designed to protect could be an impediment to its successful implementation. This has been compounded by the rapid expansion of the federal bureaucracy, which, as Halperin observes, rarely assists in the efficient implementation of policy.[28]

Despite being lauded retrospectively, therefore, the Truman administration and its policy of Containment was an all-too imperfect model for Clinton to emulate, with its internal divisions and deadly international environment. Neither had it produced a political result that Governor Clinton wished to emulate, as President Truman was driven from office with some of the lowest approval ratings in modern history. A similar fate had befallen successive Democratic presidents, including Lyndon Johnson and Jimmy Carter, who had both been seen to fail in regard to US Grand Strategy. As a result, the fate of previous administrations, the policies of Woodrow Wilson and Cordell Hull, as well as the intrinsic contradictions and political considerations of peace and trade were very much on the minds of Bill Clinton's fledgling foreign policy team as the governor of Arkansas announced his intention to seek the presidency of the United States on October 3, 1991.

The 1992 primary season

Following a remarkable career, 1992 should have been the pinnacle of George H. W. Bush's political life and a year that returned him for a second term in the White House. During his 4 years in office, the Berlin Wall had fallen; the Cold War had ended; US forces had prevailed in the 1991 Gulf War and toppled General Noriega from power in Panama. President Bush received sky-high approval ratings heading into the election season and appeared to be the logical candidate to guide the United States through the formative years of the post-Cold War era.[29] His reelection campaign questioned the capability of his opponents to deal with potential international crises and portrayed the president as being uniquely qualified to lead. His son, George W. Bush, joked with reporters, "Do you think the American people are going to turn to a Democrat now?"[30] Initially, this appeared unlikely.

However, despite President Bush's international successes, his ill-defined New World Order had failed to materialize; the USSR had disintegrated, leaving a scattering of suddenly nuclear-empowered states; civil war was raging in the former Yugoslavia, while Japanese financial preeminence appeared to be inevitable. The General Agreement on Tariffs and Trade (GATT) talks and the North American Free Trade Agreement (NAFTA) negotiations had stalled; Europe was beset by recession and dissent over further integration; China faced condemnation for its crack down on pro-democracy protests in Tiananmen Square, while South Africa was making steps toward international acceptance with the release of Nelson Mandela. Such incidents led President Bush to speculate that the world was going through changes of "biblical proportions."[31] Accordingly, there was a growing recognition that the policies of the past could not endure; that new ideas were required for the post-Cold War era. As noted by Stanley Hoffman, "the three principles that have guided foreign policy; American exceptionalism, anti-communism and world economic liberalism, will be of little help because all are less receptive, or because 'victory' has made anti-communism irrelevant, or because the market itself is the problem or provides no answers."[32] As the incumbent, President Bush needed to justify his continued relevance as powerful global forces swept established leaders from power.

This caused President Bush's advisers to consider what they called, "The Churchill Parallel," noting that "leaders are not necessarily re-elected for their foreign policy and wartime successes, even when monumental."[33] Despite the initial jubilation felt with the end of the Cold War, communism's collapse removed the unifying sense of purpose that had pervaded US society since the 1940s, leaving uncertainty in its place.[34] Senator Paul Tsongas captured the national mood when he wrote, "the Cold War is over and Japan won," while Gavin Esler noted that the United States "had conquered the world and yet . . . found little peace," as Americans were beset by political scandals and economic woes.[35]

Although elections rarely turned on issues of foreign policy, fear of the USSR had helped Republicans win 7 of the 12 presidential elections during the Cold War. The year 1988, however, proved to be the final presidential election of that era, removing a key justification for Bush's reelection. Fear of a historical analogy and the rapidly shifting geopolitical environment had a devastating impact on Bush's reelection campaign and contributed to his defeat. The president failed to campaign on his strengths in the international arena and was, instead, drawn into domestic policy debates on the state of the economy. President Bush's refusal to "dance on the Berlin Wall" and proclaim an historic victory over the USSR revealed his strong diplomatic reasoning, and also his poor domestic political touch, as he refused to utilize a vital justification for his reelection for fear of destabilizing the international situation.[36]

President Bush's position was further undermined by two unexpected domestic challenges. Former Nixon speechwriter, Patrick Buchanan, openly challenged Bush for the Republican nomination, which forced Bush to adopt a less internationalist approach to foreign policy than he wanted and to embrace more conservative domestic policies than he found agreeable. This rearguard action, necessary to secure his own nomination, forced Bush to the right, vacating the center ground of US politics where the election was decided. Secondly, driven by forces that appeared more personal than political, Texan billionaire H. Ross Perot launched an independent bid for the presidency, in a move that hemorrhaged support from the president in a three-way race.

Democrats were eager to exploit the growing mood of national discontent and benefit from Republican Party in-fighting, to fulfill Arthur Schlesinger's forecast of a decade of liberalism in the 1990s.[37] Their challenge was to present a credible case for change that encompassed foreign and domestic policy, despite being viewed as having "no coherent foreign policy" and being "widely considered pacifists."[38] However, while the Republicans were divided over the degree of internationalism to embrace, the Democratic Party was split between two foreign policy factions.[39] Exponents of New Internationalism advocated the promotion of democracy with a concentration on multilateralism and supported "an activist approach rooted in classic American values but with the cost mitigated through burden sharing with others."[40] Conversely, proponents of Retrenched Internationalism sought to promote economics on a par with diplomacy and defense, insisting that the end of the Cold War enabled the United States to "redirect [its] energy and resources towards outstanding social problems at home."[41] To succeed, the Democratic Party needed to bridge these competing views before taking their message to the country. However, President Bush's popularity in the wake of the 1991 Gulf War convinced leading Democrats to avoid the campaign and those who did run were not considered the party's most credible candidates. They were former senators, governors of small, rural states, and maverick politicians with nowhere else to go, not a field of experienced candidates who appeared qualified to compete for America's highest office.

Grand strategy on the Clinton campaign

When Arkansas Governor Bill Clinton announced his candidacy on October 3, 1991, it appeared unlikely that he would steer the United States through the emerging post-Cold War era. The idea that a 46-year-old governor from the second poorest state in the nation could unseat a president with the highest approval ratings ever recorded seemed unrealistic and it appeared likely that he was positioning himself for a more viable run in 1996 against Vice President Quayle.[42] While Clinton "had a profile as a very smart political animal," it was noted that he was looking to "succeed a president who probably knew more about foreign policy and had more foreign policy experience than many presidents in a long number of years."[43] Both individually and as a representative of the Democratic Party, it was vital for Governor Clinton to inoculate himself against charges of international inexperience as early as possible. Foreign policy could not win the presidency for Bill Clinton, but it threatened to reduce his credibility as it had for the last Democratic president, Jimmy Carter and the previous Democratic candidate, Michael Dukakis. Bill Clinton, therefore, had his work cut out for him in this area, long before he began to espouse a grand strategy of his own.

Bill Clinton's political background was exclusively domestic; he had been Governor of Arkansas, head of the Democratic Leadership Council (DLC), and Chairman of the National Governors Association. These roles convinced Clinton of the importance that international trade played in the modern world, an understanding he brought to the White House with wide-ranging implications for US Grand Strategy. His exposure to foreign affairs had been almost exclusively academic, having attended the Edmund A. Walsh School of Foreign Service at Georgetown University, worked in Senator Fulbright's office at the height of the Vietnam War, and studied at Oxford as a Rhodes Scholar. As a state governor, however, he had acted as "an international salesman for his state," which brought Clinton into contact with foreign politicians and policy makers.[44] Accordingly, "he was someone for whom the foreign world was not foreign."[45] Clinton's appreciation of the emerging concept of globalization and his willingness to seeking solutions from the wider world became central to the Clinton presidency. In the autumn of 1991, however, Clinton's rivals remained focused on domestic issues and avoided international affairs, as they believed it was unpopular with the electorate, ensuring Governor Clinton was alone in addressing foreign policy early in the campaign.[46] As he began his presidential odyssey, however, Clinton had no particular global philosophy and was, therefore, initially reliant upon a core group of advisers that played a vital role in the evolution of foreign policy during the election and later of grand strategy in the White House.

The foreign policy advisers, Anthony Lake, Samuel "Sandy" Berger, and Nancy Soderberg, formed a distinct team, separate from the core that advised Clinton on domestic issues, becoming a "wholly owned subsidiary" of the Clinton campaign, granting them "a lot of running room" on foreign policy.[47] Anthony Lake advised the campaign while teaching at Mount Holyoke College in Massachusetts, and had been recruited to the campaign to act as "the focal point" for putting together Clinton's first speech on foreign policy, to be delivered at Georgetown University in December 1991. The success of the speech led to Lake being asked to stay on and coordinate foreign policy for the campaign, which he did along with Samuel Berger, who had known Clinton since working together on the 1972 McGovern campaign and who had been Lake's deputy at the Policy Planning Staff in the 1970s. As the campaign progressed and Clinton won an increasing number of primaries, it became clear that as Lake was still teaching in Massachusetts, "it made sense to do it jointly, so Sandy and [Lake] became the co-equal or senior advisers."[48]

Lake was a proponent of Neo-Wilsonianism, which he defined as an attempt to create a world that was neither naively liberal in the Wilsonian sense nor relentlessly realist in the conservative sense. He felt that the United States "should use its moral, military, economic and political strength to engage and promote a more just, stable world."[49] It was noted that, "Tony is a moralist. He believes passionately in the moral aspect of foreign policy, he is a true Wilsonian."[50] Having spent his adult life considering the balance of American supremacy and responsibility, Lake saw the 1990s as a time to pursue "democracy's promise of a better, safer world" and unite elements of the Democratic Party that had been at odds since the Vietnam War.[51] Lake and Berger wrote the campaign's initial foreign policy speeches and brought what Clinton needed, "in terms of adding to Clinton's contacts within the foreign policy establishment, reassuring the democratic establishment that Clinton was an OK guy and making sure his ideas were not out of line or going to be attacked too much."[52]

In June 1992, Nancy Soderberg was hired as Foreign Policy Director to run foreign policy out of the campaign's Little Rock headquarters. She was "the day-to-day person," coordinating the flow of ideas and arguments from the foreign policy advisers to the candidate, while Lake and Berger were engaged in "the bigger picture stuff."[53] For a time Soderberg was the campaign's top-paid, full-time foreign policy official, since Lake and Berger remained volunteers.[54] The three were responsible for coordinating policy and "were reporting directly to Clinton or through George Stephanopoulos."[55]

The campaign consulted regularly with academics such as Michael Mandelbaum of Johns Hopkins University, Joseph Nye of Harvard, with members of the Democratic Party's foreign policy community including Madeleine Albright and Martin Indyk, as well as with Congressmen Les

Aspin, Sam Nunn, Lee Hamilton, Dave McCurdy, and Stephen Solarz.[56] Their utilization provided political coverage and revealed Clinton's willingness to court advice from the Democratic Party's foreign policy elite.[57]

In addition, many of Clinton's policy proposals originated from the Progressive Policy Institute (PPI), which helped prepare policy statements and "covered his right flank as he began campaigning from the left against Senator Tsongas."[58] PPI president, Will Marshall, argued that the United States had to "erect a whole new conceptual basis for foreign policy" after the Cold War, believing that a new age had dawned on defense issues.[59] As a member of the PPI, Clinton was a proponent of the Third Way, which posited a middle ground between liberalism and conservatism. In an expansion of this approach to the realm of foreign policy, Clinton made shrewd use of language to combine elements of New Internationalism and Retrenched Internationalism to appeal to varying elements of the Democratic Party. He stressed economic policy to the masses, while reserving discussion of US Grand Strategy for select audiences, ensuring that while Bush offered "a limited presidency in a rather unusual time of limited expectations," Clinton offered a viable alternative, far removed from the Realpolitik of the Cold War years.[60] The PPI espoused a New Internationalist philosophy, perhaps the truest indication of where Governor Clinton's instincts lay on the issue, irrespective of how his statements were refined for public consumption.

Central to that effort were Communications Director George Stephanopoulos and Campaign Manager James Carville, who developed a narrative of responsibility and growth, detailing Clinton's humble origins, his 1963 encounter with President Kennedy, and success as governor of Arkansas to advance the candidate's cause with the electorate. Governor Clinton campaigned as a New Democrat to distinguish himself from a series of Democratic presidential failures, invoked memories of President Kennedy whenever possible, and actively downplayed any reference to the Carter years. However, while the Clinton campaign sought to distinguish itself from Carter's term in office, Lake and Berger had been members of the former administration, which was reflected in several of the policies that emerged on the campaign trail.[61]

Clinton's Grand Strategy campaign addresses

With Containment of the USSR no longer a valid justification for a continued global presence, the question naturally arose, "What does a superpower do in a world no longer dominated by superpower conflict?"[62] To address this question, Governor Clinton made a series of foreign policy speeches based on three principles designed to build harmony among the disparate elements of the Democratic Party: advancing American economic competitiveness, spreading democracy, and the maintenance of a strong national defense. Clinton believed that this combination would ensure the United States stayed "secure by remaining the strongest force for peace, freedom and prosperity in the world."[63] Clinton saw these speeches as opportunities "to articulate the ideas and proposals [he] had developed over the previous decade as governor and at the Democratic Leadership Council."[64] The Clinton campaign "was very strategic about his foreign policy speeches, going to the right of Bush," and doing "slightly more than the minimum necessary to give himself foreign policy credentials and heft."[65] Foreign policy was not Clinton's *forte*, but it was manipulated to stress his progressive policies, while negating his perceived weakness in the area. Clinton's message was that "the world had changed and the government hadn't changed with it," insisting that the Bush administration "had missed the boat in trying to handle the collapse of the Soviet Union, had opposed the independence of Slovenia and Croatia," and retained "a Cold War mentality," inappropriate for the post-Cold War world.[66]

The Announcement Address

Governor Clinton introduced his campaign with an Announcement Address on October 3, 1991 in Little Rock, Arkansas. The candidate referred to his campaign manifesto as the New Covenant with echoes of FDR's New Deal and JFK's New Frontier. In a speech that dealt predominantly with domestic issues, Clinton charged that President Bush was prepared to "celebrate the death of communism abroad with the loss of the American Dream at home." This enabled Clinton to conceptualize the end of the Cold War in economic terms, noting that "national security begins at home . . . the Soviet empire never lost to us on the field of battle. Their system rotted from the inside out, from economic, political and spiritual failure." Governor Clinton presented this as a warning, stressing the inherent risks of concentrating on foreign policy at the expense of domestic affairs.

Clinton used the speech to introduce his signature concept, the linkage of foreign and domestic policy, insisting that the United States could not "build a safe and secure world unless we can first make America strong at home." Clinton sought to bring his experience of dealing with trade issues in Arkansas to the world stage, insisting that the competition for the future was "Germany and the rest of Europe, Japan and the rest of Asia" and that the United States risked losing its role as a global leader "because we're losing the American dream right here at home."[67] This stance enabled Clinton to address foreign policy by redefining its parameters and benefit from the appearance of a grand vision. However, his reference to Germany and Japan raised concerns over Clinton's future ability to forge relations with either nation and was an example of the difficulties faced by the candidates in 1992: Bush and Clinton sought to promote a domestic agenda, realizing that the outside world still needed attention after the election. However, offending foreign leaders was a risk both sides took in 1992, as President Bush urged Mikhail Gorbachev "not to pay any attention" to campaign rhetoric taking credit for ending the Cold War.[68]

Clinton's concentration on the state of the US economy enabled him to turn the incumbent's perceived strength in foreign affairs into a fatal flaw. George H. W. Bush was labeled "the foreign policy president," as Clinton promised to "focus like a laser beam on the economy."[69] Accordingly, Clinton's team strove to ensure the election focused on the economy, campaigning to President Bush's left on domestic issues and to his right on foreign affairs.[70] The campaign sought to "blunt Bush's advantage [on foreign affairs] and in boxing terms, keep a left jab in his face," ensuring that Bush was so worried about being seen as a foreign policy president, "he failed to take advantage of his strengths."[71] While pledges of an activist approach to government generated dynamic campaign speeches, however, they returned to haunt the candidate once in office.

The Georgetown University Address

On December 12, 1991, Governor Clinton spoke at Georgetown University and surveyed the challenges faced by the United States following the end of the Cold War. As prepared by Anthony Lake and Samuel Berger, this was the first foreign policy speech of the campaign, designed to attract financial, intellectual, and political support. While it was kept deliberately generic to avoid alienating individuals or groups, the speech revealed a willingness to address matters of international importance. Lake's moral influence was evident as Governor Clinton lamented the speed with which President Bush rushed "to resume cordial relations with China barely a month after the massacre in Tiananmen Square." Such an approach may have made sense during the Cold War, Clinton noted, "when China was a counterweight to Soviet power. But it makes no sense to play the China card now, when our opponents have thrown in their hand." Clinton stressed that he favored a more assertive approach toward Beijing, with implications for China's continuing most favored nation (MFN) trading status.

Clinton used the address to rally behind Boris Yeltsin and the emerging democratic movement in Russia, where he argued, "a small amount spent stabilising the emerging democracies . . . will reduce by much more the money we may have to commit to our defense in the future." Clinton was at pains to draw distinctions with the Bush campaign, lamenting that the president had "devoted his time and energy to foreign concerns and ignored dire problems here at home." This prevented him from learning from the fall of the USSR, which Clinton stressed had "collapsed from the inside out, from economic, political and spiritual failure."[72] Clinton's stance received an unexpected endorsement from President Nixon, who agreed that if Yeltsin were to fail, "the new despotism which will take [his] place will mean that the peace dividend is finished, we will have to rearm and that's going to cost infinitely more than would the aid that we provide at the present time."[73]

Governor Clinton insisted that foreign and domestic policy were "inseparable in today's world" and that the "false choice" between them placed the United States and its economy at risk, a contribution to strategic thinking that had been formulated in tandem with Anthony Lake. There was an undisguised duality in this approach to policy, which Clinton stressed could "lead to the creation of lucrative new markets, which means new American jobs."[74] The decision to emphasize the domestic element to foreign policy allowed Clinton to highlight his record and distinguish himself from President Bush. This was an astute manipulation of politics and policy that allowed Clinton to take the battle to Bush on the incumbent's apparent strongest area. It was an approach that was reprised whenever foreign policy arose on the campaign and represented an example of Clinton blending the issues to suit his strengths. Clinton's argument that the best foreign policy was a sound domestic policy and that Bush had failed by devoting so much attention to foreign affairs was "unusual, if not downright tautological, but it works as part of a jeremiadic critique because of the jeremiad's embodiment of contradictions."[75] Drawing on his experience, Clinton noted, "any governor who's tried to create jobs over the last decade knows that experience in international economics is essential and that success in the global economy must be at the core of national security in the 1990s." This shift in focus and the changes it promised for US Grand Strategy were at the heart of Clinton's insistence that in 1992, Americans should not elect "the last president of the twentieth century, but the first president of the twenty-first century."

The basic principles of Bill Clinton's eventual grand strategy were present in his Georgetown University Address of December 1991 and were outlined in language that appeared almost verbatim in future National Security Strategy Reviews; the need to "restructure our military forces for a new era . . . work with our allies to encourage the spread and consolidation of democracy abroad," and "re-establish America's economic leadership at home and in the world." These elements became the blueprint for the Clinton administration's grand strategy and the bedrock of all campaign addresses on the subject. At the forefront of this emerging strategy was Democracy Promotion, which carried the dual caveat of making the world safer while opening new markets for US exports, resulting in more American jobs. This combined Anthony Lake's moral call to enlarge democracy with Governor Clinton's pragmatic advocacy of economic expansionism and encapsulated the candidate's call to "tear down the wall in our thinking between domestic and foreign policy."[76] It also exemplified Governor Clinton's ability to combine aspects of New and Retrenched Internationalism.

Bill Clinton first encountered this approach as a student working on Capitol Hill in 1967, when he noted Senator Fulbright's preference for "multilateral cooperation over unilateral action; dialogue with, not isolation from, the Soviet Union and Warsaw Pact nations . . . and the winning of converts to American values and interests by the force of our examples and ideas, not the force of arms."[77] Governor Clinton built on this approach in his campaign speeches to advocate a distinct American engagement in the world, while stressing the practical implications of the policy.

Clinton's observation that "democracies don't go to war with each other . . . don't sponsor terrorist acts against each other" revealed the campaign's embrace of the Democratic Peace Theory, as espoused in 1795 by Immanuel Kant, who suggested that peace was not only possible, hence a moral duty, but also inevitable. Thinkers such as Hegel had challenged this approach, insisting that war was "historically and morally necessary and good," and that "the idea of perpetual peace was therefore absurd."[78] Michael Doyle had sought to advance the concept in 1983, but at a time when the end of the Cold War was not foreseen it received little serious attention. However, with the end of the Cold War, democracy was seen as a potential vehicle for peace and became central to the development of Governor Clinton's strategic thinking, guided by insights from Anthony Lake.[79]

But was democracy really the best solution to the world's challenges? Were democracies less able or willing to use power in an arbitrary and indiscriminate manner against other democracies?[80] Or were they, as Churchill dryly observed, merely "the worst form of government, except for all the others that had been tried." Even George Kennan, whose thinking did so much to define the response to the Soviet Union during the Cold War, was known to have his doubts. Speaking at the University of Chicago in 1950, Kennan spoke of democracy in the following terms:

> I sometime wonder whether . . . a democracy is not uncomfortably similar to one of those prehistoric monsters with a body as long as this room and a brain the size of a pin: he lies there in his comfortable primeval mud and pays little attention to his environment; he is slow to wrath-in fact, you practically have to whack his tail off to make him aware that his interests are being disturbed; but, once he grasps this, he lays about him with such blind determination that he not only destroys his adversary but largely wrecks his native habitat.[81]

Despite such concerns, the end of the Cold War provided an opportunity to test Kant's thesis on a global scale as the Democratic Peace concept became embraced by Democrats and Republicans alike, ensuring bipartisan support for "repeated presidential calls to promote the creation of democratic government abroad."[82]

In embracing this Kantian approach, Clinton sought to distinguish between the possibility of an Iranian nuclear arsenal and the deterrence retained by European democracies. "The French and British have nuclear weapons," Clinton insisted, "but we don't fear annihilation at their hands." Therefore, he argued that the spread of democracy was more than reassuring to Americans; it was of the utmost importance to US security. Democracy Promotion became a defining policy of the campaign, identified as "a legitimate part of our national security budget," as Clinton insisted that under his leadership an "American foreign policy of engagement for democracy will unite our interests and our values."[83]

Clinton's Georgetown University speech was important for four reasons. It was made only 2 months after the Announcement Address and 2 months before the first primary, when other candidates were dwelling on domestic issues, establishing Bill Clinton as a candidate capable of addressing international policy. This allowed Governor Clinton to gain the support of the Democratic Party's foreign policy elite before returning to domestic issues in New Hampshire and Iowa. Secondly, the speech brought New Democrat, Third Way thinking to foreign affairs, stressing the linkage of foreign and domestic policy. Thirdly, it demonstrated Clinton's mastery over a range of foreign policy issues including economics, trade, geopolitics, and defense. Finally, it enabled Clinton to demonstrate he was not a "failed governor from a poor southern state" and allowed him to "cross the threshold of understanding and competence in foreign affairs."[84]

The New York Primary Address

Governor Clinton sought to consolidate his developing international thinking in an address to the Foreign Policy Association in New York City on April 1, 1992, shortly before the state primary. Taking direct aim at the president, Clinton charged that George Bush had "invoked a new world order without enunciating a new American purpose." In addition to appeasing China, President Bush had "poured cold water on Baltic and Ukrainian aspirations for independence," failed to recognize Croatia and Slovenia, and relied too heavily on global partners, resulting in hesitancy when the world was undergoing powerful change. Governor Clinton called for greater use of multilateralism, but refused to rule out unilateral action. In a statement that became the unrecognized position of his subsequent administration, Clinton pledged, "we will never abandon our prerogative to act alone when our vital interests are at stake. Our motto in this era will be: together when we can; on our own where we must."[85] This approach was present from the earliest days of the campaign and remained in place throughout Clinton's time as president. However, the inability to convey this position successfully haunted the administration, as a perceived predilection for multilateralism led to accusations of weakness by political opponents.

The speech and accompanying remarks made during the New York Primary were an example of the use of foreign policy to gain domestic support at the potential expense of longstanding international relationships, as Clinton's foreign policies collided with the Special Relationship in a struggle for the Irish vote. Speaking on St. Patrick's Day 1992, President Bush claimed that the United States was "not in a position to dictate a solution, to in any way be the sole arbiter of this difficult situation" between London and Dublin.[86] Congressman Joseph P. Kennedy and Boston Mayor Ray Flynn condemned this position, ensuring that the president's remarks were resonating as Clinton campaigned in New York. In keeping with his campaign's multilateral approach, Clinton conceded the possibility of UN involvement in Northern Ireland, stated his intention to appoint a special envoy to Northern Ireland, and pledged to raise the subject of human rights violations with the British Prime Minister if elected.[87] Clinton also promised to consider issuing a visa to Sinn Féin leader Gerry Adams, in the full knowledge that such a move may "infuriate the British and strain our most important transatlantic relationship."[88] At this stage of the campaign, however, Clinton had no ability to implement these promises and nothing to lose by making them. In time, however, they returned to haunt him as pledges proved harder to implement in office than to make on the campaign trail.

Although the Clinton campaign was criticized for risking Anglo-American ties, it was less concerned about upsetting the British government and more focused on gaining the votes of 40 million Irish-Americans. George Stephanopoulos noted, "it obviously ticks off the Brits, but equally obviously, that is acceptable to a lot of us."[89] Prime Minister John Major's annoyance was not a matter of concern to the Clinton team, who were anticipating a Labour Party victory in the upcoming British elections of April 1992. In London, however, "there would have been an assumption that the UK government was assuming a second Bush term."[90] Thus began a series of events that saw UK consultants aid the Republican campaign and suggestions that John Major's government tried to discover whether Clinton sought British citizenship to avoid the Vietnam draft. The affair was dismissed as "a bunch of media chatter," but US Ambassador Raymond Seitz noted that such "clumsy little incidents planted the seeds of transatlantic recriminations," which haunted Anglo-American relations throughout Clinton's first term in office.[91]

Clinton's Foreign Policy Director, Nancy Soderberg, was instrumental in developing Clinton's Irish policy and sought to steer it away from its confrontational tone. "I joined in June of '92," she noted, "He made the statements April '92, in the New York Primary, not insignificantly!"[92] Her efforts met with limited success, however, as Clinton reinforced his position in October 1992, declaring that, as president, he would "take a more active role in talks on Northern Ireland and tell the British to establish more effective safeguards against the wanton use of lethal force and against further collusion between the security forces and Protestant paramilitary groups."[93] Clinton's Irish policy, cloaked in the mantle of support for human rights, was designed to attract votes not only in the primary, but also in the general election when New York's Electoral College votes would be essential. This demonstrated the inherent risk in an electoral strategy that prioritized domestic issues above global relationships and revealed the often overlooked influence that domestic political pressures place on the development of grand strategy: the need to appeal to a multicultural melting pot of competing domestic constituencies risked alienating overseas powers. While Clinton's approach helped him win the New York Primary, it placed a strain on Anglo-American relations that was not fully healed until the 1997 election of Tony Blair.

Clinton's Acceptance Address

Clinton's first speeches on the future direction of US Grand Strategy were delivered when he was a candidate in search of the Democratic Party's nomination. By the summer of 1992 that goal had been achieved, ensuring that when he next addressed the issue it was as his party's nominee for the presidency of the United States. The ensuing addresses on the subject revealed the changing nature of the campaign and of the candidate himself, as the responsibilities of power closed in and his speeches became more realistic in tone and rhetorical in style.

However, in his Acceptance Speech at the Democratic National Convention in New York on July 16, 1992, Governor Clinton devoted only 141 words to foreign affairs, among which were, "the Cold War is over. Soviet communism has collapsed and our values—freedom, democracy, individual rights, free enterprise—they have triumphed all around the world." However, as Clinton told his audience, "just as we have won the Cold War abroad, we are losing the battles for economic opportunity and social justice here at home."[94] While the brevity of his remarks reflected the view that the election was to be fought on domestic policy, it exposed Clinton to attacks that were repeated until Election Day and beyond; that he was ambivalent on foreign policy and unfit to lead a military he had actively avoided serving in during the Vietnam War. President Bush mocked Governor Clinton's lack of attention to foreign affairs, noting that his speech "spent about one minute on the national security of this Nation . . . If you blinked or had to do something else or even heated up a ham and cheese sandwich in the microwave, you missed the entire part about the national security and world peace."[95] Both men played to their perceived strengths in their acceptance speeches, however, for just as Governor

Clinton downplayed foreign policy, President Bush failed to make reference to his own economic record.

The development of what became Clinton's Grand Strategy continued with the publication of *Putting People First*, the blueprint for a potential administration. The chapter on national security insisted that the United States "cannot go four more years without a plan to lead the world," and argued that with the end of the Cold War Americans needed "a team in the White House whose goal is not to resist change, but to shape it."[96] The vital elements of Clinton's Grand Strategy were all present: an enhanced military, a role for economics in foreign affairs, and the promotion of democracy. The Carnegie Endowment for International Peace mirrored these findings in a report entitled *Changing our Ways: America and the New World*, a bipartisan critique of Bush's performance that echoed the Clinton campaign's call for an economic renaissance. As Patrick Buchanan dragged President Bush further to the right, the center ground of American politics opened up for Governor Clinton, ensuing opportunities to draw on previously unforeseen support. Former Carter aide Stuart Eizenstat prepared a memo for the Clinton campaign entitled, "Winning Back the Neo-Conservatives" that explained the group "had influence far out of proportion to their numbers" and insisting that "they can be won back in 1992 and to do so would be viewed as a major crack in the Republican armour."[97] The eventual support of several neoconservatives, though tepid, conditional, and ultimately short-lived, eased concerns about Clinton's capacity to serve as commander-in-chief and further fractured support for Bush, as Eizenstat predicted.

The Los Angeles Address

Much of the Carnegie Endowment's report fed into Governor Clinton's address to the World Affairs Council in Los Angeles (LA) on August 13, 1992. At the time, LA was in turmoil following the Rodney King verdict and for Clinton to deliver a foreign policy speech in the midst of domestic strife was a risky move, which only succeeded because of his linkage of foreign and domestic policy. The local audience was on Clinton's mind as he highlighted job losses created by the defense cuts that were a by-product of the end of the Cold War. This demonstrated the link between foreign and domestic policy and the manner in which George Bush, the "foreign policy president," had failed America. Clinton insisted that the United States required a president "who attends to prosperity at home" if the American people were "to sustain their support for engagement abroad," a role in which Clinton claimed Bush had singularly failed. Governor Clinton lamented that the Californian economy had been hurt by "the lack of a plan to convert defense cuts into domestic economic investments," contrasting his policies with those of the incumbent, who had "no serious plan to help our defense personnel make the transition to a civilian economy." Clinton promised to help "retrain defense technicians for work in critical civilian fields."[98] As the challenger, Governor Clinton had the advantage of being able to campaign on such promises, rather than on his record in office.

Congressman Lee Hamilton aided Clinton's efforts, writing in *Foreign Affairs* that the restoration of US competitiveness was critical not only to the domestic economy, but also to its foreign policy. "Our economic problems are limiting the reach of our foreign policy at a time when the rest of the world is looking to the United States for leadership," Hamilton stressed, in a deliberate echo of the Clinton campaign's central message.[99] The LA speech began a series of attacks on Bush's claims to have won the Cold War, as Clinton reminded Americans that a bipartisan effort had secured victory in the struggle with the USSR. "The notion that the Republicans won the Cold War reminds me of the rooster who took credit for the dawn," the governor said. "The truth is, from Truman to Kennedy to Carter, Democratic as well as Republican presidents held firm against the expansion of communism."

Clinton used the LA speech to set forth three tests of presidential leadership for the 1990s: "the first is to grasp how the world has changed. The second test is to assert a vision of our role in this dynamic new world. The third test is to summon all our strengths; our values, our economic power, when necessary our military might, in service of that vision." The speech was phrased to promote Clinton as a proponent of leadership and vision in contrast to the incumbent, who was accused of holding on to "old assumptions and policies, trying to prop up yesterday's status quo, failing to confront our new challenges." The idea that domestic strife was a result of an undue concentration on foreign affairs was key to understanding Clinton's foreign policy: if domestic policy was flawed, foreign policy was irrelevant, for it implied that the United States was headed for a disaster akin to that which had consumed the USSR. Governor Clinton was adamant on this central concept: "in this new era, our first foreign priority and our first domestic priority are one and the same: reviving our economy." Clinton not only outlined where President Bush had failed but also announced that he planed to "elevate economics in foreign policy; create an Economic Security Council, similar to the National Security Council; and change the State Department's culture so that economics is no longer a poor cousin to old-school diplomacy." This campaign pledge led to the establishment of the National Economic Council, which assisted Clinton as he presided over one of the most prosperous eras in the nation's history.

Clinton charged that Bush lacked "a vision of our role in this new era," arguing that "in a world of change, security flows from initiative, not inertia." The governor scolded China, whose trading privileges he promised to link to "its human rights record and its conduct on trade and weapons sales" and attacked President Bush for failing to advance US interests with the rising power. Clinton critiqued the president for appeasing Saddam Hussein, despite evidence of his brutality toward the Kurds, called for intervention in the Balkans and for the delivery of supplies to Sarajevo. Finally, he decried Bush for siding "with the status quo rather than democratic change, with familiar tyrants rather than those who would overthrow them."[100] This refrain was echoed by the authors of *Marching in Place* who referred to President Bush as "a warrior for the status quo."[101]

Clinton expanded on his notion of Democratic Enlargement, calling for Ukrainian independence, in contrast to what William Safire of the *New York Times* referred to as the "Chicken Kiev" policy of the Bush administration.[102] Clinton accused the president of moral cowardice for his refusal to support Ukrainian "emancipation from a dying communist empire" and for publicly chastising Ukrainian calls for what Bush referred to as "suicidal nationalism." In contrast, Clinton portrayed himself as an agent of change, seeking to recapture the idealism of the Peace Corps by announcing that his administration would "stand up for democracy and create a Democracy Corps to help them develop free institutions."[103] Berger, Lake, and Soderberg urged Clinton to stress Democratic Enlargement along with a strong defensive posture as they believed this was "a theme that brings together conservatives and liberals, and would be an excellent vehicle for solidifying your support from both wings of the party . . . It also provides a defining purpose for America's role in the post-Cold War world."[104] It was a combination that Clinton adopted throughout his campaign and into his presidency.

The LA speech made direct reference to the Base Force defense policy of the Bush administration and revealed the powers at work behind the campaign: "House Armed Services Chair Les Aspin is right: The administration's Base Force plan leaves us with a military that does not fit our strategy and cannot do what we ask."[105] Aspin became a key adviser to the campaign and, along with Senator Sam Nunn, provided Clinton with political coverage and vital defense-related data. Given Clinton's lack of military experience and avoidance of service during the Vietnam War, the support of such prominent individuals was a great boost to his credentials. Moreover, Aspin was right of center in the Democratic defense spectrum, offering the political protection Clinton desperately needed, as his campaign produced a post-Cold War plan for the Pentagon that could have been modeled on the views of his opponent. This hindered efforts by the Bush team to portray him as an old-style Democrat, weak on defense, or hesitant to use force. However, the candidate's repeated references to his advisers raised questions as to Clinton's personal grasp of the issues at hand.

Ultimately, Bill Clinton presented the election as a choice between two opposing outlooks: "President Bush will seek to establish his leadership by emphasizing the time he has spent, the calls he has placed and the trips he has taken in the conduct of foreign policy," Clinton noted, insisting that such criteria were no longer sufficient, since "the measure of leadership in the new era is not the conversations held or the miles travelled. It is the new realities recognized, the crises averted, the opportunities seized." With his eye on the White House, Clinton echoed Kennedy's call for a new generation of leadership that was "strategic, vigorous and grounded in America's democratic values," insisting his vision was of a world "united in peaceful commerce; a world in which nations compete more in economic and less in military terms . . . a world increasingly engaged in democracy, tolerant of diversity and respectful of human rights."[106] This exemplified the changes that had enveloped the campaign as it sought to utilize soaring rhetoric to define its aspirations; the language of the past was utilized to portray a vision of the future that was both interventionist and internationalist.

The Milwaukee Address

As the race tightened toward Election Day, Lake, Berger, and Soderberg convinced Clinton to deliver a final foreign policy address in Milwaukee. "When they walk into the voting booth . . . Americans must be able to visualise you as commander-in-chief," they noted in a memo dated August 22. "It's a threshold test. You are well positioned, but you're not there yet."[107] Seeking to regain the support of Democrats who had defected to Reagan in 1980, Clinton spoke at the University of Wisconsin in Milwaukee on October 1, 1992, asserting his belief that the United States had "a higher purpose than to coddle dictators and stand aside from the global movement toward democracy." He chided President Bush for his "ambivalence about supporting democracy," his "eagerness to befriend potentates and dictators" and for not being "in the mainstream, pro-democracy tradition of American foreign policy." In contrast, Clinton promised "a pro-democracy foreign policy" based on American principles, dedicated to "building a just, enduring and ever more democratic peace in the world."

Governor Clinton attacked Bush for his "callous disregard for democratic principles" after the Gulf War, but carefully avoided calling for a global crusade: "Every ideal, including the promotion of democracy, must be tempered with prudence and common sense," Clinton noted, stressing, "we cannot support every group's hopes for self-determination."[108] This was an indication of how much had changed since President Kennedy's promise to "pay any price, bear any burden, oppose any foe, in order to ensure the survival and the success of liberty."[109] Clinton was content to commit the United States to the promotion of democracy when and where possible, but pragmatism prevailed as this approach became not an overriding moral duty, "but one objective amongst others that would help guarantee America's place in a complex international system."[110]

The address was carefully constructed to shore up support, reach out to disaffected Democrats, and present Clinton as a credible commander-in-chief. The speech was indicative of Clinton's developing grand strategy, which now benefited from official briefings by the Central Intelligence Agency.

On September 4, 1992, Director of Central Intelligence Robert Gates met with Clinton in Arkansas to brief him on intelligence matters. The governor invited his running mate, Senator Al Gore, and the outgoing chairmen of the two congressional intelligence committees, Senator David Boren and Representative David McCurdy, to attend the session.[111] The meeting covered Russia, the former Yugoslavia, developments in Iraq, North Korea, China, and Iran, as well as weapons of mass destruction. Clinton's inclusion of his running mate was indicative of the relationship that developed between them. Former Deputy Secretary of State Warren Christopher, tasked by Clinton to identify a vice presidential candidate, felt Senator Gore had "worked hard to make himself knowledgeable in arms control, foreign affairs and the environment, all areas where Clinton needed support."[112] With a strong reputation in security matters, it was natural for Gore to speak on the issue and in September 1992 declared "George Bush does not fit the requirements of the New World Order his own speechwriters once summoned up. We require a fresh approach from a new leader of vigour and high intelligence, of courage and vision."[113] Gore's foreign policy adviser, Leon Fuerth, assisted in preparing the address, which alleged that loan guarantees and dual-use technology exports in the 1980s helped Saddam Hussein build the war machine that American soldiers had to fight in 1991.[114]

In August 1991, President Bush referred to Governor Clinton as "a very nice man," but a year later his opinion had changed, insisting, "my dog Millie knows more about foreign policy than these two bozos!"[115] However, rather than defend his actions over the course of the previous 4 years, George Bush appeared to acknowledge his predilection for foreign policy by canceling and rescheduling overseas trips and suggesting that in a second term he planned an energetic domestic agenda, the opposite of most presidencies. This, however, was viewed as being too little, too late, as the editors of New Republic noted that the Bush administration had "failed to grasp the two essential movements of its world: the growing clamour for democracy and the related impulse for national sovereignty. Its instinct has always been the status quo."[116] Such assessments enabled Anthony Lake to observe that "Bush was so worried about being seen as a foreign policy president that he failed to take advantage of his strengths."[117]

For Clinton, appearing presidential was a vital requirement in his efforts to convince Americans to elect a Democrat administration for the first time in 12 years and his foreign policy speeches helped him in this process, elevating him from a rural politician to a credible challenger.

As the campaign progressed, his speeches became more refined and rhetorical, though less ambitious. While they inflicted no harm on Clinton's electoral chances, his policy of appearing more activist than Bush led to statements that returned to haunt him, as he called for aid in Somalia, a reversal of Bush's repatriation policy toward Haitian refuges and for intervention in the Balkans. Yet for the first time in a generation, a Democratic candidate was dictating the parameters of the debate going into the final stages of a Presidential Election and the accompanying televised debates.

Grand strategy in the presidential debates

The televised presidential debates have become a vital component in modern US elections and have historically favored the challenger, of whom expectations are usually lower, since appearing on the same stage bestows equality on the contestants. They proved to be the undoing of President Ford, whose 1976 insistence that there was no Soviet domination of Eastern Europe did much to undermine confidence in him. Four years later, President Carter's revelation that he discussed arms control with his daughter did little to strengthen his reelection chances. Although George Bush was the incumbent, few doubted Clinton's debating skills, especially when contrasted to the president's garbled syntax and known disdain for debates, which he viewed as a triumph of style over substance. The debates, therefore, were an opportunity and a risk for Governor Clinton: he could reveal his intelligence, stature, and empathy, but it was an unforgiving environment where any mistake risked undermining his growing presidential credibility.

There was little difference between Clinton and Bush on the subject of defense and in the first debate both candidates attempted to trump the other in terms of cuts and the use of US forces. Clinton stressed his disagreement over the need to station 150,000 US troops in Europe, citing a report that argued for "100,000 or slightly fewer troops." Clinton continued to advance the idea of democratic promotion, insisting "we ought to be promoting the democratic impulses around the world. Democracies are our partners. They don't go to war with each other." He lambasted Bush over his China policy, but with an eye on the future, stressed that he did not wish to alienate the emerging power: "I don't want to isolate China, but I think it is a mistake for us to do what this administration did when all those kids went out there carrying the Statue of Liberty in Tiananmen Square."[118]

In the subsequent debates, Clinton stuck to his central message: "If you don't rebuild the economic strength of this country at home, we won't be a superpower . . . We need to be a force for freedom and democracy and we need to use our unique position to support freedom." Throughout, Bush mocked Clinton's experience as Chief of the Arkansas National Guard and ridiculed his equivocation over Operation Desert Storm. Bush posed the question directly: "If in the next five minutes a television announcer came on and said there is a major threat to this country, who would you choose? Who has the character, the integrity, the maturity, to get the job done?"[119] Bush made it clear that only he had the wisdom and experience to chart a course in his self-proclaimed New World Order. Governor Clinton, however, reminded the audience that the former Chairman of the Joint Chiefs, Admiral Crowe, had recently endorsed his candidacy, a move that Clinton strategist, Paul Begala, noted had an "enormous impact" on the campaign: "Having the most important military figure in America getting up and saying Clinton could be an effective commander-in-chief undermined the Republicans' fundamental argument."[120]

Crowe's endorsement was reinforced by a statement released by the Clinton campaign in October 1992, in which many leading hawks revealed their support for Clinton: "We did not agree with the stand Bill Clinton took toward the Vietnam War as a young man, but that should not disqualify him from the presidency today . . . his firm support for the democratic and anticommunist movements in the former Soviet empire and in China make him a distinctly preferable candidate to George Bush."[121] Therefore, by the time of the debates, even Bush's foreign policy credentials were in doubt, as Adam Michnik, founding member of Poland's *Solidarity* movement, suggested that the Bush administration was "sleep-walking through history."[122]

These sentiments boosted the Clinton campaign and gave credence to the belief, expressed by Leon Fuerth, that Bush's foreign policy reputation was "over-rated."[123] His administration was being referred to as "The Revlon Presidency," due to Bush's perceived ability "to identify serious problems but offer only cosmetic solutions."[124] George Stephanopoulos declared "experience isn't judgment" and insisted that the Clinton campaign intended "to question the president's judgment when it is appropriate. Bill Clinton will cede no ground on foreign policy."[125] Polls taken immediately after the debates indicated that President Bush had lost them all, while Governor Clinton was only prevented from taking a clean sweep by a strong performance from Ross Perot in the first event.[126] The debates revealed Clinton to be Bush's equal in stature and his superior in style. As Craig Allen Smith observed, "Where Bush decried the 'vision thing,' Clinton had a vision . . . and a fusion of the liberal agenda and traditional values; and where Bush 'went negative' in the campaign, Clinton was positive in his affirmation of American values."[127]

The Clinton campaign's strategy in the final weeks concentrated on domestic affairs when possible and mentioned foreign policy only when necessary and always in a manner designed to demonstrate their candidate's abilities. However, Bush had the upper hand in the dying days of the campaign in his incumbency—his power to control events—and the Clinton campaign feared that with Bush stressing the threats and dangers of the new world, an international incident could be enough to convince voters to reelect the president.[128] However, despite potential troop deployments in Somalia, Bosnia, or Iraq, no such moves materialized by Election Day, paving the way for the election of William Jefferson Clinton as the forty-second president of the United States.

Conclusion: Clinton's triumph

Contrary to the popularly held misconception that Governor Clinton's 1992 campaign for the presidency focused entirely on domestic policy, an effort was made to define a grand strategy for his administration. Clinton focused his campaign on a comprehensive worldview and articulated an assertive internationalist approach, introducing the concept of linkage between domestic and foreign policy. The campaign proposed restructuring military forces to counter post-Cold War threats, promoting democracy and restoring America's economic leadership. Governor Clinton worked to overcome the foreign policy credibility gap that he had, both as an individual and as a member of the Democratic Party, and downplay Pat Buchanan's assertion that his international experience consisted of having "had breakfast once at the International House of Pancakes."[129]

Thomas Friedman noted that the Clinton campaign's foreign policy was "hard to summarize in a single phrase," but recognized that it was "a blend of idealism and pragmatism, internationalism and protectionism, use of force and reliance on multinational institutions."[130] Certainly, the policies that emerged from the campaign were vague and unformed, but the principles that continued in office were all in place: the promotion of democracy, the importance of the economic development, and the need to maintain a strong defensive capability. These concepts permeated policy, influenced rhetoric, and helped define attitudes in the Clinton White House until the strategies became not just stand-alone objectives, but integral aspects of US Grand Strategy.

The end of the Cold War created the conditions for Clinton's domestically focused candidacy, but as a candidate and as president, he discovered that challenges from beyond America's shores were impossible to avoid. Governor Clinton and his advisers established the broad concepts around which to base US Grand Strategy, but had also created challenges for themselves in locations as diverse as China, Bosnia, and Somalia. It was these challenges that they were forced to address in office, as they struggled to implement their activist policies and come to terms with their new roles. However, they found the transition to power more complex and bewildering than any of them had imagined, exposing concerns about their level of competence even before the administration had taken office.

Notes

1 George Stephanopoulos, *All Too Human: A Political Education* (London: Hutchinson, 1999), p. 88.

2 Lawrence Freedman, *The Evolution of Nuclear Strategy* (New York: St. Martin's Press, 1981), p. xviii.

3 For a consideration of the manner in which grand strategy has been defined, see Paul Kennedy (ed.), *Grand Strategies in War and Peace* (New Haven, CT: Yale University Press, 1991); Robert Art, *A Grand Strategy for America* (Ithaca, NY: Cornell University Press, 2003); Colin Dueck, *Reluctant Crusader: Power, Culture and Change in American Grand Strategy* (Princeton, NJ: Princeton University Press, 2008); John Lewis Gaddis, *Strategies of Containment: A Critical Appraisal of American National Security Policy During the Cold War* (New York: Oxford University Press, 2005); Williamson Murray, Richard Hart Sinnreich, and James Lacey (eds), *The Shaping of Grand Strategy: Policy, Diplomacy, and War* (New York: Cambridge University Press, 2011).

4 Freedman, *The Evolution of Nuclear Strategy*, p. xvi.

5 See Sun Tzu, *The Art of War*, translated by Samuel B. Griffith (New York: Oxford University Press, 1971), p. 91 and Carl Von Clausewitz, *On War*, edited and translated by Michael Howard and Peter Paret (Princeton, NJ: Princeton University Press, 1989), p. 128.

6 John Frederick Charles Fuller, *The Generalship of Ulysses S. Grant* (New York: Dodd, Mead & Co., 1929), pp. 4–5.

7 Edward Mead Earle, "Introduction," in Edward Mead Earle (ed.), *Makers of Modern Strategy: Military Thought from Hitler to Machiavelli* (Princeton, NJ: Princeton University Press, 1943), pp. viii–x.

8 Basil Henry Liddell Hart, *Strategy*, Second Revised Edition (New York: Meridian Books, 1991), p. 336. President Eisenhower subsequently warned of the dangers inherent in a "permanent armaments industry of vast proportions" that may be necessary for victory in time of war, but which may pose a challenge to the democratic order in peacetime. See Stephen E. Ambrose, *Eisenhower Volume Two: The President* (New York: Simon & Schuster, 1984), p. 612.

9 Liddell Hart, *Strategy*, pp. 322–324.

10 Kennedy, *Grand Strategies in War and Peace*, p. 5.

11 Gary Hart, *The Fourth Power: A Grand Strategy for the United States in the Twenty-First Century* (New York: Oxford University Press, 2004), p. 33.

12 Stephen D. Krasner, "An Orienting Principle for Foreign Policy," *Policy Review* no. 163, (October 2010), p. 4.

13 As revealed by Bob Woodward, Colin Powell believed that committing strategy to paper was a flawed approach, no matter how good they were since "this had the effect of chiseling them in stone, so that whenever the United States used force, somebody was going to object; wait a minute, you didn't

follow one of your rules." See Bob Woodward, *The Commanders* (New York: Simon & Schuster, 1991), pp. 117–118.

14 For an analysis of grand strategy thinking from Truman to George W. Bush (although bypassing Clinton almost altogether), see Hal Brands, *What Good is Grand Strategy?* (Ithaca, NY: Cornell University Press, 2014).

15 John Lewis Gaddis, "What Is Grand Strategy?" Karl Van Heyden Distinguished Lecture, Duke University, February 26, 2009.

16 Amy Zegart, "A Foreign Policy for the Future," *Defining Ideas* (Stanford, CA: The Hoover Institute, November 20, 2013).

17 Thomas Paine, "Common Sense," in Nina Baym, Ronald Gottesman, Laurence B. Holland, David Kalstone, Francis Murphy, Hershel Parker, William H. Pritchard, and Patricia B. Wallace (eds), *The Norton Anthology of American Literature*, Third Edition, Volume 1 (New York: W.W. Norton, 1989), p. 621.

18 Douglas Southall Freeman, *Washington* (New York: Collier Books, 1992), pp. 701–702; Joseph J. Ellis, *American Sphinx: The Character of Thomas Jefferson* (New York: Vintage Books, 1996), pp. 214–221.

19 Henry Kissinger, *Diplomacy* (New York: Touchstone Books, 1994), p. 30.

20 Leslie H. Gelb, *Power Rules: How Common Sense Can Rescue American Foreign Policy* (New York: HarperCollins, 2009), p. 103.

21 Gaddis, *Strategies of Containment*, pp. 25–88.

22 Brands, *What Good is Grand Strategy?* p. 18.

23 "Organization Meeting on Russia," June 12, 1946, Box 298, George F. Kennan Papers, Seeley Mudd Manuscript Library, Princeton University.

24 Brands, *What Good is Grand Strategy?* p. 21; Henry Kissinger, *White House Years* (Boston, MA: Little, Brown, 1979), p. 135.

25 Dean Acheson, *Present at the Creation: My Years at the State Department* (New York: W.W. Norton, 1969), p. 209.

26 Forrestal Diary, April 26, 1947, Box 146, Forrestal Papers, Seeley Mudd Manuscript Library, Princeton University.

27 For examples of the differing interpretations of NSC-68 see Gaddis, *Strategies of Containment*, Chapters 2–4; Melvyn Leffler, *A Preponderance of Power: National Security, the Truman Administration, and the Cold War* (Stanford, CA: Stanford University Press, 1992), pp. 355–360.

28 Morton B. Halperin, *Bureaucratic Politics and Foreign Policy* (Washington, DC: The Brookings Institution, 1974).

29 Larry Berman and Bruce W. Jentleson, "Bush and the Post-Cold War World: New Challenges for American Leadership," in Colin Campbell and Bert A. Rockman (eds), *The Bush Presidency: First Appraisals* (Chatham, NJ: Chatham House, 1991), pp. 93–128.

30 Quoted in Michael Beschloss and Strobe Talbott, *At the Highest Levels: The Inside Story of the End of the Cold War* (Boston, MA: Little, Brown, 1993), p. 434.

31 *PPPGB*, vol. 1 (1992), Address Before a Joint Session of the Congress on the State of the Union, January 28, 1992, p. 156.

32 Stanley Hoffman, "A New World and Its Troubles," *Foreign Affairs* 69, Issue 4 (Fall 1990), p. 118.

33 Memorandum from Fred Steeper to Robert Teeter, "1992 Presidential Campaign: The Churchill Parallel," in Peter Goldman, Thomas M. DeFrank, Mark Miller, Andrew Murr, and Tom Matthews (eds), *Quest for the Presidency 1992* (College Station, TX: Texas A&M Press, 1994), p. 621.

34 Sidney Blumenthal, *Pledging Allegiance: The Last Campaign of the Cold War* (New York: HarperCollins, 1991); Norman J. Ornstein, "Foreign Policy and the 1992 Election," *Foreign Affairs* 71, no. 3 (Summer 1992), p. 2.

35 Paul Tsongas, *A Call to Economic Arms* (Boston, MA: Foley, Hoag & Eliot, 1991), p. 60; Gavin Esler, *The United States of Anger: The People and the American Dream* (London: Michael Joseph Ltd, 1997), p. 7.

36 Robert Schlesinger, *White House Ghosts: Presidents and their Speechwriters* (New York: Simon & Schuster, 2008), p. 375. See also Eric A. Nordlinger, *Isolationism Reconfigured: American Foreign Policy for a New Century* (Princeton, NJ: Princeton University Press, 1996). Bush's efforts went un-rewarded, but were recognized subsequently. See Herbert S. Parmet, *George Bush: The Life of a Lone Star Yankee* (New York: Scribner, 1997); Curt Smith, *George H. W. Bush: Character at the Core* (Washington, DC: Potomac Books, 2014); John Robert Greene, *The Presidency of George Bush* (Lawrence, KS: University Press of Kansas, 2000).

37 Arthur M. Schlesinger, Jr, *The Cycles of American History* (London: Andre Deutsch, 1986), p. 47.

38 Sidney Blumenthal, *The Clinton Wars: An Insider's Account of the White House Years* (London: Penguin Books, 2003), p. 12.

39 With the end of the Cold War, a range of positions were advanced across the political spectrum, from essential continuity to an effective withdrawal to a "fortress America." See Cecil V. Crabb, Leila S. Sarieddine, and Glenn J. Antizzo, *Charting a New Diplomatic Course: Alternative Approaches to America's Post-Cold War Foreign Policy* (Baton Rouge, LA: Louisiana State University Press, 2001).

40 Tim Hames, "Foreign Policy," in Paul S. Herrnson and Dilys M. Hill (eds), *The Clinton Presidency: The First Term 1992–96* (New York: St. Martin's Press, 1999), p. 127.

41 Tim Hames, "Foreign Policy and the American Elections of 1992," *International Relations* 11 (April 1993), pp. 3315–3330.

42 David Gergen, *Eyewitness to Power: The Essence of Leadership, Nixon to Clinton* (New York: Simon & Schuster, 2000), p. 255.

43 Author's interview with Sir Malcolm Rifkind, MP (UK Defence Secretary 1992–1995, UK Foreign Secretary 1995–1997), Portcullis House, Westminster, October 8, 2013.

44 Tim Hames, "Foreign Policy," p. 127.

45 Author's interview with J. F. O. McAllister (*Time* State Department Correspondent 1989–1995, White House Correspondent 1995–1997, Washington Deputy Bureau Chief 1998–1999), February 28, 2014.

46 Author's interview with Anthony Lake (Assistant to the President for National Security Affairs 1993–1997), September 14, 2004.

47 Ivo H. Daalder and I. M. Destler, *In the Shadow of the Oval Office: Profiles of the National Security Advisers and the Presidents they Served-From JFK to George W. Bush* (New York: Simon & Schuster, 2009), p. 209.

48 Author's interview with Anthony Lake.

49 Nancy Soderberg, *The Superpower Myth: The Use and Misuse of American Might* (Hoboken, NJ: John Wiley & Sons, 2005), p. 14.

50 Elizabeth Drew, *On The Edge: The Clinton Presidency* (New York: Simon & Schuster, 1994), p. 141.

51 Jason DeParle, "The Man Inside Bill Clinton's Foreign Policy," *New York Times Magazine* (August 20, 1995), p. 33.

52 Author's interview with J. F. O. McAllister.

53 Author's interview with Nancy E. Soderberg (National Security Staff Director 1993–1997, Alternative Representative to the United Nations 1997–2001), May 26, 2004.

54 R. W. Apple, Jr, "Campaign Shifts to a New Turf; Clinton Challenges Bush on His Strong Suit, Foreign Policy," *New York Times* (July 29, 1992), p. A12.

55 Author's interview with Anthony Lake.

56 Martin Fletcher, "Foreign Capitals Braced for New White House Face," *The Times* (October 14, 1992), p. 12.

57 "A Who's Who of the Men Advising Clinton," *New York Times* (September 13, 1992), p. A36.

58 Martin Walker, "How Bill Clinton is Doing Fine with a Little Help from His Friends," *Guardian* (March 21, 1992), p. 10.

59 Jamie Dettmer, "Hostile World Waits To Test Clinton's Foreign Policy Team," *The Times* (December 23, 1992), p. 8.

60 Colin Campbell and Bert A. Rockman (eds), "Introduction," in *The Clinton Presidency: First Appraisals* (Chatham, NJ: Chatham House Press, 1996), p. 2.

61 Lake and Berger had previously served together as Director and Deputy Director of the Policy Planning Staff, respectively, in the Carter administration.

62 Ornstein, "Foreign Policy and the 1992 Election," p. 1.

63 William J. Clinton, *Between Hope and History: Meeting America's Challenges for the 21st Century* (New York: Random House, 1996), p. 6.

64 William J. Clinton, *My Life* (London: Hutchinson, 2004), p. 381.

65 Author's interview with J. F. O. McAllister.

66 Author's interview with Nancy E. Soderberg.

67 William J. Clinton, "A Campaign for the Future," speech in Little Rock, Arkansas, October 3, 1991, in Smith (ed.), *Preface to the Presidency*, pp. 80–81.

68 David Remnick, "A Very Big Delusion," *New Yorker* 68, Issue 37 (November 2, 1992), p. 4.

69 Charles O. Jones, "Campaigning to Govern," in Campbell and Rockman, *The Clinton Presidency*, p. 23.

70 E. J. Dionne, "Clinton Turns Sights to Foreign Policy," *Washington Post* (July 29, 1992), p. A1.

71 Author's interview with Anthony Lake.

72 William J. Clinton, "A New Covenant for American Security," speech at Georgetown University, Washington, DC, December 12, 1991, in Smith (ed.), *Preface to the Presidency*, pp. 119–120.

73 Richard M. Nixon, "Speech on the Future of Russia," March 11, 1992, in Alvin Z. Rubinstein, Albina Shayevich, and Boris Zlotnikov (eds), *The Clinton Foreign Policy Reader: Presidential Speeches with Commentary* (New York: M.E. Sharpe, 2000), p. 44.

74 Clinton, "A New Covenant for American Security," p. 112, 120.

75 Craig Allen Smith, "The Jeremiadic Logic of Bill Clinton's Policy Speeches," in Stephen A. Smith (ed.), *Bill Clinton on Stump, State and Stage: The Rhetorical Road to the White House* (Fayetteville, AR: Arkansas University Press, 1994), p. 88.

76 Clinton, "A New Covenant for American Security," pp. 113–124.

77 Clinton, *My Life*, p. 100.

78 Stanley Hoffman, *Primacy or World Order: American Foreign Policy Since The Cold War* (New York: McGraw-Hill Book Company, 1978), p. 164.

79 Bruce Russett, *Grasping the Democratic Peace: Principles for a Democratic World* (Princeton, NJ: Princeton University Press, 1993).

80 Bruce Russett and John O'Neil, *Triangulating Peace: Democracy, Interdependence and International Organizations* (New York: Norton, 2001).

81 George F. Kennan, *American Diplomacy*, Expanded Edition (Chicago: University of Chicago Press, 1985), p. 66.

82 Tony Smith, *America's Mission: The United States and the Worldwide Struggle for Democracy in the Twentieth Century* (Princeton, NJ: Princeton University Press, 1994), p. xiii.

83 Clinton, "A New Covenant for American Security," p. 120.

84 Mary Matalin and James Carville, *All's Fair: Love, War and Running for President* (New York: Random House, 1994), p. 86; Clinton, *My Life*, p. 383.

85 William J. Clinton, "A Strategy for Foreign Policy," speech at the Foreign Policy Association in New York, April 1, 1992, in *Vital Speeches of the Day* 58, Issue 14 (May 1, 1992), pp. 422–424.

86 *PPPGB*, vol. 1 (1992), Remarks at a St. Patrick's Day Ceremony and an Exchange With Reporters, March 17, 1992, p. 467.

87   Joseph O'Grady, "An Irish Policy Born in the USA: Clinton's Break With The Past," *Foreign Affairs* 75, no. 3 (May–June 1996), p. 3.

88   Clinton, *My Life*, p. 401.

89   Conor O'Clery, *The Greening of the White House* (Dublin: Gill & Macmillan, 1997), p. 98; O'Grady, "An Irish Policy Born in the USA," p. 6.

90   Author's interview with Sir Malcolm Rifkind.

91   Author's interview with Charles A. Kupchan (Policy Planning Staff, US Department of State, 1992, National Security Council, 1993–1994), January 24, 2014; Raymond Seitz, *Over Here* (London: Weidenfeld & Nicolson, 1998), p. 321.

92   Author's interview with Nancy Soderberg.

93   O'Grady, "An Irish Policy Born in the USA," p. 3.

94   William J. Clinton, "A Vision for America: A New Covenant," speech at Democratic National Convention, New York, July 16, 1992, in Smith (ed.), *Preface to the Presidency*, p. 214.

95   *PPPGB*, vol. 1 (1992), Remarks to Odetics, Inc., Associates, Anaheim, California, July 30, 1992, p. 1204.

96   Bill Clinton and Al Gore, *Putting People First: How We Can All Change America* (New York: Random House, Times Books, 1992), pp. 129–139.

97   Memorandum from Stuart E. Eizenstat to Mickey Kantor, George Stephanopoulos, Bruce Reed, Tony Lake, Sandy Berger, and Michael Mandelbaum, "Winning Back the Neoconservatives," July 30, 1992, Anthony Lake Papers, Manuscript Division, Library of Congress, Washington, DC, Box 10, Folder 10.

98   William J. Clinton, "Strategic Security in a Changing World," speech at the Los Angeles World Affairs Council, August 13, 1992, in Smith (ed.), *Preface to the Presidency*, p. 269.

99   Lee Hamilton, "A Democrat Looks at Foreign Policy," *Foreign Affairs* 71, no. 3 (Summer 1992), p. 34.

100   Clinton, "Strategic Security in a Changing World," pp. 269–274.

101   Michael Duffy and Dan Goodgame, *Marching in Place: The Status Quo Presidency of George Bush* (New York: Simon & Schuster, 1992), pp. 134–135.

102   Quoted in Strobe Talbott, *The Russia Hand: A Memoir of Presidential Diplomacy* (New York: Random House, 2002), p. 23.

103   Clinton, "Strategic Security in a Changing World," p. 272.

104   Memo to Governor Clinton from Sandy [Berger], Tony [Lake], Nancy [Soderberg], August 22, 1992, Anthony Lake Papers, Manuscript Division, Library of Congress, Washington, DC, Box 10, Folder 10.

105   Clinton, "Strategic Security in a Changing World," p. 272.

106   Ibid., p. 276.

107   Memo to Governor Clinton from Sandy [Berger], Tony [Lake], Nancy [Soderberg], August 22, 1992, Anthony Lake Papers, Manuscript Division, Library of Congress, Washington, DC, Box 10, Folder 10.

108 William J. Clinton, "Democracy in America," speech at University of Milwaukee, Wisconsin, October 1, 1992.

109 *PPPJFK*, vol. 1 (1961), Inaugural Address, January 20, 1961, p. 1.

110 Clinton, "Democracy in America."

111 John L. Helgerson, *Getting To Know the President: CIA Briefings of Presidential Candidates, 1952–1992* (Washington, DC: The Center for the Study of Intelligence, Central Intelligence Agency, 1996), p. 6.

112 Warren Christopher, *Chances of a Lifetime* (New York: Scribner Books, 2001), p. 150.

113 Al Gore, "Remarks on Foreign Policy," Center for National Policy, September 29, 1992.

114 Bill Turque, *Inventing Al Gore: A Biography* (New York: Houghton Mifflin Company, 2000), p. 258.

115 George Bush, *All the Best, George Bush: My Life in Letters and Other Writings* (New York: Scribner, 1999), p. 532; Matalin and Carville, *All's Fair*, p. 448.

116 "What Foreign Policy?" *New Republic* (September 20, 1991), p. 6.

117 Author's interview with Anthony Lake.

118 *PPPGB*, vol. 2 (1992), Presidential Debate in St. Louis, October 11, 1992, pp. 1789–1797.

119 *PPPGB*, vol. 2 (1992), Presidential Debate in Richmond, Virginia, October 15, 1992, pp. 1838–1843.

120 Quoted in Bruce Anderson, "An Admiral at the Court of St. James's," *Stanford Magazine* (September/October 1997).

121 "Bill Clinton and the Vietnam War," Anthony Lake Papers, Manuscript Division, Library of Congress, Washington, DC, Box 11, Folder 3.

122 Martin Walker, *The Cold War and the Making of the Modern World* (London: Fourth Estate, 1993), p. 311.

123 Author's interview with Leon Fuerth.

124 Peter Edelman quoted in Burt Solomon, "Vulnerable to Events," *National Journal* (January 6, 1990), p. 7.

125 Apple, "Campaign Shifts to a New Turf," p. A12.

126 Kathleen A. Frankovic, "Public Opinion in the 1992 Campaign," in Gerald Pomper (ed.), *The Election of 1992* (Chatham, NJ: Chatham House, 1993), p. 120.

127 Smith, "The Jeremiadic Logic of Bill Clinton's Policy Speeches," p. 89.

128 Frankovic, "Public Opinion in the 1992 Campaign," p. 120.

129 Patrick J. Buchanan, Speech to the Republican National Convention, Houston, Texas, August 17, 1992.

130 Thomas L. Friedman, "Clinton's Foreign Policy Agenda Reaches Across Broad Spectrum," *New York Times* (October 4, 1992), p. A1.

CHAPTER TWO

Taking charge and taking stock

On the evening of November 3, 1992, Bill Clinton made his first appearance as President-Elect of the United States, urging his fellow citizens to face "the challenges of the end of the Cold War . . . to face problems too long ignored" and begin "the conversion of our economy, from a defense to a domestic economic giant."[1] After a yearlong campaign advocating the need for sweeping change, the mantra for Clinton's period as president-elect was "essential continuity."[2] During the 11-week transition period that followed, Clinton was forced to reassess the viability of promises and assumptions made on the campaign, ensuring that long before he set foot in the Oval Office his attempts to dwell on domestic policy were threatened by events over which he had little control. The incoming administration was forced to assemble a foreign policy team drawn from a Democratic Party that had been out of power for all but 4 of the previous 24 years and take account of their challenging geopolitical inheritance.

The transition period exposed traits that continued once the Clinton team members were in office: a reluctance to confront difficult problems; a commitment to diversity that hindered decision making; and an inclusiveness that hampered an ability to say "no." The Democratic Party's 12-year absence from the White House became apparent as the administration came to Washington with a group of people who hadn't worked together as a team, whose job descriptions weren't clear and with a foreign policy concept that was generic at best and too theoretical for many. As George Stephanopoulos noted later, "We didn't know what we didn't know."[3]

World crises came to the fore during the transition that dominated the Clinton administration's first year on office, preventing it from focusing on long-term challenges and forcing it to concentrate on peripheral issues. Administration officials, returned to power for the first time in a political generation, struggled to implement their pet projects and come to terms with a news cycle that was radically different from the 1970s. Rather than the smooth transition of previous years, inexperience and in some cases sheer exhaustion meant that many in the administration simply "hit the ground barely standing."[4] Poor planning, unexpected crises, and a lack of focus ensured that Clinton's political honeymoon was effectively over before he even took the oath of office.

Clinton's post-Cold War world

Despite President-Elect Clinton's rhetorical emphasis on continuity, change was immediately apparent as the incoming team placed its stamp on US foreign policy. Foreign heads of state calling to offer their congratulations, all received the same message: "The next President of the United States was not available, call back tomorrow."[5] This was a calculated decision to convey that Clinton would not afford foreign affairs the same priority that President Bush had. It was, however, not a decision that endeared Clinton to world leaders with whom he needed to work in the coming years. Unlike Bush, who came to office with a network of foreign contacts, "Clinton was an unknown factor" and his actions caused "a bit of naval gazing at what might be the implications of this new president."[6] However, Clinton was determined that foreign policy not disturb him during the transition and declared "the greatest gesture of goodwill any nation can make toward me is to continue their full cooperation during this period with our one president, George Bush."[7] It was a declaration that distanced Clinton from any decisions made during the transition, with profound implications for when he took office.

Bill Clinton sought to effect change, but in foreign policy he found himself a prisoner of his own past and of decisions made long before he ran for the presidency. Despite his noted experience in international relations, President Bush failed to initiate a coherent policy to deal with the post-Cold War era that began during his administration, ensuring his time in office was "an era of illusion and false hopes in American policy" culminating in "the false dawn of a New World Order."[8] As a result, the incoming Clinton administration "faced a vacuum" in foreign policy, a challenge compounded by an apparent lack of planning for what to do once in office.[9] As Morton Halperin conceded, there was no coherent foreign policy in place when the administration came to power.[10] As a result, US foreign policy was in "disarray and confusion" at this point and the lack of direction hindered Clinton during his first months in power.[11]

On the campaign trail, "foreign policy had been more a matter of words than deeds, it amounted to little more than a couple of speeches and a series of press releases."[12] Suddenly, Clinton encountered the realities of power, as campaign pledges returned to haunt him as he found himself restricted by the size of his mandate, political intransigence, and the realities of governing in the 1990s. What Clinton needed was a smooth transition and a prolonged congressional honeymoon. However, Clinton's mandate for change was not as clear as his supporters imagined. Only Arkansas gave Clinton a plurality of its ballots and, with just 43 percent of the popular vote, his was a minority presidency. Accordingly, Republican Senator Bob Dole was quick to suggest that Clinton had no mandate, no coat tails, and no excuses, stressing "the good news is he's getting a honeymoon in Washington. The bad news is that Bob Dole is going to be his chaperon."[13] Republicans were determined to complicate Clinton's arrival in Washington, eyeing the midterm elections of 1994 before Clinton had even taken his oath of office.

During the transition, Clinton's advisers drafted papers on a potential trade war with Europe, the Middle East peace talks, and the state of Russian economic reform. With two of the reports directly linked to economics, Clinton's priorities reflected the ascendancy of economics in international relations and reinforced the president-elect's assertion that US economic recovery and its ability to shape world affairs were inseparable. Leon Fuerth conceded that the incoming administration faced a bewildering array of issues to address: "Would the US take an active role in promoting Middle East peace and how deeply should the president be in this? What approach should we take towards reform and democratisation in Russia? What was America prepared to do to prevent Russia from entering a free-fall?"[14]

The Council on Foreign Relations and the Carnegie Endowment National Commission advised the president-elect to prioritize geofinance (the measurement of national power in terms of exports and currency markets) over geopolitics (in which national strength was measured in armaments).[15] The suggestion that Clinton focus on the economy as a precondition for an effective foreign policy was warmly received in Little Rock and was, in part, a reflection of the changing times. No president in the previous four decades could have elevated economics to the level of national security in the manner that Clinton aspired to, due to the ongoing Cold War. As President Kennedy remarked, "The big difference [between domestic and foreign policy] is between a bill being defeated and the country being wiped out."[16] Clinton, freed from Cold War commitments, was finally able to throw off this yoke.

However, while the incoming administration's focus may have been on domestic issues, foreign policy could not be ignored. Bill Clinton had won the election with promises of a proactive presidency to change America. However, he found the era to be a double-edged sword: the end of the Cold War created the domestic conditions for his election, and also caused a turbulent international environment that demanded more of his attention than he wished to surrender, as the departing Bush administration left a series of unresolved dilemmas: the USSR had collapsed; China was undergoing civil unrest following the Tiananmen Square protests; tensions with Iraq were unresolved; Haitians were preparing for a mass exodus to the United States; and Yugoslavia had degenerated into a civil war. These were matters of historical importance, but did not represent a direct threat to US national security and were certainly not a priority for the new administration. They did, however, need to be addressed, costing the president-elect valuable political capital as they distracted from his domestic focus.

As a consequence, many aspects of Bush's foreign policy continued under Clinton: the Middle East peace talks, START II negotiations, world trade talks, bolstering Russia's fledgling democracy, efforts to find a resolution to the conflict in the Balkans, and preventing starvation in Somalia were all policies that varied little from what George Bush had intended to address had he been reelected. President-Elect Clinton did not wish to dwell on these issues, so it made sense to continue existing programs, at least until there was time to devise new ones. Clinton also discovered during the transition that continuity was less dangerous than attempting new initiatives, as his credibility suffered due to two candid remarks that initially appeared to signify changes in US foreign policy.

When asked about future dealings with Iraq, the president-elect indicated that Saddam could be welcomed back into the family of nations, declaring that he "believed in deathbed conversions."[17] Unlike Eisenhower's dramatic decision to intervene personally to end the Korean conflict, however, Bill Clinton did not have the military experience to immediately rectify the struggle with Iraq. He had neither the military standing nor the political strength on Capitol Hill to espouse bold new initiatives in this area and discovered that his past dealings with the military forced him to acquiesce to the policies of the previous administration.

This was compounded by a furore that developed during the transition over the issues of homosexuals serving in the US military. This issue had not been a priority on the campaign and was triggered by an off the cuff remark the president-elect made to a reporter. The ensuing *mêlée* distracted attention from domestic affairs, raised doubts over the president-elect's political competence, and ensured that Bill Clinton's standing with the military eroded further before he took office.

Assembling a foreign policy team

Despite having campaigned solidly since October 1991, Bill Clinton immediately began the process of assembling a foreign policy team to implement his grand strategy for the post-Cold War world. However, in 1992 the Democratic Party had been out of power for 12 years and in power for only 4 of the past 24 years. Jimmy Carter's single term was the party's only experience in government since Lyndon Johnson left the White House in January 1969, ensuring that all senior Democrats were tainted either by their time in the Carter or Johnson administrations. Michael J. Sandel voiced the concerns of many when he noted that while Clinton was "rightly confident about his abilities in domestic affairs . . . he seems less confident about foreign policy. There is a risk, therefore, that he will embrace the conventional wisdom in foreign policy of the old Democratic Party establishment."[18]

There were also personalities to consider, for there was "the sense that Bill and Hillary thought they could do it all themselves." Both were used to being the center of attention in Arkansas and were determined to continue this at the White House. "As a result, some of the most clever and experienced Democratic Party operatives found themselves shut out of the administration or marginalized."[19] This included Richard Holbrooke, whose credentials should have made him a natural selection for a high-profile role at the State Department, but whose deteriorating relationship with Lake and reputation for being "a pain in the ass" led to his appointment as Ambassador to Germany.[20] With his domestic focus and lack of international experience, Clinton needed a strong foreign policy team to compensate for his "background, indecisiveness, and detachment."[21] The difference between what Clinton needed and what he secured was instrumental to the development and direction of US Grand Strategy in the 1990s.

Clinton wanted a competent Secretary of State who could run the department efficiently and prevent foreign policy from distracting the president from his domestic agenda. However, Clinton discovered that there was "a huge gap in age between those who would do it in the past and those who were not yet ready, but wanted to do it."[22] Having discounted senior Democrats from previous administrations, it appeared that the right candidate might be found on Capitol Hill. However, there was a reluctance to take people out of Congress due to the narrow Democratic majorities in both chambers. Additionally, the most viable candidates in the Senate were more experienced than the president-elect. Drawing on their experience during the campaign was one thing, but many were unwilling to surrender their safe seats to serve a president with a slender mandate and a perceived ambivalence toward foreign policy, especially since many believed that they could wield more power on congressional committees than in the cabinet.

Intriguingly, the successful candidate was already part of the transition team but had played no role in advising the candidate on foreign policy during the campaign. Later identified as "the only man ever to eat Presidential M&Ms on Air Force One with a knife and fork," Clinton's Transition Director Warren Christopher had been Deputy Secretary of State under President Carter and was the most senior figure in the Democratic Party's foreign policy establishment and, who, at 67, was not too old to serve and had not served at a Cabinet level before.[23] Christopher had not started out as Clinton's preference, but he had proved to be a discreet adviser on choosing the vice president. In his selection of Christopher, Bill Clinton demonstrated an ability to identify some of his own failings; his lack of standing with Washington's elite, his lack of foreign policy experience, and a perceived lack of refinement.

However, while Christopher's abilities were not inconsiderable, his critics thought they fell short, particularly for a job about to become extremely important now that the Cold War was over. It was noted that Christopher "may be a consummate manager, but is a highly unlikely architect of a new world order."[24] Few were excited by him, his view of the world or believed he had any particular ideas of his own on foreign policy. Indeed, although Christopher wanted to be Secretary of State "he seemed to have no strong beliefs or guiding philosophy."[25] This was partly why he had so few enemies, and also why many people who knew him had doubts about his selection. Madeleine Albright suggested that Christopher remained "a lawyer's lawyer," while others worried that he lacked imagination and innovation.[26] The consensus was that he was an ideal deputy, but unqualified to run the State Department and "unlikely to develop into a Metternich for the 1990s."[27]

In a move that had serious repercussions for Clinton's presidency, Christopher advised the president-elect to ignore suggestions that an overarching, single-word doctrine for US foreign policy be identified to replace Containment. Christopher stressed that the post-Cold War challenges were too diverse to be summarized in a neatly defined doctrine. Although this stance was not without its supporters, it revealed a lack of appreciation for the need to present a coherent strategic vision that became an impediment to the development of Clinton's Grand Strategy.

Samuel "Sandy" Berger was offered the top job at the National Security Council (NSC), but realized that the foreign policy establishment perceived him as a Washington trade lawyer with strong Democratic Party connections. In a move that endeared him to the president-elect, Berger recommended Anthony Lake, his old boss from the Policy Planning Staff, for the position. Lake had not lobbied for the position, nor worked on the transition, but agreed to serve, despite reservations about the potential impact on his home life and general contentment working in Massachusetts and living on his farm.[28] Lake and Berger became the central components of Clinton's foreign policy team, "the principals, working with the issues and dealing with the president . . . Tony and Sandy were the CEO and deputy CEO; they were the decision makers, the ones making judgments and briefing the president."[29] Lake and Berger agreed on the need for US foreign engagement and the support for human rights, although Berger brought "a less academic and more political approach to the table."[30]

Nancy Soderberg joined Lake and Berger, serving as Deputy Assistant to the President for National Security Affairs, the third ranking official at the NSC, or "the COO of the NSC" from 1993 to 1997.[31] However, the appointment of Lake and Berger proved frustrating to Michael Mandelbaum, who had advised the Clinton campaign on Russian affairs, contributed to early speeches, and had a relationship with Clinton dating back to their university days in England. It was believed, however, that his thinking was more Realist than Wilsonian, placing him at odds with the central core of advisers on the campaign. Having been denied the job he sought at the NSC, he rejected the Directorship of the Policy Planning Staff and remained at Johns Hopkins University.[32]

Due to Clinton's past dealings with the military and his lack of a service record, the task of running the Pentagon was always likely to be contentious. Senator Sam Nunn was considered, but his conservative voting record made him anathema to the liberal wing of the Democratic Party. Despite the reluctance to take people out of the Congress, Les Aspin, the Chairman of the House Armed Services Committee, had helped on the campaign and was a *bona fide* defense intellectual, was selected. He was also a Democrat who disagreed with calls for dramatic reductions in the US defense budget and was initially well regarded by the professional military.[33] However, doubts were raised as to whether Aspin was too abrasive to run the Pentagon and, although he was selected, his time in office was neither happy nor protracted. The same was true for Clinton's appointment as CIA Director. Clinton had intended to nominate the Chairman of the House Intelligence Committee, Dave McCurdy, but he refused to resign his seat to run the CIA. The only job that interested him was at the Pentagon, where he was Clinton's second choice. After considering Tom Pickering, Clinton was persuaded to name neoconservative James Woolsey, whose credentials were a mystery to Clinton's closest advisers—as Press Secretary Dee Dee Myers mistook him for an admiral.[34]

Clinton initially invited his friend and Russian expert Strobe Talbott to be ambassador to Moscow; however, Talbott urged Clinton to consider Condoleezza Rice, who served as President Bush's senior Russia adviser on the NSC. Talbott believed that her appointment might address the lack of bipartisanship in the foreign policy team and provide continuity in a vital area of foreign policy.[35] Instead, Clinton heeded Warren Christopher's advice that a seasoned professional diplomat was needed in Moscow, and appointed Tom Pickering.[36] Talbott took a role at the State Department where he came to assist with broader policy toward Russia, although within a year he was promoted to Deputy Secretary of State.[37] Clinton again considered Dr Rice for the UN Ambassadorship, but decided to stay within the Democratic Party, naming another Carter administration alum, Madeleine Albright.[38]

"In a time of great change and challenges, the world is no longer a simple place with clear choices," Clinton said as he introduced his foreign policy team. In the post-Cold War era, he noted, "we need bold thinking to advance our American values."[39] The foreign policy team had been assembled for their capability to do the job with as little fuss as possible. To many, however, the appointments represented a poor choice to devise US policy in a time of rapid and unpredictable change, and were widely viewed as a collection of "Carter administration retreads."[40] Even Clinton supporters expressed concern over the team, which many New Democrats felt looked a lot like Old Democrats. Joe Klein lamented that there was "a blandness, a lack of personal intensity in positions of great power that seems, well, weird."[41] Republicans, uniformly excluded from the cabinet, feared an obsession with negotiations, angst over the use of military force and, from their point of view, too low an intellectual level.[42] Even the desire to avoid "the total chaos and disillusion and misery" caused by in-fighting during the Carter years was not avoided, as personal feuding and the desire to define policy continued unabated.[43]

Bill Clinton had sought a diverse group of cabinet officers that resembled the United States, but it appeared that their defining qualities were membership of the Council on Foreign Relations, their time together at a subcabinet level under President Carter, and the fact that they "were not attuned to the rigours of the new twenty-four hour news cycle or the harsh partisan politics that pervaded the Congress."[44] Suddenly, the "essential continuity" that Clinton spoke of appeared to be with the 1970s, rather than with the early 1990s. It was not an auspicious beginning.[45]

The return to Georgetown

Having named his foreign policy team, President-Elect Clinton outlined his administration's priorities in an address to members of the Diplomatic Corps at Georgetown University, 2 days before he took the oath of office. He had spoken at the university 13 months earlier to unveil the New Covenant concepts that formed the ideological basis of his campaign for the presidency. Now Bill Clinton had arrived at a position of unrivalled power to dictate grand strategy for the coming 4 years, a moment he referred to as "an era of both peril and promise," during which "the future for millions and millions of people around the globe can be better than the present." It could be an age when "the dreams of freedom and democracy and economic prosperity and human rights can become real," but Clinton stressed that much depended on what path the United States adopted. Having spent the previous year attacking the Bush administration, the president-elect announced that he intended to build on his predecessor's work in the Middle East, nuclear arms reduction, Somalia, and reform in the former USSR, raising questions about the degree of change that could be expected under this New Democrat.

However, the central narrative of Clinton's foreign policy remained consistent from the Georgetown Address of December 1991 and was reiterated once more on the eve of his presidency. Clinton formalized the place of economic security within US Grand Strategy and collapsed the barrier between domestic and foreign policy, since the United States could no longer "sustain an active engagement abroad without a sound economy at home." Having not served in the military, the president-elect sought to stress the most robust element to his foreign policy initiative: maintaining US national security through superior firepower. Clinton insisted that grand strategy would be "based on a restructuring of our armed forces to meet new and continuing threats to our security interests and the international peace." The end of the Cold War allowed the new administration to "continue prudently to reduce defense spending," but the incoming commander-in-chief stressed that "potential aggressors should be clear about American resolve." Clinton did not relish the prospect of military engagement, but stressed that he would do so "when all appropriate diplomatic measures have been exhausted."

Clinton announced that his grand strategy was to be dedicated to "the democratic principles and institutions which unite our own country and to which so many now around the world aspire." The president-elect insisted "America cannot and should not bear the world's burdens alone. But if we work together, we can make great progress in making this a better world." He committed his administration to the defense of freedom and democracy, noting that "whenever possible we will support those who share our values, because it is in the interests of America and the world at large for us to do so." Finally, Clinton advocated the promotion of democracy, insisting, "history has borne out these enduring truths: Democracies do not wage war against one another; they make better partners in trade and . . . offer the best guarantee for the protection of human rights."[46]

This utilization of Kant's Democratic Peace concept proved to be pivotal to the grand strategy adopted by the United States in the post-Cold War era and was central not only to Clinton, but also to his successor. The capacity of the United States to implement sweeping Democracy Promotion was severely tested in Clinton's time in office and the moral justification for it came to be disputed during his successor's tenure. In 1993, however, few questioned this commitment to freedom and democracy so soon after the collapse of the Berlin Wall.[47]

Bill Clinton's decision to address the diplomatic corps at Georgetown University on the eve of his presidency should not be overlooked. The combination of location, audience, and timing sent a variety of messages, both domestically and internationally. It signified a new era in grand strategy was imminent, with new priorities and a new focus in which economics were central, along with Wilsonian concepts of Democracy Promotion. However, this was not going to be an administration that shrank from military confrontation when necessary and Clinton was eager to highlight this, lest his opponents, foreign or domestic, thought otherwise. In the coming weeks, Clinton would refer darkly to a passage from Machiavelli's *The Prince*: "There is nothing more difficult to plan, more doubtful of success, nor more dangerous to manage, than a creation of a new order of things" as he discovered the difference between campaigning and governing, and pledges returned to haunt him in the partisan atmosphere of Washington, DC.[48]

Following an efficient campaign, Clinton's transition period was "considered by many historians and by more than a few staff members who suffered through it, as the worst in modern history."[49] A chaotic management style and the president-elect's insistence on approving all White House appointments resulted in vital time being lost. Morton Halperin insists that Clinton's approach reflected the priorities of the president as well as the changing geopolitical environment: "The president had his domestic agenda and foreign policy was not as imposing or as pressing then as when Kennedy had come to power. The Cold War was over so he spent less time dealing with foreign policy." Halperin acknowledged that this was hindered by the Bush administration, which left "a mess in Somalia that demanded more attention than we would have liked."[50] However, these were "eleven lost weeks, a time irretrievably squandered," which raised concerns about the new administration's preparedness for power.[51] Eisenhower's critique of the Kennedy White House appeared apt: "Good organization does not guarantee good policy. But bad organization guarantees bad policy."[52] The momentum behind Clinton's early agenda was taken from him and he spent his first months in office struggling to get it back.

Talking the talk . . .

The first opportunity for Bill Clinton to address grand strategy as president of the United States was in his inaugural address. As a student of history, Clinton was aware of those who had gone before him and of the opportunity that lay ahead, telling readers of *Time* that he aimed to be "somewhere between Roosevelt and Kennedy" since "there's a sense that we need to get the country moving again."[53] What Roosevelt and Kennedy had brought to the White House, however, was an eloquence that Clinton had not been blessed with in the past. He had been jeered while nominating Michael Dukakis in 1988 and his own acceptance speech had been criticized for lasting over an hour. George Stephanopoulos understood that Clinton's inaugural address had to be "crisp, concise,

Kennedyesque."[54] For the previous 40 years, inaugural addresses had dwelt on foreign affairs, as presidents declared their intentions to the world. However, this was not to be the case with President William Jefferson Clinton—as he was to be known officially. Due to Clinton's domestic agenda, foreign policy did not dominate the address and was only referenced in the context of linkage to domestic policy. Over the course of at least 20 drafts, Michael Waldman and David Kusnet prepared a speech that focused on campaign pledges to renew American democracy and stressed the themes of economic renewal, government reform, and increased personal responsibility.[55] However, the word of the day was "change," which was mentioned nine times. Clinton's campaign speeches were abridged into an inaugural address of 1,557 words, making it, "the third shortest inaugural speech in history by the third youngest man to make one."[56]

On the campaign, Governor Bill Clinton insisted that his foreign and domestic priorities were "one and the same: reviving our economy."[57] Now, as president, Clinton used his inaugural address to insist "there is no longer a clear division between what is foreign and what is domestic. The world economy, the world environment, the world arms race—they affect us all." This became a recurring theme in Clinton's presidency as an increasing dependence on international commerce to bolster the domestic economy ensured that trade became an integral aspect of US Grand Strategy. Clinton redefined the parameters of American power to utilize foreign policy for domestic purposes. However, he insisted that, "While America rebuilds at home, we will not shrink from the challenges nor fail to seize the opportunities of this new world." Clinton was adamant that a US global presence would not be forfeited in favor of domestic renewal, but instead would be used to assist in strengthening the nation, confirming that America "must continue to lead the world [it] did so much to make."

However, in an inaugural address dedicated almost entirely to domestic affairs, the line concerning foreign affairs received most focus, as Clinton announced, "when our vital interests are challenged, we will act, with peaceful diplomacy whenever possible, with force when necessary."[58] In this oblique reference to Iraq came confirmation that if foreign issues arose that were not economic in nature, the Clinton administration planned to resort to classic power politics. However, although the new administration's view of foreign policy rejected a preponderance of power philosophy in favor of a multilateral approach, its overall methodology was unclear at this stage. Bill Clinton had campaigned stressing an activist approach to government, but his inaugural address lacked direction, ensuring that questions remained concerning the focus and intent of US Grand Strategy.

The new geopolitical environment was of little help to the administration in this regard. Two years before Clinton took office,

Theodore H. Moran predicted that in the coming decade, US national security would face "not clear and present dangers requiring great sacrifices, but dim and distant dangers calling for small sacrifice."[59] The sudden absence of a single foe presented the Clinton administration with a challenge, since discerning the national interest was complicated by the lack of an external threat. This ensured the White House "faced a choice instead of compulsion" as it sought to define America's new role in the world.[60] Kissinger noted at the time that Clinton "must find a role for an America that can neither dominate nor retreat."[61] The president needed to do so while fulfilling his pledge to concentrate on domestic policy, a balancing act that was initially achieved by delegating authority to National Security Advisor Anthony Lake, Secretary of State Warren Christopher, and Defense Secretary Les Aspin. This, however, quickly led to claims that the president was not in control of foreign policy, a charge that hindered his efforts to implement sweeping change in the direction of international affairs. "I might have to spend all my time on foreign policy," Clinton admitted, "and I don't want that to happen."[62] However, Clinton's presidential inheritance beckoned and the world was not about to wait for his new team to settle in. All too quickly, President Clinton "became surprised by how quickly the in-box filed up with stuff that he didn't put there."[63]

Having devoted barely 200 words to foreign affairs in a 7,000-word address to a joint session of Congress on February 17, 1993, President Clinton's speech at the American University 9 days later was intended to compensate. This was the first national security speech drafted following Anthony Lake's successful effort to ensure that the NSC prepared such addresses rather than the White House speechwriters. On the day of the event, speechwriter Jeremy Rosner was concerned that the president had not practiced enough and could flounder, drawing upon varying drafts. However, as Rosner noted, Clinton "ad-libbed some sections, he found the key paragraphs. And it was this gorgeous speech . . . much better than anything we wrote."[64]

Speaking on February 26, Clinton reminded his audience that President Kennedy had spoken at the same university at the height of the Cold War on "the imperative of pursuing peace in the face of nuclear confrontation." Having drawn the historical comparison and raised the image of his political hero, President Clinton used similar language to address "the great challenge of this day: the imperative of American leadership in the face of global change." Clinton insisted that the great question of the time was whether the United States would adopt an isolationist stance as it had in the 1920s and 1930s, or "repeat the successes of the 1940s and the 1950s by reaching outward and improving ourselves as well." The president made clear that definitions of national security were changing in the new era and that economic leadership was a priority. In light of this, the debate over GATT and NAFTA took on new meaning. They were no longer seen as trade agreements, but as strategic initiates vital to the continued economic security of the United States.

It was already apparent that capital and services had become global and the new president summoned his countrymen to see the future as a land of opportunity, intoning, "in the face of all the pressures to do the reverse, we must compete, not retreat." The address revealed the understanding of globalization that Bill Clinton brought to the presidency as he analyzed the problems to be overcome and presented a series of remedies. Neither globalization nor Clinton's prescribed solutions were necessarily new, but his move to define economic security as vital to US national security was indicative of the new post-Cold War environment in which he sought to define US Grand Strategy. The president insisted his concept was based on established principles, for "as philosophers from Thucydides to Adam Smith have noted, the habits of commerce run counter to the habits of war."[65] This, at least, was a philosophical basis for Clinton's policies, but his referencing of an ancient Greek historian best known for his *History of the Peloponnesian War*, and an eighteenth-century Scottish philosopher raised questions about the originality of Clinton's New Democrat concepts and their suitability for the late twentieth century.

Tough talk with the Pentagon

As the Clinton administration sought to develop grand strategy during 1993, the Bottom Up Review was underway at the Pentagon, drafted from position papers prepared by Les Aspin's staff from the House Armed Services Committee. The goal was to implement Clinton's "pledge to cut forces by 200,000 troops and tens of billions of dollars."[66] More immediate was the "pledge to slash $60 billion from George Bush's defense budget over five years, beginning with $5.7 billion in 1994."[67] There was a public expectation that millions of dollars could be diverted from the military to domestic spending, thus delivering a peace dividend. However, on the campaign Clinton had been attacked as a draft dodging, pot smoking, military-bashing liberal. Now, as commander-in-chief, Clinton desperately needed to avoid an open clash with the military, finding himself caught between political expediency and ideology.

On March 12, 1993, Bill Clinton made his first visit to a military establishment as president. Aboard the aircraft carrier *USS Theodore Roosevelt*, he addressed the issues facing the US military and declared that a "changed security environment demands not less security but a change in our security arrangements." The trip was designed to address the belief that Clinton's avoidance of military service in Vietnam disqualified him from serving as commander-in-chief, as well as allay fears of impending reductions in military spending. The two did not play well together, especially when compounded by the furore over gays in the military that enveloped the administration. The president stressed, "you have the services working together in new ways. That enables you to operate perhaps with fewer ships and personnel, but with greater efficiency and effectiveness." It was unclear how many of the assembled sailors were convinced, but the commander-in-chief reminded them that defense spending had been declining since 1986.

The downsized military needed to react to a growing number of regional crises where US interests were not directly involved, as the conflicts of the era became focused on the periphery of what could broadly be defined as America's area of strategic interest. One of Clinton's greatest challenges was in defining exactly where US interests lay in the absence of a single, formidable foe and his efforts to reconfigure the economy or the armed forces remained impeded by an inability to do so. The world environment, however, meant the US military "must also be agile, with an emphasis on manoeuvre, on speed, on technological superiority." The president referred to the world as "a hopeful time, yet one still full of challenges."[68] Not all agreed with this sunny assessment of the international situation and their pessimism soon found focus in the Horn of Africa.

The president sought to build on his remarks concerning US military priorities in a Commencement Address at West Point Military Academy on May 29, 1993. He conceded that the collapse of the Soviet Union had not resulted in utopia and that the end of the Cold War left America "with unfamiliar threats, not the absence of danger." The new era heralded the return of older forces; "ethnic and religious conflict, the violent turmoil of dissolving or newly created states, the random violence of the assassin and the terrorist." It was these forces that Clinton saw unleashed; "from the former Soviet Union and Yugoslavia to Armenia to Sudan, the dynamics of the Cold War have been replaced by many of the dynamics of old war." However, even at the crucible of America's military machine, Clinton could not ignore the economy, insisting that "what ultimately enabled us to prevail in the Cold War was the simple fact that our free political and economic institutions had produced more prosperity and more personal human happiness than did the confining institutions of communism."[69] The speeches were only the first in a series that Clinton gave during his presidency in a vain effort to gain the support of the military.

New structures

Among his very first acts as president, Bill Clinton initiated a number of changes to the national security architecture. Awaiting his signature immediately after taking the oath of office were two Presidential Decision Directives. The first (PDD-1) established the Clinton-era Presidential Review Directive (PRD) and the Presidential Decision Directive (PDD) series.[70] The second (PDD-2) enlarged the membership of the NSC to include the Secretary of the Treasury, thereby placing a greater emphasis on economic issues in the formulation of national security policy. PDD-2 also granted the Deputies Committee responsibility for day-to-day crisis management (CM), when it was designated Deputies Committee/CM. This was a decision with implications for operations in Somalia, Rwanda, and Bosnia in the years ahead and led to allegations of disengagement at the senior level of the administration.

Despite the yearlong campaign against the Bush administration's policies, Clinton's team saw no reason to unnecessarily alter what was widely perceived to have been an efficient and coherent NSC structure.[71] As a result, Clinton's NSC structure built on changes implemented by his predecessor and included a Principals Committee as a forum available to cabinet-level officials to address issues not requiring the president's participation, as well as a Deputies Committee for considering national security policy issues at a subcabinet level.[72] Initially, Clinton's NSC "was not a hierarchical structure," but was "open access" and "user friendly," a situation that enabled increased access to the president, but did not necessarily make for an effective operation.[73]

Somalia and Assertive Multilateralism

No administration inherits a clean slate; however, the Clinton team took office in the midst of an ongoing operation in Somalia. The plight of the Somali people became apparent during 1992 while America's focus was on the presidential campaign. Only after his defeat did President Bush declare the Somali deployment, "necessary to address a major humanitarian calamity and avert related threats to international peace and security and protect the safety of Americans and others engaged in relief operations."[74] On December 9, 1992, US troops landed in Somalia under the auspices of Security Council Resolution 794, as United Task Force (UNITAF) codenamed Operation Restore Hope.

The deployment ensured that the Clinton administration entered office with more than 25,000 troops deployed in an ill-conceived mission and needed to develop a strategy to deal with the situation, since the mission was "inherited" and "not thought out."[75] Dick Moose, Clinton's Under-Secretary of State for Management, drafted a memo examining options in Somalia that recommended a withdrawal. However, when his report received a muted response from Anthony Lake and Sandy Berger "he suspected he was saying something that Lake . . . did not want to hear."[76]

Moose was not alone in his concerns, however; Morton Halperin, at that point working for Defense Secretary Aspin, suggested a pragmatic approach: "I felt that we should get out of Mogadishu, since we had no stake in that fight. I felt that we should establish a base in the countryside and tell the people if you want to come and get food, its here, if you want to stay in Mogadishu and shoot each other, then stay in Mogadishu and shoot each other."[77]

However, Lake and Berger were proponents of a humanitarian-led foreign policy and feared that such actions might return Somalia to a state of anarchy. Lake in particular had a special interest in the plight of Africa and was committed to the operation's completion. In addition to Lake and Berger, Ambassador to the United Nations, Madeleine Albright, was committed to the mission, having spent the 1980s on the Georgetown University faculty developing the concept of Assertive Multilateralism.[78] This posited that if the United States no longer had the political will or the resources to act as a global policeman, it should form coalitions to do so. It meant, "that when America acted with others, [America] should lead in establishing goals and ensuring success."[79] Vitally, this did not preclude unilateral action in self-defense or safeguard vital interests. The United Nations appeared to offer the best forum for such an approach in the 1990s, enabling the United States to lead while simultaneously reducing its defense expenditure. Albright was adamant that Assertive Multilateralism was a tactic, not a goal and a continuation of President Bush's actions in the 1991 Gulf War. It was an approach that the administration believed would receive strong bipartisan support. As late as June 1993, Albright was insistent that Assertive Multilateralism was in America's best interests.[80]

However, the advice from Moose and Halperin should have been heeded. Instead, an ideological determination by the administration's senior foreign policy advisors caused them to reject pragmatic options and pursue policies that bore no resemblance to anything that had been espoused on the campaign trail and which had no place in the grand strategy that eventually emerged. It was a decision that contributed to tragic results in Somalia and the nadir of foreign intervention for the entire Clinton presidency.

In May 1993, the United States handed over operational command of the Somali mission to the United Nations and reduced its contingent to just 1,100 rapid reaction troops and 3,000 logistical support personnel. UNITAF morphed into UNOSOM II as the Clinton administration endorsed Security Council Resolution 814, authorizing the United Nations to rebuild Somalia. President Clinton hosted a reception on the South Lawn of the White House to honor service personnel returning from Somalia on May 5, at which point only eight Americans had been lost during the deployment. This had been "the largest humanitarian relief operation in history" and an operation that the president believed, had "written an important new chapter in the international annals of peacekeeping and humanitarian assistance."[81] However, leaving personnel in Somalia ensured the United States retained a lingering commitment to a mission that was of minimal importance to the administration. The mission remained multilateral at this point, but US involvement was anything but assertive. Retaining even a token commitment guaranteed that what was initiated under Resolution 814 became associated with the administration, despite the lead taken on the issue by UN Secretary General Boutros Boutros-Ghali, whose commitment to social engineering led to a shift in the mission's parameters.

The US withdrawal emboldened Somali warlords, including General Mohammed Aideed, who targeted the multinational peacekeeping force on June 5, killing 23 Pakistani peacekeepers. This resulted in calls to arrest Aideed "pursuant to Security Council Resolution 837."[82] Having withdrawn more than 20,000 troops from Somalia, President Clinton acquiesced to the recommendation of Chairman of the Joint Chiefs, Colin Powell, and the Deputies Committee of the NSC to deploy Task Force Ranger to Somalia to prevent further losses to the UN detachment.[83] This rapid decision, made at a subcabinet level, drew American forces deeper into a land where US interests were impossible to define and in an operation that had nothing to do with the administration's priorities.

On October 3, 1993, American Special Forces, dispatched to apprehend Aideed, became embroiled in a mission that dragged on throughout the night, as two Black Hawk helicopters were lost. The ensuing battle cost 18 American lives in the worst day of battlefield casualties in the entire Clinton presidency. It contributed to the abandonment of Assertive Multilateralism as a model of policy implementation and began a shift in focus away from the United Nations as the organization of choice for future US initiatives. The White House was "totally blindsided by Somalia" and the mission raised serious questions about the administration's commitment to its publicly declared principles.[84]

The Bush administration's decision to intervene in Somalia was recommended by the Deputies Committee of the National Security Council. This process continued under the Clinton administration as the Deputies Committee, rather than the full National Security Council, oversaw events in Somalia.[85] There was no Principals Meetings on Somalia until tragedy struck, because "the operation seemed to be going well. The mission seemed on track for transfer to the UN, with US forces scheduled to be out by early to mid-1994."[86] This ensured that cabinet-level officials were "not sufficiently attentive" to the Somali operation and that President Clinton was removed from the policy-making process.[87] Nancy Soderberg, Staff Director of the National Security Council at the time, conceded the administration "weren't really paying attention" and "didn't focus enough on the political track as it was being shifted over to the United Nations, so that was a huge mistake."[88] This created a self-perpetuating situation; focus on domestic priorities led to inattention to the Somali mission, contributing to American fatalities, which ensured political adversaries could exploit the Somali debacle for their own ends and derail the administration's domestic policy programs. Clearly, "wild assumptions were made and no one was paying attention."[89]

President Clinton's well-documented, but well-hidden temper erupted at this stage, as he "felt betrayed by his top team and the intelligence community, whom he blamed for soft-peddling the threat just days before the raid."[90] The president's anger at the US deaths in Somalia reflected his realization that the incident threatened to dominate the news, overshadowing his domestic agenda and his entire presidency. Clinton's fears were realized in a *TIME/CNN* poll that indicated only 43 percent supported a continued US presence in Somalia, down from 79 percent in January 1993.[91] The administration's problems were compounded when a ship loaded with lightly armed US soldiers seeking to assist in the return of Haitian President Aristide chose not to dock in Port-au-Prince due to the presence of an armed gang. The incidents caused the House Appropriations Committee to impede future humanitarian operations by demanding that presidents give 15 days notice before dispatching troops and provide estimated costs, projected duration, operational goals, and defined US interest. These moves, by a Democratically controlled Congress, reinforced growing concerns about President Clinton's ability to serve as commander-in-chief.

However, President Clinton was in the difficult situation of having to rectify mistakes made by his own team and members of the former Bush administration. The Somalia tragedy "shocked Clinton into taking control of his foreign policy and his bureaucracy."[92] Clinton had acted on the advice of his senior military officers, including Colin Powell, and therefore saw the incident as his own Bay of Pigs. He ordered all US troops out of Somalia by March 31, 1994 and dispatched a contingent of 1,700 troops to facilitate the withdrawal. As Anthony Lake conceded, the decision made itself, since "to do otherwise would have made it open season on Americans around the world. The potential message: Kill and humiliate our people and the United States will immediately retreat."[93]

It was recognized that "the scale of the foreign policy reversals in Somalia destroyed the administration's willingness to pursue foreign policy goals aggressively."[94] It led to a change in philosophy at the White House and negatively impacted the internal debate surrounding the use of US troops for peacekeeping operations. Officials who had previously been enthusiastic about the idea acknowledged that "there was a pulling back from this idea from that point onwards."[95] A State Department official said "We'll get back to it at some point and hopefully some sort of concept of collaborative action with the UN will emerge, but it is not going to be what it was."[96] Despite this hopeful assertion, US policy toward the United Nations failed to recover from the incident and resulted in a relationship of mutual suspicion that endures.[97]

The fallout from Somalia impacted not only the policy of Assertive Multilateralism but also the administration's capacity to engage in multilateral action. Leon Fuerth lamented that the events in Somalia "created on over-hang that was a consistent reminder in other events. It provided a realization that future losses or casualties would produce a response in Congress similar to that provided by the events in Mogadishu."[98] The crisis ensured that President Clinton was initially unable to recommend a deployment of US troops to Bosnia under a UN peacekeeping role, for fear of crossing "the Mogadishu Line."[99] Similarly, the fallout from Somalia coincided with the massacres in Rwanda, as the UN plan to send 5,500 troops to alleviate the situation was vetoed by Madeline Albright, operating under instructions from Washington. Despite protests from the White House that the plan had received limited support from other nations, the reality was that "it was politically impossible to go into central Africa" following the events in Somalia.[100] Nancy Soderberg noted, "After Somali there was just no enthusiasm for putting troops on the ground anywhere. I think it delayed aggressive engagement in Bosnia, it certainly delayed any response in Rwanda, but I don't think we ever really stepped away from multilateralism, it was more a question of assessing where multilateralism worked and where it didn't work."[101] The eventual PDD document on this issue directed that any involvement in future peacekeeping operations required that vital national or allied interests be at stake and that a clear commitment to win existed.

Assertive Multilateralism appeared to offer the Clinton administration a way to share expenditure, casualties, and divert the focus of hostility away from the United States and on to the shoulders of a global organization that had the potential to live up to its mandate in the post-Cold War era. However, this was predicated on the expectation that the American people would tolerate casualties in distant lands when no national interest was at stake and that Congress would continue its Cold War era support of the president in matters of world affairs. Neither assumption proved to be viable as the administration's efforts met congressional opposition in the face of public dismay over the deaths in Somalia. The administration noted that mistakes had been made, both operationally and in terms of presentation. Tara Sonenshine of the NSC lamented, "we have failed to explain why multilateralism is NOT and does NOT have to be a substitute for US leadership or an excuse NOT to act."[102] Such issues continued to plague the administration for years to come, while overseas, it was recognized that "having his fingers burnt in Somalia," was seen to have had "a very sobering impact," on the president.[103] Rather than reinforcing US efforts to export human rights and engage in conflict resolution, events in Somalia convinced Americans that internal disputes were of no concern to the world's sole superpower.

Events in Somalia confirmed President Clinton's worst fears about foreign policy being "a murky business, outside the reach of domestic presidential control, with greater possibility for negatives than positives, out of which relatively little good could come."[104] There would be no further deployment of ground forces to locations where US national interest did not exist, or could not be adequately defined, as peacekeeping operations were not considered a justifiable cause for American casualties. The death of 18 American servicemen on October 3, 1993, a number that Colin Powell noted would not have even warranted a press conference during the Vietnam War, was instrumental in ending a brief era of bipartisan support for multilateral operations under the United Nations, and caused the Clinton administration to reconsider its commitment to the organization and to peacekeeping operations in general.[105]

Iran, Iraq, and dual containment

The Somali mission was far from being Clinton's sole concern during his first months in power. Before he even entered office, Bill Clinton was forced to confront Iraq. Intelligence reports indicated that Saddam Hussein had amassed forces in northern Iraq in an effort to challenge US resolve by mounting military strikes against Iraqi Kurds in the safe havens along the Turkish border. A spokesman for the president-elect said Saddam "should take no comfort in the fact that Bill Clinton is heading towards the presidency."[106] The incoming team were determined to demonstrate solidarity with Bush over Saddam, least they be portrayed as weak on foreign policy, a slight that had blighted the Democratic Party. When allied forces shot down an Iraqi MiG that violated the No-Fly-Zone, the president-elect supported the action in terms almost identical to those used by President Bush, as advisers emphasized the "fundamental continuity between the policy of a Clinton administration and the policy of the Bush administration on Iraq."[107]

To Clinton, however, Iraq was not a personal matter, as it appeared to have been for President Bush and his philosophical approach to Saddam was apparent from his comments to the *New York Times*. Clinton freely admitted, "I am not obsessed with the man." Clinton's view was that "the people of Iraq would be better off if they had a different ruler. But my job is not to pick their rulers for them." Clinton appeared open to a new relationship, stating, "if he wants a different relationship with the United States and the United Nations, all he has to do is change his behaviour."[108] Clinton was not alone in suggesting that a *rapprochement* with Saddam may be possible. British Foreign Secretary Douglas Hurd insisted that the coalition had never planned to drive Saddam from power and that the normalization of relations with Iraq with Saddam in power could be achieved "with difficulty."[109] Britain's Gulf War Commander General Sir Peter De La Billiere maintained that the West was not trying to destroy Iraq, but rather "to point out to Saddam Hussein that unless he complies with the United Nations, then he must expect retribution, in the form of force."[110] There was, however, a world of difference between Clinton's views and those of the British; the president set western policy, Hurd and De La Billiere merely followed it.

Almost immediately, Clinton's remark, totally in keeping with his personality, was seized upon by political opponents and portrayed as a weakening of American resolve. Within 24 hours, Clinton backed away from any suggestion of peaceful relations with Saddam in a retreat that did little to inspire confidence in the incoming administration or its capacity to stand by stated principles or policies. Having been attacked for appearing to move to the left on the issue, Clinton could not veer too far to the right without escalating the situation to a point that forced the United States to act unilaterally. Iraq and its leaders remained an irritant, but not a priority and regime change was not an option for the Clinton administration in its first term. Faced with a multilateral framework and with pressing domestic priorities upon which to focus political capital and attention, the Clinton administration had little or no room to maneuver in regard to Iraq.

Despite this setback, new policies began to emerge following meetings conducted by Secretary of State Christopher in the Middle East and a review requested by President Clinton shortly after he took office.[111] In April 1993, Vice President Gore and senior officials met with representatives from the Iraqi National Congress (INC), a group of exiled Iraqi dissidents dedicated to the overthrow of Saddam. Despite concerns in the previous administration about their ability to bridge religious and ethnic rivalries, the Clinton's White House believed that the INC had "succeeded in broadening its base" and allayed US concerns by pledging to maintain current Iraqi borders. Washington was "keen to ensure that the INC [received] more regional recognition and support," particularly from Persian Gulf nations, to present a "vision of an alternative, democratic future" in Iraq.[112] The administration was also encouraged by reports of unrest within Saddam's inner circle, since such trends could lead "to new conditions for the citizens of Iraq and new opportunities to build a more peaceful and normal relationship between Iraq and the outside world."

Just as Iraq and Saddam was the *bête noire* for Republicans, so Iran loomed large for Democrats. This was especially true of the Clinton administration's senior foreign policy team who left government service when President Carter's tenure ended so ingloriously, partly due to the Iranian hostage crisis. The administration was forthright in stating its case against the Iranian regime, which it viewed as being "the foremost sponsor of terrorism and assassination worldwide."[113] Secretary of State Christopher alleged that Iran had established terrorist training camps in Lebanon and Sudan and assisted groups trying to overthrow the governments of Egypt,

Algeria, and Tunisia. Christopher was certain that Iran was the world's "most significant state sponsor of terrorism and the most ardent opponent of the Middle East peace process." Due partially to the focus on Iraq, he argued that the international community had been "far too tolerant of Iran's outlaw behaviour" claiming that Iran was "intent on projecting terror and extremism across the Middle East and beyond."[114]

The administration believed that a window of opportunity existed "to prevent Iran from becoming in five years time what Iraq was five years ago." The White House stressed that it did not oppose Islamic government, nor seek the regime's overthrow. Instead, it remained "ready for an authoritative dialogue" with the Iranian regime. The administration's desire to remove religion from the equation was of importance, as Lake noted, "Washington does not take issue with the 'Islamic' dimension of the Islamic Republic of Iran. It is extremism, whether religious or secular, that we oppose." The administration believed that it had a new approach to Iran and Iraq, which it felt was both realistic and sustainable, as well as one that took into account both "US interests and the realities of the Persian Gulf region."[115]

The Clinton administration's policy for addressing Iran and Iraq was Dual Containment, announced on May 18, 1993. However, in a pattern that continued to reduce confidence in the administration's commitment to its policies, the plan was not unveiled by the Secretary of State, or by the President, or even by the National Security Adviser, but by Martin S. Indyk, then Senior Director for Middle East policy at the National Security Council. Dual Containment sought to persuade allies to halt loans, investment, and arms sales to Tehran and prevent Iran gaining access to materials required to achieve a military renaissance. Indyk said, "If we fail in our efforts to modify Iranian behaviour, five years from now Iran will be much more capable of posing a real threat to Israel and to Western interests in the Middle East."[116] Compounding fears of a revitalized Iran were concerns over links to the bombing of the World Trade Center on February 26, 1993.[117] In addition, the CIA reported Iranian meetings with Chinese and Russian delegations for the purchase of nuclear material, leading to speculation that Iran could become a nuclear power by the end of the twentieth century. Robert Gallucci, Assistant Secretary of State for Political-Military Affairs, argued that "No country ought to cooperate with Iran in the nuclear area."

Iran, however, had negotiated trade deals with nations as diverse as Russia, China, and members of the European Union. Therefore, the administration brought pressure not only on Iran and Iraq, but also on its own allies by arguing that, "the income supported Iranian terrorism and that Iran's steadily worsening economy made it a bad investment."[118] The administration stressed the risks in dealing with Iran, referencing the $25 billion it had borrowed over the previous 4 years and the $5 billion it had already fallen behind in repayments: clearly, Iran was "no longer a good commercial proposition."[119] The policy had domestic implications, blocking a bid by Boeing to sell 20 jets to Iran in a deal worth more than $750 million.[120] However, with high inflation and unemployment, it was believed that Iran was "more vulnerable than it has been in the past or is likely to be in the future." Indyk insisted that the White House did not seek a confrontation, but refused to normalize relations "until and unless Iran's policies change across the board."

In regard to Iraq, Indyk explained that the administration sought Baghdad's "full compliance with all UN resolutions" and was "committed to ensuring Iraq's compliance with UN Resolution 688, which calls upon the regime to end its repression of the Iraqi people." The administration did not "seek or expect a reconciliation with Saddam Hussein's regime" and called for a UN commission to investigate Iraqi war crimes and human rights abuses "to establish clearly and unequivocally that the current regime in Iraq is a criminal regime, beyond the pale of international society and, in our judgment, irredeemable."[121] Since the end of the Gulf War, the United States had enforced the No-Fly-Zone above Iraq, requiring the positioning of aircraft carriers in the region. Containing Iraq was, therefore, proving to be a costly role, requiring increased military expenditure in the Gulf when the administration was looking to reduce costs.[122]

The administration may have unveiled a new policy to deal with Iran and Iraq, but it did not view the two nations as a monolithic power to be handled identically. Instead, it recognized the different cultural and religious influences and attempted to tailor its policy accordingly: "In Saddam Hussein's regime, Washington faces an aggressive, modernist, secular avarice; in Iran, it is challenged by a theocratic regime with a sense of cultural and political destiny and an abiding antagonism toward the United States."[123] The nations were challenging enough alone, but in the early 1990s fears emerged that they could attempt a reconciliation: Iran imported refined Iraqi oil and was believed to have obtained a shipment of Iraqi steel, acts that violated the UN trade embargo.[124] In addition, 1993 saw a repatriation of Iraqi prisoners of war from Iran. The administration was dismissive of suggestions that by combining Washington's approach to Iran and Iraq, the White House risked driving the two nations together: "The prospects for reconciliation will remain limited for a simple reason: they mistrust each other more than they mistrust the United States."

The administration believed that Dual Containment was a viable concept for a number of reasons. The end of the Cold War removed fears of a potential Soviet incursion into the Persian Gulf, significantly reducing the strategic importance of Iraq and Iran, since "their ability to play the superpowers off each other has been eliminated." Secondly, Iraq's victory in the Iran–Iraq War "substantially reduced Iran's conventional offensive capabilities, whilst Iraq's defeat in Desert Storm significantly diminished its offensive capabilities and brought its weapons of mass destruction under tight control."[125] Thirdly, following the Gulf War, the Gulf Cooperation Council (GCC) states were more inclined to enter into pre-positioning arrangements with the United States, enabling forces to be deployed locally against future threats. However, the administration was wary of accusations that the policy was religiously motivated. Eager to reject a fashionable concept, Anthony Lake stressed, "This is not a clash of civilizations . . . it is a contest that pits nations and individuals guided by openness, responsive government and moderation against those animated by isolation, repression and extremism."[126]

There was a wider dimension to the policy: in 1993, the Middle East stood at the threshold of a more promising era that heralded Arab–Israeli peace, Israeli security, and unimpeded access to Persian Gulf oil. Before Clinton's first year was over, he presided over the signing of a peace treaty between Israel and the Palestine Liberation Organization. A year later, a similar ceremony was held between Israel and Jordan. However, there were some that would stop at nothing to disrupt the peace process and it was believed that Iran was the main sponsor of groups dedicated to such an outcome.

The *Boston Globe* believed the administration had unveiled "a clear, forceful policy adapted to the transformations wrought by the implosion of the Soviet Union and by Saddam Hussein's failure to annex Kuwait."[127] Paul Wolfowitz, the former Undersecretary of Defense for Policy, referred to Dual Containment as having provided "a much-needed break with old notions of depending on a balance between the two to protect security in the gulf."[128] Despite this initial praise, however, Wolfowitz questioned the commitment to the policy, the degree of interest shown in the matter at a senior level, and the effect that an Iraqi victory in overcoming sanctions may have on the prestige of the United States. Considering that Martin Indyk announced the policy, Wolfowitz's concern about senior level interest (itself a thinly veiled reference to the president) was perhaps not wide of the mark. President Bush's former National Security Adviser Brent Scowcroft felt the administration had "behaved as if the principal issues of the region, Iraq, Iran and the [stalled Israeli–Palestinian] peace process, have no relation to each other."[129] However, concern that Iranian-sponsored terrorism and Iraqi-inspired instability was affecting the Middle East peace process was at the heart of the Dual Containment policy. The administration sought to enforce UN sanctions that were being flouted and to prevent the sale of nuclear materials to Iran in violation of various nonproliferation accords.

Daniel Pipes, editor of the *Middle East Quarterly*, believed that the Iranian threat was being underestimated: "They'd want to take control of Iraq, at least, if Saddam were gone, but they'd likely create a classic satrapy rather than move to an outright annexation." A senior Kuwaiti official added, "it's exactly because they're so much more clever than Saddam that the Iranians pose the more serious long-term threat."[130] Therefore, while the containment of Iraq struck many as logical, the decision to impose similar constraints on Iran appeared to others as less than wise. Critics pointed to the size of Iran, its population of almost 60 million, and a leadership determined to be preeminent in the Gulf as factors suggesting that an embargo may struggle to succeed.[131] Others argued that rather than isolate the nations, a move toward *rapprochement* served all interests. Highlighting US policy toward China, it was suggested that a more tolerant stance could lead to economic liberalization and political democratization. However, despite the Chinese precedent, the administration believed that such an approach was flawed in regard to two nations that remained openly hostile to Western interests, insisting that "fuelling their economic resurgence would only permit them to rearm and become more adventurous."[132] These suggestions also failed to consider the long-standing hostilities between the United States and Iran and the increasing pressure from Congress to take a strong line in the region.

Critics suggested that Dual Containment was "more a slogan than a strategy," that lacked "strategic viability" and had a "high financial and diplomatic cost."[133] It was suggested that the policy was "shot through with logical flaws and practical inconsistencies" and was "based on faulty geopolitical premises," since it was "hard to see how either Iraq or Iran could be contained, in the administration's sense, without the cooperation of its hostile counterpart." A major debate arose over the viability of implementing the policy simultaneously, since "containment of Iran requires a relatively strong and unified Iraq on its long western border . . . a weak Iraq is an inviting target for an Iran 'contained' and isolated." However, the containment of Iraq was "hard to imagine without some kind of Iranian cooperation," since Iran was "an important element in keeping the pressure on his regime."[134] Fears of an Iranian super state at the heart of the region were prevalent, but this worst-case scenario failed to materialize. Additionally, despite the valid notion that "the security and independence of the region is a vital US interest" suggestions that "a recommitment by President Clinton to the principles of the Carter Doctrine—a renewal of US vows to the Gulf—might be both welcome and appropriate" appeared self-serving on behalf of Brzezinski who had helped to prepare the unloved, unlamented doctrine.[135]

In Dual Containment the Clinton administration had a policy, which along with arms control and Arab–Israeli peace, formed a three-strand Middle East strategy, the successful implementation of which could have bought sweeping change in a vital part of the world. Like the eventual grand strategy of Engagement and Enlargement, however, the biggest hurdle came not in devising the initiative but in implementing the policy. For Dual Containment to be effective, the United States needed to convince Russia and China not to sell Iran weapons and nuclear reactors and to persuade Germany, the United Kingdom, and Japan to cut off loans. Not surprisingly, these countries were hesitant to do so at a time of economic instability when it meant "forgoing a market whose imports from Europe were over $10 billion and from Japan over $2.5 billion in 1992."[136] Neither was the administration's cause aided when the World Bank loaned Iran $165 million to upgrade its electrical power system in March 1993.[137] Given this environment, it is perhaps not surprising that the policy was unable to produce the result that was hoped for.

However, during the Clinton years, neither Iran nor Iraq made forays into foreign lands, as Dual Containment effectively kept Saddam "in his box" for the remainder of the decade. This, however, was a short-term solution that did little to end Iran's support for Hezbollah. In Iraq, Saddam's conventional forces were rebuilt following his defeat in Desert Storm, allowing him to impose his will over Shiite Muslim rebels in southern Iraq and the Kurdish rebels in the north. Gradual alterations to Dual Containment led to its eventual demise, and by November 1998 the administration changed its policy to containment plus regime change. Martin Indyk insisted that the objective was not only to contain Saddam, "but also to help the Iraqi people remove him and set up a different kind of government." The administration took the opposite approach to Iran. Viewing the changes implemented following the election of Khatami, the administration indicated that it was ready to move toward an engagement with Iran. Regretfully, the Tehran regime failed to respond as hoped. The policy continued unabated, but Indyk declared that "Whereas what we're saying is on the Iraqi side it's containment plus regime change, we're saying on the Iranian side it's containment until they are ready for engagement."

Dual Containment maintained the sanctions imposed by the United Nations in the aftermath of the Gulf War. This policy did not initially endorse regime change since the administration believed that doing so would invite an armed conflict that had no backing from Congress, the population or within the administration itself. Dual Containment, therefore, fitted the administration's overall approach to the Middle East, which was viewed as a two-way process: "The more we succeeded with making peace, the easier it would be to contain these two regimes that were threatening our interests. The more we succeeded in containing them, the easier it would be to pursue comprehensive peace."[138] Anthony Lake was more direct: "It was more 'These guys can screw up what's going on in the rest of the world and we need to contain them and implement the change.'"[139] Dual Containment did not provide a lasting solution, but throughout the 1990s it proved effective at restricting both Iran and Iraq without strengthening either side, demonstrating a theoretical alternative to a balance of power strategy in the Persian Gulf.

The Tarnoff doctrine

The Clinton administration's position was not eased on May 25, 1993, when Under Secretary of State for Policy, Peter Tarnoff, appeared to reverse

US foreign policy that had endured for more than 40 years.[140] Washington, DC is renowned for "official and unofficial information leaks as well as trial balloons for new initiatives," but what became known as the Tarnoff Doctrine was especially problematic for the Clinton administration.[141] Tarnoff was attempting to explain the new administration's approach to foreign policy, however, by making his remarks off-the-record, he unnecessarily caused editors to seek verification. This led to denials and confusion that could have been avoided had the administration been more adroit in its dealings with the Washington press corps.

In remarks that reflected Bill Clinton's campaign pledge to focus on the economy, Tarnoff insisted America's "economic interests are paramount" and would cause the United States to "define the extent of its commitment and make a commitment commensurate with those realities," that may "fall short of what some Americans would like and others would hope for."[142] Tarnoff was forthright, as he believed he was presenting a nonattributable briefing: "We're talking about new rules of engagement for the United States and new limits," he noted, since "we don't have the money."[143] This was a pragmatic approach to policy in which financial considerations were weighed. Tarnoff insisted "there may be occasions in the future where the United States acts unilaterally—if we perceive an imminent danger very close to home."[144] When such situations arose, the administration planned to act, but every deployment had to be considered "case by case," with the administration being prepared to limit foreign intervention to "what we think is appropriate."[145] This approach was the result of economic realities and the administration's decision to prioritize domestic spending, which impacted the funds available to foreign initiatives. Tarnoff stressed that in a time of deficits the "importance of money" ensured a "constant preoccupation" with expenditure.[146]

Tarnoff appeared to advocate a less interventionist foreign policy, arguing that the United States was not the world's policeman: "We simply don't have the leverage, we don't have the influence, we don't have the inclination to use military force, we certainly don't have the money to bring to bear the kind of pressure which will produce positive results anytime soon."[147] This was a new administration with new priorities, which Tarnoff acknowledged may not be universally welcomed and may be "difficult for our friends to understand," but noted "it's not different by accident; it's different by design."[148] Financial realities and new priorities ensured that a new era was inevitable, in which roles and responsibilities were changing and in which "there will have to be genuine power-sharing and responsibility sharing."[149] Tarnoff used the debate over intervention in Bosnia to explain that inaction represented a calculated withdrawal from overseas commitments, not a policy failure: the administration was "determined not to go in there and take over Bosnia policy," Tarnoff insisted, adding that the United States would not "take over" if other nations could do so.[150]

Tarnoff's briefing was in keeping with statements that had been issued previously by the Clinton White House and those that followed for the next 8 years: together when possible, alone when necessary—but this was not how the briefing was reported. Instead, headlines screamed "Reduced US World Role Outlined But Soon Altered" (*Washington Post*), "Clinton Foreign Policy Appears to Retreat From Decades of US World Leadership" (*Baltimore Sun*). Almost a year later, the *New York Times* continued to misquote Tarnoff, as evidence that the United States had "an administration that does not believe in the commitment of American power, purpose and resolve to keep the peace."[151] Paul Wolfowitz, who addressed the briefing in his assessment of Clinton's first year in office, exacerbated this, noting that it was "simply common sense" for the United States "to summon as much international support as possible and spread the burden of action to as many partners as possible" as it had throughout the Cold War. Wolfowitz warned darkly, however, that "it is something else to say, as Undersecretary of State Peter Tarnoff apparently did, that the United States can no longer afford to act except multilaterally."[152] Except, of course, that this is not what Tarnoff had said.

Tarnoff's briefing did not stay off-the-record for long, as its implications demanded an official statement. When it came, it was an apparent rebuke from Warren Christopher, who insisted that the remarks did not represent official policy "if the implication is that we'd step back from our leadership role." Christopher added, "there is no derogation of our powers and our responsibility to lead."[153] When a White House official stressed Tarnoff's statement was "not our foreign policy," it appeared that the undersecretary had been tasked with issuing a statement that served as a reminder of the new rules of engagement, while being plausibly deniable.[154] Despite Christopher's rebuke, many viewed Tarnoff's remarks as an accurate reflection of the administration's approach to foreign policy, suggesting that Clinton's "abdication of American leadership and his reluctance to sustain attention on a US Grand Strategy, all gave rise to the impression that Washington was locked in a policy of inertia and drift."[155] The situation was exacerbated by the response from the White House; although the State Department inadvertently released Tarnoff's schedule that included the briefing, White House Press Secretary Dee Dee Myers refused to identify him as the source because the briefing had been off-the-record and nonattributable.[156] State Department Press Secretary Richard Boucher faced the bizarre situation of journalists offering him transcripts of the briefings, derived from their own recordings, for the administration to comment upon in circumstances that did little to boost confidence.

The Tarnoff briefing caused a rewrite for a speech the secretary of state gave in Minneapolis 3 days later, which made 23 references to American leadership in an effort "to dispel any suggestion at home or abroad that the first Democratic administration in a dozen years was sounding a retreat."[157] Christopher noted that the United States faced "many challenges" that were "unlike any in the nation's history." He insisted, however, that this meant the United States "must be more engaged internationally, not less; more ardent in our promotion of democracy, not less; more inspired in our leadership, not less."[158] The speech reinforced Tarnoff's comments, which reflected Clinton's campaign statements that successful foreign policies needed to be based on solid economic foundations. Neither Tarnoff, nor his colleagues in the administration, were advocating anything that had not previously been espoused by officials dating back several decades; that America's allies should take a greater role in their own protection; and that US intervention depended on the circumstances of each situation. However, "since the president had not yet made a major pronouncement about his foreign policy principles or priorities, Tarnoff's words filled a conceptual vacuum."[159] Tarnoff's announcement was in keeping with the attempt to have foreign policy dealt with by a specific element of the administration (as it had been on the campaign), allowing the president and his key advisers to focus on domestic affairs. However, while this avoided the necessity of involving the president in the rigmaroles associated with such a high-profile declaration, it raised questions about the administration's dedication to the policy and reduced the credibility of its senior members who appeared to be upstaged by subordinates.

Tarnoff's statement was in line with stated policy, but its delivery, subsequent denial, and attempts at explanation exacerbated the sense of an administration out of control. The *New York Times* argued that Tarnoff's explanation was "a defensible, even sensible doctrine" but asked why its defense was left to "covert briefings by unnamed senior officials?" The paper argued that what was needed was a clear statement of intent: "A thoughtful Presidential speech on American values, interests and priorities in the world could also help enormously—especially if he then matches deeds to words."[160] Matching words to deeds became the administration's central challenge in the months ahead as it sought to quell doubts over its ability to lead in the post-Cold War world.

Conclusion: Clinton's poisoned chalice

All administrations inherit the detritus of their predecessors. However, in Clinton's case, the presidential chalice was particularly toxic, if not altogether poisoned. Clinton assumed responsibility for US forces engaged in Somalia, off the Haitian coast, in Bosnia, and in the skies above Iraq. Little wonder, perhaps, that his first year in office appeared to be more concerned with "putting out fires" than devising a new grand strategy.[161] However, foreign policy was arguably the one area in which President Clinton appeared to lack self-confidence and, during the 1990s, there was a belief that foreign affairs were so remote to Americans that "success would bring only fleeting advantage, much as George Bush's Gulf War victory was unable to rescue his presidency."[162] When President Clinton addressed foreign policy he did so in relation to domestic and economic matters, which did little to inspire confidence. As informed as President Clinton could be in domestic matters, he seemed unengaged in his response to foreign policy issues. This is not to suggest that the commander-in-chief was disengaged from international relations, for clearly President Clinton "was not the foreign policy innocent he is often portrayed as." However, it is clear that in his initial months in office 'his primary concern was to revert the direction of the American economy."[163] The president's foreign policy advisers advised him, but there was no clear plan emerging as attention was focused on the domestic agenda due to the lack of a discernable threat from overseas. The communications team did what they could with the material they had, but as Halperin observed, "I don't feel that there was a problem communicating, there just was no specific policy to communicate since there was no doctrine at the time."[164]

As smart as Clinton was in domestic matters, he seemed unfocused on foreign policy issues, where critics lamented the absence of a strategic outlook. Even the US ambassador to Great Britain noted the administration "almost turned foreign policy into a vaudeville act," as international repercussions demonstrated that the president couldn't abdicate interest over one area of government for the benefit of another.[165] Clinton's presidential inheritance was a world in flux that demanded close and immediate attention. Neither were forthcoming in the first months as the administration plunged from crisis to crisis, struggling with its new responsibilities and lacking focus and leadership. The best efforts of Clinton's foreign policy team to espouse a new approach to foreign policy failed to generate enthusiasm as global events provided "real wake up calls for the administration. They may have been thinking about big strategic things, but when you are the big giant that's the problem: you are vulnerable in places that people don't know exist."[166]

Notes

1   William J. Clinton, "A New Beginning," speech in Little Rock, Arkansas, November 3, 1992, in Smith (ed.), *Preface to the Presidency*, pp. 417–419.

2   William J. Clinton, "Remarks in Little Rock," speech in Little Rock, Arkansas, November 4, 1992.

3   Stephanopoulos, *All Too Human*, p. 120.

4   Drew, *On The Edge*, p. 36.

5   Martin Walker, *Clinton: The President They Deserve* (London: Forth Estate, 1996), p. 161.

6   Author's interview with Sir Malcolm Rifkind.

7   Clinton, "Remarks in Little Rock."

8   Walter Russell Mead, "An American Grand Strategy: The Quest for Order in a Disordered World," *World Policy Journal* 10 (Spring 1993), p. 9.

9   Author's interview with Leon Fuerth.

10 Author's interview with Morton Halperin (Consultant to the Secretary of Defense and the Under Secretary of Defense for Policy 1993; Special Assistant to the President and Senior Director for Democracy at the National Security Council 1994–1996; Director of the Policy Planning Staff 1998–2001), June 22, 2004.

11 David C. Hendrickson, "The Recovery of Internationalism," *Foreign Affairs* 73, no. 5 (September–October 1994), p. 26.

12 Stephanopoulos, *All Too Human*, p. 157.

13 Quoted in Blumenthal, *The Clinton Wars*, p. 159.

14 Author's interview with Leon Fuerth.

15 "Special Report: Policymaking For a New Era," *Foreign Affairs* 71, no. 5 (Winter 1992), pp. 175–189.

16 Quoted in Theodore C. Sorensen, *Kennedy* (New York: Konecky & Konecky, 1965), p. 573.

17 Thomas L. Friedman, "Clinton Backs Raid but Muses About a New Start," *New York Times*, January 14, 1993, p. A1.

18 Quoted in Friedman, "Clinton's Foreign-Policy Agenda Reaches Across Broad Spectrum," p. A1.

19 Joe Klein, *The Natural: The Misunderstood Presidency of Bill Clinton* (New York: Doubleday, 2002), p. 47.

20 Author's interview with J. F. O. McAllister.

21 John Brummett, *Highwire: From The Backwoods to the Beltway—The Education of Bill Clinton* (New York: Hyperion, 1994), p. 210.

22 Vernon Jordan, quoted in David Halberstam, *War in a Time of Peace: Bush, Clinton and the Generals* (New York: Random House, 2001), p. 172.

23 *PPPWJC*, vol. 2 (1996), Remarks on the Resignation of Secretary of State Warren Christopher and an Exchange With Reporters, November 7, 1996, p. 2089.

24 Martin Fletcher, "World of Disorder Undermines Domestic Agenda," *The Times* (January 18, 1993), p. 10.

25 Drew, *On The Edge*, p. 140.

26 Madeleine Albright, *Madam Secretary: A Memoir* (London: Macmillan, 2003), p. 132; Author's interview with J. F. O. McAllister.

27 Dettmer, "Hostile World Waits to Test Clinton's Foreign Policy Team," p. 8.

28 Author's interview with Anthony Lake.

29 Author's interview with Charles A. Kupchan.

30 Soderberg, *The Superpower Myth*, p. 15.

31 Author's interview with Charles A. Kupchan.

32 Blumenthal, *The Clinton Wars*, p. 154.

33 Paul Y. Hammond, "Central Organization in the Transition from Bush to Clinton," in Charles E. Hermann (ed.), *American Defense Annual: 1994* (New York: Lexington Books 1994), pp. 163–181.

34 Halberstam, *War In A Time Of Peace*, pp. 192–193.

35 Talbot, *The Russia Hand*, p. 38.

36 *PPPWJC*, vol. 1 (1993), Nomination for Ambassador to Russia, January 26, 1993, p. 16.

37 *PPPWJC*, vol. 2 (1993), Statement on the Nomination of Strobe Talbott To Be Deputy Secretary of State, December 28, 1993, p. 2206.

38 Michael Dobbs, *Madeleine Albright: A Twentieth Century Odyssey* (New York: Henry Holt & Company, 1999), p. 220; Drew, *On The Edge*, p. 28.

39 Quoted in Simon Tisdall, "Clinton Team Draws on the Carter Years," *Guardian* (December 23, 1992), p. 8.

40 Christopher, *Chances of a Lifetime*, p. 175.

41 Joe Klein, "A High Risk Presidency," *Newsweek* 121, Issue 18 (March 5, 1993), p. 32.

42 Fred Barnes, "Neoconned," *New Republic* (January 25, 1993), p. 14–15.

43 Author's interview with J. F. O. McAllister.

44 Soderberg, *The Superpower Myth*, p. 14.

45 See Kurt M. Campbell and James B. Steinberg, *Difficult Transitions: Foreign Policy Troubles at the Outset of Presidential Power* (Washington, DC: Brookings Institution Press, 2008).

46 William J. Clinton, "A New Era of Peril and Promise," Address Before the Diplomatic Corps, Georgetown University, Washington, DC, January 18, 1993, *US Department of State Dispatch* 4 (February 1), p. 58.

47 There were dissenters. See David Spiro, "The Insignificance of the Liberal Peace," *International Security* 19, no. 2 (Fall 1994), pp. 50–86; Christopher Layne, "Kant or Cant: Myths of the Democratic Peace," *International Security* 19, no. 2 (Fall 1994), pp. 5–49.

48 Niccolò Machiavelli, *The Prince and The Discourses* (New York: Random House, 1950), p. 21; see also Blumenthal, *The Clinton Wars*, p. 45.

49 Klein, *The Natural*, p. 44.

50 Author's interview with Morton Halperin.

51 Gergen, *Eyewitness to Power*, p. 258.

52 Quoted in Lawrence Korb, "The Department of Defense: The First Half Century," in David Jablonsky, Ronald Steel, Lawrence Korb, Morton H. Halperin, and Robert Ellsworth (eds), *US National Security: Beyond the Cold War* (Carlisle, PA: Strategic Studies Institute, US Army War College, 1997), p. 69.

53 Quoted in Henry Muller and John F. Stacks, "First, We Have to Roll Up Our Sleeves," *Time* 141, no. 1 (January 4, 1993), p. 34.

54 Stephanopoulos, *All Too Human*, p. 114.

55 Schlesinger, *White Hose Ghosts*, pp. 402–404.

56 Martin Fletcher, "New Leader Borrows Kennedy's Lofty Themes," *The Times* (January 21, 1993), p. 2.

57 Clinton, "Strategic Security in a Changing World," p. 268.

58 *PPPWJC*, vol. 1 (1993), Inaugural Address, January 20, 1993, p. 2.

59 Theodore H. Moran, "International Economics and National Security," *Foreign Affairs* 69, no. 5 (Winter 1990/1991), p. 74.

60 Larry Berman and Emily Goldman, "Clinton's Foreign Policy at Midterm," in Campbell and Rockman, *The Clinton Presidency*, p. 295.

61 Kissinger, "Clinton and the World," p. 45.

62 Lance Morrow, "Man of the Year: The Torch is Passed," *Time* 141, no. 1 (January 4, 1993), p. 26.

63 Author's interview with J. F. O. McAllister.

64 Quoted in Schlesinger, *White House Ghosts*, pp. 410–411.

65 *PPPWJC*, vol. 1 (1993), Remarks at American University Centennial Celebration, February 26, 1993, pp. 207–210.

66 Colin Powell, *My American Journey* (New York: Random House, 1995), p. 579.

67 George J. Church and Dan Goodgame, "His Seven Most Urgent Decisions," *Time* 141, no. 4 (January 25, 1993), p. 30.

68 *PPPWJC*, vol. 1 (1993), Remarks to the Crew of the *USS Theodore Roosevelt*, March 12, 1993, pp. 281–282.

69 *PPPWJC*, vol. 1 (1993), Remarks at the United States Military Academy Commencement Ceremony in West Point, New York, May 29, 1993, pp. 781–782.

70 PDD-1: Establishment of Presidential Review and Decision Series, January 20, 1993. The Clinton administration established the PRD mechanism to direct specific reviews to be undertaken by various governmental departments and agencies. The conclusions often helped formulate PDDs that provided specific policy direction.

71 For more on the Bush era NSC, see David Rothkopf, *Running the World: The Inside Story of the National Security Council and the Architects of American Power* (New York: Public Affairs, 2004); John Prados, *Keepers of the Keys: A History of the National Security Council from Truman to Bush* (New York: William Morrow, 1991). For an insiders'perspective, see George Bush and Brent Scowcroft, *A World Transformed* (New York: Alfred A. Knopf, 1998).

72 PDD-2: Organization of the National Security Council, January 20, 1993. The NSC structure was subsequently amended via PDD-45 (March 1, 1996), PDD-51 (October 12, 1996), and on January 9, 1997 via PDD-53 when the Assistant to the Vice President for National Security Affairs was added to the Principal's Committee. On June 23, 1998, PDD-65 further amended the NSC structure when arms control experts were added to the list of invited officials.

73   Author's interview with Charles A. Kupchan.

74   *PPPGB*, vol. 2 (1992), Letter to Congressional Leaders on the Situation in Somalia, December 10, 1992, pp. 2179–2180.

75   Author's interview with Morton Halperin.

76   Halberstam, *War In A Time Of Peace*, p. 254.

77   Author's interview with Morton Halperin.

78   James D. Boys, "A Lost Opportunity: The Flawed Implementation of Assertive Multilateralism (1991–1993)," *European Journal of American Studies* 7, no. 1 (December 2012), pp. 2–14.

79   Albright, *Madame Secretary*, p. 176.

80   Madeleine Albright, "Myths of Peace-Keeping," *US Department of State Dispatch* 4, no. 26 (June 28, 1993), p. 464.

81   *PPPWJC*, vol. 1 (1993), Remarks on Welcoming Military Personnel Returning From Somalia, May 5, 1993, p. 565.

82   *PPPWJC*, vol. 1 (1993), Letter to Congressional Leaders on Somalia, July 1, 1993, pp. 669–970.

83   Michael R. Gordon with John H. Cushman, Jr, "After Supporting Hunt for Aidid, US Is Blaming UN For Losses," *New York Times* (October 18, 1993), p. A1.

84   Author's interview with J. F. O. McAllister.

85   Author's interview with Leon Fuerth. By October 3, 1993, the NSC had held 38 Principal Committee Meetings (none of which had addressed Somalia) and 60 Deputies Committee meetings (9 of which had addressed Somalia).

86   Soderberg, *The Superpower Myth*, p. 38.

87   Quoted in Gordon with Cushman, Jr, "After Supporting Hunt for Aidid, US Is Blaming UN For Losses," p. A1.

88   Author's interview with Nancy Soderberg.

89   Author's interview with J. F. O. McAllister.

90   Derek Chollet and James Goldgeiger, *America Between The Wars: From 11/9 to 9/11 The Misunderstood Years Between the Fall of the Berlin Wall and the Start of the War on Terror* (New York: Public Affairs Books, 2008), p. 76.

91   J. F. O. McAllister and James L. Graff, "When to Go, When to Stay," *Time* 142, no. 14 (October 4, 1993), p. 40.

92   Soderberg, *The Superpower Myth*, p. 40.

93   Anthony Lake, *Six Nightmares: Real Threats in a Dangerous World and How America Can Meet Them* (Boston, MA: Little Brown, 2000), p. 129.

94   James Adams, "Clinton Foreign Policy in Tatters," *Sunday Times*, October 17, 1993, Overseas Section.

95   Author's interview with Morton Halperin.

96   Michael R. Gordon with Thomas L. Friedman, "Details of US Raid in Somalia: Success So Near, a Loss So Deep," *New York Times* (October 25, 1993), p. A1.

97 James D. Boys, "What's So Extraordinary About Rendition?" *The International Journal of Human Rights* 15, no. 4 (May 2011), p. 591.

98 Author's interview with Leon Fuerth.

99 Walter Clarke and Jeffrey Herbst, "Somalia and the Future of Humanitarian Intervention," *Foreign Affairs* 75, no. 2 (March–April 1996), p. 70.

100 Mike Sheehan, military adviser to Madeleine Albright, quoted in Dobbs, *Madeleine Albright*, p. 357.

101 Author's interview with Nancy Soderberg.

102 Tara Sonenshine to Bob Boorstin; re: Some Random Thoughts on the UNGA Speech, Clinton Presidential Records, National Security Council, Robert Boorstin (Speechwriting), OA/Box Number: 422, UNGA '94—NSC Memos, William J. Clinton Presidential Library.

103 Author's interview with Sir Malcolm Rifkind.

104 Halberstam, *War in a Time of Peace*, pp. 264–265.

105 Mark Bowden, *Black Hawk Down* (London: Bantam Press, 1999), p. 497.

106 Quoted in Martin Fletcher and Ian Brodie, "West Warns Saddam as Iraq Moves Missiles," *The Times* (January 6, 1993), p. 11.

107 Jamie Dettmer, "Clinton's Advisers Struggle to Gauge Baghdad Strategy," *The Times* (January 13, 1993), p. 11.

108 Friedman, "Clinton Backs Raid but Muses About a New Start," p. A1.

109 Daniel Pederson, "The World Crowds In: An Interview with Douglas Hurd," *Newsweek* 121, Issue 4 (January 25, 1993), p. 48.

110 General Sir Peter De La Billiere, "Choosing Our Next Target," *Newsweek* 121, Issue 4 (January 25, 1993), p. 46.

111 Douglas Jehl, "US Seeks Ways to Isolate Iran; Describes Leaders as Dangerous," *New York Times* (May 27, 1993), p. A1.

112 R. Jeffrey Smith and Daniel Williams, "White House to Step Up Plans to Isolate Iran, Iraq; Administration to Try 'Dual Containment,'" *Washington Post* (May 23, 1993), p. A26.

113 Anthony Lake, "Confronting Backlash States," *Foreign Affairs* 73 (March–April, 1994), p. 52.

114 Warren Christopher, "America's Leadership, America's Opportunity," *Foreign Policy* 98 (Spring 1995), p. 22.

115 Lake, "Confronting Backlash States," pp. 50–54.

116 Martin Indyk, *Clinton Administration Policy toward the Middle East*, Washington Institute for Near East Policy, May 18, 1993.

117 Jehl, "US Seeks Ways to Isolate Iran," p. A1.

118 Smith and Williams, "White House to Step Up Plans to Isolate Iran, Iraq," p. A26.

119 Indyk, *Clinton Administration Policy toward the Middle East*.

120 Jehl, "US Seeks Ways to Isolate Iran," p. A1.

121 Indyk, *Clinton Administration Policy toward the Middle East*.

122 Russell Watson with John Barry and Douglas Waller, "A New Kind of Containment," *Newsweek* 122, Issue 2 (July 12, 1993), p. 30.

123 Lake, "Confronting Backlash States," p. 49.

124 Smith and Williams, "White House to Step Up Plans to Isolate Iran, Iraq," p. A26.

125 Lake, "Confronting Backlash States," pp. 48–54.

126 Anthony Lake, "The Reach of Democracy: Tying Power To Diplomacy," *New York Times* (September 23, 1994), p. A35.

127 "Containing Iraq and Iran," *Boston Globe* (March 23, 1994), p. 74.

128 Paul D. Wolfowitz, "Clinton's First Year," *Foreign Affairs* 73, no. 1 (January–February 1994), p. 40.

129 Thomas W. Lippman, "Critics Want US to Re-evaluate 'Dual Containment' Policy on Iran and Iraq," *Washington Post* (December 7, 1997), p. A33.

130 Michael Kramer, "The Cost of Removing Saddam," *Time* (October 24, 1994), p. 39.

131 Such fears were reported in "Containing Iraq and Iran," *Boston Globe* (March 23, 1994), p. 74.

132 Kramer, "The Cost of Removing Saddam," p. 39.

133 Zbigniew Brzezinski, Brent Scowcroft, and Richard Murphy, "Differentiated Containment," *Foreign Affairs* 76, no. 3 (May–June 1997), p. 20.

134 F. Gregory Gause III, "The Illogic of Dual Containment," *Foreign Affairs* 73, no. 2 (March–April 1994), pp. 56–60.

135 Brzezinski, Scowcroft, and Murphy, "Differentiated Containment," p. 30.

136 Gause III, "The Illogic of Dual Containment," p. 61.

137 Jehl, "US Seeks Ways to Isolate Iran," p. A1.

138 Martin Indyk, Interview, *Al-Qabas*, January 31, 1999.

139 Author's interview with Anthony Lake.

140 For an excellent analysis of the event, see Jim Anderson, "The Tarnoff Affair," *American Journalism Review* 16 (March 1994), pp. 40–44.

141 Thomas H. Henriksen, *Clinton's Foreign Policy in Somalia, Bosnia, Haiti and North Korea* (Stanford, CA: Stanford University Press, 1996), p. 20. The briefing, initially cited as being by a "Senior State Department Official," was revealed as having been delivered by Peter Tarnoff. The story was developed over the coming days, see Daniel Williams and John M. Goshko, "Administration Rushes to 'Clarify' US Policy Statements by 'Brand X,'" *Washington Post* (May 27, 1993), p. A45; Lloyd Grove, "Who Was That Masked Official?" *Washington Post* (May 27, 1993), pp. D1–D2.

142 Quoted in Heinz A. J. Kern, "The Clinton Doctrine: A New Foreign Policy," *Christian Science Monitor* (June 18, 1993).

143 Quoted in Williams and Goshko, "Reduced US World Role Outlined But Soon Altered," p. A1.

144 Quoted in Kern, "The Clinton Doctrine."

145 Quoted in Mark Matthews, "Clinton Foreign Policy Appears To Retreat From Decades of US World Leadership," *Baltimore Sun* (May 27, 1993).

146 Quoted in Scott Thompson and Edward Spannaus, "Is the 'Tarnoff Doctrine' Now US Strategic Policy?" *Executive Intelligence Review* 20, no. 23 (June 11, 1993), p. 51.

147 Martin Fletcher, "White House Denies US Will Withdraw from Leadership Role," *New York Times* (May 27, 1993).

148 Williams and Goshko, "Reduced US World Role Outlined But Soon Altered," p. A1.

149 Quoted in Kern, "The Clinton Doctrine."

150 Quoted in Williams and Goshko, "Reduced US World Role Outlined But Soon Altered," p. A1.

151 Anthony Lewis, "Abroad At Home; Peace At Any Price," *New York Times* (April 18, 1994), p. A15.

152 Wolfowitz, "Clinton's First Year," p. 36.

153 Ian Brodie, "President's Men Labour to Forge Clinton Doctrine," *The Times* (August 27, 1993), p. 13.

154 Williams and Goshko, "Reduced US World Role Outlined but Soon Altered," p. A1.

155 Henriksen, *Clinton's Foreign Policy in Somalia, Bosnia, Haiti and North Korea*, p. 21.

156 "A Brand X Foreign Policy," *New York Times* (May 28, 1993), p. A28.

157 Warren Christopher, *In The Stream of History: Shaping Foreign Policy for a New Era* (Stanford, CA: Stanford University Press, 1998), p. 40.

158 Warren Christopher, "US Support for Russian Reform: An Investment in America's Security," *US Department of State Dispatch* 4, Issue 22 (May 31, 1993), p. 389.

159 Chollet and Goldgeiger, *America Between The Wars*, p. 65.

160 "A Brand X Foreign Policy," p. A28.

161 Stephen E. Ambrose and Douglas G. Brinkley, *Rise to Globalism: American Foreign Policy Since 1938*, Eighth Revised Edition (New York: Penguin Books, 1997), p. 403.

162 Jonathan Clarke, "Contempt for Foreign Policy is Showing," *Los Angeles Times* (October 26, 1993), p. B7.

163 Author's interview with Leon Fuerth.

164 Author's interview with Morton Halperin.

165 Raymond Seitz, *Over Here* (London: Weidenfeld & Nicolson, 1998), p. 332.

166 Author's interview with J. F. O. McAllister.

CHAPTER THREE

A grand strategy emerges

By August 1993 the Berlin Wall was becoming a memory, but the Clinton administration had yet to announce a grand strategy to account for the shift in world events. However, while foreign policy appeared to be of secondary importance to the administration, this did not mean that international issues were not addressed. The Dual Containment policy for dealing with Iran and Iraq was developed at the State Department; Bob Bell's team on the National Security Council were preparing the first drafts of the Nation Security Strategy Review; and the president had delivered a series of addresses that considered aspects of foreign policy.[1] However, the policy initiatives were developed and unveiled discreetly by Clinton's national security team, while the president's speeches had been too content to couch foreign policy in terms of economic issues. Therefore, despite the fact that the new evolving strategies were far more interlinked than was appreciated at the time, the public perception of the Clinton administration was far from positive. To address these growing concerns surrounding the direction of US Grand Strategy, the Clinton administration devised a series of policy announcements in September 1993. All too quickly, however, the White House discovered how policy declarations could be neutered, as their theoretical efforts were overshadowed by real world events that challenged Clinton's attempt to provide global leadership in the post-Cold War world.

The growing mood of unrest

During its first 8 months in office, the Clinton administration actively advanced domestic policies at the expense of foreign affairs. President Clinton's Inaugural Address had all but ignored foreign policy and his speeches in the spring of 1993 approached the issue in terms of its relationship to the economy. On each occasion the president referenced incidents and nations of concern, but failed to espouse a specific policy with which to address the world. By May 1993, Clinton's public approval was 36 percent, "the lowest for any postwar president at a comparable point in his first year."[2] The lack of a Clinton foreign policy produced what *Time* called, "That Sinking Feeling," while *Newsweek* felt the nation was on "The Road to Indecision." Writing in September 1993, Jonathan Clarke lamented that the Clinton administration, "bristling as it is with academic talent," was "content to live hand to mouth on foreign policy, embracing stale concepts from the bygone era of the Cold War." Clarke noted that despite Clinton's criticism of President Bush's "lack of vision and despite promises of a "fresh assessment" of US foreign policy, the president, it seems, either doesn't comprehend or doesn't wish to grapple with the fact that in foreign policy terms he stands at a historic crossroads."[3] Within the White House, President Clinton was growing increasingly tired of constant references to the "post-Cold War" era, believing the expression to be "agnostic, provincial, backward-looking." Worse still, "it was an admission that while everyone knew what was finished, no one knew what had taken its place, to say nothing of what would or should come next. He didn't want his presidency to coincide with an age of uncertainty."[4] Providing a new definition for the era was becoming almost as pressing a matter as providing a new grand strategy.

The president's predicament was not aided by his disregard for cabinet-level structures, including the National Security Council, as formal meetings chaired by the president became rare. Although he immersed himself in domestic affairs, President Clinton tended to avoid meetings with his foreign policy advisers. Anthony Lake attempted to set a specific time to brief the president and met weekly for lunch with Warren Christopher, but Clinton's dedication to domestic affairs prevented him from being sufficiently engaged in the "larger contemplative discussions."[5] Lake, although experienced in Washington, lacked the relationship with Clinton that was needed to serve as a surrogate for a president focused on domestic policy.[6] This was not helped by his decision to adopt "the lowest profile of any national security adviser since Reagan's immortal Judge Clark."[7]

It was clear that many within the administration were ambiguous about foreign policy; the fact that President Bush had been hindered in his bid for reelection by a perceived preoccupation with foreign affairs convinced them the subject was potentially toxic. The administration, therefore, sought to keep foreign policy contained so the president could "put more than half [of his] energies and intensity into these other things."[8] However, the belief that foreign policy was being delegated to subordinates led to concerns that Clinton had "spent too little time schooling himself in the vagaries of foreign policy."[9] Foreign policy was drafted and enacted in the first months of the Clinton administration, but it was done quietly and without the president's active involvement.

This was not something that most were aware of, so that by the summer of 1993 it was suggested that the administration lacked even a basic foreign policy and the president's "ideas about the world and his policy preferences were mostly borrowed."[10] To get away from his "reactive, seat-of-the-pants" approach to foreign policy, Clinton needed to construct a concept of America's place in the world in order to "protect the interests and project the values of the United States." This needed to be done "while simultaneously finding significant savings in those sections of the budget devoted to defense and international discretionary spending."[11] However, the world was not about to wait for the administration to perform such a political juggling act.

Within the NSC, a growing realization emerged in the summer of 1993 that change was needed. Experts were "looking to hear an overarching theme and to sense that this administration has a coherent, strategic vision for its foreign policy." The White House began to appreciate a growing concern that Clinton was "comfortable with 'ad hocery' and . . . content to say that the post-Cold War era does not lend itself to an overall strategy and theme, and we will simply have to make policy case-by-case." Despite the repeated assertions of Warren Christopher, internal memos expressed concern over a perceived lack of direction and structure: "Most foreign policy thinkers are NOT prepared to accept the notion of an administration without a central, overarching strategy and not ready to concede that the world simply does not lend itself to gameplans anymore." This was a total repudiation of Warren Christopher's most basic approach to his position and after 6 months in the job the NSC were reporting that "There is still an expectation that we can articulate and deliver on a long-range plan that gives people a comfortable feeling that we are not simply managing crises, but organizing the world."[12]

Contrary to reports at the time suggesting that US foreign policy was in "disarray and confusion" and that "flips and flops of policy toward Bosnia, Somalia, Haiti, North Korea and China . . . have elicited ridicule from all points on the political spectrum," the administration did have specific foreign policy aspirations.[13] Its aim was to place the US relationship with Russia "on a very strong footing" and to pass "a new and streamlined defense programme."[14] Neither the administration nor the president failed to recognize the significance of foreign policy, but in the initial months it was "too busy trying to do, rather than to sort out a pre-existing doctrine."[15] The administration also unashamedly prioritized the promise of domestic reform that was credited with securing its election. As the president noted, "I wanted to be able to devote most of the first year to dealing with the domestic problems of the country that I thought were necessary to strengthen us so that we could formulate and carry out a successful foreign policy in the post-Cold War world."[16] Yet, conversely, it was recognized that the administration had a unique opportunity. As Morton Halperin noted, "there was the perception at the end of the Cold War that there was the lack of a threat and so we had an opportunity to deal with longer-term problems and opportunity to do things in keeping with our interests and values." Bringing these interests and values to bear in a rapidly evolving geopolitical environment proved to be the central challenge for the Clinton White House.

Devising Clinton's doctrine

The Clinton administration came to Washington openly divided on the wisdom of espousing a presidential doctrine. Throughout US history and particularly during the Cold War, administrations developed a series of principles to guide their global conduct. The concept of a presidential doctrine is largely predicated on the belief that only by articulating such a vision can an administration claim to be directing events, rather than being at the whim of history. During the initial months of the administration, President Clinton "was content to focus on his domestic agenda rather than formulate a doctrine. There was a preference to deal with events rather than formulate doctrines."[17] With a world in flux, many believed that such a doctrine risked offering a hostage to fortune that may be rendered irrelevant by a rapidly transforming world environment. In his confirmation hearing, Warren Christopher refused "to fit the foreign policy of the next four years into the straitjacket of some neatly tailored doctrine."[18] Others, however, felt a doctrine was needed that was "adoptive to the impulses at work in the world . . . that would encapsulate the conclusions of those working in the foreign policy team."[19]

The necessity of devising a new strategy was compounded by internal debate concerning the validity of previous strategies. President Clinton was convinced that no grand strategies had sufficiently explained "how to exert American leadership against the global threats posed by Hitler and Stalin." Instead, he believed that FDR and Truman had "powerful instincts about what had to be done, and they just made it up as they went along." The president suggested that the sense of an overarching policy had been applied retrospectively, as the victors wrote their own histories, a practice that continued unabated and which perpetuated the "huge myth that we always knew what we were doing during the Cold War." Despite this, the president recognized that the public needed to have policy explained to them in a simple, coherent fashion: "You've still got to be able to crystallize complexity in a way people get right away." Clinton realized in 1993 that this was not happening. Instead, he complained, "The operative problem of the moment is that a bunch of smart people haven't been able to come up with a new slogan."[20]

Differences of opinion within the administration regarding the relative benefits of a presidential doctrine were compounded by bureaucratic and personal challenges. In June 1993 Bob Boorstin of the NSC expressed his concern to Mark Gearan, Assistant to the President and Director of Communications and Strategic Planning, that "there is little or no coordination between domestic and foreign policy messages . . . our external communications failures are grounded in dysfunctional internal communications in the Executive Office of the President." The impact of such issues was that "people don't talk to each other. Meetings don't include relevant parties. People don't show up at meetings, and then countermand decisions. Decisions are made, remade and then reversed." The result of this was "confusion, both in message and policy." The NSC sought to rectify this and called for the integration of the administration's foreign policy message with its domestic message. It recognized that this was "a hazardous and complicated undertaking," but stressed that the administration had thus far "not developed an easy to understand 'Clinton doctrine' that is in line with our domestic themes." As a result, the "haphazard approach threatens to bury domestic events that we want to stress or to highlight foreign policy issues that we could muffle with domestic pronouncements."[21]

The operational logic behind such a document was open to question. While a grand strategy document may have been congressionally mandated, the actual benefit may have been purely for public consumption. As Anthony Lake conceded,

> These strategy papers are seen as opportunities to provide coherence for the bureaucracy for what the strategy is and to make public statements of what the strategy is and to inform the Congress, as legally required at the time, as to what the strategy is and in the process of working on them to get the very senior folks together. But the process involves putting together a lot of the things that you are doing with the general strategy. It is not a process of saying, "OK, first, what's our strategy and then secondly, what are all of our polices," because the world just doesn't work that way.[22]

However, as criticism mounted over his apparent disengagement, President Clinton ordered his foreign policy advisers to combine the administration's policies into a discernable concept to capture the public attention and provide a rallying call for politicians. The plan called for the president to unveil the strategy in his address to the UN General Assembly in September 1993 and be underscored in speeches by Warren Christopher, Anthony Lake, and Madeleine Albright. The speeches were designed to do more than inform the public and Washington elite about the direction of policy; they were used "to drive decisions and focus the bureaucracy" and specifically designed "to force consensus internally."[23] However, as a senior administration official said, "with no Cold War, the threats are more amorphous. The rallying ground is more difficult to find. It's tough to put US policy goals on a bumper sticker."[24]

The NSC had been drafting material for a grand strategy document, but with no success. As Morton Halperin revealed: "There is no general staff to do stuff like this at the NSC. At State they'd have the Policy Planning Staff do it. At the NSC it fell under the Defense Directorate and Robert Bell's people were involved in drafting it, but Lake was unsatisfied with it."[25] As a result Halperin was asked to come up with a coherent policy. Accordingly, Halperin, Anthony Lake, and NSC staff members Jeremy Rosner, Donald Steinberg, and Leon Fuerth began the task of "devising a strategic vision with an accompanying catchphrase."[26] The challenge was to produce a doctrine that embodied the foreign policy ideas articulated on the campaign: reconstructing US military and security capabilities, elevating the role of economics in international affairs, and promoting democracy. The aim was to dispel the perception that the administration had an *ad hoc* foreign policy while making it "simple so people would understand the heart of the strategy, while writing a fairly nuanced speech that did not overstate what we could do."[27]

Leon Fuerth advocated "Global Civilization," a concept Al Gore developed in his book, *Earth in the Balance*.[28] It emphasized continued US leadership in the post-Cold War world and insisted that failure to do so invited "a decent towards chaos." The philosophy fitted with the administration's position that the United States needed to discharge its "obligation to world leadership," since the end of the Cold War should cause the West "to do more than merely indulge in self-congratulation." Gore's position was in keeping with Anthony Lake's philosophy that "Enlightened governments and their leaders must play a major role in spreading awareness of the problems, in framing practical solutions, in offering a vision of the future we want to create." Yet Gore also introduced a Clintonesque rationale as he stressed the "substantial economic and geopolitical benefits for the United States."[29] Despite this, Lake felt "Global Civilization" failed to convey the scale of the new policies the administration was seeking to unveil. It was also a concept associated closely with the vice president, recognized for his work in foreign policy and the exercise would have backfired if it were believed that Gore was defining and devising foreign policy.

At the height of the internal quest for a definition of policy, George Kennan advised the Clinton administration to reconsider their actions. He lamented that in retrospect he "had tried to pack so much diagnosis and prescription into three syllables," a folly that led to "great and misleading oversimplification of analysis and policy." Instead, Kennan recommended drafting a "thoughtful paragraph or more, rather than trying to come up with a bumper sticker." When notified, President Clinton observed wryly, "That's why Kennan's a great diplomat and scholar and not a politician."[30]

Eventually "Democratic Enlargement" emerged as Lake's chosen description of policies required in the post-Cold War world. It fell to the NSC's Senior Director for Legislative Affairs, Jeremy Rosner to prepare the documents that stressed the US intention to "remain the world's pre-eminent military power and its chief advocate for liberalizing the global economy" a ploy to be unveiled in a series of speeches in September 1993.[31] President Clinton appreciated that Democratic Enlargement signified the notion that as free states grew, the international order became more prosperous, more secure, and likened the concept to the Domino Theory in reverse.[32] Democratic Enlargement posited that where command economies collapsed, free markets may rise and flourish: "What Clinton liked best about Lake's Enlargement policy was the way it was inextricably linked to economic renewal with its emphasis on making sure the United States remained the number one exporter."[33] Lake and the NSC staff had tailored a bespoke foreign policy to match the aspirations of the president and his domestic agenda. The administration finally appeared to have an agreed upon grand strategy concept with which to engage the post-Cold War world. In September 1993, in a week of high-profile speeches, it was unveiled to a waiting world.

Warren Christopher's address

The policy announcements got off to a poor start, however, as the first official to address the issue was Secretary of State, Warren Christopher, whose support for the new concept was less than total. Speaking at Columbia University on September 20, 1993, Christopher alluded to Democratic Enlargement, but without any enthusiasm and singularly failed to reference it directly, revealing the "typical" and "cautious" approach of the department.[34] The focus of Christopher's remarks was the Middle East peace process, which had been energized by agreements between Israel and the Palestinians. This was promoted as a priority for the administration since "the real barrier to peace between the Israelis and Palestinians—the psychological barrier—has been breached."[35] Christopher revealed plans to provide $250 million to the Palestinians over the next 2 years. While conceding that the money would come from the foreign aid budget, leaving less for other countries, Christopher confirmed that aid to Israel and Egypt would remain at current levels, which in 1993 totaled $3 billion and $2.1 billion a year respectfully, accounting for more than one-third of the US foreign aid budget.[36] Christopher also revealed the administration had decided it could not count on the United Nations to keep order in the post-Cold War world, since it was often unwilling to take military action except in instances where the US had demonstrated a willingness to act unilaterally if necessary.

Christopher appeared to be a warm up act for Anthony Lake and gave notice that the national security adviser's speech would "address the broad outlines of our foreign policy. His speech will reflect broad policy discussions within our administration and I commend it to your attention."[37] He did not indicate that Lake would unveil specifics or agreed upon concepts. Christopher was used to dealing with traditional foreign policy concepts and believed that the theories developed by Anthony Lake and the NSC staff went too far.[38] As Nancy Soderberg noted, "The State Department tried its own hand at defining America's doctrine and put forth its own plan, everyone was trying to find something, all coming up with their own ways of trying to get at the same idea of what the United States had to do."[39] The lack of overall policy coordination was revealing.

Rather than endorsing Democratic Enlargement, Christopher offered a policy of Engagement, which he referenced five times. His speech utilized a false construct as the secretary of state insisted "in the latest round in a century-old debate between engagement and isolationism, the United States chooses Engagement." Yet this was a false debate since no one was seriously advocating a policy of isolationism, while Engagement was a concept previously espoused by James Baker and Gary Hart. Christopher intoned that the central purpose of US foreign policy was "to ensure the security of our nation and to ensure its economic prosperity as well—and to promote democratic values." His second justification for Engagement was security, in a concession to classic power politics where Christopher felt at ease. US national interest was spelt out in the ensuing national security strategy documents, but Christopher asserted that the United States "must maintain its military strength and reinvigorate its economy so that we can retain the option to act alone when that is best for us." In defending its interests, the United States would not necessarily act alone and Christopher was at pains to stress the pragmatic approach the administration intended to adopt. He discussed how collective action could "advance American foreign policy interests. It can bolster our efforts to stem the proliferation of weapons of mass destruction, to knock down barriers to global trade and to protect the environment. We have also seen that collective action requires—and cannot replace—American leadership."

Christopher sounded a scornful note when he suggested that the speculation surrounding policy development was of secondary importance to the implementation of diplomacy, noting that while "this largely tactical debate on the means of American engagement has proceeded, President Clinton has been meeting the key foreign policy tests and challenges." It was, however, a debate that had been brewing within the administration itself, both between and within departments. Clinton's challenges included addressing potential crises that could threaten the United States in the future, such as democratic reversals in Russia and the risk of ethnic conflict in Europe. As Christopher noted, "If any of these things comes to pass-then our own security and our ability to focus on domestic renewal will be directly put at risk." These potential developments were highlighted to justify Christopher's stance regarding continued US engagement. The alternative, he stressed, must be rejected "for the dangerous argument that it is . . . the pied pipers of isolationism misread the history of this century . . . they minimize the threats to our security."[40] However, suggestions that the alternative to Engagement was isolationism dramatically overstated the case. Calls for isolationism had been heard only from Pat Buchanan and the defeated fringe of the Republican Party and no one anticipated that such a policy would be enacted by the Clinton administration.

Christopher's lack of reference to the agreed upon concept of Democratic Enlargement was noticeable. The missing element in Christopher's speech was indicative of differences at the heart of the administration, between those who espoused an embrace of Democratic Enlargement and those who felt it was a step too far. It seemed that this was an effort by the State Department to dampen expectations in regard to US adventurism in the 1990s and betrayed Christopher's pedigree as a Cold War diplomat, ill prepared for the realities through which President Clinton was governing. This was a fact that had already dawned on the White House; "The idea that you're going to get independent thinking from Warren Christopher is ridiculous," lamented a Clinton adviser.[41] The Berlin Wall may have fallen but the Cold War mentality of a state-based approach to foreign policy remained constant, for as Nancy Soderberg noted after leaving office, "The world had changed and the government hadn't changed with it."[42] Christopher personified this mentality, a shortcoming that hindered the administration and reduced its standing around the globe, repeatedly confirming fears that "his personality was too restrained for him to be effective."[43] The fact that the secretary of state failed to publicly endorse the new policy spoke volumes about the level of support the initiative had within the administration. It was indicative not only of the challenges that the policy faced, but also of tensions within the administration between the State Department and the National Security Council.

Madeleine Albright's address

While Warren Christopher could be accused of paying lip service to the new policy, the same could not be said of US Ambassador to the United Nations, Madeleine Albright. In her address at the National War College on September 23, Albright openly supported the idea of enhancing democracy and empowering nations to take steps toward human rights and political reform. This stance marked her as a dove to many, however, as a firm advocate of military intervention when necessary, she was viewed as a hawk within the Clinton administration. Eight months into office and with questions being asked about the direction of foreign policy at the White House, Albright noted that "a debate has raged about whether it is necessary to spell out a set of specific circumstances—a checklist—describing when America will or will not contemplate the use of military force." Despite these having been issued in the past, Albright suggested that "Too much precision in public, however well-intentioned, can impinge on the flexibility of the commander-in-chief or generate dangerous miscalculations abroad."[44] Perhaps not surprisingly, she has subsequently stated her belief that the search for a new doctrine was "merely a public relations device and not very helpful in practical terms."[45]

Notwithstanding such concerns, Albright's speech developed the themes that the administration had chosen to unveil, announcing the policy goals as being "to strengthen the bonds among those countries that make up the growing community of major market democracies . . . to help emerging democracies get on their feet . . . to reform or isolate the rogue states . . . to contain the chaos and ease the suffering in regions of greatest humanitarian concern." Unlike Christopher, Albright made specific reference to the policy, insisting that "taken together, our strategy looks to the enlargement of democracy and markets abroad" and presented a *tour de force* of the administration's view of the world.

Albright was quick to note that while few mourned the passing of the Cold War and its Containment policy, "anyone who concludes that foreign adversaries, conflicts and disasters do not affect us misreads the past, misunderstands the present and will miss the boat in the future." Whereas Christopher felt Lake's Democratic Enlargement concept went too far, Ambassador Albright appeared to suggest that it could have gone much farther. Her previously espoused concept of Assertive Multilateralism adopted a liberal internationalist approach that sought to preserve US involvement abroad at a reduced cost by working through alliances and international organizations, enabling a sharing of the burdens. Albright acknowledged that "some say we must make rigid choices between unilateral and multilateral, global and regional, force and diplomacy. But that is not true . . . We have a full range of foreign policy tools with which to work and we will choose those that will be most effective in each case."

Albright continued her use of the "assertive" prefix, insisting that "as a result of our assertive diplomacy," the United States had garnered "global support for sanctions against Libya for shielding the alleged saboteurs of Pan Am 103, against Iraq for its continued failure to meet its obligations following the Persian Gulf War and against Haiti prior to the agreement reached recently to restore democratic rule." Despite her personal preference for multilateral action, Albright stressed the unilateral options that the United States was willing to initiate when necessary, highlighting President Clinton's strike on Saddam Hussein's military intelligence headquarters in response to an attempt to kill President Bush. She also placed Clinton's willingness to embrace unilateral action in a wider context: "If America's vital economic interests are at risk . . . or if terrorists need to be tracked down . . . President Clinton will not hesitate to act as a commander-in-chief to protect America." It was, however, revealing that Albright was chosen to speak about the use of military force in the post-Cold War world, as she was not representing the Pentagon and her direct reporting line was to the State Department. The content, tone, and location of the speech indicated that it could, and perhaps should, have been delivered by Defense Secretary Aspin who was noticeably absent from the high-profile addresses that were made that September.

Despite the military component of the speech, the central focus of Albright's remarks was the future of the United States within a UN framework. Albright was at pains to highlight the benefits and the drawbacks of continued cooperation, particularly in the area of peacekeeping operations. The administration saw the benefits that such missions brought by way of reducing rivalry with the former USSR, but expressed concern at the expansion of such missions, particularly in addressing ethnic conflicts: "More peace-keeping operations in the past five years than in the previous forty-three; a sevenfold increase in troops; a tenfold increase in budget; and a dramatic but immeasurable increase in danger and complexity." At best, Albright insisted, such missions "have the potential to act as a 'force multiplier' in promoting the interests in peace and stability that we share with other nations." Despite these potential benefits, Albright was forthright in her observations regarding the flaws in peacekeeping operations, insisting that "UN peace-keepers need reformed budget procedures, more dependable sources of military and civilian personnel, better training, better intelligence, better command and control, better equipment and more money." Accordingly, the administration expected reform of the UN decision-making process on peacekeeping and insisted that key issues be addressed prior to any future commitment. These included ensuring that a cease-fire was already in place, that an exit strategy was agreed upon, that the mission had clearly defined objectives, and that sufficient resources be made available to ensure success. Albright announced that the administration was "preparing guidelines for American participation that will promise greater assistance in specialized areas such as logistics, training, intelligence, communications, and public affairs." Notable in their absence was reference to troops or to the latest technology.

The speech occurred at a time when the administration was being critiqued for its embrace of the United Nations, forcing Albright to walk a fine line between support for the organization and a defense of US sovereignty and determination to act unilaterally when necessary. Ambassador Albright outlined the administration's policy on multinational peacekeeping operations within a framework of Democratic Enlargement. The administration, she insisted, supported the United Nations, but understood "that there are limits to what that partnership can achieve for the United States . . . we cannot rely on the UN as a substitute guarantor for the vital interests of the United States." Pragmatism reigned supreme in the Clinton White House and "The tools that America will use to carry out its foreign policy will be both unilateral and multilateral." Albright wanted to leave no doubt that the United States had "strong reason to help build a United Nations that is increasingly able and effective. But America will never entrust its destiny to other than American hands."[46]

The Clinton administration initially believed that US participation in UN-led actions may remove some of the military burden shouldered by the United States and allow the president to concentrate on his domestic agenda. That did not mean that America intended to surrender her right to act alone and Albright asserted the nation's right to act unilaterally where its interests were at stake. Such declarations, however, were included primarily to appease the administration's domestic critics and belied the fact that the evolving US Grand Strategy reflected a Wilsonian belief in multilateralism and a sense that action through international institutions could foster global peace. However, not all were convinced by such Wilsonian principles. Unilateralists felt that America should and could act alone and rejected involvement where humanitarian needs did not represent a challenge to American self-interest. They feared the Clinton administration was ceding too much authority to the United Nations in what Senator Robert Dole called "an abdication of American leadership."[47] Ambassador Albright's address was an attempt to refute such allegations, while stressing the limits to America's embrace of multilateralism.

The speech also reflected a Senate Foreign Relations Committee report of August 1993 that stipulated clear mandates should be provided to troops going into war zones and that a realistic time frame of action should be prepared so that operations could be properly planned and implemented. However, neither Albright nor the Senate ruled out using American troops in multinational peacekeeping operations where US interests were not threatened. Despite the attempt at a coordinated effort the administration was accused of "patching together, amid much internal squabbling, a policy framework," with which to engage with the world.[48]

The presidential address

The presidential address at the United Nations on September 27, 1993 should have been an historic event, as Bill Clinton became the first US president born after the foundation of the organization to address the General Assembly. With a new era, a new president and a new global strategy to deliver, this could have been a key moment in UN history. However, the president was under congressional pressure to justify continued involvement in UN peacekeeping operations and was forced to neuter his advocacy of multilateralism. The president faced two distinct challenges: the need to reveal policies that adhered to his campaign promise of putting domestic affairs first and the need to outline a vision for America's place in the world, which he had struggled to do in his first 8 months in office. While an American withdrawal from the world was never in question, the domestic focus of the administration and the anti-UN tone of Congress forced the president to dispel fears about continued US involvement in international affairs. The president advocated an activist foreign policy and full cooperation with the United Nations in a speech that called for the bolstering of democracy around the globe, new initiatives on weapons proliferation, environmental protection, and population control.

Never one to shy away from a Kennedy reference, Clinton attempted to cloak himself in the mantle of his fallen hero, telling the gathered dignitaries, "Thirty-two years ago, President Kennedy warned this Chamber that humanity lived under a nuclear sword of Damocles that hung by the slenderest of threads." Under Clinton's leadership, the United States was striving to heed Kennedy's warning by "working with Russia, Ukraine, Belarus and others to take that sword down, to lock it away in a secure vault where we hope and pray it will remain forever." While the threats that Kennedy spoke of may have been reduced, the end of the Cold War "removed the lid from many cauldrons of ethnic, religious and territorial animosity." Clinton believed that this ensured nations must "work together more effectively in pursuit of our national interests and to think anew about whether our institutions of international cooperation are adequate."[49]

Continuing a theme from the campaign, the president rejected the distinction between the domestic and international systems, describing them as inseparable, insisting that this was necessary if America was to compete economically and promote a more stable international system. To Clinton, domestic and foreign, as well as political and economic issues, were inextricably intertwined and what was needed "was an integrated approach in which foreign policy would take its place as part of an overall strategy for guaranteeing the security of present and future generations of Americans."[50] As a result, while this may have been an address on foreign policy, economics were never far from the surface. By 1993, the US economy was entwined in the global economy and its security with global security. Therefore, Clinton insisted that "a thriving and democratic Russia not only makes the world safer, it also can help to expand the world's economy. And the growing economic power of China, coupled with greater political openness, could bring enormous benefits to all of Asia and to the rest of the world." The administration believed that domestic problems should be prioritized, but that in an interdependent world foreign policy could not be considered in isolation.

It was on such a note that President Clinton introduced the policy of Democratic Enlargement. He insisted that America's "overriding purpose" must be to "expand and strengthen the world's community of market-based democracies," since democracy and free markets were "reducing suffering, fostering sustainable development, and improving health and living conditions." This was a new policy for a new era. During the Cold War, the West "sought to contain a threat to the survival of free institutions"; now it should "seek to enlarge the circle of nations that live under those free institutions." Democratic Enlargement was presented as a worldwide effort in which the United States supported "the consolidation of market democracy where it is taking new root, as in the states of the former Soviet Union and all over Latin America." This was not to be a pax-Americana, however, as the president demanded this was "no crusade to force our way of life and doing things on others." It was necessarily, however, a policy that depended on multilateral support, something that was soon to be in short supply as the future of the US relationship with the United Nations came into question.

Despite praising the United Nations for its peacekeeping activities and hailing it as the instrument that "holds the promise to resolve many of this era's conflicts," President Clinton used his address to demand changes in the way the United Nations embarked on and operated peacekeeping operations.[51] The UN budget was of concern to many in Washington, despite its total budget being "roughly what the Pentagon spends every thirty-two hours."[52] There was a duality to the president's speech, therefore, which insisted that the United States intended to continue to be engaged globally, while indicating to the Congress that future participation in UN peacekeeping was to be restricted. President Clinton may have believed in the United Nations, but he was forced to inoculate himself from congressional critics. He insisted that the United States had not supported peacekeeping missions "as some critics in the United States have charged, to subcontract American foreign policy," but rather "to strengthen our security . . . and to share . . . the costs and effort of pursuing peace." Despite the ambiguity in the president's message, it was clear that the administration was ideologically committed to the United Nations in a way that many of its predecessors were not. Yet while Clinton supported the concept of multilateralism, he refused to surrender his powers as commander-in-chief, insisting that the United States intended to "work in partnership with others and through multilateral institutions," while refusing to hesitate "when there is a threat to our core interests or to those of our allies."[53] This had long been US policy and remained so during the Clinton administration, as revealed in speeches and documents released during the campaign and its time in office.

Although time and events put the administration's faith in multilateralism to the test, President Clinton's UN address demonstrated that he was more than just a domestic president and the results were immediate—his approval rating jumped to 56 percent, the highest since shortly after taking office.[54] However, the mood in Washington prevented President Clinton from making a Kennedyesque call for sacrifice "to assure the survival and success of liberty" and this lack of absolute commitment led some to question his dedication to the international order.[55] Indeed, despite the jump in his approval ratings, it was noted that his delivery "gave away the difference within him [between] domestic or foreign policy issues . . . He was wooden and projected little confidence."[56] It was further noted that, "If the belief takes hold in Washington that America need only provide the technology while others die on the ground, Clinton's hopes of providing leadership will quickly dissipate."[57] After US losses in Somalia, however, this approach effectively became the operating principal for US forces for the remainder of the decade.

Anthony Lake's address

While the president spoke of America's global status and its relationship with the United Nations, the speech was short on specifics. As a result, the clearest explanation of the Clinton administration's foreign policy came not from the president but from Anthony Lake, in a speech delivered on September 21, 1993 entitled "From Containment to Enlargement." It was to be the most succinct foreign policy statement to come out of the Clinton White House in its 8 years and set forth the administration's view of the world and how it intended to shape it. Speaking at the School of Advanced International Studies at Johns Hopkins University, Lake argued that the end of the Cold War presented an opportunity to reassess America's place in the world, as the United States returned to "debates about our role in the world that are as old as our Republic."

Communism's collapse presented a challenge that Lake believed was one of the greatest America could face: "whether we will be significantly engaged abroad at all." As it enabled him to identify with the architects of the modern world, Lake was eager to highlight a similar debate after the Second World War that had "pitted those Democrats and Republicans whose creativity produced the architectures of postwar prosperity and security against those in both parties who would have had us retreat within the isolated shell we occupied in the 1920s and 1930s." Lake may have made an ally of history, but he recognized that times had changed, for in 1993, "rallying Americans to bear the costs and burdens of international engagement is no less important. But it is much more difficult." Americans were anticipating a peace dividend, not a call to arms, which hindered advocacy of an activist foreign policy. This public sentiment had contributed to Clinton's election and, despite this paradox, Lake placed such concerns in their historical context, recognizing that with the end of the Cold War, "there is no longer a consensus among the American people about why and even whether, our nation should remain engaged in the world."

Lake was eager to dismiss two fashionable foreign policy concepts, insisting the United States faced neither the end of history nor a clash of civilizations, but rather "a moment of immense democratic and entrepreneurial opportunity." What was needed was a policy that took account of the rapidly changing geopolitical circumstances, leading Lake to insist, "the successor to a doctrine of Containment must be a strategy of Enlargement, enlargement of the world's free community of market democracies." This policy promoted global democracy, isolated Iran and Iraq, and worked with the United Nations to implement international policies that combined America's "broad goals of fostering democracy and markets with our more traditional geopolitical interests."

As Lake surveyed the initial months of the Clinton administration, he implied that a policy of Democratic Enlargement was already in effect. The administration had "completed a sweeping review of our military strategy and forces . . . led a global effort to support the historic reforms in Russia . . . helped defend democracy in Haiti [and] facilitated major advances in the Middle East peace process." However, he insisted that such an approach no longer sufficed; a doctrine was required to prevent dire consequences. If not, "foreign events can seem disconnected; individual setbacks may appear to define the whole," resulting in "unwise cuts to our military force structure or readiness, a loss of the resources necessary for our diplomacy and thus erosion of US influence abroad." Lake's unveiling of a doctrinal approach was intended to shore up support and provide direction for future US foreign policy initiatives.

However, the Clinton administration was reliant on the United Nations to implement various aspects of its far-reaching Democratic Enlargement program and it was feared that this risked ceding too much power to the UN Secretary General. In this instance, Lake stressed that the argument between unilateralists and multilateralists was misplaced. Since both agreed that the United States had important interests abroad it should rely on a pragmatic use of both approaches: "We should act multilaterally where doing so advances our interests and . . . act unilaterally when that will serve our purpose. The simple question in each instance is: What works best?" This pragmatic approach to policy defined the Clinton administration, though it infuriated many and confounded others. On the policy of Democratic Enlargement, however, Lake was adamant: "I believe strongly that our foreign policies must marry principle and pragmatism." Lake emphasized that the new policy had its roots in the history of the twentieth century, since "throughout the Cold War, we contained a global threat to market democracies; now we should seek to enlarge their reach, particularly in places of special significance to us." Clearly Democratic Enlargement was designed to have a special meaning to those with an East European heritage, a region that eventually benefited greatly from these new policies.

Underlying the policy of Democratic Enlargement was the notion of neo-Wilsonianism, which Lake attempted to implement, fully conscious of the historical parallel he was attempting to draw. Wilson, Lake explained, "understood that our own security is shaped by the character of foreign regimes." The League of Nations failed, but "most presidents who followed, Republicans and Democrats alike, understood we must promote democracy and market economics in the world, because it protects our interests and security and because it reflects values that are both American and universal." The Clinton administration built on Wilson's legacy, and also drew inspiration from the post-Second World War generation, whose spirit America "needed to recapture in forging a coalition of the center."[58] To demonstrate his efforts in this direction, Lake consulted with Newt Gingrich on the formulation of Democratic Enlargement and attempted to fulfill his self-imposed mandate of delivering a concept that was "simple so that people would understand the heart of the strategy."[59] To do so, he equated the modern struggle with that of the Cold War, when Americans "knew we were trying to contain the creeping expansion of that big, red blob." Now, Lake explained, "we might visualize our security mission as promoting the enlargement of the 'blue areas' of market democracies."[60] Gingrich concurred that no Republican could oppose the spread of democracy, but despite Gingrich's "interesting comments, [he was not] committed to supporting us publicly."[61] The future Speaker of the House may have been a dedicated internationalist, but as the White House discovered, neither he nor his fellow Republicans hesitated to use foreign policy initiatives against the administration if it promised electoral reward.

Lake stressed that practical interests, not starry-eyed idealism, defined the Clinton administration: "This is not a democratic crusade; it is a pragmatic commitment to see freedom take hold where that will help us most." For the plan to work, America needed to target its efforts "to assist states that affect our strategic interests, such as those with large economies, critical locations, nuclear weapons, or the potential to generate refugee flows into our own nation or into key friends and allies." The policy was open to interpretation, so while Democratic Enlargement was presented as a challenge to the growing mood of neo-isolationism and a way to maintain American global leadership, Lake insisted that the United States was to be selective in its interventions. In this respect, Lake's statement echoed the Tarnoff Doctrine, with implications for the global implementation of policy. It was this pragmatic approach that did much to raise doubts about the policy, as it granted the administration the right not to intervene when the mood suited. Indeed, the strategy rejected the belief that the United States was duty bound to promote constitutional democracy and human rights everywhere, as this was not a politically viable approach. Rather,

Democratic Enlargement was aimed at US strategic and economic interests: "We cannot impose democracy on regimes that appear to be opting for liberalization, but we may be able to help steer some of them down that path while providing penalties that raise the costs of repression and aggressive behaviour."[62] For those hoping for a return to the ideology of the Carter years, the Clinton administration proved to be disappointing as it placed economic considerations ahead of human rights concerns, despite early rhetoric to the contrary.

The backlash from rogue states of concern

For all of the administration's hopes for Democratic Enlargement, it recognized that certain states fell beyond its capacity to enact social and political reform.[63] In his speech and subsequent writings, Lake developed the idea that the United States was threatened by the Backlash States of Cuba, North Korea, Iran, Iraq, and Libya, which sought "to traffic in the weapons of mass destruction, support terrorism and are dedicated to the destruction of the tolerant society."[64] Lake may have been a neo-Wilsonian, but he was not blind to the threats that such nations posed to his policy. In a passage that had great resonance 8 years after its delivery, Lake insisted America "respects the many contributions Islam has made to the world . . . but we will provide every resistance to militants who distort Islamic doctrines and seek to expand their influence by force." Islamic Fundamentalism was a growing threat during the 1990s, but Lake believed the Backlash States posed a more immediate threat and that the United States should "expect the advance of democracy and markets to trigger forceful reactions from those whose power is not popularly derived."[65]

The Backlash States concept built on the Dual Containment policy unveiled by Martin Indyk and posited that certain states needed to be targeted for radical change, in a precursor for the Regime Change policy that evolved during Clinton's second term and was implemented in Iraq by his successor. It was the repressive nature of the ruling bodies, as opposed to the ethnicity or creed of the population that best underscored the rationale for the Backlash States concept, of which Iran and Iraq were but two. Lake believed such nations had defining characteristics: they were "ruled by cliques that control power through coercion, they suppress basic human rights and promote radical ideologies . . . their leaders share a common antipathy toward popular participation that might undermine the existing regimes."[66] There was a general consensus within the administration that the term defined "all those who would return newly free societies to the intolerant ways of the past."

Therefore, years before President George W. Bush announced an Axis of Evil, the Clinton administration prepared a similar list of similar states, against which it would fight for "small victories, through persistence and pragmatism." Such initiatives were "the hallmarks of determination, of a nation engaged in the long struggle for democracy and the freedom and tolerance it brings."[67] The Backlash States threatened their neighbors, US allies, and vital American interests and met the full resistance of the United States, though not necessarily via military engagement. "Our policy toward such states must seek to isolate them diplomatically, militarily, economically and technologically," Lake insisted and it was via such a policy that Saddam Hussein was to be "kept in his box" for the remainder of the decade.[68]

The ideology that motivated the Cold War may have gone, but the Clinton administration recognized that it faced "a struggle between freedom and tyranny . . . between those who would build free societies governed by laws and those who would impose their will by force."[69] While conceding that in the short term the Backlash States lacked the resources to "enable them to seriously threaten the democratic order," it was feared that "the ties between them are growing as they seek to thwart or quarantine themselves from a global trend to which they seem incapable of adapting." The administration sought to solve what it viewed as "a strategic puzzle" that had confounded the three previous administrations, yet one it believed the United States could resolve and, in doing so, "transform these Backlash States into constructive members of the international community." Lake was aware that there were those who advocated a more conciliatory approach, but the administration believed that these nations were "on the wrong side of history" and that an opportunity existed to rectify this. This, he insisted, was "not a crusade, but a genuine and responsible effort, over time, to protect American strategic interests, stabilize the international system and enlarge the community of nations committed to democracy, free markets and peace." As stressed in the eventual National Security Strategy Reviews, the administration recognized the need to tailor policy specifically to address the history, culture, and circumstances of each nation. In regard to the Backlash States, however, the White House sought "to contain the influence of these states, sometimes by isolation, sometimes through pressure, sometimes by diplomatic and economic measures" and encouraged the international community "to join in a concerted effort."[70]

This, however, remained a state-based approach to issues that failed to take into account the rise in importance of non-state-based actors. Eventually, the policy evolved to one of States of Concern, since "Rogue States suggests a state that you fundamentally cannot deal with. States of Concern are states that you have strong concerns about but will continue to deal with, Pakistan was one, Saudi was another."[71] The announcements highlighted the administration's recognition that all nations needed to be dealt with independently, depending upon their status, a vital element in the policy announcements and one that fitted the administration's world view. Lake identified challenges and advocated a manner in which to deal with them, something that was missing in many pronouncements from the White House in this era. All too often it appeared that a great deal of attention had been lavished upon defining policy, but with far less attention paid to how such policies were to be implemented.

Reaction

Democratic Enlargement was conceptually simple, acknowledged the potential unleashed by the end of the Cold War and, "unlike all the self-proclaimed competitors like Clash of Civilizations, it had a positive rather than a negative sound to it."[72] It was an important message that some felt was overdue, but the Clinton administration had only been in office 8 months, was the first in 45 years not to be able to rely on a policy of Containment, and had a mandate to concentrate on domestic reform. Anthony Lake was adamant that US foreign policy had "to be based on ideas as well as on interests, ideas, not ideals" and, despite the apparent differences between them, this philosophy was clear in the speeches of September 1993. If the speeches lacked operational specificity, they nevertheless conveyed the message that America intended to remain engaged in world affairs, albeit selectively. The speeches refuted allegations of an overdependence on multilateralism and left no doubt that the Clinton administration intended to pursue an activist foreign policy and remain internationalist in perspective, adopting a multilateral approach when possible, but acting unilaterally when necessary. Lake insisted that the concept was simple: "together when we can, alone when we must."[73]

That was not to say that President Clinton planned to engage US forces recklessly. An underlying theme of the speeches was that the administration sought to be selective about where and when it posted its resources. As such, the speeches reflected a caution about military engagement that characterized the Clinton years. However, while the administration wished to be cautious in its execution of military operations, this did not mean that it adopted a passive foreign policy. The speeches emphasized a proactive effort to introduce positive change to the world, roll-back the remaining influences of the Cold War, and usher in a new era of democracy. The difficulty came not in convincing policy makers of the righteousness of the concept, but in its implementation. The lack of an external threat ensured that the administration could focus less on foreign policy. This also meant that when the White House sought to address international affairs, it found that congressional support was far more difficult to generate, as there was relatively little to focus against. This was apparent in the emerging Clinton Grand Strategy, which had no specific focus against an overseas aggressor. The administration's repeated efforts "were really inadequate to describe America's role in the world because people wanted a containment theory for the post-Cold War and there wasn't one."[74]

In this environment the policy announcements failed to appease critics who argued that an opportunity had been lost, as the speeches "fell short. And they received little attention."[75] Democratic Enlargement was branded "a strained attempt," to replace Containment, with much of the criticism reserved for Anthony Lake, whom opponents concluded was "no Henry Kissinger or even a Zbigniew Brzezinski."[76] Kissinger contrasted Lake's Democratic Enlargement policy with Containment, noting "Lake's speech contained very elevated attitudes, yet he gave it no operational definition. When George Kennan put forward Containment . . . that was an operational definition, being something that one could actually do."[77] The man who had set out to devise a new foreign policy for the post-Cold War world was branded, "Lake Inferior" and his policy critiqued as "academic and abstract, that while seemingly high-minded, failed to explain anything beyond Americans' good intentions [and] aspiration to morality."[78] This was exacerbated by a failure to coordinate the speeches and ensure that the same policies were advocated with the same phraseology. Lake "had wanted the whole team to deliver a single message, but he was unable to get his colleagues on board, since none of them shared his passion to find a single concept to replace Containment."[79]

The criticism leveled at Lake seemed more personal than professional and certainly went beyond what may have been expected or anticipated for a presidential adviser who made no effort to conceal his disdain for publicity or the limelight. He had, of course, burnt bridges by his decision to resign from the National Security Council in protest at the Cambodia operations during the Nixon administration. However, the vitriol that his philosophical approach to policy attracted was all the more perplexing considering the complex nature of Wilson, whose political and philosophical approach to foreign policy Lake sought to update for a late twentieth-century administration.

It was suggested that Lake had invoked a singular reading of history. Gaddis remarked that Wilson had not sought universal democracy, but rather "democracy and capitalism where possible within a framework of great power cooperation; but he was not so naive as to believe that the other great powers' interests would automatically accord with his own."[80] However, what appear to be contradictions in the Clinton administration's interpretation of Wilsonianism are less problematic than initially appear when Wilson's record is examined. Much like the widely accepted interpretation of Clinton, the single dimensional view of Wilson distorts the historical record, which is far more complex than either his supporters or detractors care to concede.[81]

Wilson's democratic crusade of 1917 can be seen as an idealist veneer to conceal the realist principles behind US entry to the First World War, as he blended realist policies with an idealistic rhetoric to inspire the American people to engage in a conflict that many believed was of little consequence to them. Wilson's much-vaunted idealism was certainly not on display in his address to the Senate in January 1917, as he told the assembled lawmakers that a "peace forced upon the loser, a victor's terms imposed upon the vanquished . . . would be accepted in humiliation, under duress, at an intolerable sacrifice and would leave a sting, a resentment, a biter memory upon which terms of peace would rest . . . as upon quicksand."[82]

Wilson had previously praised the Kaiser's system of government as a "shining model" of efficiency.[83] The man credited with making the world "safe for democracy" had also dismissed the role of elections within democracies and resorted to force in Mexico, Haiti, the Dominican Republic, in the First World War, northern Russia, and Siberia between 1914 and 1918.[84] As Cox reminds us, "Wilson was neither a fool nor a saint and to portray him as if he was one or the other only serves to distort his place in history."[85]

On April 2, 1917, however, the same president insisted that "the world must be made safe for democracy," a rallying call that defined Wilson and provide his ideological legacy. Rousing a peaceful populace in the name of balance of power or geostrategic leverage is unlikely to succeed. Urging them to fight to defend liberty and democracy, the very bedrock of American political life, proved to be a successful model that has been emulated ever since, despite what George Kennan later bemoaned as the "legalistic–moralistic approach to international affairs" that become synonymous with Wilsonianism.[86]

The concept of Wilsonianism has been adopted, interpreted, and utilized ever since and the Clinton administration's attempt to do so was merely the latest example. Interpretations have differed considerably, but it has been suggested that they have fallen into two camps: liberals embrace a "soft" interpretation of Wilsonianism and seek to rely on treaties and international organizations to foster peace and secure US ambitions. A conservative approach embraces a "hard" interpretation of Wilsonianism with which to use US power to advance national interests and ideals.[87] However it was interpreted, it was a clear break with the previous model that had endured since the founding era. It has been suggested that Wilson's fate was that of "a man who let his ideals exceed his grasp and whose immodesty for America led to his fall."[88] It was a fate Bill Clinton was determined to avoid as he sought to make the world safe not only for democracy, but also for American commerce.

Considering the transition from the Cold War to the Age of Clinton, however, the reaction was to some extent to be expected: "For a generation hand-reared on the truths of realism and the doctrine of power politics, the idea that a change in the form of other countries' governments would enhance US security must have sounded a little odd, especially coming from someone so inexperienced in the ways of the world as Bill Clinton."[89]

Worryingly, however, the speeches exposed differences that existed between the National Security Council and the State Department, which viewed Democratic Enlargement as naive and self-aggrandizing on the part of Anthony Lake. "Was it enlargement or engorgement?" one official asked.[90] As the reaction against the speeches gathered pace, the president turned on its architect, insisting that the speeches of September had been "weak, pathetic . . . I just didn't get it; it just didn't grab."[91]

By dividing the speech writing process between the State Department and the NSC, the administration inadvertently highlighted internal divisions in relation to the direction of policy. These differences undermined the credibility of the efforts to launch a cohesive approach to foreign policy. Yet Leon Fuerth later explained, "we all believed in engagement and the expansion of democracy. We viewed it as a Ratchet Principal, a guard against the situation slipping back to the previous situation, particularly in the former Soviet Union."[92] However, differences clearly existed. The NSC's Jeremy Rosner, described by Don Baer as a "tremendous writer with force and punch," had prepared the addresses for Lake and the president, while the State Department had prepared Christopher and Albright's remarks.[93] Both bodies were meant to support administration policy, but the feuding that left Madeleine Albright feeling like Anthony Lake's student had repercussions beyond personality and into the realm of policy making.[94] The speeches had been coordinated "but they didn't write them for each other" and the failure to ensure that the speeches were watertight ensured that while they may have been policy-coordinated, "the rhetorical gap was not closed."[95]

The difficult birth of Clinton's Grand Strategy

Having delivered a series of high-profile speeches, the administration recognized that its foreign policy credibility rested on its ability to formulate a credible, coherent strategy with which to address the new geopolitical environment. The administration had dealt with issue-specific polices to address regions and organizations and had formulated approaches to policy through PDDs, but had yet to demonstrate a capacity for linked-up thinking. This process did not constitute a grand strategy, but it was the first step toward the formulation of an overall policy, which began to take shape during the autumn of 1993 and into 1994.

Under the 1986 Goldwater-Nichols Department of Defense Reorganization Act, the White House was mandated to produce an annual National Security Strategy Report (NSSR) even if it was naturally inclined to focus on domestic policy. Having espoused policies of Democratic Enlargement, Engagement, Dual Containment, Assertive Multilateralism, and the Tarnoff Doctrine, the NSSR process gave the administration an opportunity to demonstrate its capacity to produce a strategy for dealing with the world at large. Clearly, there were many competing concepts to amalgamate and the risk was producing a report of "mushy 'globaloney' to be fed to Congress."[96] This was not a problem unique to the Clinton administration. As Richard K. Betts has noted, the report "has sometimes been a Christmas tree on which every interest groups hangs its foreign policy concerns." As a result, the NSSR reports "rarely says much that really illuminates national security strategy."[97]

The Goldwater-Nichols Act was an attempt by Congress to encourage the White House to formulate a coherent national security strategy. While few in the Congress at that time doubted that such a concept existed, what was in doubt "was its focus in terms of values, interests and objectives; its coherence in terms of relating means to ends; its integration in terms of the elements of power; and its time horizon."[98] The concern was that too few administrations gave too little serious thought to medium- or long-term foreign policy initiatives and failed to elucidate a coherent strategy with which to engage the world. It was hoped that requiring a written report would focus the attention of the White House and generate horizon-scanning perspectives with regard to foreign policy, which would assist in annual budget planning and resource allocation. Each report was expected to include the worldwide interests, goals, and objectives of the United States that were judged vital to its national security; the foreign policy, worldwide commitments, and national defense capabilities necessary to deter aggression and to implement the national security strategy; the proposed short-term and long-term uses of the political, economic, military, and other elements of national power; and the adequacy of the capabilities of the United States to carry out the national security strategy.[99]

However, "even when submitted," the reports had "generally been late," noted Senator Strom Thurmond in 1994, who added that the documents had "seldom met the expectations" of those who had drafted the legislation.[100] The NSSR was supposed to be presented to Congress along with the annual budget in February, but exceptions have occurred, usually when the date conflicts with military deployments or a presidential transition. At the start of the Clinton administration, five previous documents had been prepared; two by the Reagan administration in 1987 and 1988 and three by the Bush administration in 1990, 1991, and 1992. Intriguingly, the Clinton administration came to make more use of the NSSR process than any administration before or since, as it sought to present a strategic vision for the role of the United States in the post-Cold War world.

Ultimately going through 21 drafts, the administration's first National Security Strategy Report was quietly released in July 1994. Elements of the December 1991 Georgetown University Address, the 1993 Inaugural Address, the speeches of September 1993 and the 1994 State of the Union all found their way into the report. As had been the case since the 1991 Georgetown speech, Clinton's Grand Strategy was based around three central pillars: national security, prosperity promotion, and democracy promotion. Yet just as Lake's specific policy of Democratic Enlargement blended the apparently opposing policies of Wilsonianism with a post 1945 realism, so now the administration combined Lake's policy of Democratic Enlargement with the State Department's notion of Engagement, a term Lake felt to be "rather wimpy, because of course we were going to be engaged" and which "became a part of it just to make everyone happy."[101] The competing policies of Engagement and Democratic Enlargement were brought together to form the 1994 National Security Strategy of Engagement and Enlargement. Accordingly, the document appeared to be both a composite and a compromise, a collection of policies developed during the previous 18 months brought together under a title that combined opposing notions. The document's unceremonial unveiling led some to conclude "it was intended to be missed, or it was eminently missable."[102] Clinton may have been searching for a pragmatic policy, but many saw flaws in its principles even before it could be implemented.

The 1994 report revealed a broad approach to foreign policy that was decidedly more muted than Clinton had anticipated earlier in his administration and was seen as little more than "watered-down versions of earlier White House pronouncements."[103] Gaddis suggested later that such reports "tended to be restatements of existing positions, cobbled together by committees, blandly worded and quickly forgotten. None sparked significant public debate."[104] The report also revealed the bureaucratic challenges involved in its preparation. While Leon Fuerth viewed Clinton's NSC as "an ensemble" in which "there was a collective sense of what tasks we faced, consistent with our views of the world and of the administrations," the NSSR faced the organizational hurdle of the US national security structure.[105] The strategy document had been written within the Defense Directorate of the NSC, but it had to be cleared by every office in State and the Pentagon. This is where Morton Halperin's "Australia Phenomenon" emerged:

> What I mean by this is that the Australia desk at the State Department will demand that Australia be mentioned, else they may refuse to send her 450 troops next time we need them in a peace operation. But then once you mention Australia fourteen other desks demand that their countries be included. Then you get a document that simply goes around the world and results in an unfocused policy.[106]

In addition to the bureaucratic challenges, personal traits presented problems. In an effort to avoid the open warfare that defined the Carter years, Anthony Lake was eager to "preserve harmony among the key players" within the administration "and if that meant living with decisions that were not pushed to a logical conclusion then that was OK in the name of not upsetting the apple cart." Such an approach was evident in the eventual production of the National Security Strategy Review, which was devoid of "a lot of sharp edges," in keeping with Lake's effort to build "an inclusive, open tent and to good working relationships across the interagency process."[107]

In his statement unveiling the grand strategy, President Clinton insisted that although the Cold War was over, American leadership remained essential. Accordingly, the administration's policy was founded on three principles: "maintaining a defense capability strong enough to underwrite our commitments credibly," American economic strength at home and abroad, and the assertion that "the best way to advance America's interests worldwide is to enlarge the community of democracies and free markets throughout the world." These were seen as being mutually supportive:

> Democratic states are less likely to threaten our interests and more likely to cooperate with us to meet security threats and promote sustainable development. Secure nations are more likely to maintain democratic structures and to support free trade. And even with the cold war over, our Nation's security depends upon the maintenance of military forces that are sufficient to deter diverse threats and, when necessary, fight and win against our adversaries.[108]

The document was the foundation of grand strategy for the Clinton years, which remained largely consistent throughout the two terms of the administration. As Lake observed, "It's always the case that the first one is the most interesting and then the others are always looking for places to amend it."[109] This proved to be the case as the policy evolved throughout the administration to reveal the pragmatic nature of the Clinton presidency. It was also a tacit acknowledgment that a liberal grand strategy based on the view that "American security and national interests can be best advanced by promoting international order organised around democracy, open markets, multilateral institutions and binding security ties," would continue to prevail under the new administration.[110] Such strategy was not prepared in an intellectual vacuum, however and world events and the reaction to them influenced the drafting of the annual reports. The impact of events was to be found in every incarnation of the US Grand Strategy documents as reality repeatedly forced the administration to trim back its initial ambitions.

Problems of policy and presentation

Having espoused a grand strategy initiative in a series of high-profile speeches and in a fully fledged national security strategy, the Clinton administration may have been forgiven for thinking that their problems in the area had been solved. Instead, they were only beginning, as time and again their efforts to guide the United States through what Anthony Lake referred to as "a radically new international environment" were hindered by problems as much to do with presentation as with policy.[111] In December 1993, pollster Stan Greenberg briefed the president on the public perception of the administration's grand strategy thus far. "Foreign affairs," he conceded, "is not our strongest area." Although the signing of the Middle East peace agreement between Israel and the PLO was viewed as an important accomplishment by 67 percent of respondents, other foreign policy initiatives fared less well. Only 46 percent saw the administration's support for Boris Yeltsin in making the transition to democracy in Russia as an important accomplishment, and less (44%) thought similarly about the passage of NAFTA.[112] The following month, following a meeting of academics and administration officials, Greenberg urged the president to "use his educative role to shape people's understanding of this new world."[113]

As the White House prepared for the State of the Union address in 1994, it courted the opinion of leading historians and foreign policy experts. White House Deputy Communications Director David Dreyer advised Clinton to consider the input of Walter Russell Mead, whose work Dreyer believed, "succeeds brilliantly on history and theme."[114] Mead stressed that the State of the Union "should explain the overall guiding strategy of American foreign policy and put it in the context of the current world situation. Second, it should show how this overall strategic foreign policy supports the overall domestic reform and renewal agenda of the administration." Mead noted that "it is, frankly, not easy for the average American citizen to see why chasing warlords in Somalia or sending the marines to Haiti would serve his or her interests." However, he suggested that "if global economic growth is properly appreciated as the strategic centerpiece of your quest for peace and democracy abroad, then your foreign and domestic policies will be seen to be complementary." Mead observed "Foreign policy is not a diversion from the domestic agenda." Instead, he suggested, it should be harnessed as "a method to reach the central Administration goal of renewed prosperity for the American middle class.[115]

By September 1994, Bob Borrstin of the NSC briefed Lake that the president needed to "set out US interests in clear terms for the American people, and to convince the media/foreign policy elite to take a fresh look at the President's leadership and policies."[116] Doing so was seen as being vital to the future of the administration, as the NSC urged Clinton to remind voters "of what he stands for and what his Presidency is fundamentally about."[117] The administration required "a deep commitment to explain, explain and explain again, in simple and concrete terms, the ideals that drive our overseas agenda and how that agenda relates to life at home."

It is clear from declassified internal memos that the NSC saw the lack of communications as a serious impediment to the administration's ability to establish a credible grand strategy initiative. The NSC feared that the administration had allowed its critics "to draw old, outdated lines between domestic and foreign policy without making a strong case for why the distinction is no longer valid." Despite this, the Clinton administration failed "to build a strong bridge between national security and international security and to explain why and how in an interdependent world it no longer makes sense to look at foreign policy in isolation from domestic issues and vice versa," despite repeated efforts by the president and his advisers to do so.

These conclusions make it clear that the White House believed its challenges were not in the devising of policy, but in its communication: "Neither those who make foreign policy nor those whose responsibility it is to articulate the policy are consistently doing so in a way that communicates strength, clarity and decisiveness." The administration had a variety of media outlets to utilize, however, and the NSC feared that "too much of that reporting and analysis takes places without an administration point of view. We are, therefore, constantly on the defensive." Much of this was viewed as being a continuation of interdepartmental infighting, as "too much happens at State and Defense without White House knowledge." As a result, "too many journalists now find they can play one agency off another."[118]

Anthony Lake had attempted to prevent this by ensuring that the NSC wrote the president's national security speeches, a move that both Kissinger and Brzezinski had sought, but which Lake had implemented in what was described by Jeremy Rosner as "the biggest turf grab in White House history." Lake insisted that this move had been made for "simple efficiency" wanting speeches to be drafted "in the NSC by a speechwriter who [knew] the substance behind foreign policy so that you're not then getting behind and trying to fight over nuance."[119] This may have taken national security speechwriting away from the White House, but not from the State Department, resulting in a continued lack of policy coordination.

In the wake of the Somali disaster, special assistant to White House Chief of Staff, Roderick K. Von Lipsey, prepared a memo for his boss, Thomas McLarty, highlighting the continuing flaws in the administration's presentation of grand strategy initiatives. Von Lipsey noted that widespread media coverage "insinuates that the administration lacks viable foreign and security policies," and that without "clear and coherent statements of national interest and policy objectives by senior administration officials," the administration's entire grand strategy initiative "is put at risk." Von Lipsey recommended McLarty "provide guidelines or talking points to all cabinet officials which clearly outline our interest in, and policy toward Bosnia, Somalia and Haiti."

Von Lipsey urged McLarty to "convene a working group to define, in plain language, the administration's overarching foreign and security policy objectives, and . . . relate these objectives to an overall Presidential strategy which includes NAFTA, Health Care Reform, the Crime Bill and Deficit Reduction."[120] Once the American public understood the interconnectivity of policy, it was believed, they would fall in line behind the administration. The fact that such a coordinated response had only been unveiled weeks beforehand, however, spoke volumes as to its impact with the American public.

Indeed, the coordinated outreach that Von Lipsey envisioned was rendered less likely by the president's own actions. Tara Sonenshine and Tom Ross of the NSC argued further that President Clinton "should not be placed in the position of articulating foreign policy on the run. He needs to communicate our foreign policy in carefully structured and dignified settings on matters of great importance." All too often in his first year in office, President Clinton had addressed policy while literally on the run, as he jogged around Washington. Such impromptu incidents ended, but not before they eroded some of the majesty of the presidency. In their place, the president was urged to deliver "well-crafted speeches, appropriately placed and well-timed," to ensure that foreign policy issues were dealt with "in a proactive, not reactive manner."[121]

Conclusion: Clashes on the road to grand strategy

The addresses of September 1993 were the tip of an intellectual iceberg that betrayed the different priorities key members of the administration sought to promote. The central themes in the speeches had been Lake's concept of Democratic Enlargement and Christopher's policy of Engagement. Despite Leon Fuerth's insistence that he didn't "recall any clash between State and the NSC" and that he failed to "see any great distinction between Engagement and Enlargement," the lack of coordination and differing emphasis revealed clear divisions between personalities and departments. Bill Clinton had campaigned on a promise to strengthen America's global standing by promoting democratic values, while embracing the need for a continued strong defense—themes of the speeches of September 1993 and the initial NSSR document were intended to espouse.

Having been out of power for a political generation, it was not surprising that Clinton's foreign policy team had differing views on how best to define grand strategy. However, rather than attempting to coordinate policy, it appeared that there was intense internal competition to define policy. The speeches of September 1993 were intended to convince critics that the White House had a grasp of foreign policy and put an end to accusations of incompetence in this area. However, rather than heralding the prompt publication of a National Security Strategy Report, the White House became embroiled in a debacle that saw the report delayed until July 1994, during which time Fuerth conceded the administration was "busy wrestling with crocodiles!"[122] Rather than ushering in a new era of calm, the speeches coincided with a flare up of violence in Somalia and accusations of double standards in Bosnia. Having considered the manner in which policy was devised on the campaign trail and during the Clinton administration's initial months in office, it is vital to consider the manner in which it was implemented under these conditions and the degree to which it adhered to the three central policies espoused in its grand strategy.

Notes

1 Robert G. Bell served as the Defense Policy and Arms Control expert on the National Security Council from 1993 to 2000.

2 Chollet and Goldgeiger, *America Between The Wars*, p. 64.

3 Jonathan Clarke, "The Conceptual Poverty of US Foreign Policy," *The Atlantic Monthly* 272, no. 3 (September 1993), p. 54.

4 Talbot, *The Russia Hand*, p. 133.

5 Thomas L. Friedman, "Clinton's Foreign Policy: Top Adviser Speaks Up," *New York Times* (October 13, 1993), p. A8.

6 See DeParle, "The Man Inside Bill Clinton's Foreign Policy," pp. 32–39; Leslie H. Gelb, "Where's Bill?" *New York Times* (March 11, 1993), p. A23; Friedman, "Clinton's Foreign Policy," p. A8.

7 Joe Klein, "A High Risk Presidency," p. 32.

8 Quoted in Brummett, *Highwire*, p. 277.

9 Klein, *The Natural*, p. 68.

10 Michael Clough, "A President Bedevilled By a Lack of Vision," *Los Angeles Times* (October 17, 1993), p. M1.

11 Clarke, "The Conceptual Poverty of US Foreign Policy," p. 54.

12 "Thoughts for Your Breakfast Tomorrow," Clinton Presidential Records, National Security Council, Robert Boorstin (Speechwriting), OA/Box Number: 415, Clinton Doctrine—Articles, William J. Clinton Presidential Library.

13 Hendrickson, "The Recovery of Internationalism," p. 26.

14 Quoted in Brummett, *Highwire*, p. 276.

15 Author's interview with Leon Fuerth.

16 Quoted in Brummett, *Highwire*, p. 276.

17 Author's interview with Morton Halperin.

18 Warren Christopher, "Statement at Senate Confirmation Hearing," *US Department of State Dispatch* 4, Issue 4 (January 25, 1993), p. 45.

19 Author's interview with Leon Fuerth.

20 Talbot, *The Russia Hand*, pp. 133–134.

21 Bob Boorstin to Mark Gearan; re: Job Description/Suggestions, June 18, 1993, Clinton Presidential Records, National Security Council, Robert Boorstin (Speechwriting), OA/Box Number: 416, Communications Department–Structure, William J. Clinton Presidential Library.

22 Author's interview with Anthony Lake.

23 Chollet and Goldgeiger, *America Between The Wars*, p. 65.

24 Brodie, "President's Men Labour to Forge Clinton Doctrine," p. 13.

25 Author's interview with Morton Halperin.

26 Douglas Brinkley, "Democratic Enlargement: The Clinton Doctrine," *Foreign Policy* 106, (Spring 1997), p. 114.

27 Author's interview with Anthony Lake.

28 Author's interview with Leon Fuerth.

29 Al Gore, *Earth in the Balance: Ecology and the Human Spirit* (New York: Houghton Mifflin, 1992), pp. 172–179.

30 Talbot, *The Russia Hand*, p. 134.

31 Jeremy D. Rosner served as Senior Director for Legislative Affairs and Counsellor on the National Security Council (1993 to 1994); Brinkley, "Democratic Enlargement," p. 115.

32 During the Cold War, the Domino Theory posited that Communist conquest of one country would have a knock-on effect in neighboring countries.

33 Brinkley, "Democratic Enlargement," p. 117.

34 Author's interview with Morton Halperin.

35 Warren Christopher, "Building Peace in the Middle East," *US Department of State Dispatch* 4, no. 39 (September 27, 1993), p. 654.

36 Elaine Sciolino, "US to Contribute $250 Million in Aid for Palestinians," *New York Times* (September 21, 1993), p. A1.

37 Christopher, "Building Peace in the Middle East," p. 654.

38 Brinkley, "Democratic Enlargement," pp. 121–122.

39 Author's interview with Nancy Soderberg.

40 Christopher, "Building Peace in the Middle East," pp. 654.

41 J. F. O. McAllister and William Mader, "Secretary Of Shhhhh!" *Time* 141, no. 23 (June 7, 1993), pp. 32–34.

42 Author's interview with Nancy Soderberg.

43 Clinton, *My Life*, p. 455.

44 Madeleine Albright, "Use of Force in a Post-Cold War World," *US Department of State Dispatch* 4, no. 39 (September 27, 1993), p. 665.

45 Chollet and Goldgeiger, *America Between The Wars*, p. 69.

46 Albright, "Use of Force in a Post-Cold War World," p. 665.

47 Quoted in Martin Walker, "Clinton Fudges Plans for Peace Troops," *Guardian* (September 25, 1993), p. 14.

48 John M. Broder, "US Clarifies Its Policy on Peacekeeping," *Los Angeles Times* (September 24, 1993), p. A12.

49 *PPPWJC*, vol. 1 (1993), Remarks to the 48th Session of the United Nations General Assembly in New York City, September 27, 1993, pp. 1613–1616.

50 Edward Mortimer, "Sights Set on a Wider World: The Imperatives Guiding America's Hesitant Foreign Policy," *Financial Times* (September 27, 1993), p. 17.

51 *PPPWJC*, vol. 1 (1993), Remarks to the 48th Session of the United Nations General Assembly in New York City, September 27, 1993, pp. 1614–1616.

52 Madeleine Albright, "United Nations," *Foreign Policy* 138 (September–October 2003), p. 22.

53 *PPPWJC*, vol. 1 (1993), Remarks to the 48th Session of the United Nations General Assembly in New York City, pp. 1615–1616.

54 Martin Fletcher, "Clinton Launches Crusade for Peace With Democracy," *The Times* (September 28, 1993), p. 1.

55 *PPPJFK*, vol. 1 (1961), Inaugural Address, January 20, 1961, p. 1.

56 Drew, *On The Edge*, p. 325.

57 "Clinton the Internationalist," *Independent* (September 28, 1993), p. 19.

58 Anthony Lake, "From Containment to Enlargement," Address at the School of Advanced International Studies, Johns Hopkins University, Washington, DC, September 21, 1993, *US Department of State Dispatch* 4, no. 39 (September 27, 1993), p. 658.

59 Author's interview with Anthony Lake.

60 Lake, "From Containment to Enlargement," p. 658.

61 Author's interview with Anthony Lake.

62 Lake, "From Containment to Enlargement," p. 658.

63 For analysis of the Clinton administration's approach to such nations, see Alex Miles, *US Foreign Policy and the Rogue State Doctrine* (Abingdon, Oxon: Routledge, 2013).

64 Anthony Lake, "The Reach of Democracy: Tying Power To Diplomacy," *New York Times* (September 23, 1993), p. A35.

65 Lake, "From Containment to Enlargement," p. 658.

66 Lake, "Confronting Backlash States," p. 46.

67 Lake, "The Reach of Democracy," p. A35.

68 Lake, "From Containment to Enlargement," p. 658; Henry Kissinger, *Does American Need A Foreign Policy? Towards A Diplomacy for the Twenty-First Century* (New York: Simon & Schuster, 2001), p. 181.

69 Christopher, "America's Leadership, America's Opportunity," p. 7.

70 Lake, "Confronting Backlash States," pp. 45–55.

71 Author's interview with Morton Halperin.

72 Michael Cox, "Wilsonianism Resurgent? The Clinton Administration and the Promotion of Democracy" in Michael Cox, G. John Ikenberry, and Takashi

Inoguchi (eds), *American Democracy Promotion: Impulses, Strategies, and Impacts* (Oxford: Oxford University Press, 2000), pp. 223–224.

73 Author's interview with Anthony Lake.

74 Author's interview with Nancy Soderberg.

75 Drew, *On The Edge*, p. 324.

76 Walker, *Clinton: The President They Deserve*, p. 259; Cox, "Wilsonianism Resurgent? The Clinton Administration and the Promotion of Democracy," p. 225.

77 Anthony Day and Doyle McManus, "Kissinger on Clinton: No Clear Idea Where We're Going," *Los Angeles Times* (February 7, 1994), p. B7.

78 Jacob Heilbrunn, "Lake Inferior: The Pedigree of Anthony Lake," *New Republic* (September 27, 1993), pp. 29–35; Blumenthal, *The Clinton Wars*, p. 154.

79 Chollet and Goldgeiger, *America Between The Wars*, p. 69.

80 John Lewis Gaddis, "Foreign Policy by Autopilot," *Hoover Digest* no. 3 (2000), http://www.hoover.org/research/foreign-policy-autopilot.

81 Robert W. Tucker, "The Triumph of Wilsonianism," *World Policy Journal* 10, no. 4 (Winter 1993–1994), pp. 83–99; Lloyd Gardner, *Safe for Democracy: The Anglo-American Response to Revolution, 1913–1923* (New York: Oxford University Press, 1984).

82 Woodrow Wilson, Address to the Senate of the United States: "A World League for Peace," January 22, 1917.

83 Ido Oren, "The Subjectivity of the 'Democratic Peace': Changing US Perceptions of Imperial Germany," *International Security* 20, no. 2 (1995), p. 178.

84 Sidney Bell, *Righteous Conquest: Woodrow Wilson and the Evolution of the New Diplomacy* (Port Washington, NY: Kennikast Press, 1972), pp. 10–28.

85 Cox, "Wilsonianism Resurgent? The Clinton Administration and the Promotion of Democracy," p. 238.

86 Kennan, "Diplomacy in the Modern World," p. 95.

87 Max Boot, "What the Heck Is a 'Neocon'?" *Wall Street Journal* (December 30, 2002).

88 Hoffman, *Primacy or World Order*, p. 228.

89 Cox, "Wilsonianism Resurgent? The Clinton Administration and the Promotion of Democracy," p. 225.

90 Ann Devroy and Daniel Williams, "Christopher Remains in Limbo Despite Clinton's Reassurance," *Washington Post* (October 9, 1994), p. A40.

91 Chollet and Goldgeiger, *America Between The Wars*, p. 79.

92 Author's interview with Leon Fuerth.

93 Baer quoted in Schlesinger, *White House Ghosts*, p. 409.

94 Albright, *Madam Secretary*, p. 166.

95 Author's interview with Anthony Lake; William Safire, "Leaping the Rhetorical Gap," *New York Times* (October 10, 1993), p. F16.

96 Don M. Snider and John A. Nagl, "The National Security Strategy: Documenting Strategic Vision," in Joseph R. Cerami and James F. Holcomb, Jr (eds), *US Army College Guide to Strategy* (Carlisle Barracks, PA: Strategic Studies Institute, US Army War College, 2001), p. 129.

97 Richard K. Betts, *US National Security Strategy: Lenses and Landmarks* (Princeton, NJ: Woodrow Wilson School of Public and International Affairs, 2004), p. 8.

98 Don M. Snider, *The National Security Strategy: Documenting Strategic Vision*, Second Edition (US Army War College, Strategic Studies Institute, March 15, 1995), p. 2.

99 50 US Code 404a.

100 John Lewis Gaddis, "A Grand Strategy of Transformation," *Foreign Policy* 133 (November–December 2002), p. 53.

101 Author's interview with Anthony Lake.

102 Author's interview with J. F. O. McAllister.

103 Art Pine, "Clinton Issues Muted National Security Report," *Los Angeles Times* (July 22, 1994), p. 17.

104 Gaddis, "A Grand Strategy of Transformation," p. 50.

105 Author's interview with Leon Fuerth.

106 Author's interview with Morton Halperin.

107 Author's interview with Charles A. Kupchan.

108 *PPPWJC*, vol. 1 (1994), Statement on the National Security Strategy Report, July 21, 1994, p. 1297.

109 Author's interview with Anthony Lake.

110 G. John Ikenberry, "American Grand Strategy in the Age of Terror," *Survival* 43, no. 4 (Winter 2001–2002), p. 26.

111 Address by Anthony Lake, National Security Advisor—The Council on Foreign Relations (Rob edits—new version—extensive comments), September 12, 1994, Clinton Presidential Records, National Security Council, Robert Boorstin (Speechwriting), OA/Box Number: 420, [Anthony] Lake—Council on Foreign Relations—9/12/94 [1], William J. Clinton Presidential Library.

112 Stan Greenberg to Clinton Communications re: Accomplishments: 1993, December 7, 1993, Clinton Presidential Records, Speechwriting, Carter Wilkie, OA/Box Number: 4273: Accomplishments, William J. Clinton Presidential Library.

113 Stan Greenberg to POTUS et al.; re: The Academic Retreat, January 4, 1994, Clinton Presidential Records, National Security Council, Robert Boorstin (Speechwriting) OA/Box Number: 419, SOTU 1994—Theme Memos, William J. Clinton Presidential Library.

114 David Dreyer to President Clinton; re: State of the Union, December 30, 1993, Clinton Presidential Records, Speechwriting, Carter Wilkie, OA/Box Number: 4273: State of the Union 1994 [I], William J. Clinton Presidential Library.

115 Walter Russell Mead to President Clinton; re: Foreign Policy and the State of the Union Address, December 30, 1993, Clinton Presidential Records, Speechwriting, Carter Wilkie, OA/Box Number: 4273 State of the Union 1994 [I], William J. Clinton Presidential Library.

116 Bob Boorstin to Anthony Lake; re: POTUS Speeches September–December, Clinton Presidential Records, National Security Council, Robert Boorstin (Speechwriting), OA/Box Number: 420, 1994 Principals Schedules, William J. Clinton Presidential Library.

117 Carter Wilkie to Don Baer; re: Major Speeches in September, August 17, 1994, Clinton Presidential Records, National Security Council, Robert Boorstin (Speechwriting), OA/Box Number: 420, NSC—Public Affairs Strategy, William J. Clinton Presidential Library.

118 Tara Sonenshine and Tom Ross to Mark Gearan; re: Six-Month Public Affairs Strategy, June 10, 1994, Clinton Presidential Records, National Security Council, Robert Boorstin (Speechwriting), OA/Box Number: 420, NSC—Public Affairs Strategy, William J. Clinton Presidential Library.

119 Schlesinger, *White House Ghosts*, p. 410.

120 Roderick Von Lipsey to Fax at 15:35:00.00. Subject: Foreign/Security Policy Meme, October 25, 1993, Clinton Presidential Records, Automated Records Management System (Email), WHO ([Somalia]), OA/Box Number: 500000: [03/29/1993–10/25/1993], William J. Clinton Presidential Library.

121 Sonenshine and Ross to Gearan, Clinton Presidential Records, OA/Box Number: 420, NSC—Public Affairs Strategy, William J. Clinton Presidential Library.

122 Author's interview with Leon Fuerth.

CHAPTER FOUR

Enhancing security

Despite being the first administration elected to the post-Cold War world, the Clinton White House noted that its primary responsibility was to defend the United States by maintaining "a strong defense capability of forces ready to fight." This had been central to Bill Clinton's foreign policy speeches on the campaign and remained at the heart of his administration's grand strategy throughout his time in office. The Clinton administration's national security team prepared a rolling policy that addressed key geographical regions and identified the vital components of national security to promote and defend including the US nuclear posture, national missile defense (NMD), the role of intelligence, and counter-terrorism. The Clinton era grand strategy documents provide an insight into the evolving relationship with the United Nations and NATO, organizations viewed as central to the implementation of US Grand Strategy at varying times in the 1990s.

The Clinton administration recognized that the national interest continued to dictate the need for "unparalleled military capabilities" and the capacity to project firepower. It had no plans to withdraw to a Fortress America and appreciated the need to maintain forces overseas to deter aggression and advance US interests, arguing that such deployments demonstrated a commitment to its allies, ensured regional stability, and permitted prompt responses in times of crisis. The administration sought to ensure the United States was "the security partner of choice in many regions," enabling it to act as "a foundation for regional stability through mutually beneficial security partnerships." This was an essential aspect of grand strategy, designed to ensure the United States remained integral in political, military, and economic affairs, a role it could best maintain by retaining "the military wherewithal to underwrite [its] commitments credibly."[1] The evolving nature of Clinton's Grand Strategy revealed the manner in which state-centered threats diminished during his time in office and how they were replaced by threats of a more nomadic, but no less devastating nature.

National security in the Clinton administration

The Clinton administration may have come to power after the end of the Cold War, but the world it inherited was anything but stable. The collapse of the USSR, the rise of China, the emerging European Union, the rise of nationalism in the Balkans, ongoing tensions with Iran and Iraq, and the threat of nuclear proliferation, all ensured that the maintenance of US national security remained vital to Clinton's Grand Strategy. Despite the many challenges it faced, however, one of the administration's greatest tests was defining America's adversaries in the 1990s and convincing the American people of their credibility in the absence of a single, unifying foe. Applying a grand vision to US national security in the 1990s was one of Clinton's most formidable challenges, as Anthony Lake admitted this was the first president since Truman whose foreign policy "has not had a single defining issue against which it could define itself."[2]

As a former governor of a southern, rural state, Clinton was typical of most presidents who enter office with little experience in foreign affairs. Indeed due to his actions during the Vietnam era, "Clinton was perhaps a little bit more gun-shy than the others."[3] This improved with time, but it hurt him in the initial months of the administration. Clinton's national security team was comprised of his selected Cabinet officers and serving members of the armed forces. In neither case could Clinton's initial tenure be descried as ideal. Key civilian advisers proved to be ineffectual and Clinton's relationship with the armed forces was problematic long before he became commander-in-chief. His southern charm appeared to fail him in his relations with the military and the tension was reciprocated. A letter he had written in 1969, referencing his "loathing of the military" and desire to "maintain [his] political viability," emerged during the 1992 New Hampshire Primary, confirming what critics saw as his "Slick Willie" reputation.[4]

President Clinton inherited Colin Powell as Chairman of the Joint Chiefs of Staff and he clearly daunted Clinton to a degree that was inappropriate for the nature of their relationship. Tension between the civilian leadership and the uniformed officers at the Pentagon was not unique to the Clinton administration, but it was exacerbated by a series of factors, not least of which was the fact that Powell had a greater international standing than the new president. In London, Powell was viewed as "a very powerful asset for the Clinton administration" since he was "very highly respected and he was better known than most people in that position usually are."[5] Domestically, however, President Clinton's lack of military service and active avoidance of the Vietnam War hurt his standing with the military. It was also acknowledged that Powell disagreed with Clinton over the policy of gays in the military, which had dominated the president's first weeks in office, utterly overwhelmed his first news conference and created an impression at odds with the New Democrat approach espoused on the campaign.[6] It was believed that Powell considered resigning over the issue, something Clinton could ill-afford, as he had "limited political capital and [could not] afford to alienate Powell."[7] Polling also revealed that Powell would beat Clinton 42 percent to 38 percent in a campaign for president in 1996, which did little to ease tension.[8] President Clinton's dealings with the military eased considerably when General Shalikashvili succeeded Powell as Chairman of the Joint Chiefs. "You cannot exaggerate the influence, both military and political, that Colin Powell had on the early administration," a senior official said once Powell retired; "Everything we did effectively over the following two or three years, we did without the shadow of Colin Powell and the so-called Powell doctrine."[9]

Clinton's dealings with his civilian advisers proved to be equally frustrating. Les Aspin had been selected as Defense Secretary due to his help on the campaign and his reputation in the House of Representatives. However, his rumpled style and absent-minded demeanor did not endear him to the Pentagon. Aspin's poor health caused him to have a pacemaker fitted in March 1993, prompting questions about his continued capacity to serve after less than 2 months in office.[10] It became clear to those both near and far that Aspin was "not in great health . . . not at the top of his game . . . not completely vigorous."[11] From across the Atlantic, Malcolm Rifkind, British Defence Secretary at the time, noted that Aspin "just couldn't cope with the pressures of that particular department" and that "quite apart from his health, he was finding it a great personal strain."[12] Events in Somalia compounded Aspin's situation and opened up a breach between the Defense Secretary, members of Congress, and senior officers at the Pentagon, where "the uniformed guys hated Aspin . . . they found him loathsome."[13] The situation became untenable, leading to Aspin's departure in December 1993, after less than a year in post.[14] President Clinton's relationship with the military finally found equilibrium by 1994 as William Perry replaced Aspin at the Pentagon, bringing stability to the department for the remainder of Clinton's first term. The moves reinforced the image of an administration coming to grips with power, and defining the parameters of future deployment as Bill Clinton "became a foreign policy president and found his readiness to stand up to the Pentagon."[15]

In an attempt to avoid the warfare that had affected Carter's foreign policy team, President Clinton arranged for Secretary of State Christopher and National Security Adviser Lake to meet every Wednesday. Despite these good intentions and the fact that both men "subscribed to the tenets of economic liberalism and a strong strain of Wilsonian idealism permeated their outlooks," differences emerged as both sought to define policy.[16]

The incompatibility between Lake and Christopher contributed to delays in publishing the administration's key foreign policy declaration, which diminished the White House in the eyes of many observers. Much of the fault lay with the president who sought consensus from the various options presented to him by advisers. This was exacerbated by a psychological and political determination to avoid conflict and ensure harmonious relations, both on the part of the president and his senior foreign policy advisers. Clinton's tendency toward empathy and conflict-avoidance was matched by a determination to avoid bureaucratic clashes within the national security team. Lake in particular was seen to have "over compensated for the internal division of the Carter years." His low profile and cerebral management style ensured that, as informed as the administration was on events, it appeared to lack energy and drive.[17]

It was also clear that as focused as Clinton could be in domestic matters, he seemed unfocused on foreign policy issues, despite longer daily briefings being introduced to remedy this. In 1994, foreign policy became a "more disciplined, tightly focused process," as the daily national security briefing was increased by "another fifteen minutes to thirty minutes over and above the base-line time we normally give it." President Clinton noted that such sessions now lasted "normally . . . forty-five minutes." Incredibly, this implied that the president had previously spent less than 15 minutes a day on foreign policy matters.[18] Therefore, 1994 began with the president spending 30 minutes in daily foreign policy briefings, which comprised of a 10-minute presentation from the CIA and a 20-minute update from Anthony Lake.[19] However, even the timing of these briefings, at 8 a.m., ill-suited the personality of the president they were designed to aid. This "was defiantly not the time that Clinton was at his best" ensuring that the president "was often groggy and wanted to cancel his NSC briefing," further contributing to a lack of rapport with Anthony Lake.[20]

UN peace operations

The Clinton administration had initially viewed the United Nations as the organization of choice for the execution of US foreign policy in the 1990s, allowing the president to concentrate on domestic policy. This required a new United Nations for a new age and the president planned a reformed Security Council to reflect the new balance of power in the world. Warren Christopher announced that the time had come for a reorganization of the UN Security Council, which he declared should be brought "into tune with 1993 realities rather than with 1946 realities." The main alteration proposed the appointment of Germany and Japan as permanent members of the Security Council. The British Foreign Office was appalled by the suggestion, realizing the detrimental impact it would have on UK global influence: "To make any changes would take years and every country, not just Germany and Japan, would want to be on the council." The British pledged to use "all necessary means, including our right of veto, to ensure we retain our rightful position on the council." The suggested changes also raised serious questions about military capability. Britain and France were the only powers apart from the United States with substantial overseas military forces, while Germany's constitution-bound forces were dismissed as "a joke" and Japan did not have a minister of defense.[21] The administration's dealings with the United Nations and the organization's standing within the United States deteriorated further over time, as the administration's initial aspirations gave way to distrust and dissent.

As a candidate, Clinton had suggested that a UN Rapid Deployment Force be initiated "for purposes beyond traditional peacekeeping, such as standing guard at the borders of countries threatened by aggression; preventing attacks on civilians; providing humanitarian relief; and combating terrorism and drug trafficking."[22] However, as president, he was forced to consider the implications of such a proposal in terms of national sovereignty and his role as commander-in-chief. Clinton believed the United States "had to strengthen the institutions-and habits-of international cooperation, while preserving our ability to act alone if necessary to protect America's security" and that US foreign policy should be constructed around a coherent approach to international cooperation and the use of international institutions, particularly the United Nations.[23] Implementing this was a central challenge in Clinton's first years in office, as the president's ambitions for the United Nations simply unraveled. The man who came to be blamed for this was UN General Secretary, Boutros Boutros-Ghali, a character with an ability to alienate people and draw personal criticism for the organization's failings. His lack of empathy collided with the will of the United States, preventing the relationship from developing as Clinton had envisaged.

The Clinton administration entered office committed to the principle of UN-led peacekeeping operations, but immediately recognized the need to review such initiatives, having inherited the Somali mission from the Bush administration. On February 9, 1993, Richard Clarke and Michael Sheehan initiated PRD-13 on Multilateral Peacekeeping Operations for Anthony Lake. It addressed both the broad concept of UN peacekeeping operations and the specific viability of US participation in future missions. The report's conclusions were incorporated into the 1994 National Security Strategy Review as well as the eventual PDD-25 that emerged in May 1994.

The initial grand strategy document of 1994 established the basis for future US multilateral action and attempted to demonstrate that the administration had learned from the lessons of Somalia. "The lesson we must take away" it reported, was not to "foreswear such operations but that we should employ this tool selectively and more effectively." The administration identified peace operations "as a means to support our national security strategy, not as a strategy unto itself."[24] Despite efforts to portray this as a profound shift in policy, Clinton's approach had long been one of "multilateral if possible, unilateral if necessary" and this was reiterated in the 1994 grand strategy document. When vital or survival interests were at stake, the use of force would be "decisive and, if necessary, unilateral." However, in less threatening situations, US military engagement would be "targeted selectively on those areas that most affect our national interests."[25] In the aftermath of the Somali operation, humanitarianism became a category that could justify the use of armed intervention, but the administration noted that the military was not necessarily the best tool to use in such instances.[26]

The administration sought to ensure that when possible, US intervention accompanied a multilateral force, "especially on those matters touching directly the interests of our allies," in which case the White House believed that there should be "a proportional commitment from them." Such multilateral action spread the financial and political burden of intervention—an important consideration since "the costs and risks of US military involvement must be judged to be commensurate with the stakes involved."[27] During an era of economic restrictions, "Working together increases the effectiveness of each nation's actions, and sharing the responsibilities lessens everyone's load."[28] As identified in PRD-13, financial considerations had to be weighed alongside military maneuvers as the administration pondered future troop deployments and the need to balance interests against costs. The interrelated economic restrictions that the administration operated under and its domestic economic priorities are an often-overlooked aspect of Clinton's Grand Strategy. The budget had been capped; so in any circumstance where troop deployments were a consideration the Pentagon provided a cost estimate that required congressional approval for extra funds: "The problem with this was that if we did this, it would break the budget cap and end the president's efforts to reduce the deficit and help the bond and stock market and improve the US domestic economy."[29] This was further evidence of the linkage between foreign and domestic policy and between the three central elements of Clinton's Grand Strategy.

These were the principles and limitations governing peace operations in Clinton's Grand Strategy, as the administration sought to balance "interests against costs" and "put power behind [US] diplomacy."[30] The administration's efforts to gain control over UN peacekeeping operation were inspired in part by congressional efforts to assert increasing control over foreign policy in general and over multilateral operations in particular. In the Senate, Bob Dole attempted to initiate a Peace Powers Act to curb the commitment of troops and cash abroad and to "rein in" what he viewed as the "misguided, if not dangerous, peacekeeping efforts" of the administration.[31] Of particular concern to Republicans was the question of command of US forces and their operation under UN control.

The National Security Revitalization Act, a tenet of the Contract With America, sought to prevent American units from serving under foreign officers anywhere in the chain of command. Ambassador Albright ventured that if Republican efforts succeeded in barring the United States from UN peacekeeping, the United States may be unable to launch another Desert Storm-style operation: "If we put the UN out of business, our costs will go up, not down, for our interests will require that we act on our own more often," she warned.[32]

Grand strategy remained firm in regard to concerns over command and control, insisting that "There may be times when it is in our interest to place US troops under the temporary operational control of a competent UN or allied commander." However, "Under no circumstances will the President ever relinquish his command authority over US forces."[33] Former Clinton campaign adviser Michael Mandelbaum denounced both parties as being "incoherent," suggesting that Democrats favored multilateralism but blamed the United Nations "for its own failures in Somalia," while Republicans favored unilateralism but their budget cutting threatened the US global reach.[34] Such was the nature of politics for the remainder of the twentieth century and well into the next.

The policy response to the Somali mission took the form of PDD-25: "Reforming Multilateral Peace Operations." Delivered to the president in May 1994, this was the first comprehensive policy on multilateral peace operations in the post-Cold War era. It developed new standards to determine future participation in peacekeeping operations and restated the importance of congressional support for such missions. PDD-25 stressed that multilateral peace operations must be "placed in perspective among the instruments of US foreign policy." Following congressional criticism in this area, PDD-25 restated President Clinton's insistence that, "As President, I retain and will not relinquish command authority over U.S. forces." However, when necessary he would "consider placing appropriate US forces and personnel under the operational control of a competent UN commander for specific UN operations authorized by the Security Council."[35] PDD-25 made it clear that such a situation would only arise under certain conditions and be consistent with the US Constitution, US federal law, and the Uniform Code of Military Justice. Therefore, if and when US combat units became necessary in the future and when national interests justified this, the findings of PDD-25 would define their involvement.[36] This was not designed to present the United Nations with an ultimatum, but rather "to maximise the benefits of UN peace operations," allowing the United States to make "highly disciplined choices about when and under what circumstances to support or participate in them."[37] The administration retained its commitment to utilize multilateral options and to participate in peacekeeping operations, but PDD-25 established new parameters for such involvement. In doing so, the administration ensured its grand strategy undulated between one of cooperative security and of selective engagement.[38] In future, the administration would support such initiatives when it believed "the operation's political and military objectives are clear and feasible; and when UN involvement represents the best means to advance US interests." The question of US interests was to be the key-determining factor in any future deployment, as the administration noted that it would not support UN involvement in situations "when it would interfere with US interests."[39]

Somalia did not convince the White House of the need to withdraw from a multilateral embrace of peacekeeping, "but that if we were going to sustain it either in substantive terms, or in political terms, we had to become more precise in how we thought about it." Accordingly, PDD-25 was not an end to multilateralism, "it was saying we've got to get multilateralism right, if we're going to a) do it right and b) be able to sell it politically to show that we know what we're doing, and Somalia certainly led to that."[40] Accordingly, the drafting of PDD-25 was a tacit admission that while the Clinton administration may have wished to solve the world's problems, neither the United States nor the international community had the resources or the mandate to do so. Involvement in peacekeeping operations required that vital national or allied interests be at stake and that a clear commitment to win existed. PDD-25 placed intense restrictions on the US involvement in future operations and "if taken at face value, would ensure the US is seldom actually engaged."[41] From now on, it was clear that "the responsibility for peace ultimately rests with the people of the country in question."[42]

Morton Halperin acknowledged that Somalia "interrupted an important policy debate upon the use of peacekeeping troops in operations. People had been very enthusiastic about the concept but it was seen as a bad idea after Somalia."[43] In the aftermath of the Somali debacle, a new pragmatism was present in the administration's policy on peacekeeping. The administration expressed its hope to move beyond the debacle and to return to a constructive relationship with the United Nations, but such aspirations proved fruitless. In spite of the multilateral aspirations of many in the White House, the administration's dealings with the UN never truly recovered, as suspicion and finger pointing prevailed.

Whatever the benefits of such operations, participation in UN peace operations could "never substitute for the necessity of fighting and winning our own wars, nor can we allow it to reduce our capability to meet that imperative." Quite simply, "peacekeeping became a dirty word after Somalia," as reflected in the language of the directive.[44] The report concluded that while peacekeeping remained a component of US foreign policy it would be "a part of our national security strategy, not the centerpiece."[45] Following the initial ambitions of the Clinton administration, PDD-25 severely restricted US participation in future peacekeeping operations. Following its drafting, Clinton sent forces abroad on 15 occasions. Between January 1993 and 1995, US troops deployed overseas eight times, all in conjuncture with the United Nations. For the remaining years of the Clinton presidency, they did so only on four more occasions—an indication of the change that PDD-25 introduced.

A nuclear grand strategy

Rather than fighting the Cold War, the Clinton administration was required to tidy up its diplomatic and military mess. A key component of Clinton's Grand Strategy, therefore, involved continuing efforts initiated by previous administrations in the field of arms control, viewed by the White House as being "defense by other means."[46] Accordingly, the "full and faithful implantation of existing arms control agreements," including the Anti-Ballistic Missile (ABM) Treaty, Strategic Arms Reduction Talks (START), Biological Weapons Convention (BWC), Intermediate-range Nuclear Forces (INF) Treaty, and the Conventional Forces in Europe (CFE) Treaty, became central to US Grand Strategy.[47]

Defense Secretary Aspin observed that the threats posed by nuclear, chemical, biological, and ballistic missile systems required a five-point counter-proliferation drive to ensure international cooperation in curtailing such threats. These points involved viewing the era as distinct and not the continuation of the Cold War; focused intelligence efforts on detecting weapons of mass destruction (WMD); reengineering plans to use against these threats; purchasing the correct weaponry to destroy WMD; and ensuring international cooperation with allies.[48] The administration entered into bilateral negotiations with former Soviet states and multilateral agreements with international organizations to combat the threat from WMD as early meetings of the National Security Council sought to identify actionable solutions. In March 1993, PDD-3 urged the ratification and implementation of START I and START II and the denuclearization of Ukraine, Belarus, and Kazakhstan. In May 1993, PRD-34 initiated a review of policy on nuclear arms control beyond START I and START II, conducted by the Interagency Working Group (IWG) on Arms Control, that was reviewed by the NSC Deputies Committee on September 9, 1994.

On October 29, 1993, Defense Secretary Aspin announced the Nuclear Posture Review (NPR) to build on the findings of the Bottom Up Review (BUR). The findings were incorporated into PDD-30, dated September 1994, along with findings from PRD-34, which established the US nuclear posture beyond START I and II. The central premise of the NPR was that the United States should "retain a triad of strategic nuclear forces" designed to deter potential adversaries from acting against US interests and against seeking a nuclear advantage. While remaining true to its commitments under the START I and II agreements, Clinton's Grand Strategy ensured the United States continued to maintain nuclear forces of "sufficient size and capability to hold at risk a broad range of assets valued by such political and military leaders."[49] These options ensured that the United States could eliminate its surface ship nuclear capability by the end of the administration's first term.[50]

Despite the end of the Cold War, the focus of US arms control remained the former USSR, ensuring that Clinton's most striking example of the overlap between domestic and foreign policy was in relation to Russia, where President Yeltsin's democratic initiatives not only made the world safer, but also allowed the United States to prosper: "The reductions in our defense spending that are an important part of our economic programme . . . are only tenable as long as Russia and the other nuclear republics pose a diminishing threat to our security," the president insisted in February 1993. Despite the costs involved, the figures were negligible compared to past expenditure. "If we were willing to spend trillions of dollars to ensure communism's defeat in the Cold War, surely we should be willing to invest a tiny fraction of that to support democracy's success where communism failed."[51]

During the Cold War, the White House had been able to deal directly with the Kremlin in regard to Soviet nuclear forces. With the breakup of the USSR, however, the White House was required to deal with a host of newly empowered nuclear states including Ukraine, Belarus, and Kazakhstan. National Security Council memos reveal the extent of anxiety over the proliferation of nuclear materials and the threat of nuclear smuggling. Declassified NSC communiqués note the threat this posed to the United States and warned that "failure to address this danger could ultimately become a crisis powerful enough to define this administration, just as the Iranian hostage incident defined the Carter Presidency."[52] By 1995, however, many of these concerns had been placated due to the quiet diplomacy of the United States, which had secured much of the nuclear material that had been inherited by the former Soviet Republics. One of the tools that brought this about was the Nunn-Lugar Cooperative Threat Reduction effort.

The Nunn-Lugar process was one of the most successful initiatives of the post-Cold War era and proved to be a vital component in the effort to secure nuclear material and build "a more secure international environment by combating the threat posed by the possible theft or diversion of nuclear warheads or their components." The initiative safeguarded nuclear materials from the former USSR in a variety of ways that were designed to ensure increased security and stability. As a direct result, nearly 600 kilograms of nuclear material, including uranium, was transferred from Kazakhstan to the United States in 1994 alone, in a joint mission undertaken by the Departments of Defense and Energy. Similar agreements ensured that by the end of the administration's first term all nuclear warheads had been removed from Kazakhstan under

Operation Sapphire, most had been removed from Belarus, while Ukraine had agreed to transfer its nuclear warheads to Russia for dismantlement "in return for fair compensation."[53] Finally, an agreement was reached for Russia to convert highly enriched uranium from dismantled weapons into commercial reactor fuel to be delivered to the United States. This approach continued into the second term as the administration oversaw the removal of 34 metric tons of plutonium from Russia's nuclear weapons program and worked to refashion former Soviet WMD sites, along with transferring thousands of former scientists in Eastern Europe and Eurasia from military activities to civilian research.[54]

The central components of Clinton's Grand Strategy of Engagement and Enlargement were present in this agreement: The deal made the world safer by removing nuclear materials from unsecured locations; it enhanced both the Russian economy and the relationship between the two nations, while providing the United States with much needed reactor fuel, thus aiding its domestic economy. These efforts ensured that in January 1995, President Clinton delivered the first State of the Union Address since the beginning of the Cold War "when not a single Russian missile [was] pointed at the children of America."[55] Despite the success of these initiatives, there was increasing frustration that White House efforts were not being recognized, as declassified NSC memos reveal: "It is high time that the administration gets the credit it deserves for its important accomplishments, such as Operation Sapphire in Kazakhstan, or the lab-to-lab efforts improving nuclear security in Russia right now."[56] The public relations battle was one that continued to rage for the duration of the administration.

On taking office, the Clinton administration prioritized efforts to secure the "indefinite and unconditional extension" of the Treaty on the Non Proliferation of Nuclear Weapons (NPT) as well as "its universal application."[57] This was achieved in May 1995 and formed the bedrock of grand strategy initiatives aimed at reducing the global nuclear threat Clinton inherited. The Clinton administration secured bilateral agreements with Ukraine, Russia, and South Africa that ensured adherence to the guidelines of the Missile Technology Control Regime (MTCR) and convinced China to observe MTCR guidelines, as well as a commitment not to transfer MTCR-controlled ground-to-ground missiles.

START I came into effect in December 1994 following Ukraine's accession to the Nuclear Non-Proliferation Treaty and the rejection of nuclear weapons by Belarus and Kazakhstan. Progress immediately began on gaining congressional approval for START II, designed to leave the United States and Russia with between 3,000 and 3,500 deployed strategic nuclear warheads, a two-thirds reduction from the Cold War peak.[58] On January 26, 1996, the Senate voted to ratify the START II Treaty, designed to "eliminate additional US and Russian strategic launchers and will effectively remove an additional 5,000 deployed warheads, leaving each side with no more than 3,500."[59] Such a move to reduce the deployed strategic arsenals of the United States and Russia by two-thirds was unimaginable only 10 years beforehand, but progress had been so sweeping that the announcement was barely noticed. It was agreed at the March 1997 Helsinki Summit that following ratification of START II, negotiations could begin on START III, designed to leave the United States and Russia with between 2,000 and 2,500 missiles by the end of 2007, a reduction of 80 percent from the height of the Cold War.[60]

The next step was a Comprehensive Test Ban Treaty (CTBT). President Bush had signed the Energy and Water Appropriations Bill, which included a 9-month moratorium on US nuclear testing and required the president to submit a plan for achieving a multilateral test ban by September 30, 1996. Yeltsin and Clinton confirmed their intention to adhere to the moratoria as the Clinton administration issued a number of directives that addressed nuclear testing. PDD-11, dated July 4, 1993, announced the intent to negotiate a nuclear test ban treaty and extend the moratorium on US nuclear testing until September 30, 1994, in accordance with the 1992 Hatfield-Exon-Mitchell Amendment. Following Chinese nuclear tests in October 1993, the Clinton administration prepared PDD-15 that confirmed the president's decision to place the United States in a state of readiness to resume nuclear testing and addressed the stewardship of nuclear weapons stockpiles.

Negotiations for the CTBT commenced at the Conference on Disarmament in Geneva in January 1994 and concluded in August 1996. The UN General Assembly adopted it on September 10, 1996, but despite being the first world leader to sign the treaty, President Clinton failed to secure Senate ratification. The chamber voted 51–48 on October 13, 1999, falling well short of the two-thirds majority needed, demonstrating how grand strategy was beholden to domestic politics, as Senator Jessie Helms, Chairman of the Senate Foreign Relations Committee, targeted the treaty for defeat. When Matt Gobush of the NSC suggested holding Helms publicly accountable for being unprepared to discuss the CTBT in his committee, he was reminded by Counselor to the National Security Advisor, Mara Rudman, that "Taking Helms on directly in the press is the surest way to ensure that you never see any CTBT hearings, let alone moving the ratification through his committee." Rudman noted that "If later on in the summer we decide we want to just make a public case KNOWING we will get nothing from the Senate, and nothing likely as long as Helms is the chair, then we may want to use that kind of frontal attack. Otherwise, I don't think it makes a lot of sense."[61] The *Financial Times* observed that the rejection was "the clearest indication yet of the radical change in US politics and the country's view of its role in the world. Thumbing its nose at the rest of the world was not an option open to the US during its struggle with communism."[62] Clearly, much had changed in the post-Cold War world.

National Missile Defense

Despite a solid commitment to reducing nuclear threat levels, the Clinton administration demonstrated an ambiguous record in regard to NMD. As revealed by President Reagan, the concept of a space shield to intercept incoming long-range missiles entered the zeitgeist in the 1980s. Having placed its faith in the fledgling program, the US government continued to spend heavily on research despite the end of the Cold War. The Clinton administration never abandoned the project, but it placed a reduced level of intensity on the initiative than previous administrations and sought instead to reduce the likelihood of such missiles being fired on the United States. On April 26, 1993, the Clinton administration issued PRD-31, initiating a review of US Ballistic Missile Defenses (BMD). Following a review of the findings, PDD-17 was signed on December 11, 1993 to address the future direction of both BMD and the ABM Treaty. The document was mindful of changes underway in Russia, but was explicit in its insistence that missile defense cooperation with the Kremlin was dependent on their "continued progress in political and economic reform" as well as their "adherence to arms control agreements . . . and a willingness to enter into and abide by a bilateral agreement on cooperative activities."[63] In his 1994 State of the Union Address, President Clinton announced that due to agreements that had been reached, Russia's strategic nuclear missiles "soon will no longer be pointed at the United States, nor will we point ours at them. Instead of building weapons in space, Russian scientists will help us to build the international space station."[64] This was seen as a more productive way to protect the nation from any potential missile strike and an effective way to pre-empt such attacks.

Initially, therefore, the administration argued that the best form of defense against missile attack was to "locate, identify and disable arsenals of WMD, production and storage facilities for such weapons and their delivery systems."[65] Rather than seeking to deploy NMD, the Clinton administration committed to utilizing localized, theatre missile defense capabilities. Such a stance was based on findings from the US intelligence community, which concluded no rogue states would be capable of launching an ICBM attack on the United States "in the foreseeable future." Despite this, the administration continued to fund research into "a national missile defense deployable program" that could be launched "quickly (within two–three years) should a sooner-than-expected threat materialize."[66] Such a timescale revealed the lack of dedication to a national program during the administration's first term in office.

With a second term, however, came an increasingly robust approach to NMD, as the Clinton administration notably increased its interest in the initiative as its time in office went on. This was in part due to the changed atmosphere in Washington following the Republican takeover of Congress. Speaker of the House Newt Gingrich placed a commitment to NMD at the heart of his 1994 Contract with America and insisted that this revealed, "the difference between those who would rely on lawyers to defend America and those who rely on engineers and scientists."[67] However, Republican efforts to hold the administration to account for not committing to NMD backfired, as many Americans "refused to believe that the United States did not already have such a system in place." A participant in a focus group, when told no missile shield existed, stated, "I don't believe you, you couldn't pay me enough to believe you . . .you see it in the movies."[68] Bizarrely, therefore, the Clinton administration appeared to benefit from the lack of public engagement on the issue as well as from an increasingly blurred line between factual and fictional presentations of the presidency and national security scenarios in the 1990s.[69]

The administration highlighted its "highly effective missile defense development programs" designed to protect the nation, its armed forces, as well as its allies, "against ballistic missiles armed with conventional weapons or WMD."[70] However, the administration noted in 1998 that it was unlikely that Russia, China, or North Korea could target the United States with an ICBM within 20 years. This was amended a year later, as the White House claimed that "during the next fifteen years the United States will most likely face an ICBM threat from North Korea, probably from Iran and possibly from Iraq."[71] This was a conclusion reached, in part, from evidence provided by a commission headed by Donald Rumsfeld. Therefore, political pressure and global events, including the August 1998 North Korean test of a Taepo Dong I missile, contributed to the administration's increasing focus on NMD.

On July 23, 1999, President Clinton signed the National Missile Defense Act, stating that, "It is the policy of the United States to deploy an effective NMD system as soon as technologically possible." Despite the steadfastness of this declaration, the act contained two amendments that appeared to suggest otherwise. First, any NMD deployment had to be "subject to the authorization and appropriations process and thus . . . no decision on deployment has been made." Secondly, US policy remained committed to seeking "negotiated reductions in Russian nuclear forces, putting Congress on record as continuing to support negotiated reductions in strategic nuclear arms, reaffirming the administration's position that missile defense policy must take into account important arms control and nuclear non-proliferation objectives." Despite these ambiguities, in August 1999, President Clinton announced that the initial NMD architecture was to be based in Alaska, to include 100 ground-based interceptors, 1 ABM radar, and 5 upgraded early warning radar.[72]

As the administration entered its final year in office, it adopted an increasingly strident approach to NMD and increased Pentagon spending by $10.5 billion over a 6-year period for a limited NMD program.[73] By the publication of its final NSSR document, the Clinton administration defined itself as being "committed to the development" of a limited NMD system designed "to counter the emerging ballistic missile threat from states that threaten international peace and security." However, despite this commitment, the president announced on September 1, 2000 that while the technology was promising, the system was not yet proven and he was therefore not prepared to proceed with its deployment. Instead, the Pentagon was granted permission to continue the research and development of a potential NMD system, ensuring that the process developed, but was not deployed. NMD was promoted as being "part of the administration's comprehensive national security strategy to prevent potential adversaries from acquiring and/or threatening the United States with such weapons." The White House, however, recognized that continuing arms control agreements with Russia also formed an integral aspect of this strategy, since they helped to "ensure stability and predictability between the United States and Russia, promote the dismantling of nuclear weapons and help complete the transition from confrontation to cooperation with Russia."

The contradiction between these two positions was apparent in the language of the 1972 ABM Treaty that limited anti-missile defenses according to the following principle: "Neither side should deploy defenses that would undermine the other's nuclear deterrent and thus tempt the other to strike first in a crisis or take countermeasures that would make both our countries less secure."[74] In March 1997, Clinton and Yeltsin met in Helsinki and agreed to adapt "to meet the threat posed by shorter-range missiles, a threat we seek to counter through our theatre missile defense (TMD) systems."[75] Both leaders committed to the continuation of the ABM Treaty, which remained "a cornerstone" of US "strategic stability" as late as December 2000.[76] President Clinton's decision to delay the implementation of a limited NMD system was made, at least in part, to provide more time to negotiate how to deploy such a system without undermining the existing ABM Treaty. It was a position that would not long endure following his departure from office.

Intelligence

With the end of the Cold War, questions were raised at the highest level with regard to the future of the US intelligence services. Senator Daniel Patrick Moynihan raged that the failure to predict the demise of the USSR was reason enough to abolish the CIA and give its functions to the State Department.[77] In a new geopolitical environment, sweeping changes to the US intelligence community were considered, as it was noted that if changes were not implemented the community risked becoming "an expensive and irrelevant dinosaur just when America most needs information and insight into the complex new challenges that it faces."[78] Efforts were made to pass the Boren-McCurdy Omnibus Act to restructure the intelligence community in a move that mirrored the 1986 Goldwater-Nichols Act. Senator Boren, Chairman of the Senate Intelligence Panel, argued in 1992 that reform was vital: "It is clear that as the world becomes more . . . complex and no longer understandable through the prism of Soviet competition, more intelligence—not less—will be needed." The solution, he insisted, was "to change the existing community, including the CIA."[79]

Plans to eradicate the CIA, however, never materialized and carried no favor within the administration, as Joseph Nye observed, "eliminating the community's chief source of nondepartmental analysis would weaken estimates. In policy circles the old adage is that where you stand depends on where you sit. In intelligence, what you foresee is often affected by where you work. The primary duty of departmental analysts is to respond to the needs of their organizations."[80] From the beginning of its time in office, the Clinton administration noted that national security had taken on "a much broader definition" in the post-Cold War era and that "intelligence must address a much wider range of threats and dangers." The information provided by the intelligence community was seen as being an "essential complement" to data accessed from "foreign service reporting, media reports and private analysts who rely entirely on open sources."[81] All aspects of Clinton's Grand Strategy depended on strong intelligence capabilities, recognized by the administration as being "critical instruments of our national power and integral to implementing our national security strategy."

In the first term, the administration focused on ways the intelligence community could enhance its domestic economic initiatives. However, as it moved into its second term, the White House appeared more willing to recognize the CIA's more traditional remit. In terms of the national security component of Clinton's Grand Strategy, the intelligence priorities included, but were not limited to, rogue states, belligerent nuclear powered nation states, nuclear proliferation, drug smuggling, terrorism, and organized crime. The administration acknowledged that the intelligence community needed to be assigned specific roles for dealing with such threats and defined them as being the support of US military and diplomatic efforts worldwide and the thwarting of efforts to develop WMD and terrorism.[82]

On June 18, 1993, PDD-9 tasked the Director Of Central Intelligence with "responsibility for foreign intelligence in support of interdiction efforts" by the Coast Guard and Immigration and Naturalisation Service to prevent alien smuggling into the United States.[83] On August 5, 1993, President Clinton signed PDD-12 addressing security awareness in an attempt to thwart foreign intelligence gathering operations within the United States. In May 1994 President Clinton signed PDD-24, designed to enhance "cooperation, coordination and accountability among all US counterintelligence agencies."[84] This focus on intelligence followed the Aldrich Ames espionage case and led to the establishment of the National Counterintelligence Center.[85] The administration also sought to initiate the "exchange of senior managers between the CIA and the FBI to ensure timely and close coordination between the intelligence and law enforcement communities."[86]

With the end of the Cold War, the US intelligence services underwent a decade of upheaval. Consistent with the provisions of the 1995 Intelligence Authorization Act, President Clinton directed the Chairman of the Foreign Intelligence Advisory Board to conduct a review of the roles and missions of the intelligence community to define its needs in the post-Cold War world. In March 1995, President Clinton signed PDD-35 to establish the Intelligence Priorities IWG, which served as a forum for identifying issues that required specific attention from the intelligence community and supplemented the President's Foreign Intelligence Advisory Board. Regardless of changes in focus, however, Clinton's second CIA Director, John Deutch, insisted that the primary mission of intelligence remained the need to provide the president with the best possible information: "We have to maintain an unassailable reputation for unvarnished treatment of the facts, never allowing ourselves to tailor our analysis to meet some policy conclusion that may be of convenience to one of our leaders at one time or another. If we do so, it will quickly destroy [our] credibility."[87]

The second term's intelligence priorities extended to include "transnational threats; potential regional conflicts that might affect US national security interests; intensified counterintelligence against foreign intelligence collection inimical to US interests; and threats to US forces and citizens abroad."[88] The administration utilized technology to enhance its grand strategy, including the use of "continuous, non-intrusive, space-based imaging and information processing," designed to "monitor treaty compliance, military movements and the development, testing and deployment of weapons of mass destruction" and to "support diplomatic and military action" initiated by the White House. Such efforts, however, were reliant on Human Intelligence (HUMINT) and the administration recognized the need to "continue to attract and retain" qualified staff to provide much-needed regional analysis and to develop relations with private enterprises and public institutions whose expertise was deemed to be "especially critical."[89]

The evolving national security threat

Throughout its 8 years in office, the Clinton administration's policies evolved to reveal a shift in focus from a state-centered approach to a growing recognition of the dangers posed by non-state actors in the post-Cold War world. Grand strategy accepted, however, that certain nation states retained the desire to challenge US interests and that in some instances these states were "actively improving their offensive capabilities, including efforts to obtain nuclear, biological or chemical weapons."[90] Accordingly, US Grand Strategy focused on major theatre conflict and identified North Korea, Iran, and Iraq, as nations it anticipated may need to be resisted. The strategy called for a multilateral response if possible, but recognized that unilateral action might be required.

Accordingly, the administration advocated "forces that can deploy quickly and supplement US forward based and forward deployed forces, along with regional allies, in halting an invasion and defeating the aggressor." Such a strategy was utilized during the October 1994 operation when Iraq threatened to invade Kuwait. With continuing global commitments and operational requirements, the Clinton administration recognized that "An aggressor in one region might be tempted to take advantage when US forces are heavily committed elsewhere."[91] Accordingly, it adopted a Two War philosophy, designed to repel such a threat "in concert with regional allies." The justification for such a stance was revealed "by the real prospect of near simultaneous hostilities with Iraq and North Korea in the late summer of 1994."[92] By the second term, it was clear that the administration was presiding through a transitional era, one in which it needed to lead a "revolution in military affairs and to restructure the defense budget" to ensure continued "dominance of information systems, awareness technologies and directed energy weapons." To do otherwise risked enabling competitors "to keep us out of regions of vital national interest, checkmating anything else we might do with the rest of our military establishment."[93]

Despite Republican concerns, Clinton's defense budget continued to equal the total defense spending of France, Russia, Japan, China, and Germany, despite the defense budget having been steadily reduced by 35 percent between 1985 and 1995. Military budgetary requests of $1.7 billion for 1994 and $2.6 billion for 1995 were made to ensure training readiness was not impaired by the costs of "unanticipated contingencies," while the administration added $25 billion to the defense budget over a 6-year period to increase funding for readiness and improve the quality of life for military personnel and their families.[94] Such moves were a concession to Republicans and the military, two groups the administration were keen to sway, but to little avail. In April 1997, the Republican controlled House National Security Committee reported that "Declining defense budgets, a smaller force structure, fewer personnel and aging equipment, all in the context of an increase in the pace of operations, are stretching US military forces to the breaking point."[95] Despite the president's lack of inroads with the military, Labor Secretary Robert Reich revealed "everyone . . . knows that the Defense Department will get what it wants. [Clinton] won't stand in the way of the Pentagon."[96]

Into its second term, the administration continued to advocate an integrated approach to the challenges it faced in the international arena. In addition to military force, this included "a strong diplomatic corps and a foreign assistance program" to ensure the United States continued to "shape the international environment, respond to the full spectrum of potential crises and prepare against future threats."[97] The administration noted that the threats posed to the United States grew more diverse as its time in power drew to a close, justifying its calls for an integrated approach "to defend the nation, shape the international environment, respond to crises, and prepare for an uncertain future."[98] The administration's stated ambition was "a stable, peaceful" world in which the United States continued to "prosper through increasingly open international markets and sustainable growth in the global economy," and in which, "democratic values and respect for human rights and the rule of law are increasingly accepted." To achieve this meant ensuring "close cooperative relations with the world's most influential countries," in order to "shape the policies and actions" of those who could negatively impact US national security.[99]

The Clinton administration governed not only in the post-Cold War era, but also at the dawn of the Information Age, which presented "new challenges to US strategy even as it [offered] extraordinary opportunities to build a better future." Technology had benefits and shortcomings, since it brought the world closer "as information, money and ideas move around the globe at record speed" but it also enabled "terrorism, organized crime and drug trafficking to challenge the security of our borders and that of our citizens in new ways."[100] As early as April 1993, the Clinton administration recognized the dilemma of the times; advances in technology made life easier for Americans, while modern technology in the hands of terrorists posed a major challenge to the security of the United States.

To address this, the administration prepared PDD-5 to address advances in telephone encryption technology. It introduced Clipper Chip technology to address "encryption's dual-edged sword," to enable secure transactions and privacy for citizens, while preventing it from acting as a "shield" for criminals and terrorists.[101] It also drafted PRD-27 that committed the administration "to the development of an information superhighway and National Information Infrastructure."[102] Five years later, on May 20, 1998, the administration produced PDD-63, dedicated to the protection of the US critical infrastructure, in an indication of how far the information revolution had progressed.[103] The administration conceded that the internet had "increased the ability of citizens and organizations to influence the policies of governments" and sought, therefore, to use public diplomacy as a tool to leverage foreign opinion in favor of US directives and, in doing so, increase pressure on their leaders.[104]

However, in an indication of the pre-9/11 environment through which the Clinton administration sought to introduce such changes, Congress slashed the White House spending request for Critical Infrastructure Protection by 55 percent in September 2000.[105]

While technological advancements benefited many, they also demonstrated what Bill Clinton later referred to as "the dark side of this new age of global interdependence."[106] Such was the way of things in the new era, for "the demise of communism not only lifted the lid on age-old conflicts but it opened the door to new dangers, such as the spread of weapons of mass destruction to non-state, as well as state, forces." The administration recognized in 1996 that America's "freedom, democracy, security, and prosperity were threatened by regional aggressors; the spread of weapons of mass destruction, ethnic, religious, and national rivalries; and the forces of terrorism, drug trafficking and international organized crime."[107] Long before September 2001, the Clinton administration recognized it was engaged in a new kind of battle; a covert quest to prevent death and destruction unleashing themselves upon the streets of the United States.

Counter-terrorism

If threats from former adversaries were receding, time demonstrated that dangers to the United States remained real and present. At home and abroad, the Clinton administration fought a war that went unnoticed by many until it exploded above the streets of Manhattan in 2001. Since that day terrorism has become "an indispensable part of the argot of the late twentieth century," about which, however, "most people have a vague idea or impression . . . but lack a more precise, concrete and truly explanatory definition."[108]

President Clinton spoke many times on terrorism, including at the 1995 General Assembly of the United Nations. In 1996, he convened a Summit of Peacemakers in Egypt devoted to counterterrorism and raised it at the G-7 in Lyons. On August 5, 1996, he addressed the issue at George Washington University, lamenting, "fascism and communism may be dead or discredited . . . but the forces of destruction live on."[109] Clinton had not campaigned stressing threats from terrorism, but his administration came to appreciate its dangers very quickly. Four days into its time in office, CIA employees were targeted on their way to work and a month later the World Trade Center was bombed.[110] Therefore, as early as 1994 the administration noted that "from time to time," it may be necessary "to strike terrorists at their bases abroad, or to attack assets valued by the governments that support them."

This was far from a theoretical exercise. On June 26, 1993, following a determination that Iraq had plotted to assassinate George Bush, Clinton ordered a cruise missile attack against the headquarters of Iraq's intelligence service. Similarly, on March 4, 1994, the United States secured convictions against four defendants in the bombing of the World Trade Center.[111] Speaking at a groundbreaking ceremony for a memorial to victims of the Pan Am flight 103 bombing over Lockerbie, Scotland, President Clinton weaved the administration's stance on terrorism into a wider narrative relating to the direction of history. Terrorists, he insisted, realized that history and "the rising tide of democracy seen everywhere in the world, is turning against them. And so with terrorism and any other means at their disposal, they lash back."[112] Speaking 2 years later at the opening of the memorial, the president insisted, "America is more determined than ever to stand against terrorism, to fight it, to bring terrorists to answer for their crimes."[113]

The administration addressed counterterrorism in a series of PDDs that were later incorporated into the annual National Security Strategy Review documents. In May 1994, PDD-24 was prepared to "foster increased cooperation, coordination and accountability among all US counterintelligence agencies" and established a new national counterintelligence policy structure.[114] The directive also led to the creation of the National Counterintelligence Center, which operated until President Clinton replaced it in January 2001 with the Office of the National Counterintelligence Executive. In June 1995, PDD-39 directed all federal agencies to review their security requirements and take necessary steps to ensure the continued safety of the American people. It also committed the government to "pursue vigorously efforts to deter and pre-empt, apprehend and prosecute, or assist other governments to prosecute, individuals who perpetrate or plan to perpetrate" terrorists attacks. The directive was based on reducing vulnerabilities, deterring terrorist acts, responding to terrorist incidents, and preventing the use of WMD.[115]

On August 8, 1995, the Transportation Secretary advised the White House Chief of Staff, Leon Panetta, that the Federal Aviation Administration would increase airport and airline security in accordance with PDD-39 and following input from law enforcement and intelligence sources. Intriguingly, the Transport Secretary relayed the concerns of the Air Transport Association about "the potential impact on their industry if civil aviation alone is the focal point for increased security" and proposed that the White House publicly acknowledge that the measures were "part of an administration-wide effort in response to a general increase in the potential for anti-American terrorism."[116] In 1997, the Clinton administration publicized its efforts to improve aviation security at airports in the United States and worldwide to "ensure better security for all US transportation systems; and improve protection for our personnel assigned overseas."[117]

In the aftermath of September 2001, international terrorism obtained a new dimension. In the years prior to the attack, however, the Clinton administration was not irresolute in its efforts. Since 1993, it had arrested and extradited more terrorists to the United States "than during the totality of the previous three administrations."[118] In addition to such legal maneuvers, covert operations were utilized to expel terrorists to nations that had less stringent human rights policies: "If we do not receive adequate cooperation from a state that harbors a terrorist whose extradition we are seeking, we shall take appropriate measures to induce cooperation. Return of suspects by force may be effected without the cooperation of the host government, consistent with the procedures outlined in NSD-77, which shall remain in effect."[119] Such language reveals the extent to which rendition was utilized prior to September 2001 and had been put in place prior to the Clinton administration, in classified documentation prepared for George H. W. Bush in January 1993.[120] Beginning in 1996, the Clinton administration persuaded allies to apprehend terrorists and ship them to a third country, without legal process. More than 50 terrorists were forcibly removed in this fashion with a view to breaking organizations "brick by brick."[121] The administration stressed that "foreign terrorists will not be allowed to enter the United States, and the full force of legal authorities will be used to remove foreign terrorists from the United States and prevent fundraising within the United States to support foreign terrorist activity." Definitions of what defined a terrorist, however, were open to interpretation, as Yasser Arafat became the most regular visitor to the White House during the Clinton presidency and Sinn Féin president, Gerry Adams, was granted a visa despite protests from the British government.

Clinton's Grand Strategy was committed to eliminating foreign terrorists and their support networks in the United States, destroying terrorist sanctuaries and confronting state-sponsored terrorism using "diplomatic, law enforcement, economic, military and intelligence activities."[122] Domestically, the administration proposed legislation designed to provide law enforcement officials with the tools to combat terrorism including additional manpower and training, methods to mark and trace explosives, as well as legal mobile wiretaps.[123] Although the language focused on international terrorism, the major threats faced by the Clinton administration were home grown: the destruction left by the Unabomber, the attacks at the Atlanta Olympics, and the Oklahoma City bombing were all perpetuated by Americans. Indeed, it was President Clinton's reaction to the devastation in Oklahoma that enabled him to find his presidential voice, and his role as Empathiser in Chief. This was a task he was forced to return to time and again during his presidency, noting, "you have lost too much, but you have not lost everything. And you have certainly not lost America, for we will stand with you for as many tomorrows as it takes."[124]

Following the destruction in Oklahoma, the administration urged Congress to pass anti-terrorism measures. The Senate approved a bill in June 1995 by a wide margin of 91–8, but similar legislation languished in the House of Representatives. In March 1996, the chamber approved a series of amendments proposed by Congressman Bob Barr (R-GA), including one to ban the use of wiretap evidence obtained without a warrant to prosecute terrorists. The amendments caused the bill's sponsor, Congressman Henry Hyde (R-IL), chairman of the House Judiciary Committee, to observe, "this is no longer a real anti-terrorism bill." John Conyers, Jr (D-MI) agreed that the move "eviscerated the heart and soul of the anti-terrorism bill."[125] The White House shared the sentiment, where Alan J. Kreczko, legal adviser to the National Security Council, advised Anthony Lake that the amendments "effectively gut an already-weakened anti-terrorism bill."[126]

The Clinton administration was eager to stress its focus on preventing terrorism as much as its determination to seek revenge for attacks once they had occurred. This included "active diplomatic and military engagement, political pressure, economic sanctions and bolstering allies' political and security capabilities." In language that reflected pre-9/11 era priorities, the administration noted the need to continue to devote "the necessary resources for America's strategy to combat terrorism, which integrates preventive and responsive measures and encompasses a graduated scale of enhanced law enforcement and intelligence gathering, vigorous diplomacy and, where needed, military action."[127] Despite what was retrospectively critiqued as a dependence on law enforcement to counter terrorist threats, the administration noted that there would be times when these were not sufficient and that when national security was challenged it would take "extraordinary steps" to protect US citizens.[128] It insisted that "a coalition of nations is imperative to the international effort to contain and fight the terrorism that threatens American interests."[129] However, in language that echoed that of its successor, the Clinton administration insisted that "as long as terrorists continue to target American citizens, we reserve the right to act in self-defense by striking at their bases and those who sponsor, assist or actively support them."

The Clinton administration addressed terrorism throughout its time in office and sought to re-task the federal government to address this gathering threat. However, the risks posed by bureaucratic resistance were apparent to the administration as it insisted that countering the terrorist threat required the "day-to-day coordination within the US Government and close cooperation with other governments and international organizations." It noted improvements in such efforts between the Departments of State, Justice, Defense, Treasury, Energy, Transportation, the CIA, and other intelligence agencies and sought extra funding and manpower from Congress to increase the ability of these agencies to combat terrorism.[130] In a move that revealed the lackadaisical approach to this issue, however, President Clinton was advised on September 11, 2000 that Congress had slashed administration requests for counter-terrorist activities. The House cut the funding request by $225 million (10%), while the Senate cut funding by $664 million (29%) from a total $2.34 billion request.[131]

While Clinton's Grand Strategy was designed to prevent the use of force against the United States, it accepted that such an eventuality must be planned for and initiated a policy of National Security Emergency Preparedness. Such a plan was necessary in the event of an emergency "in order to ensure the survivability of our institutions and national infrastructure, protect lives and property and preserve our way of life." This initiative was enshrined in PDD-67 "Enduring Constitutional Government and Continuity of Government Operations," dated October 21, 1998. Continuity of Government became an area of increasing concern in the second term of the administration as officials recognized the need to ensure the continued function of the federal government in the event of a national emergency. While this did not constitute the creation of a new department for National Security, it was the first step in the direction of the eventual Homeland Security Department established in the wake of the attacks of September 11, 2001. Until then, the Clinton administration continued to build up resources to ensure "comprehensive, all-hazard emergency preparedness planning by all federal departments and agencies continues to be a crucial national security requirement."[132]

The Clinton administration continued to address terrorism through the use of PDDs. President Clinton signed PDD-62 in May 1998, which created a new approach to fighting terrorism and reinforced the mission of the agencies charged with defeating terrorism. It "codified and clarified their activities in the wide range of US counter-terrorism programs, including apprehension and prosecution of terrorists, increasing transportation security and enhancing incident response capabilities."[133] Vitally, it established the Office of the National Coordinator for Security, Infrastructure Protection, and Counter-Terrorism, designed to oversee a "broad variety of relevant polices and programs including such areas as counter-terrorism, protection of critical infrastructure, preparedness and consequence management for weapons of mass destruction."[134]

The administration led efforts at G-7 conferences to coordinate international efforts to counter threats from terrorism. At the G-7 Summit in 1995, leaders agreed to work more closely in combating terrorism and at a December 1995 meeting in Ottawa, eight nations pledged to adopt counter-terrorism treaties by the year 2000, "to cooperate more closely in detecting forged documents and strengthening border surveillance, to share information more fully and effectively and to work together in preventing the use by terrorists of nuclear, biological and chemical weapons." The Clinton administration identified Iran as the main state sponsor of terrorism, noting in 1996, "Iran's support of terrorism is a primary threat to peace in the Middle East and a major threat to innocent citizens everywhere."[135] On August 5, 1996, the president signed the Iran and Libya Sanctions Act, designed "to deny those countries the money they need to finance international terrorism. It will limit the flow of resources necessary to obtain weapons of mass destruction." This was, in part, a continuation of policies initiated under the Dual Containment policy and revealed the extent to which the administration was seeking to address terrorism on three fronts: "first, abroad, through closer cooperation with our allies;

second, at home, by giving our law enforcement officials the most powerful counter-terrorism tools available; and, third, by improving security in our airports and on our airplanes."[136]

To counter potential threats, the administration imposed an embargo against Iran as part of the Dual Containment strategy, designed to deprive Tehran of "the benefits of trade and investment with the United States." The primary result of this embargo "was to further disrupt an Iranian economy already reeling from mismanagement, corruption and stagnant oil prices." Importantly, the United States did not act unilaterally in its actions against Iran as the G-7 joined in condemning Iran's support for terrorism. The United States also gained commitments from Russia not to sell weapons to Iran that had dual-use technologies with military end-uses.[137] As late as November 24, 2000, the Clinton administration sought to enforce restrictions on Iraq. When Shaykh Hamad bin Ali bin Jaber Al Thani made a gift of a Boeing 747 airplane to Saddam Hussein, Secretary of State Albright and Secretary of Commerce Mineta announced immediate measures. In accordance with UN Security Council Resolutions designed to prevent the diversion of US-origin goods to Iraq, the Department of Commerce moved to "restrict export and re-exports of a broad category of US-origin goods" to the Shaykh or his commercial entities. The State department also moved "to ensure that those directly responsible for the transfer of this airplane [would] not enjoy the privilege of travel to the United States."[138]

Vitally, the Clinton administration stressed its readiness to defend US interests "by striking at terrorist bases and states that support terrorist acts."[139] On August 20, 1998, President Clinton authorized air strikes against facilities in Afghanistan in an effort to confront "the network of radical groups affiliated with Osama bin Laden," identified in the 1998 NSSR as "perhaps the pre-eminent organizer and financier of international terrorism in the world."[140] The attacks also included a strike on a factory in Sudan that was believed to have been involved in the production of materials for chemical weapons, in what was deemed "a necessary and proportionate response to the imminent threat of further terrorist attacks against US personnel and facilities."[141] The strike targeted bin Laden's "network of radical groups" that came "from diverse places but share a hatred for democracy, a fanatical glorification of violence and a horrible distortion of their religion to justify the murder of innocents."[142] The language of the Clinton era reports was revealing. A 1996 CIA report entitled "Usama bin Laden: Islamic Extremist Financier" did not emphasize the relevance (if indeed there was any) of the term "al-Qaeda."[143] As Jason Burke notes, State Department memos from the era make no reference to any single group that bin Laden was fronting, identifying him purely as an "ex-Saudi financier and radical Islamist."[144]

The administration was at pains to stress that its efforts were not new and that the United States had "battled terrorism for many years" and had done so using the tools at its disposal. "Where possible, we've used law enforcement and diplomatic tools to wage the fight. The long arm of American law has reached out around the world and brought to trial those guilty of attacks in New York and Virginia and in the Pacific." But it noted that legal niceties may not always be viable: "There have been and will be times when law enforcement and diplomatic tools are simply not enough, when our very national security is challenged and when we must take extraordinary steps to protect the safety of our citizens." Such was the case with "the bin Ladin network of terrorist groups."[145] Again, the language is important, for as Burke stresses, "sensibly, Clinton talks of 'the network' not of 'al-Qaeda.'"[146]

The administration committed its 1998 address to the UN General Assembly to the subject of terrorism, identified as being "a clear and present danger to tolerant and open societies and innocent people everywhere." The president argued that "terror has become the world's problem" and took issue with those who noted that "the number of deaths from terrorism is comparatively small, sometimes less than the number of people killed by lightning in a single year." Terrorists were exploiting the benefits of the sweeping technological revolution that the administration was so eager to advance and of the "greater openness and the explosion of information and weapons technology." This raised the "chilling prospects of vulnerability to chemical, biological and other kinds of attacks, bringing each of us into the category of possible victim." Rather than acceding to popular theories of the time, however, the president rejected suggestions of "an inevitable clash between Western civilization and Western values and Islamic civilizations and values." Instead, Clinton argued that potential threats represented "a clash between the forces of the past and the forces of the future, between those who tear down and those who build up, between hope and fear, chaos and community."[147] This was highlighted in an un-dated note urging the administration to "Find a Muslim! This effort will get us to the real issue: 'Terrorism' vs. A perceived issue of religion. (Muslims against us and vice versa.)" It is not clear what event this was relating to, but there was a clear recognition of the need to "find a prominent Muslim associate directly or indirectly with the US Gov" so as to not appear to be making a racial issue out of the situation at a time that was at least months, if not years prior to the attacks of September 2001.[148]

As the administration prepared to leave office, its final grand strategy document revealed the extent of its anti-terrorism program. Noticeably more robust than in 1994, the document's language and tone repeated the greater threat faced by the United States. The document claimed to have "mounted an aggressive response to terrorism," a statement that came under close scrutiny 9 months later. It also claimed to combine "enhanced law enforcement and intelligence efforts; vigorous diplomacy and economic sanctions; and, when necessary, military force."[149] The priorities of the United States soon reversed, however, as military force took precedence over law enforcement initiatives. The dramatic nature of the September 2001 attacks enabled a focus on anti-terrorism initiatives that were unimaginable during the Clinton presidency as initiatives designed to thwart equally spectacular actions, such as the Millennium Eve celebrations, were largely overlooked.[150]

Enhancing security: NATO expansion

Clinton's Grand Strategy depended on utilizing existing international organizations and nowhere was this more evident than in Europe, which remained "at the center of America's geopolitical map of the world" in the 1990s.[151] The administration identified several entities that it sought to work with including the European Union, the Council of Europe, the Western European Union, and the Organization for Security and Cooperation in Europe. The utilization of these entities, working "together in harmony on common problems and opportunities," was identified by the administration as a way to demonstrate its commitment "to building a united, free and secure Europe."[152] However, the North Atlantic Treaty Organization (NATO) was central to the administration's plans in Europe. Indeed, despite initial European fears that the Clinton administration was focusing its attention on the Pacific, Europe saw the most tangible example of US Grand Strategy when NATO expanded during Clinton's second term.[153]

NATO enlargement was the most profound foreign policy undertaking of the Clinton presidency, designed to do for Europe's East what NATO had already done for Europe's West, to "create a secure environment for prosperity and deter violence in the region where two world wars and the Cold War began."[154] This ambition had been highlighted in 1994 when the White House announced that NATO's expansion "will not be to draw a new line in Europe further east, but to expand stability, democracy, prosperity and security cooperation to an ever-broader Europe."[155] When the administration took office, however, such a move was far from certain, as many questioned the continuing need for NATO. In the words of Lord Ismay, the organization had proved adept at keeping "the Americans in, the Russians out and the Germans down," but as a collective defense arrangement, based on an external threat from the USSR, the end of the Cold War raised questions about NATO's continued necessity.[156]

Intriguingly, the Clinton administration, with its apparent domestic focus and uncertain relationship with the military, was responsible for the enlargement of what it referred to as "history's greatest political–military alliance."[157] This was in part due to the presence within the administration of individuals such as Morton Halperin, William Perry, and Ashton Carter, who were known for their advocacy of cooperative security, of which NATO enlargement was seen as a perfect example. Therefore, rather than extinguish the alliance, the United States sought to expand it by incorporating those nations of Central and Eastern Europe previously segregated by the Iron Curtain, insisting that NATO alone had "the military forces, the integrated command structure, the broad legitimacy and the habits of cooperation that [were] essential to draw in new participants and respond to new challenges."[158] The twentieth century had twice been disrupted by conflicts originating in these areas and so expanding to this region was viewed as a way to consolidate the end of the Cold War and reduce the chance of conflict by providing democratic foundations for the newly independent states. The Clinton administration declared that the organization had always "looked to the addition of members, who shared the Alliance's purposes and its values, its commitment to respect borders and international law and who could add to its strength."[159] This concept was embraced by the administration in its efforts to push the boundaries of Europe further east.

The drive to expand NATO was informally proposed on October 21, 1993 by Defense Secretary Les Aspin at a meeting of NATO defense ministers. Three months later, on January 10, 1994, President Clinton made it official at a NATO summit meeting in Brussels, declaring "the Soviet Union is gone, but our community of interest endures. And now it is up to us to build a new security for a new future for the Atlantic people in the twenty-first century."[160] Speaking on his first trip to Europe, Clinton declared, "I have come here today to declare and to demonstrate that Europe remains central to the interests of the United States and that we will help to work with our partners in seizing the opportunities before us all."[161] Six months later NATO enlargement was enshrined in the 1994 National Security Strategy Review and gathered momentum during Clinton's first term. With the end of the Cold War, the Clinton administration recognized the opportunity "to complete the construction of a truly integrated, democratic and secure Europe, with a democratic Russia as a full participant." In doing so, the administration believed that it "would complete the mission the United States launched fifty years ago with the Marshall Plan and the creation of the North Atlantic Treaty Organization."[162] It sought to work with Europe to "address global challenges . . . consolidate the region's historic transition in favour of democracy and free markets . . . and to build a more open world economy without barriers to transatlantic trade and investment."[163]

The primary aspect of US Grand Strategy in Europe was "security through military strength and cooperation," for while the Cold War had ended, "war itself is not over."[164] The Clinton administration insisted that the NATO alliance remained "the anchor of American engagement in Europe and the linchpin of transatlantic security" as it sought to keep the organization "strong, vital and relevant."[165] NATO's continued relevance was defended robustly by the administration. Ambassador Albright insisted that "no other institution had comparable clout," while the 1995 grand strategy report referred to NATO as "a guarantor of European democracy and a force for European stability . . . its mission endures even though the Cold War has receded into the past."[166] The concept of using NATO, identified as "the sword and shield of democracy," as a force for the promotion of democracy as well as increased security, addressed two of the three central elements at the heart of US Grand Strategy.[167] Strobe Talbott noted that "enlargement of NATO would be a force for the rule of law both within Europe's new democracies and among them . . . An expanded NATO is likely to extend the area in which conflicts like the one in the Balkans simply do not happen."[168]

Just as the administration sought to expand NATO, it also strove to utilize it as the organization of choice for US foreign policy, in a move that mirrored the relative decline of the United Nations. Despite the administration's philosophical belief in multilateralism, the diluted power of the United States within the United Nations and the actions of fellow members of the Security Council tainted the organization in the eyes of many. Unlike the United Nations, where the United States was but one of five nations with a veto, the United States could control NATO without fear of sanction. As the most powerful military contributor, NATO depends on US hardware and the organization's chief military commander is by design an American. As Anthony Lake revealed,

> The problem with the Security Council was that the threat of vetoes made it difficult to do things in a classic multilateral way and, therefore, it's not that we made a conceptual choice for NATO over the UN, it is that if we could have done it through the UN effectively it would have been better, but when the UN couldn't act we had to find other ways to do things . . . but that was just because of events and the nature of the Security Council.[169]

When NATO expansion was first considered, critics feared that it would discriminate against those states that were not accepted.[170] However, advocates such as former National Security Adviser Zbigniew Brzezinski, argued that NATO's existing boundaries were outdated and that 'Preserving NATO on the basis of the lines that were drawn by Stalin in 1945 would doom the alliance to atrophy."[171] Two schools of thought quickly emerged: The first advocated rapid NATO expansion to preserve democratic and capitalist institutions in Central and Eastern Europe. Delay, it was suggested, would be fatal since "a Russia facing a divided Europe would find the temptation to fill the vacuum irresistible."[172] Others favored "taking gradual steps toward expanding the alliance, while at the same time encouraging Russia to join NATO in co-operative security arrangements."[173] The latter approach had the support of the Clinton White House, but the very concept of NATO expansion met with vocal opposition.

A collection of politicians and academics believed that NATO's time had passed. Irving Kristol of the American Enterprise Institute argued NATO had become "a vast irrelevance" that should be allowed to "slide into obsolescence."[174] George Kennan criticized the initiative as "the most fateful error of American policy in the entire post-Cold War era" and viewed it as "a badly conceived strategy designed to counter a highly artificial, unforeseeable and improbable military conflict."[175] Kennan feared NATO enlargement would have an adverse effect on Russian democracy and lead to another Cold War due to Russian militarism. Opponents saw the administration's decision as an *ad hoc* response to events over which it had no control and were appalled at the costs involved. The Congressional Budget Office (CBO) estimated that NATO expansion would cost $61 billion to $125 billion between 1996 and 2010.[176] British Foreign Secretary Malcolm Rifkind called such costs "a small price to pay for the security of the continent," while NATO Secretary General Solana suggested "opening NATO to new members is a good bargain, a sound investment."[177] It was suggested that no matter how much of a bargain it seemed, NATO expansion threatened to provoke a costly reaction from the Russians, who historically had most to fear from the organization.

Russia had lost large segments of the Soviet-era early warning network, leaving her vulnerable to the increasingly sophisticated capabilities of US conventional forces. The situation contributed to what Brzezinski referred to as an "oblong of maximum danger" from the Adriatic to China, from the Persian Gulf to the Russian–Kazakh border.[178] Given the domestic priorities of Yeltsin's government in the mid-1990s, there were no prospects to redress this imbalance. Rather, the question arose over the extent to which Yeltsin could compensate by increasing Russia's reliance on tactical nuclear weapons. The official Russian military doctrine appeared to indicate an intention to react in this manner and it was acknowledged that NATO enlargement could seriously jeopardize both the START treaties and the Conventional Forces in Europe Treaty, producing new divisions in Europe and restoring Cold War tensions. There was also concern within the administration, as the NSC's Charles A. Kupchan argued that it was a mistake to "push a geopolitical dividing line up into Russia's face."[179] The administration concluded, however, that "The end of the Cold War cannot mean the end of NATO and it cannot mean a NATO frozen in the past, because there is no other cornerstone for an integrated, secure and stable Europe for the future."[180] Despite Kupchan's concerns, NATO expansion, as championed by Anthony Lake, became a high priority for the administration, as "the consensus was that NATO should be expanded."[181]

Questions arose, however, over how to enlarge NATO without antagonizing Russia or threatening its interests, since "the prize, was anchoring Russia in Europe."[182] Accordingly, the Clinton administration sought to placate the Kremlin by declaring that NATO expansion was not "aimed at replacing one division of Europe with a new one, but to enhance the security of all European states, members and non-members alike."[183] While the administration was eager to calm Russian concerns, they refused to allow Moscow to dictate terms, asserting, "NATO will not automatically exclude any nation from joining. At the same time, no country outside will be allowed to veto expansion."[184] No one was under any illusions about whom this was directed toward, despite claims that "the enlargement of NATO is not directed against any state."[185] While the White House did not require Russian jubilation at NATO expansion, its begrudging consent was a prerequisite and Clinton was insistent that Russia should be recognized as "a vital participant in European security affairs."[186] Such tensions, however, raised questions about the focus of the NATO expansion program as some members of the administration expressed concerns that the policy risked being overlooked due to the methods used to pursue a more open and democratic Europe.

The Partnership for Peace

To remedy this situation, the Partnership for Peace (PfP) was created, enabling NATO military cooperation with "all former members of the Warsaw Pact as well as other European states" and bestowing the status of partner on all former Warsaw Pact nations, including Russia.[187] By the summer of 1994, 21 nations including Russia had joined the partnership, paving the way for a growing program of military cooperation and political consultation. Richard Holbrooke, by this point serving as Assistant Secretary of State for European and Eurasian Affairs, called PfP "an invaluable tool that encourages NATO and individual partners to work together. It helps newly democratic states restructure and establish democratic control of their military forces and learn new forms of military doctrine, environmental control and disaster relief."[188] The administration viewed PfP as "a dynamic instrument for transforming former adversaries into lasting partners and for consolidating, strengthening and extending peace for generations to come."[189]

The move enabled the administration to justify a continued military deployment in Europe in the face of calls to repatriate US troops, a point reiterated by the Brookings Institution, since "If the United States intends to lead and shape this process, then we will have to retain significant American ground forces in Europe."[190] The White House stressed that participation was no "guarantee that a participant [would] be invited to begin accession talks with NATO."[191] With the end of the Cold War, the Clinton administration was determined not to lose the ensuing peace and PfP became a vehicle to achieve this, ensuring that the United States remained "a vital participant in European security affairs."

US Grand Strategy in Europe, therefore, was driven by a desire for "a growing, healthy NATO–Russia relationship" that had Russia "closely involved" in PfP.[192] It is clear to see how the development of NATO fit within the grand strategy of Engagement and Enlargement: Bringing nations into NATO ensured that the organization had to depend less on American troop deployments, allowing the administration to reduce the military budget, which assisted efforts to reduce the budget deficit. NATO membership increased the likelihood of nations joining the European Union, thereby opening up more markets for US exports, which would in turn lead to more American jobs. Membership of the European Union depended upon specific forms of governmental structures for member states, thereby ensuring the enlargement of democracy to Central and Eastern Europe.

This was not the first time NATO's configuration had been altered: France withdrew from the integrated military command structure in 1966; Greece withdrew in August 1974 after Turkey's invasion of Cyprus, but rejoined in 1980. Finally, Spain was admitted to the alliance in 1982. In the 1990s, however, the overriding dilemma arose over which nations to admit and when. It was decided that NATO membership be dependent on five criteria: an established democracy, respect for human rights, a market-based economy, armed forces under full civilian control, and good relations with neighboring states. It was intended that the choice of country to be invited for membership should be based on the strength of their candidacy, but the United States also insisted that candidates confirm their military and political integration into NATO and contribute to the financial cost of expansion.

Such decisions carried the possibility that other factors may play a part in determining which nations would be invited to join and, ultimately, geopolitical factors became involved. Technically, since East Germany had become part of a unified Germany, in practice, it had become the first new contingent of NATO, albeit by a different route. The official rationale for the expansion of NATO was to provide the stability and security required for democratic and free market reforms in Eastern Europe; "But it was always assumed that Poland in particular was by far the strongest claimant and of course Poland, unlike most of the others, had a military contribution to make to NATO."[193] The first new members, Poland, Hungary, and the Czech Republic, were the states in which such reforms required the least encouragement or protection and were selected because of their strategic value. Slovenia was at least as far along the path of democratic reform but was not selected because it did not offer as much strategic value to NATO. The countries where reforms were needed the most: Russia, Belarus, Ukraine, the Baltic States, and Slovakia were excluded from the first round of the process. NATO enlargement followed the Clinton principle of pragmatic realism first, idealism always a close second, as defined by Dick Morris: "When you lead in an idealistic direction, the most important thing to do is to be highly pragmatic about it."[194]

In allegations that reveal a lack of comprehension not only about how grand strategy was constructed, but also of the policy formulation process, it was suggested that President Clinton enlarged NATO merely to gain electoral favor with the immigrant population in the Great Lake States. However, NATO Enlargement had been championed by Anthony Lake in 1994 when he referred to PfP as "the lighthouse at the entrance to NATO's harbour, offering real, practical military and defense cooperation with NATO" for the new European democracies.[195] The policy had been espoused at the January 1994 NATO conference and was the cornerstone of European policy in every NSSR document. However, in October 1996 the President announced his determination to admit the first group of countries in 1999, on "NATO's fiftieth anniversary and ten years after the fall of the Berlin Wall."[196] He made the speech in Detroit, Michigan, 2 weeks prior to Election Day and here the claims of politicization have some merit, as there had been no consultation with the Congress or the European allies and Clinton had previously stated that there was no consensus to enlarge NATO. However, the impact of the policy was of questionable electoral impact, as "only 10% of Americans could name even one of the three countries granted a US nuclear guarantee via their admission to NATO on 12 March 1999."[197]

The White House believed that NATO expansion reduced the risk of instability in Europe, assured that no part of Europe could revert to a Russian sphere of influence, built confidence, and gave new democracies incentives to consolidate reforms.[198] The policy had wide ranging support, as the president told the people of Berlin in 1998, "This is the opportunity of generations. Together, we must seize it. We must build a Europe like Germany itself, whole and free, prosperous and peaceful, increasingly integrated and always globally engaged."[199] Five months earlier President Clinton noted in his State of the Union Address that this was also the commitment of a decades-long pledge: "For fifty years, NATO contained communism and kept America and Europe secure. Now, these three formerly Communist countries have said yes to democracy . . . by taking in new members and working closely with new partners, including Russia and Ukraine, NATO can help to assure that Europe is a stronghold for peace in the twenty-first century."[200] By the time it left office, the administration could reflect on a policy that had helped to establish "an undivided, peaceful Europe."[201] As noted in 2013 by former British Foreign Secretary Sir Malcolm Rifkind, "the extent to which Central and Eastern Europe is now firmly part of the European mainstream with democratic government, not perfect rule of law, but certainly infinitely better than it was in the past and getting better as the years go by. That has been a huge achievement."[202]

An assessment of National Security Policy 1993–2001

The national security aspect of US Grand Strategy enabled Bill Clinton to establish a credible foreign policy that moved beyond the disappointment of Somalia to a point where, by 1996, he had become the embodiment of what President Bush had strived to achieve: "a president visibly confident of re-election, facing a parade of unconvincing campaign rivals, presiding over the world's healthiest economy and the very embodiment of global leadership."[203] The Clinton administration was adamant that its grand strategy helped to "shape the international environment in ways favorable to US interests and global security."[204] It had done so using "diplomacy, economic cooperation, international assistance, arms control and non-proliferation efforts, military presence and engagement activities," in an attempt to "strengthen alliances, maintain US influence in key regions and encourage adherence to international norms."[205]

However, many remained unconvinced by such calls and by the attempt to redefine concepts of national security. Former Deputy Under Secretary of Defense Dov Zakheim critiqued components of the strategy as being, "primarily non-military and [focused] on economic, social and even environmental concerns." References to the environment reflected the presence of Al Gore in the administration and, while there were sections devoted to economic, social, and environmental issues, it was far from non-military. Perhaps a more appropriate complaint was that when military matters were raised it was often in relation to multilateral operations, which many opposed, due to fears centering on command and control issues. Zakheim remained unconvinced by the strategy, suggesting that "This radical revision of the notion of national security goes to the heart . . . of the administration's understanding and employment of military means."[206]

Clinton's Grand Strategy walked a fine line between defending the administration's natural inclination toward multilateralism, which it viewed as "an important component of our strategy" and the fact that events caused a need to articulate a more robust unilateral approach to foreign policy.[207] The intellectual divide between aspiration and political reality was evident in an evolving policy that repeatedly stressed the philosophical commitment to international engagement, while insisting that the United States could not "become involved in every problem."[208] The continued interaction with allies was essential during the 1990s as the administration engaged in "combined training and exercises, coordinating military plans and preparations, sharing intelligence, jointly developing new systems and controlling exports of sensitive technologies according to common standards."[209] Only by leading, the strategy concluded, could the administration ensure a safer and more prosperous United States. This could only be achieved by "fostering the peaceful resolution of dangerous conflicts, opening foreign markets, helping democratic regimes and tackling global problems."[210]

Much of this was lost on the administration's critics, who saw a grand strategy light on military supremacy and dominated by notions of trade and democracy. However, the strategy was pragmatic in its stance: "We can and must make the difference through our engagement; but our involvement must be carefully tailored to serve our interests and priorities."[211] This point was vital to the understanding of the concept: idealism when possible, realism when necessary; the prioritizing of human rights where feasible, the elevation of the national interest at all times; multilateralism when possible, unilateralism if necessary. Such was the policy for the coming decade and arguably beyond. From 1994 onward, Clinton's Grand Strategy documentation insisted, "It is clear we cannot police the world; but is it equally clear we must exercise global leadership."[212] Questions remained over the administration's willingness to use force, however, and Nancy Soderberg's admission that it took 2 years to devise an approach to the use of force was compounded in the second term by Secretary of State Albright's insistence that, "We're talking about using military force, but we are not talking abut a war."[213] As Andrew Bacevich noted, "the cause of peace may from time to time impel the United States to use force; but peace-loving Americans did not start war on others: That was Albright' Rule."[214]

The capacity to deliver upon grandiose ambitions of global leadership may appear fanciful in retrospect. However, as Kupchan noted, in the 1990s there remained a lingering attachment to Fukuyama's *End of History* thesis and in "the degree to which the American way would be bought hook line and sinker around the world." With the sudden end of the Cold War, the victory in the Gulf War, and the unrivalled global status of the American economy and its accompanying military firepower, such optimism appeared justified. It is clear, however, that such a stance was flawed, as the administration "mistook that there was a true geo-political quiescence at the time and I think we understood it as a deeply grounded linear historical advance, whereas I think it was a pause."[215] It was a pause that was to out-last the administration by fewer than 9 months.

Conclusion

From December 1991, until his last day in office, national security considerations remained one of three central pillars to Clinton's Grand Strategy, which was committed to ensuring the United States continued to lead the world that it had done so much to create. Its national security component recognized, however, that the end of the Cold War had unleashed forces that were beyond the power of any nation to control. Whether threats were from groups, individuals, states, or rogue regimes, the Clinton administration was adamant that working with allies was a more viable option than operating alone. Accordingly, Clinton's Grand Strategy was committed to adapting security relationships with allies to address common threats, while retaining the right to act unilaterally in support of US national interests.

The strategy's integrated approach also applied to the federal government, for just as the president sought to break down the wall between foreign and domestic policy, so too did his grand strategy, requiring elements of the US government to work together in common cause. As noted in 1997, "at a time when domestic and foreign policies are increasingly blurred," grand strategy placed "a premium on integrated interagency efforts to enhance US security."[216] By attempting to integrate the components of the federal government, the Clinton administration sought to maximize the tools at its disposal as it moved to shape the international community in the new geopolitical era. Diplomacy, international assistance, arms control programs, non-proliferation initiatives, and overseas military presence were all adopted to shape the new era, while the United States maintained its ability to respond to any potential military crisis.

Clinton's Grand Strategy committed the United States to a full and vital role in world affairs and active promotion of its national security structures, unperturbed by calls for a more truncated approach to foreign policy. As President Clinton stated at George Washington University, "Where our interests and values demand it and where we can make a difference, America must act and lead."[217] Anthony Lake was adamant that continued American leadership in the world was a prerequisite: "It can mean more democracies and fewer dictatorships" and he called on Congress to help the administration "shape a second American Century of security and prosperity."[218] Lake's optimistic, ideological philosophy was clear: "If we can help lead the dozens of nations . . . who are trying to adapt to democracy and free markets, we help to create the conditions for the greatest expansion of prosperity and security the world has ever witnessed."[219] By the end of Clinton's second term in office, with the nation at peace and with the longest economic boom in American history, few argued with such an ambition. In hindsight, it is possible to see a certain naivety to the stance adopted in the 1990s as the United States dominated the world in an era of sudden unipolarity. Yet the Clinton administration did not seek to enforce its military might on the world. It rejected a preponderance of power approach and presided over an era of peace and prosperity. This was an era ruptured all too suddenly, but during its time in office, the Clinton administration's optimism and cautious use of its military capacity were certainly justified.

Notes

1 *NSSR94*, p. 6.

2 Friedman, "Clinton's Foreign Policy: Top Adviser Speaks Up," p. A8.

3 Author's interview with Charles A. Kupchan.

4 Nigel Hamilton, *Bill Clinton: An American Journey* (London: Century, 2003), p. 633; Meredith L. Oakley, *On the Make: The Rise of Bill Clinton* (Washington, DC: Regnery Publishing, 1994), p. 14.

5 Author's interview with Sir Malcolm Rifkind.

6 *PPPWJC*, vol. 1 (1993), The President's News Conference, January 29, 1993, pp. 20–22.

7 James Adams, "Gays In Services Set Clinton His First Policy Trial," *Sunday Times*, November 15, 1992, p. 20.

8 Steven V. Roberts and Bruce B. Auster, "Colin Powell-Superstar," *US News and World Report*, September 20, 1993, p. 48.

9 Steven Erlanger and David E. Sanger, "On World Stage, Many Lessons for Clinton," *New York Times*, July 29, 1996, p. A1.

10 *PPPWJC*, vol. 1 (1993), Remarks at a Saint Patrick's Day Ceremony with Prime Minister Albert Reynolds of Ireland and an Exchange With Reporters, March 17, 1993, p. 317.

11 Author's interview with Charles A. Kupchan.

12 Author's interview with Sir Malcolm Rifkind.

13 Author's interview with J. F. O. McAllister.

14 *PPPWJC*, vol. 2 (1993), Remarks on the Resignation of Les Aspin as Secretary of Defense, December 15, 1993, p. 2177.

15 Author's interview with Charles A. Kupchan.

16 Rubinstein et al., *The Clinton Foreign Policy Reader*, p. 5.

17 Author's interview with Charles A. Kupchan.

18 Quoted in Dan Goodgame and Michael Duffy, "Clinton On His Foreign Policy Gains: Blending Force With Diplomacy," *Time* 144, no. 18 (October 31, 1994), p. 35.

19 Douglas Jehl with Elaine Sciolino, "Sharper Focus: Genesis of Clinton's Hard Line," *New York Times* (April 24, 1994), p. A14.

20 Author's interview with J. F. O. McAllister.

21 James Adams, "The Special Relationship: Clinton and Major," *Sunday Times* (January 31, 1993), p. 11.

22 Clinton, "A New Covenant for American Security," p. 118.

23 William J. Clinton, "Foreword," in Soderberg, *The Superpower Myth*, p. vii.

24 *NSSR94*, p. 13.

25 *NSSR94*, p. 10.

26 *NSSR95*, p. 12.

27 *NSSR94*, p. 10.

28 *NSSR95*, p. 13.

29 Author's interview with Leon Fuerth.

30 *NSSR95*, p. 13.

31 Helen Dewar, "Dole Seeks Curbs on Use of Troops for UN Efforts," *Washington Post* (January 9, 1995), p. A7.

32 Martin Walker, "Home Alone: Ancient Regime Fights for the Old Order and America Firsters Look to Their Own," *Guardian* (February 20, 1995), p. 9.

33 *NSSR94*, p. 13.

34 Ann Devroy and Daniel Williams, "In Foreign Policy Debate, Parties Are Parting at Water's Edge," *Washington Post* (May 1, 1995), p. A4.

35 PDD-25: "Reforming Multilateral Peace Operations," May 3, 1994, pp. 2–3.

36 *NSSR94*, p. 13.

37 *NSSR95*, p. 16.

38 Barry R. Posen and Andrew L. Ross, "Competing Visions for US Grand Strategy," *International Security* 21, no. 3 (Winter 1996/1997), p. 44.

39 PDD-25: "Reforming Multilateral Peace Operations," May 3, 1994, p. 2.

40 Author's interview with Anthony Lake.

41 Posen and Ross, "Competing Visions for US Grand Strategy," p. 45.

42 *NSSR95*, p. 17.

43 Author's interview with Morton Halperin.

44 Author's interview with Charles A. Kupchan.

45 Lake, *Six Nightmares*, p. 153.

46 *NSSR98*, p. 9.

47 *NSSR94*, p. 12.

48 Les Aspin, The "Counter Proliferation Initiative," speech at the National Academy of Science, Committee on International Security, December 7, 1993, in Barry R. Schneider and Jim A. Davis (eds), *Avoiding the Abyss: Progress, Shortfalls and the Way Ahead in Combating the WMD Threat* (Westport, CT: Praeger Security International, 2006), pp. 333–338.

49 *NSSR95*, p. 15.

50 *NSSR96*, p. 21.

51 *PPPWJC*, vol. 1 (1993), Remarks at American University Centennial Celebration, February 26, 1993, p. 213.

52 Jane Wales to Billy Webster; re: Presidential Speech on Nuclear Smuggling & Non-proliferation, January 11, 1995, Clinton Presidential Records, National Security Council, Robert Boorstin (Speechwriting), OA/Box Number: 420, [Anthony] Lake—Non-Proliferation Speech—[1/30/95], William J. Clinton Presidential Library.

53 *NSSR96*, pp. 19–20.

54 *NSSR99*, p. 9.

55 *PPPWJC*, vol. 1 (1995), Address Before a Joint Session of the Congress on the State of the Union, January 24, 1995, p. 83.

56 Wales to Webster; re: Presidential Speech on Nuclear Smuggling & Non-proliferation, OA/Box Number: 420, [Anthony] Lake—Non-Proliferation Speech—[1/30/95], William J. Clinton Presidential Library.

57 *NSSR95*, p. 14.

58 *NSSR96*, pp. 20–21.

59 *NSSR96*, p. 5.

60 *NSSR98*, p. 9.

61 Mara Rudman to John Caravelli re: Press on START/ABM, June 21, 1999, Clinton Presidential Records, NSC Emails, Exchange-Non-Record (March 1997–January 2001) (Kennedy and Assassination), OA/Box Number: 630000 [06/2111999–01/18/2001], William J. Clinton Presidential Library.

62 Gerald Baker and David Buchan, "American Isolationism Put to the Test," *Financial Times* (October 15, 1999), p. 23.

63 PDD-17: US Policy on Ballistic Missile Defenses and the Future of the ABM Treaty, December 11, 1993, p. 4.

64 *PPPWJC*, vol. 1 (1994), Address Before a Joint Session of the Congress on the State of the Union, January 25, 1994, p.132.

65 *NSSR95*, p. 15.

66 *NSSR96*, p. 21.

67 Stephen Fidler, "Conservatives Determined to Carry Torch for US Missile Defence," *Financial Times* (July 12, 2001), p. 7.

68 Glenn P. Hastedt, *American Foreign Policy: Past, Present, Future*, Fifth Edition (Upper Saddle River, NJ: Prentice Hall, 2003), p. 140.

69 Over 60 motion pictures featured a presidential character of one sort or another in the 1990s compared to less than 40 in the 1980s.

70 *NSSR97*, p. 14.

71 *NSSR99*, p. 16.

72 *NSSR2000*, p. 21.

73 William C. Berman, *From the Center to the Edge: The Politics and Policies of the Clinton Presidency* (Lanham, MD: Rowman & Littlefield Publishers, Inc., 2001), p. 113.

74 *NSSR2000*, pp. 20–21.

75 *NSSR97*, p. 14.

76 *NSSR2000*, p. 12.

77 Joseph S. Nye, Jr, "Peering into the Future," *Foreign Affairs* 73, no. 4 (July–August 1994), p. 85.

78 David L. Boren, "The Intelligence Community: How Crucial?" *Foreign Affairs* 71, no. 3 (Summer 1992), p. 53.

79 Richard A. Best, Jr and Herbert Andrew Boerstling, "Proposals for Intelligence Reorganization, 1949–1996," Report Prepared for the Permanent Select Committee on Intelligence, House of Representatives (Washington, DC: Congressional Research Service, February 28, 1996), p. 29.

80 Nye, "Peering into the Future," p. 85.

81 *NSSR94*, p. 14.

82 *NSSR96*, pp. 23–24.

83 PDD-9: Alien Smuggling, June 18, 1993, p. 2.

84 PDD-24: US Counterintelligence Effectiveness, May 3, 1994.

85 In 1994, CIA officer Aldrich Ames was convicted of spying for the Soviet Union and Russia. Sentenced to life imprisonment, it is believed that Ames compromised at least 100 US intelligence operations, resulting in the execution of at least 10 sources.

86 *PPPWJC*, vol. 1 (1994), Statement by the Press Secretary on United States Counterintelligence Effectiveness, May 3, 1994, p. 834.

87 Deutch was named DCI following James Woolsey's resignation in December 1994. Quoted in Melvin A. Goodman, "Ending the CIA's Cold War Legacy," *Foreign Policy* 106 (Spring 1997), p. 142.

88 *NSSR97*, p. 14.

89 *NSSR98*, p. 25.

90 *NSSR97*, pp. 5–6.

91 *NSSR94*, p. 7.

92 *NSSR96*, p. 14.

93 Robert F. Ellsworth, "American National Security in the Early 21st Century," in David Jablonsky, Ronald Steel, Lawrence Korb, Morton H. Halperin, and Robert Ellsworth (eds), *US National Security: Beyond the Cold War*, p. 82.

94 *NSSR95*, p. 3.

95 Bradley Graham, "Military Forces are 'Near Breaking Point,' GOP Report Charges," *Washington Post*, April 9, 1997, p. A14.

96 Robert B. Reich, *Locked In The Cabinet* (New York: Alfred A. Knopf, 1997), p. 135.

97 *NSSR97*, p. 5.

98 *NSSR98*, p. 6.

99 *NSSR99*, p. 5.

100 *NSSR96*, p. 1.

101 *Statement by the Press Secretary on PDD-5 Public Encryption Management*, The White House, April 16, 1993.

102 PRD-27: Advanced Telecommunications and Encryption, April 16, 1993, p. 1.

103 PDD-63: Critical Infrastructure Protection, May 22, 1998.

104 *NSSR99*, p. 6.

105 Memorandum for the President from Samuel Berger, September 11, 2000, International Affairs Funding Issues, Clinton Presidential Records,

Speechwriting, Heather Hurlburt, John Pollack OA/Box Number: 24510: [Berger National Security Reform] 9/27/00 [1], William J. Clinton Presidential Library.

106 William J. Clinton, The Richard Dimbleby Lecture, "The Struggle for the Soul of the 21st Century," December 14, 2001.

107 *NSSR96*, p. 2.

108 Bruce Hoffman, *Inside Terrorism*, Revised and Expanded Edition (New York: Columbia University Press, 2006), p. 1.

109 *PPPWJC*, vol. 2 (1996), Remarks on International Security Issues at George Washington University, August 5, 1996, p. 1256.

110 For details of the Clinton administration's struggle with political violence, see Richard A. Clarke, *Against All Enemies: Inside America's War on Terror* (London: Simon & Schuster, 2004), pp. 73–226.

111 *NSSR94*, pp. 8–9.

112 *PPPWJC*, vol. 2 (1993), Remarks at the Ground-breaking Ceremony for the Pan Am Flight 103 Memorial in Arlington, Virginia, December 21, 1993, p. 2195.

113 *PPPWJC*, vol. 2 (1995), Remarks at the Dedication of the Pan American Flight 103 Memorial Cairn in Arlington, Virginia, November 3, 1995, p. 1717.

114 PDD-24: US Counterintelligence Effectiveness, May 3, 1994.

115 PDD-39: US Policy on Counterterrorism, June 21, 1995.

116 Federico Pena to the White House Chief of Staff, re: DOT Security, August 8, 1995, Clinton Presidential Records, National Security Council, Trans-national Threats (Richard Clarke), OA/Box Number: 3547: Terrorism-FAA [Federal Aviation Administration] [1], William J. Clinton Presidential Library.

117 *NSSR97*, p. 10.

118 *NSSR97*, p. 16.

119 PDD-39, p. 4.

120 See Boys, "What's So Extraordinary About Rendition?"

121 Barton Gellman, "Broad Effort Launched After '98 Attacks," *Washington Post* (December 19, 2001), p. A1.

122 *NSSR98*, p. 15.

123 *NSSR96*, p. 6.

124 *PPPWJC*, vol. 1 (1995), Remarks at a Memorial Service for the Bombing Victims in Oklahoma City, Oklahoma, April 23, 1995, p. 573.

125 Robert L. Jackson, "House Approves Amendment to Weaken Anti-Terrorism Bill," *Los Angeles Times* (March 14, 1996).

126 Alan Kreczko to Anthony Lake. Subject: Terrorism Bill, March 14, 1996, Clinton Presidential Records, Speechwriting, David Shipley, OA/Box Number: 12006: Terrorism Radio Attack, William J. Clinton Presidential Library.

127 *NSSR2000*, p. 23.

128 *NSSR98*, p. 15.

129 *NSSR2000*, p. 22.

130 *NSSR98*, pp. 15–16.

131 Memorandum for the President from Samuel Berger, September 11, 2000, International Affairs Funding Issues, Clinton Presidential Records, Speechwriting, Heather Hurlburt, John Pollack OA/Box Number: 24510: [Berger National Security Reform] 9/27/00 [1], William J. Clinton Presidential Library. In a move that carried even greater significance following the events in Benghazi during 2012, it emerged that $420M of the Senate cuts came from a request for extra funding for embassy security.

132 *NSSR96*, p. 26.

133 *NSSR98*, p. 15.

134 PDD-62, Combating Terrorism, Fact Sheet, Office of the Press Secretary, May 22, 1998.

135 *NSSR96*, p. 16.

136 *PPPWJC*, vol. 2 (1996), Remarks on Signing the Iran and Libya Sanctions Act of 1996 and an Exchange With Reporters, August 5, 1996, p. 1254.

137 *NSSR96*, p. 16.

138 National Security Affairs Guidance, November 28, 2000, Clinton Presidential Records Automated Records Management System (Email) WHO 2000/10–2001/01 ([Lieberman]), OA/Box Number: 900000 [11/28/2000] [2], William J. Clinton Presidential Library.

139 *NSSR96*, p. 7.

140 *PPPWJC*, vol. 2 (1998), Address to the Nation on Military Action Against Terrorist Sites in Afghanistan and Sudan, August 20, 1998, p. 1460.

141 *NSSR96*, p. 16.

142 *PPPWJC*, vol. 2 (1998), Address to the Nation on Military Action Against Terrorist Sites in Afghanistan and Sudan, August 20, 1998, p. 1460.

143 Jason Burke, *Al-Qaeda* (London: Penguin Books, 2007), p. 5.

144 Burke, *Al-Qaeda*, p. 5.

145 *PPPWJC*, vol. 2 (1998), Address to the Nation on Military Action Against Terrorist Sites in Afghanistan and Sudan, August 20, 1998, p. 1461.

146 Burke, *Al-Qaeda*, p. 6.

147 *PPPWJC*, vol. 2 (1998), Remarks to the 53rd Session of the United Nations General Assembly in New York City, September 21, 1998, pp. 1630–1632.

148 Terrorism, Clinton Presidential Records, National Security Council, Transnational Threats (Richard Clarke), OA/Box Number: 3546: Terrorism [Folder 2] [6], William J. Clinton Presidential Library.

149 *NSSR2000*, p. 22.

150 See Steve Coll, *Ghost Wars* (New York: Penguin, 2004).

151 Author's interview with Charles A. Kupchan.

152 *PPPWJC*, vol. 2 (1994), Remarks to the Conference on Security and Cooperation in Europe in Budapest, Hungary, December 5, 1994, p. 2144.

153 See James Goldgeier, *Not Whether, But When: The US Decision to Enlarge NATO* (Washington, DC: Brookings Institution Press, 1999).

154 Madeleine Albright, "Enlarging NATO: Bigger Is Better," *Economist* (February 15, 1997), p. 22.

155 *NSSR94*, p. 22.

156 Quoted in Michael Lind, *The American Way of Strategy: U.S. Foreign Policy and the American Way of Life* (Oxford: Oxford University Press, 2008), p. 134.

157 *NSSR95*, p. 26.

158 *NSSR94*, p. 22.

159 *NSSR95*, p. 26.

160 *NSSR95*, p. 21.

161 *PPPWJC*, vol. 1 (1994), Remarks to Future Leaders of Europe in Brussels, January 9, 1994, p. 10.

162 *NSSR97*, p. 21.

163 *NSSR99*, p. 29.

164 *NSSR94*, p. 21.

165 *NSSR95*, p. 26.

166 Albright, *Madam Secretary*, p. 167; *NSSR95*, p. 26.

167 *PPPWJC*, vol. 2 (1995), Remarks to the Parliament of the United Kingdom in London, November 29, 1995, p. 1799.

168 Strobe Talbott, "Why NATO Should Grow," *New York Review of Books* 42, no. 13 (August 10, 1995), p. 28.

169 Author's interview with Anthony Lake.

170 John Steinbruner, "Russia Faces An Unsafe Reliance on Nukes," *Los Angeles Times* (March 3, 1997).

171 Quoted by Michael Dobbs, "Clinton's NATO Effort Risky," *Washington Post* (July 8, 1997), p. A1.

172 Henry Kissinger, "Expand NATO Now," *Washington Post* (December 19, 1994), p. A27.

173 Michael Dobbs, "Turmoil Over NATO's Makeup and Mandate," *International Herald Tribune* (July 7, 1995), p. 16.

174 Quoted in Martin Walker, "Home Alone: What Matters Now is Trade not the Cold Not Tanks but Toyotas," *Guardian* (February 22, 1995), p. 12.

175 George Kennan, "NATO Expansion: Most Important International Issue," *Los Angeles Times* (March 11, 1997).

176 Congressional Budget Office, CBO Paper, "The Cost of Expanding the NATO Alliance," (Washington, DC: Congressional Budget Office, March 1996).

177 Malcolm Rifkind, "Europe's Future Security," speech to the Carnegie Endowment, March 10, 1997; Javier Solana, "Chatham House Address," speech to the Royal Institute of International Affairs, Chatham House, March 4, 1997.

178 Zbigniew Brzezinski, *Out of Control: Global Turmoil on the Eve of the Twenty-First Century* (New York: Collier, 1993), pp. 163–166.

179 Author's interview with Charles A. Kupchan.

180 *PPPWJC*, vol. 2 (1995), Remarks at the Harry S. Truman Library Institute Legacy of Leadership Dinner, October 25, 1995, p. 1683.

181 Author's interview with Leon Fuerth.

182 Author's interview with Charles A. Kupchan.

183 *NSSR95*, p. 27.

184 *PPPWJC*, vol. 2 (1994), Remarks to the Conference on Security and Cooperation in Europe in Budapest, Hungary, December 5, 1994, p. 2145.

185 *PPPWJC*, vol. 1 (1997), Letter to Congressional Leaders Transmitting a Report on the Enlargement of the North Atlantic Treaty Organization, February 24, 1997, p. 196.

186 *NSSR95*, p. 27.

187 *NSSR94*, p. 22.

188 Richard Holbrooke, "America, A European Power," *Foreign Affairs* 74, no. 2 (March–April 1995), p. 43.

189 *PPPWJC*, vol. 2 (1994), Letter to Congressional Leaders Transmitting a Report on the Partnership For Peace, August 18, 1994, p. 1477.

190 M. Thomas Davis, "Goodwill Is the Mission, Too," *Los Angeles Times* (December 4, 1996).

191 *NSSR96*, p. 44.

192 *NSSR95*, p. 27.

193 Author's interview with Sir Malcolm Rifkind.

194 Quoted in David Maraniss, *First in His Class: The Biography of Bill Clinton* (New York: Simon & Schuster, 1996), p. 407.

195 Address by Anthony Lake, National Security Advisor—The Council on Foreign Relations (Rob edits—new version—extensive comments), September 12, 1994, Clinton Presidential Records, National Security Council, Robert Boorstin (Speechwriting), OA/Box Number: 420, [Anthony] Lake-Council on Foreign Relations—9/12/94 [1], William J. Clinton Presidential Library.

196 *PPPWJC*, vol. 2 (1996), Remarks to the Community in Detroit, October 22, 1996, p. 1895.

197 Quoted in Charles A. Kupchan, *The End of the American Era* (New York: Random House, 2002), p. 18.

198 *NSSR95*, p. 27.

199 *PPPWJC*, vol. 1 (1998), Remarks to the People of Germany in Berlin, May 13, 1998, p. 751.

200 *PPPWJC*, vol. 1 (1998), Address Before a Joint Session of the Congress on the State of the Union, January 27, 1998, p. 117.

201 *NSSR2000*, p. 41.

202 Author's interview with Sir Malcolm Rifkind.

203 Walker, *Clinton: The President They Deserve*, p. 281.

204 *NSSR98*, p. 8.

205 *NSSR2000*, p. 9.

206 Dov S. Zakheim, "US Defense And Its National Strategy," speech at Bar-Ilan University, Israel, February 25, 1999.

207 *NSSR94*, p. 13.

208 *NSSR96*, p. 9.

209 *NSSR94*, p. 6.

210 *NSSR95*, p. 2.

211 *NSSR94*, p. i.

212 *NSSR94*, p. 5.

213 Author's interview with Nancy Soderberg; Albright, quoted in Andrew Bacevich, *American Empire: The Realities and Consequences of US Diplomacy* (Cambridge, MA: Harvard University Press, 2002), p. 48.

214 Bacevich, *American Empire*, p. 48.

215 Author's interview with Charles A. Kupchan.

216 *NSSR97*, p. 6.

217 *PPPWJC*, vol. 2 (1996), Remarks on International Security Issues at George Washington University, August 5, 1996, p. 1257.

218 Anthony Lake, "A Second American Century," *Washington Post* (May 3, 1996), p. A21.

219 *NSSR96*, p. 9.

CHAPTER FIVE

Prosperity promotion

Of the three central aspects of US Grand Strategy, it was prosperity promotion that most revealed President Clinton's hand in foreign policy developments in the post-Cold War world. Other administrations had addressed economic policy and the importance of foreign trade, but the Clinton administration took this to a new level by incorporating them into US Grand Strategy. The administration's embrace of economic policy within the international sphere ensured it was at the vanguard of foreign policy initiatives, in a timely combination of a new era, a new administration and a new approach to grand strategy. The decision to bring economic policy into grand strategy was a way to redefine policy to minimize the president's lack of experience in international relations as it had been practiced throughout the Cold War. With a new geopolitical era, the administration claimed that old definitions of international relations were no longer valid and it was time for new ideas and concepts. Prosperity promotion as a part of grand strategy had a profound impact on other nations and institutions, giving direction and impetus to the CIA, driving US policy with a new Europe, an emerging China, and new international trading blocks.

Promoting prosperity in US history

The Clinton administration was not the first in US history to harness the power of national economic might. Indeed, its ability to emphasize trade and economic power as an element of grand strategy stemmed in part from the manipulation of economic interests by previous administrations in their effort to win the Cold War. However, while this had been the case, prosperity promotion had not previously been placed at the center of US Grand Strategy.

For 80 years following the American Revolution the United States was, for the most part, content with expansion into the Western territories of North America. The Civil War further ensured that any notions of foreign economic excursions were placed on hold until the 1880s when, with a continent peopled, a constitution defended and a new century looming, the United States began to look overseas for economic growth. US manufacturing output, which greatly assisted in the construction of the nation's railroad network, grew to a point where it was in surplus and in need of markets, as US Gross National Product rose from $13 billion in 1890 to $35 billion in 1910, contributing to a rise in overseas trade, from $93 million in 1880 to $223 million by 1898.[1]

With the dawn of the Industrial Age a more confident United States emerged, which adopted an entrepreneurial approach to the Western hemisphere in particular. The Monroe Doctrine was used to ward off not only unwelcome imperial armadas, but also competition for US economic domination. With European powers seemingly content to colonize Africa and Asia, future Secretary of State James G. Blaine declared it to be "the especial province" of the United States "to improve and expand its trade with the nations of America."[2] The lack of infrastructure ensured that US efforts to establish an economic foothold did not occur immediately, but Blaine's efforts to establish a customs union to ensure that the United States became "the industrial provider of the agricultural nations of Latin America" was a harbinger of policy to come.[3] It was also a sign of change in foreign policy, as the United States deviated from what Secretary of State Gresham called its "traditional and well-established policy of avoiding entangling alliances with foreign powers in relation to objects remote from this hemisphere."[4] By 1895, Gresham's successor at the State Department, Richard Olney, noted that the United States' "infinite resources combined with its isolated position render it master of the situation and invulnerable against any or all other powers."[5] Three years later, Albert Beveridge insisted, "fate has written our policy for us; the trade of the world must and shall be ours."[6]

Throughout the twentieth century, successive administrations stressed the importance of international trade, as "foreign commercial expansion and national prosperity seemed intertwined." It was suggested that governments had an obligation to "take every step possible towards the extension of foreign trade" and ensure domestic employment.[7] Politicians of all persuasions agreed; during the 1920s, Calvin Coolidge insisted that "the chief business of the American people is business" while in 1934, FDR appointed Cordell Hull to his administration and passed the Trade Agreements Act, prompting Henry F. Grady to observe that the United States was "to a greater degree than ever before meshing our domestic economy into the world economy."[8] Two decades later, Defense Secretary Charles Wilson noted that "what was good for our country was good for General Motors."[9]

Throughout its history, therefore, the United States had encouraged economic expansionism and had, on occasion, militarized such a commitment. Some presidents had even put their names to doctrines designed to maximize this, but this was quite distinct from what the Clinton administration attempted with its grand strategy. The growing importance of economics in the post-Cold War era was becoming apparent during the 1992 campaign, as Michael Mandelbaum noted: "If the US is to play a useful role in the reconstruction of the world's economies . . . a far greater public appreciation of the importance of particular economic policies will have to be developed."[10] In Bill Clinton, the United States had a president determined to do all he could to educate the populace as to the role of economics in the post-Cold War world, referencing the economy in a public setting 12,798 times in 8 years, or around 133 times a month.[11]

Prosperity promotion in the Clinton administration

Governor Clinton had stressed the need to base national security on a sound economic footing from the first moments of his campaign for the presidency. In his Announcement Address, Clinton spoke of the economic challenges posed by Europe and Japan and of the risks to US international standing due to domestic economic decline. In his December 1991 address at Georgetown University, he reiterated his belief that a continued refusal to blend foreign and domestic policy risked harming the economy. Affirming this approach, Warren Christopher told the Senate Foreign Relations Committee at his confirmation hearings that economic growth was the president's highest foreign policy.[12] The administration utilized economic policy to enhance the nation's finances and end a mild recession that had contributed to George Bush's electoral defeat in 1992; it subsequently sought to utilize this element of foreign policy for domestic purposes, to assist in Clinton's bid for reelection in 1996 and to serve as a powerful legacy once the administration left office in 2001.[13]

Clinton's domestically focused campaign and his administration's focus on the economy were both made possible by the end of the Cold War. Beforehand, national survival had dominated policy as successive administrations sought to contain Soviet advances. With the end of the Cold War, the Clinton administration sought to reinforce strategic gains. Whereas a Domino Theory once existed to explain the spread of communism, now such a process was attempted in reverse. The Clinton administration sought to ensure that free markets flourished and replaced command economies. Such thinking was apparent during the campaign and reflected not only the personal view of Governor Clinton, but also that of foreign policy advisers such as Michael Mandelbaum, who observed that in the post-Cold War world "economic issues will predominate, particularly as former Communist Europe and countries in other regions move toward market institutions and practices."[14] Mandelbaum may not have joined the eventual Clinton administration, but his thinking was incorporated into policy nevertheless.

Combining economics with foreign policy enabled President Clinton to engage more fully in the subject, finally exclaiming "'I get it, this is as interesting as domestic policy,' and from that point on he was deeply engaged. But it didn't begin on day one."[15] Blending economics with foreign policy also enabled President Clinton to maintain his commitment to focus on the economy, while initiating a foreign policy that was in tune with the geopolitical realities of the post-Cold War world. Mickey Kantor may have reached too far in his assertion that Clinton was "the first president to really make trade the bridge between foreign and domestic policy" since commerce and foreign policy have long been entwined in the American experience, but Clinton was, however, able to elevate the importance of such issues, freed from the Cold War constraints, to ensure that "trade and international economics have joined the foreign policy table."[16]

To implement the prosperity promotion element of its grand strategy, the Clinton administration sought to implement a variety of structural changes, designed to enhance the status of geoeconomics. This involved changes to the federal bureaucracy as well as to international bodies. Existing entities were adopted and new organizations created to ensure the viability of the policy. New, emerging markets were targeted and a variety of organizations utilized as the administration looked to engage in both multilateral and bilateral negotiations to promote prosperity.

The National Economic Council

The most concrete structural change was the creation of the National Economic Council (NEC) by Executive Order 12835 on January 25, 1993, designed to coordinate domestic and foreign economic policy making. Although previous administrations had sought to coordinate national and international economic policy, President Clinton was determined to have better control of economic strategy than his predecessors and less infighting. Clinton had promised such an entity on the campaign trail, insisting in *Putting People First* that the United States required an "Economic Security Council, similar in status to the National Security Council, with responsibility for coordinating America's international economic policy."[17] A memo drafted during the transition noted that the end of the Cold War and the nation's economic woes demanded "a shift of priority and resources away from national security as traditionally defined, toward the broader problems of making America competitive in a fiercely competitive world." The NEC, it insisted, "would be your instrument for assuring that economic policy gets attention equal to traditional national security, working extremely closely with the NSC and its staff when international economic issues are under consideration, and with the Domestic Policy Council and its staff on domestic policy matters."[18]

The NEC was designed to manage the flow of economic advice to the president, direct economic policy making, and ensure that policies and programs were implemented in accordance with the administration's stated ambitions. President Clinton was adamant that members of his economic team "use this instrument to harmonise their efforts and coordinate policy," adding his personal stamp of approval to the NEC.[19] The name of the new body was specifically intended to reflect Clinton's insistence that it enjoy a status akin to the National Security Council. Indeed, "the goal was to do for economic policy what the National Security Council has done for national security policy."[20] The NEC was structured to coordinate both domestic and international economic policy, but with a far smaller staff than the NSC. However, the NSC provided an existing framework that the NEC deliberately mirrored, with a principals committee, a deputies committee, and various *ad hoc* interagency working groups. President Clinton later viewed the successful establishment of the NEC as having been "the most important innovation in White House decision making in decades."[21]

Economic appointees

The shift from Cold War militarism to post-Cold War economics was apparent in the Cabinet announcements that followed President Clinton's election. Four years earlier, President-Elect Bush named "one of the strongest foreign policy teams ever fielded in Washington: a group that cast a heavy shadow over the president's less impressive domestic advisers."[22] The opposite was true under Clinton, who promised to "focus like a laser beam on the economy" and defied convention by prioritizing members of the Cabinet with financial responsibilities.[23] With the precarious state of the US economy and the new priorities of the administration, the appointment of the Treasury Secretary was considered more important than the appointment of the Secretary of State.

Managing the NEC called for a particular individual, respected by economists and politicians alike. President Clinton found such a person in Robert Rubin, co-chairman of Goldman Sachs and a major adviser and fund-raiser to his campaign. Rubin noted that his time at the NSC presented a series of daunting challenges: "we had to define it, we had to create its acceptance within the government process, and then we had to staff it, all at the same time that we were working on the economic plan."[24]

Rubin was part of an economic team recruited from academia, business, and politics, designed to inspire confidence in the administration and its economic aspirations, which became responsible for the longest period of economic growth in US history.[25]

To head the Treasury Department, Clinton selected the Chairman of the Senate Finance Committee, Lloyd Bentsen, whose appointment was, in part, designed to convey a sense of maturity and counter the impression of a young, inexperienced administration. His reputation proved essential in gaining Republican support for NAFTA and GATT and mirrored the appointment of Warren Christopher as a respectable, fatherly figure whom the president found reassuring. Clinton named his fellow Rhodes Scholar Robert Reich as Labor Secretary, since his personal politics precluded him from serious consideration as Treasury Secretary. Although he contributed material to Clinton's campaign and headed the economic transition team, Reich's tenure at the Labor Department was later revealed as having been less than satisfying. Reich and Bentsen clashed over the direction of economic policy and both departed the administration before the start of the second term. Filling out the economic team were Commerce Secretary Ron Brown—who aided Clinton's campaign as Chairman of the Democratic National Committee—and Federal Reserve Chairman, Alan Greenspan, whom Clinton saw no reason to remove, despite his ties to the Republican administrations he had campaigned against. Mickey Kantor was appointed US Trade Representative, while California Congressman Leon Pannetta was appointed to head the Office of Management and Budget, the first in a series of roles that he came to fill in the coming years as his reputation for efficiency blossomed.

Vice President Gore was a key supporter of prosperity promotion, drawing his inspiration from fellow Tennessean, Cordell Hull, who served as Franklin Roosevelt's Secretary of State from 1933 to 1944. Gore often invoked Hull's Trade, Prosperity, and Peace concept, arguing that trade agreements increased global economic stability.[26] Gore's influence on policy was further demonstrated by the unprecedented participation of his foreign policy adviser, Leon Fuerth, on the National Security Council. His long-standing participation was cemented on January 9, 1997, when PDD-53 established him as a member of the Principals Committee. President Clinton noted Gore's contribution to the administration, referring to him as "the most influential and constructive force ever to occupy the Vice-Presidency's office."[27]

Clinton's economic inheritance

Despite having secured the presidency in part due to a pledge to focus on the domestic economy, the administration quickly discovered that the economic conditions they had inherited were far worse than had been revealed and their ability to rectify the situation was more diminished than they could have imagined. The state of the economy posed "a cancerous threat to the long-term vitality of the American economy."[28] Chairman Greenspan made it clear that the Bond Markets were looking for a clear sign of intent to deal with the deficit as a matter of urgency. If this was not forthcoming, Greenspan warned of spiraling interest rates and an economic downturn that would spell disaster for Clinton's reelection ambitions. The ensuing debate between deficit reduction and investment caused tension within the administration, particularly between Treasury Secretary Bentsen and Labor Secretary Reich.

As a long standing Friend of Bill (FOB), Reich had been instrumental in devising the economic blueprint for his campaign that called for investment spending and infrastructure development to spur the domestic economy. Reich, along with James Carville, argued that Clinton had campaigned on a pledge to invest in the US infrastructure and that this had the approval of the American people. J. Thomas Cochran, executive director of the United States Conference of Mayors, reminded the White House that the president had promised "an annual increase of $20 billion to rebuild America and the mayors believe that this promise should be kept."[29] Secretary Bentsen, Robert Rubin, Leon Panetta, and Alan Greenspan, however, cautioned the president to deal with the financial markets first: "By the time he took office, the deficit hawks inside the new administration were winning the debate" to shape its financial priorities.[30]

The administration's economic plan was presented to Congress in February 1993, projecting a deficit of $500 billion over a 5-year period and reduced military spending by $112 billion over the same period. A major component of this was the deficit reduction plan—initiated as a signal to the markets and the Federal Reserve Chairman that the administration was serious about economic reform. Under these initiatives, the federal deficit fell for 3 years between 1992 and 1995 for the fist time since Truman's presidency and the deficit as a percentage of GDP sank to its lowest level since 1979, from 4.9 percent to 2.4 percent.[31] Joseph Stiglitz, appointed as Chairman of the Council of Economic Advisers by President Clinton, later observed that "everybody seemed to be benefiting from . . . this *Economia Americana*, which brought unprecedented flows of money from developed countries to the developing world—sixfold increases in 6 years—unprecedented trade—an increase of over 90 percent over the decade—and unprecedented growth.[32]

However, the administration's ability to deliver on its pledges was placed in doubt by the Democratic Congress, which imposed a nonbinding budget resolution that retained spending caps. This limit on increased spending for domestic programs unless cuts were made elsewhere left the administration with less than $1 billion for new investments in 1994 and less than $6 billion in 1995.[33] Outraged, Clinton asked, "Where are all the Democrats? We are all Eisenhower Republicans here and we are fighting Reagan Republicans. We stand for lower deficits and free trade and the bond market. Isn't that great?"[34] This was hardly the reason that Clinton had sought the presidency and these new priorities were indicative of the faltering party unity in Washington as well as further evidence that President Clinton, "the policy wonk, entered the candy store just as its shelves had been emptied."[35]

The Big Emerging Markets

An early and continuing approach to promoting prosperity was the Big Emerging Markets (BEMs) concept, developed at the Commerce Department, under the guidance of Secretary Ron Brown and Under Secretary Jeffrey E. Garten. The policy was based on a forecast that the ten markets involved held remarkable potential for economic growth and political development in the medium term. Due, in part, to the scale of the development projects that were proposed and required in these nations, estimated at over $1 trillion over 10 years, the White House sought to assist US businesses secure valuable contracts in a discernable break from previous practice.

The individual locations selected emerged from early horizon-scanning efforts by the Clinton administration to discern innovative ways to aid US companies compete and win in overseas markets. Despite the "developing" nature of the economies in question (Argentina, Brazil, China, India, Indonesia, Mexico, Poland, Turkey, South Africa, and South Korea), they played a role arguably disproportionate to their stature, indicative of the potential for future growth. Maximizing the potential profit for US companies was the basis for the BEM concept of the Clinton administration.

The administration calculated that by the end of its time in office, the BEM nations would collectively be importing more from the United States than either Japan or the European Union and that those import numbers could jump to total more than the figures for the European Union and Japan combined by 2001.[36] The Clinton administration envisioned the role that US companies could play in the establishment of new airports, infrastructure projects, telecommunications systems, and financial entities. To ensure that this was achieved, the administration recognized the need to ensure market access to these nations that had historically proved difficult to penetrate due to trade barriers. In this endeavor, the administration revealed its capacity to work in tandem with private enterprise and, in doing so, maximize opportunity for increased outlets for US goods and services.

It was apparent that the nations under scrutiny could well provide a vast outlet for US business opportunities. However, the BEMs also served as regions of potential political development in keeping with the administration's democracy promotion policy, and by extension proved to be a focus of the administration's security policy, demonstrating once again, the interconnectivity of Clinton's Grand Strategy initiative. In determining where to place emphasis, it was believed that the policy "has the balance about right between aggressively selling (with its inevitable bilateral orientation) and a longer-term effort to liberalize the trade practices of these countries (with an emphasis on World Trade Organization membership and improvements in the treatment of services and intellectual property)." It was feared, however, that viewing these nations solely in terms of commercial exploitation brought with it risks associated with income inequality, governmental corruption, and environmental degradation. "If these issues are not taken seriously in our policies towards these countries, they at least need to be factored into our expectations about how stable they are as commercial partners."[37] To succeed, the Clinton administration required the latest data from the nations involved, not all of which was openly available.

The CIA and prosperity promotion

The combination of economics and security was most vividly demonstrated in the administration's use of the US intelligence services, as Clinton's Grand Strategy provided an unlikely solution regarding the future of the CIA. The Clinton administration recognized the need to draw on all aspects of the federal government to enact its policies; redrafting the role of intelligence recognized the need to retain the agency's services, and also to adapt to changing times. In an age with no discernable enemy, the continued rationale for the agency was in doubt. Indeed, as the new administration took office, it was suggested that "to many in Congress and perhaps to the incoming president, the CIA seemed to have lost its traditional enemy and not yet found a role."[38]

Clinton's Grand Strategy re-tasked the agency to assume new responsibilities in the area of economic intelligence. The administration believed that such a role would "play an increasingly important role in helping policy makers understand economic trends" and that "economic intelligence can support US trade negotiators and help level the economic playing field by identifying threats to US companies from foreign intelligence services and unfair trading practices."[39] Elements of the new mission were consistent with their previous tasking, such as the need to assist in military and diplomatic missions and combat terrorism. However, in tasking the CIA to "contribute where appropriate to policy efforts aimed at bolstering our economic prosperity" and to provide "timely information necessary to monitor treaties, promote democracy and free markets and forge alliances and track emerging threats," the administration specifically utilized the CIA in its grand strategy of Engagement and Enlargement.[40]

It was Clinton's predecessor, however, who initiated many of these changes. In 1991, President Bush began the reallocation of CIA resources away from its previous focus "toward new economic targets, as the world marketplace became an ever more important battlefield for America."[41] Previously, up to 60 percent of CIA resources had been targeted on the USSR, a figure that dropped to 13 percent by 1993.[42] Intelligence analysts continued to address weapons proliferation, counter-terrorism, and traditional espionage activities, but the Clinton administration tasked the CIA with aiding American companies in the global market. During the Cold War, economic intelligence accounted for 10 percent of CIA activity, a figure that rose to 40 percent under Clinton. The intelligence community had always engaged in economic intelligence gathering, but under Clinton this new role helped justify the CIA budget and assist the administration in its efforts to forge domestic renewal. Business intelligence played a crucial role during the Cold War; now intelligence assisted business in the post-Cold War era, as the full weight of the US national security apparatus was brought to bear in maintaining economic security. This was an example of the policy's duality: Clinton's Grand Strategy gave new direction to the CIA, ensuring its continued relevance and, in doing so, the agency's new remit helped revitalize the economy. Such changes were required in a time of uncertainty and change "because national security has taken on a much broader definition in this post-Cold War era, intelligence must address a much wider range of threats and dangers."[43]

Structural approach

Despite concerns expressed in Congress regarding the administration's adoption of a multilateral approach to national security policy, the White House identified multilateralism more readily with its plans for prosperity promotion. The administration recognized the need for American business to gain access to international markets and the 96 percent of global consumers that lived outside the United States. This was necessary not only to ensure continued innovation and productivity, but also as a means to improve American living standards by improving access to foreign markets. Internal NSC memos reveal the extent to which the administration sought to present President Clinton "as a pioneer in making antiquated institutions fit the new realities of the post-Cold War world and giving birth to brand new institutions and mechanisms for solving international problems."

Therefore, the administration devised a three pronged approach for prosperity promotion: US participation in the development of regional economic bodies including NAFTA and the Asia-Pacific Economic Cooperation forum (APEC); the utilization of and influence over a series of multilateral organizations including the International Monetary Fund

(IMF), the World Trade Organization (WTO), and the World Bank; and bilateral agreements with trading partners. The challenge would be in ensuring that neither the administration, nor the United States was "held hostage to an international bureaucracy and to make global institutions active agents of change."[44]

Prosperity promotion and regional bodies: NAFTA and APEC

Establishing regional economic bodies was a major focus of the Clinton administration in its initial time in office. The primary focus was securing agreement for NAFTA, designed to create a free-trade zone among the United States, Canada, and Mexico. Negotiations had been initiated by the Bush administration, but were opposed by trade unions and Democrats over fears they would negatively impact US manufacturing. Ross Perot also emerged as a leading sceptic of the initiative and forecasted "a great flushing sound" as jobs and industries headed south to Mexico, leaving their US counterparts decimated.[45] There was also internal White House concern in July 1993 over the amount of initiatives underway and the implications involved: "In the cases of health care and NAFTA, failure to take immediate action threatens the ability of policy teams to present final proposals in time for September action. Failure to decide also means that we could return to the 'loss of focus' theme that injured the president's standing during the spring" with wide ranging ramifications for the administration.[46]

In addition to the domestic opposition to NAFTA, the administration faced the added challenge of Mexican perception, as a White House memo dated July 23, 1993 insisted, "those working on NAFTA argue that it needs to be launched as early as possible because attacks by NAFTA foes are damaging it and because President Salinas of Mexico will regard the delay as an abandonment, and may tilt in a more nationalist direction."[47] The Clinton administration's support for NAFTA revealed several factors: its readiness to defy union pressure and the Democratic congressional leadership in defense of its New Democrat philosophy, its strategic vision of free trade and free markets, and its concept of prosperity promotion as a component of grand strategy. The White House viewed the agreement as "vital to the national interest and to our ability to compete in the global economy" and as a "pro-growth, pro-jobs, pro-exports agreement."[48] The president was adamant; "NAFTA means exports; exports means jobs. No wealthy country in the world is growing more jobs without expanding exports . . . This is a job winner for our country, more jobs with Latin America, even more jobs when we have a new world trade agreement. It all begins with NAFTA."[49]

Vice President Gore was an early champion of NAFTA and debated the issue with Ross Perot on "Larry King Live," identifying the trade pact as "a starting point for dealing with the common challenges of the Americas." The administration viewed NAFTA as a core element of its grand strategy as it advanced all three of its objectives: "Not only does it mean new jobs and new opportunities for American workers and business, but it also represents an important step in solidifying the hemispheric community of democracies."[50] The White House defied congressional Democrats to gain support for NAFTA from Republicans and passed the North American Free Trade Act in December 1993, providing a much-needed boost at the end of its first year in office. It also demonstrated that Clinton "was willing to take unpopular foreign policy positions—but not often, and almost always to promote the US economy, such as NAFTA."[51]

Passed in the face of overwhelming hostility from members of the Democratic Party, NAFTA had already created more than 100,000 American jobs by 1995, a figure that jumped to almost 310,000 by 1996.[52] The agreement created the world's largest free trade area and increased trade among its member nations by over 85 percent. In 1997 the Clinton administration anticipated that by 2010, US exports to Latin America and Canada would exceed those to Europe and Japan combined.[53] By 1999 US merchandise exports to Mexico had nearly doubled, as Mexico became the second-largest export market for the United States.[54] By the end of the Clinton administration, Mexico and Canada imported almost 40 percent of all US exports.[55] Beyond the economic benefits, NAFTA also aided US national security by increasing Mexico's ability to cooperate with the United States on a range of issues including the environment, narcotics trafficking, and illegal immigration.[56]

NAFTA was one of the administration's most recognized successes, described by Henry Kissinger as being "the most innovative American policy toward Latin America in history."[57] Even administration critic Richard Haass was forced to note that in its first 5 years, NAFTA helped to almost double trade with the US's two largest trading partners and insulate Mexico from recession and political instability.[58] Paul Wolfowitz conceded, "President Clinton's foreign policy already looks much stronger than it did before his recent victory in the battle over the NAFTA."[59] The success caused the administration to advocate expanding NAFTA across the Western hemisphere, which in 1995 accounted for over 35 percent of all US overseas sales.[60] In 1994, hemispheric leaders agreed to negotiate the Free Trade Area of the Americas (FTAA) by 2005.[61] The 1995 Denver Trade Ministerial and Commerce Forum encouraged the decision "to promote trade liberalization and business facilitation throughout the Western hemisphere."[62] Plans for the FTAA were particularly important as it could, "accelerate progress toward free, integrated markets, which will create new high-wage jobs and sustain economic growth for America."[63]

The administration also sought to bring Chile into the existing NAFTA agreement.

However, despite its success in securing passage of NAFTA, the establishment of Chile as a NAFTA partner and eventual its success in successfully negotiating more than 300 trade agreements during its time in office, the Clinton administration was unable to leverage support for a regional free trade agreement to cover the Western hemisphere, or for full Chilean accession.[64] Despite Republican plaudits for ensuring that "one of the most important political successes of this young president challenged the argument that the United States can no longer afford to play an active and engaged role in the world," the administration's capacity to expand NAFTA further fell victim to domestic political maneuvering surrounding Fast Track Authority.[65]

Between 1975 and 1994, Fast Track negotiating authority had enabled successive presidents to negotiate international trade agreements that Congress could vote to accept or reject, but not filibuster or amend. President Clinton had inherited Fast Track negotiating authority; however, this lapsed in April 1994 and his efforts to secure its re-instatement were hampered by organized labor and disaffected Democrats, angered over the passage of GATT and NAFTA. The issue had been a major concern to other administrations. Former Secretary of State James Baker expressed his concerns over the expiration of an earlier agreement in 1991, noting, "without it, individual members [of Congress] could literally amend an agreement to death. Opponents of NAFTA saw the Fast Track vote as a chance to derail negotiations almost before they had begun."[66] The Clinton administration viewed trade-negotiating authority as essential in its remit to enhance US economic interests. In 1997, the administration observed that securing Fast Track negotiating authority was "a litmus test for trade expansion and US interest in leading the hemisphere toward the creation of the FTAA."[67] However, despite it being in place from 1975 until 1994 and again from 2002 to 2007, the Clinton administration was unable to secure congressional support for such powers as "renewal of Fast Track authority languished because of irreconcilable differences between the opponents and supporters of globalization."[68]

The administration observed that "Congress has consistently recognized that the President must have the authority to break down foreign trade barriers and create good jobs," but despite this, the Republican-controlled Congress denied the administration Fast Track Authority for the remainder of its time in office, before finally bestowing it on President George W. Bush in 2002.[69] Clinton's inability to secure continued Fast Track negotiating authority and the impeachment hearings in his second term did little to assist the situation, despite the advantages that such authority promised for the US economy and broader aspirations of US Grand Strategy. In an example of domestic politics impacting foreign affairs, the FTAA and expansion of NAFTA became victims of the political tensions caused by the impeachment process that cast a shadow over the Clinton administration's second term in office.

NAFTA proved to be so successful that by 1995 European leaders made enquiries about expanding it across the Atlantic. The Clinton administration considered the concept of a Transatlantic Free Trade Area (TAFTA) following an October 1994 meeting with UK Prime Minister John Major.[70] Assistant Secretary of State Richard Holbrooke suggested TAFTA would be "part of the intense dialogue on the future of Europe" that would develop in the years ahead, but noted, "it's a good idea whose time hasn't quite come yet."[71] Despite this, President Clinton launched the New Transatlantic Agenda at the US–EU Summit in December 1995 to reduce barriers to trade and investment beyond what had already been agreed in the Uruguay Round of GATT. The move made economic sense as Europe and the United States produced over half of all global goods and services. As President Clinton told the people of Berlin in 1998, transatlantic commerce was already "the largest economic relationship in the world, encompassing more than half a trillion US dollars each year, supporting millions of jobs in both America and Europe . . . Europe's investment in America has now created so many jobs that one of twelve US factory workers is employed by a European-owned firm."[72]

Beyond Europe, the Pacific Rim was vitally important to the prosperity promotion element of Clinton's Grand Strategy. When the administration came to power, Asia-Pacific was the world's fastest growing economic region. Asia had accounted for just 8 percent of the world's gross domestic product in the 1960s, a figure that jumped to 25 percent by 1994, as Asian economies grew at three times the rate of established industrial nations.[73] The Clinton administration announced that the United States, Mexico, and Canada were key members of the Asia-Pacific Economic region, enabling the White House to identify the region as accounting for half of the world's GDP and a third of the global population. The administration convened the first APEC summit in November 1993 to "open new opportunities for economic co-operation and commit US companies to become involved in substantial infrastructure planning and construction" in the area as it sought to promote "open regionalism."[74]

Since 1989 US exports to Asian nations had increased by over 50 percent and, by 1994, US exports to APEC economies accounted for $300 billion, supporting nearly 2.6 million American jobs. By 1995, US investments in the APEC region reached in excess of $140 million, almost one-third of all US direct foreign investment.[75] By 1996, 60 percent of US merchandise exports went to APEC economies and half of these went to Asian countries.[76] The influence of the APEC economies was felt most evidently in California, Washington, and Oregon, where sales to Asia accounted for more than half of each state's total exports.[77] Between 1989 and 1994, US exports to many Asian nations increased by 50 percent or more as Asia became America's largest trading partner, with exports accounting for 2.5 million American jobs. With such figures at stake, the change of heart on China's MFN status becomes understandable: "Three decades ago, Asia had only 8% of the world's gross domestic product. Today it exceeds 25%."[78] Understandably, a prosperous and freely trading Asia Pacific region was key to the economic health of the United States.

The Clinton administration envisioned a New Pacific Community, "cementing America's role as a stabilizing force in a more integrated Asia Pacific region."[79] At the second APEC summit, leaders agreed in principle to "free and open trade and investment throughout the region by early in the twenty-first century," as the administration continued to lock the United States into the heart of free trading areas.[80] Doing so enabled the United States to benefit from and exert influence over, the organization and the region, with the pragmatic aspect of grand strategy never being far from the surface. In 1999, the administration acknowledged that US initiatives in APEC promised "new opportunities for economic cooperation and [would] permit US companies to expand their involvement in substantial infrastructure planning and construction throughout the region."[81] The administration, therefore, continued to utilize foreign initiatives to assist the domestic economy late in its term.

US Grand Strategy reflected the domestic requirements of the administration as the White House increased exports to the APEC region "through market-opening measures and levelling the playing field for US business."[82] During the administration's 8 years in office, its grand strategy in the region remained consistent in purpose, based on the premise that "a stable and prosperous East Asia and Pacific" was vital to US national security interests. Despite regional economic crises, the administration continued to advocate its approach of "promoting democracy and human rights, advancing economic integration and rules-based trade and enhancing security" on the basis that the three pillar approach was "mutually reinforcing" and provided a framework for its bilateral and multilateral initiatives in Asia.[83]

NAFTA and APEC were examples of the United States locking itself into the global economy, at the heart of the global structures that dictated the future direction of global trade. The initiatives allowed the administration to unite domestic growth with a foreign policy that advocated free trade and US exports. It was this concept of linking foreign policy to domestic renewal that most appealed to the president. This was the establishment of an international core, including "the major industrial democracies of Europe, North America and East Asia—a community of states with stable governments, liberal societies and advanced market economies, linked by security alliances, economic interdependence and a variety of multilateral governance institutions."[84] Through its utilization of international trading blocks, the Clinton administration locked the United States into closer trading positions than had been achieved previously and positioned the United States for the twenty-first century.

Prosperity promotion and multilateral organizations

The second aspect of the Clinton administration's structural approach to prosperity promotion was to utilize and influence a series of multilateral organizations including the IMF, the WTO, and the World Bank. These relationships proved to be essential for the economic revitalization the president envisaged for the United States and formed an essential element of US Grand Strategy. However, it would not be enough to passively participate in such organizations; the United States actively sought to influence them and the list of organizations grew during the Clinton years. The concept of seeking multinational solutions was a continuation of policy espoused on the 1992 campaign and was enshrined in grand strategy: "Whether the problem is nuclear proliferation, regional instability, the reversal of reform in the former Soviet empire, or unfair trade practices, the threats and challenges we face demand cooperative, multinational solutions." The administration was forthright in its assertion that, "The only responsible US strategy is one that seeks to ensure US influence over and participation in collective decision making in a wide and growing range of circumstances."[85]

Despite widespread criticism for Clinton's multilateral approach to military engagement, it was in the economic sphere that the administration's true multilateral intentions were most evident. Yet here, too, there were concerns about the manner in which the policies were perceived. Tara Sonenshine, Deputy Director of Communications at the NSC, noted, "the reality is that our administration has come to rely more and more on global, international, multilateral institutions and mechanisms for addressing world problems." This, she explained was not a problem. However, she feared that the administration had "failed to explain why and how we view these institutions and the role of American leadership both in driving these bodies to act, and reforming them in ways that increase their effectiveness."[86] For the most part, however, the success of this endeavor mitigated any perceived doubts about the viability of Clinton's aspirations in this area.

The administration benefited from excellent timing with respect to economic affairs. It came to power partly due to a mild recession that was effectively over by the time it took office, but which had undermined confidence in the Bush administration. Clinton also inherited a number of negotiation positions that had been initiated during the Bush years. The president's team successfully continued these negotiations to their eventual implementation, enabling the administration to make a series of rapid developments by building on existing foundations. Chief among these were the NAFTA deal and the conclusion of the Uruguay Round of GATT that led to the establishment of the WTO. Clinton argued that the GATT agreement "not only tears down trade barriers, it also bulldozes differences of party, philosophy and ideology . . . It is an American agreement, designed to benefit all the American people in every region of our country from every walk of life."[87]

The Uruguay Round of the General Agreement on Tariffs and Trade was concluded in December 1993 at the end of the Clinton administration's first year in office. It was hailed as "the largest, most comprehensive trade agreement in history," that promised to create "hundreds of thousands of new US jobs and expand opportunities for US businesses."[88] The deal resulted in the establishment of the WTO, designed to provide a forum for dispute resolution. The administration anticipated that the new entity would add $100–200 billion and hundreds of thousands of jobs each year to the US economy, as well as "provide a new institutional lever" for securing access to new markets.[89] The Uruguay Round had another unexpected impact according to administration insiders. At a meeting on the issue President Clinton said, "you know, I'm starting to get this!" Charles A. Kupchan recalls "the light bulb going on and him starting to show deepening interest and knowledge and passion for foreign policy issues."[90] The agreement had an impact above and beyond the president's own comfort levels in foreign affairs; however, even administration critic Richard Haass conceded that the WTO "provided a set of rules to govern important areas of world trade and a mechanism for resolving disputes among member countries."[91]

It was clear that the Clinton administration did not see itself as a mere member of the WTO, but as the driving force promoting progressive change, particularly with regard to the admission of new member states. In 1997, it insisted that it was "setting high standards for accession in terms of adherence to the rules and market access. Accessions offer an opportunity to help ground new economies in the rules-based trading system."[92] In this respect, no nations were more prominent than China and Russia. At the start of its second term, the administration insisted that it was in America's interest that China join the WTO, but remained "steadfast" in its effort to ensure China's membership occurred on "a commercial basis." This was because China retained "many barriers that must be eliminated" and the administration sought to ensure that necessary reforms were agreed to before accession occurred. Similarly, the administration believed that Russia's accession to the WTO would play a "crucial part in confirming and assuring Russia's transition to a market economy, enhanced competitiveness and successful integration into the world economy."[93] Such statements revealed the multidimensional approach that was necessary to global trade initiatives in the post-Cold War world, as the United States sought to deal with nations via multilateral organizations, as well as on more traditional, bilateral terms.

Bilateral agreements

The third component of the Clinton administration's structural approach to prosperity promotion was bilateral agreements, enacted with key trading partners including Japan. When the Clinton administration came to power, Japan was America's second largest export market. At his first news conference with Japan's Prime Minister Kiichi Miyazawa, Clinton insisted "there is no more important relationship for the United States than our alliance with Japan. We are the world's largest economies, with forty percent of the world's GNP between us."[94] Despite this, tensions simmered over the difficulties involved in accessing key sectors of the Japanese domestic market. The concept of Japan-bashing emerged during the Bush era as the US domestic economic situation soured. During the 1992 campaign, Democrats and Republican attempted to gain national prominence by blaming Japan for the US economic slowdown.[95] In addition, Japan's current-account surpluses created problems in the global economy.

Accordingly, the Clinton administration viewed moves to address the trade imbalance with Japan as a priority in its first years in office and continued efforts that had been initiated by the Bush White House. Following years of trade wars, the prosperity promotion aspect of grand strategy sought to ensure that such skirmishes were as much a part of history as the Cold War. Despite initial tensions that led to questions over the administration's commitment to a multilateral trading system—with former US ambassador to Japan Michael H. Armacost lamenting that "trade frictions generated mistrust and resentment that threatened to contaminate our security relations," US Grand Strategy recognized Japan as a major target for prosperity promotion in the 1990s.[96] Accordingly the administration sought to ensure that "competitive American goods and services" gained access to the Japanese market and sought to ensure that opening its markets stimulated the Japanese economy "both to benefit its own people and to fulfil its international responsibilities."[97]

In July 1993, the Clinton administration and Japanese Prime Minister Miyazawa established the US–Japan Framework for Economic Partnership, designed to address outstanding issues of trade imbalance. By the end of Clinton's first term, 20 market access agreements had been reached under the Framework Agreement that included medical technologies and insurance, as US exports to Japan in these sectors doubled.[98] Between 1993 and 1996, US exports to Japan increased from $47.9 billion to $67.6 billion while the bilateral trade deficit fell from $59.4 billion to $47.6 billion.[99] By 1999, the United States and Japan had signed 38 agreements to open Japan further to American goods and services.[100]

The bargaining position of the United States was enhanced by an economic downturn in the Japanese economy. Having entered the 1990s with a vibrant economy that appeared capable of dominating for decades to come, Japan suffered an ignominious collapse: the bilateral trade deficit with the United States for the first four months of 1998 rose to $20.8 billion, up 32 percent from the same period in 1996. By 1998, US Grand Strategy advocated reform of Japan's financial sector, efforts to stimulate domestic demand, the deregulation of its economy, and greater efforts to open its markets to US goods and services.[101] This combination of a domestic demand-led recovery, a restored financial sector, and deregulation coupled with greater US access to markets defined US Grand Strategy toward Japan in the second term of the Clinton administration.

Prosperity promotion in the post-Cold War world

While Cold War tensions had subsided, the world faced by the Clinton administration was far from stable. The collapse of communism ushered in an era of instability and opened a Pandora's Box of regional conflicts. As the president noted in his Inaugural Address, his administration governed "in a world warmed by the sunshine of freedom but threatened still by ancient hatreds and new plagues."[102] While the administration wanted to enhance the US domestic economy by increasing exports, it recognized the potential dangers involved in selling certain technologies to foreign nations. As a leading manufacturer of technology with potential military applications, the United States was mindful to avoid these products being used by states or organizations in a manner that could threaten American national security. The debate resulted in divisions within the administration over the best course of action: "The Commerce Department actually was constantly trying to argue that foreign direct investment by the United States was the best foreign policy. It was basically the Labor Department verses the Commerce Department verses the Defense and State Department. Defense were worried about Chinese access to technology."[103]

However, it also noted that placing "excessive restrictions" on such exports in a competitive global market did not limit the availability of such goods, but would instead "make US high technology companies less competitive globally, thus losing market share and becoming less able to produce cutting-edge products for the US military and our allies." Clearly, a balance was required in regard to dual-use technology that enabled US sales to flourish overseas while ensuring that export controls continued to protect US national security—without making American companies less competitive globally. This represented a challenge for a nation that led the world in defense contractors, whose sales helped to sustain the domestic economy in key congressional districts and who were themselves part of a corporate structure that included influential media corporations.

Clinton's Grand Strategy resulted in the signing of the Information Technology Agreement to remove tariffs on technology exports, as well as increased US cooperation through the Nuclear Suppliers Group, the Missile Technology Control Regime, the Zangger Committee, the Australia Group for the control of chemical and biological weapons-related items, and the Wassenaar Arrangement for greater transparency in conventional arms transfers.[104] These initiatives were part of a coordinated grand strategy to open markets, restrict WMD proliferation, and ensure US manufacturers remained competitive.

Clinton's Grand Strategy recognized that the US economy was susceptible to events overseas and sought not only to improve the economy of the United States, but also to improve global macroeconomic performance through the G7. The initial aspiration was to initiate a growth strategy by complementing a reduced US budget deficit with lower German interest rates and reduced current account surpluses in Japan. The administration believed that working at a macroeconomic level increased the ability "to prevent and mitigate international financial crises."[105] Indeed, it was the effort to address developing economic turmoil that most drove policy in this area. The administration recognized that although the influence of globalization provided new opportunities for the American economy, it also exposed the US financial markets to increased risks from overseas, with the ensuing dangers to the US domestic economy that the administration had won office pledging to fix: "Global economic turmoil today threatens to undermine confidence in free markets and democracy. Those of us who benefit particularly from this economy have a special responsibility to do more to minimize the turmoil and extend the benefits of global markets to all citizens."[106] Prosperity promotion, therefore, included a decidedly pragmatic domestic element, designed to ensure that the administration did not suffer politically due to foreign economic incidents beyond its control.

In this approach to policy, it is possible to recognize the rationale for the grand strategy's declared policy of seeking to exert control over an ever-increasing number of international entities: control meant the power to influence and direct policy in the best interest of the administration and the United States. By 1998, American unemployment stood at a 28-year low and inflation at a 32-year low. Wages were rising at twice the rate of inflation and the budget was balanced for the fist time in 29 years.[107] Despite such positive results, President Clinton remained vigilant, reminding the nation that it must "never lose sight of what the fundamental problem is—we need . . . more growth in this world today."[108] The Clinton administration believed that its implementation of grand strategy contributed to the establishment of a "stable, resilient global financial system" designed to promote "strong global economic growth while providing broad benefits in all countries."[109] Clinton's Grand Strategy was devised to ensure that the future was one of free trade, so that the United States could thrive, but also the world as well: "As the world's premier economic and military power and its premier practitioner of democratic values, the US is indispensable to the forging of stable political relations and open trade."[110] By 1999, the administration saw itself as being involved in nothing less than the "worldwide transition from military industrial economies reliant upon government capitol to information-based economies reliant on intellectual capital."[111]

Global implementation

Beyond the structural approaches to prosperity promotion, Clinton's Grand Strategy contained a series of philosophical elements, based around the concept of Free Trade and Free Markets. The principle of free trade was at the core of Clinton's concept of security. The White House acknowledged that the post-Cold War world demanded that economics, rather than military power, become the most efficient tool to implement US global leverage. It was in this light that the administration's focus on NAFTA, GATT, APEC, and the US–EU Transatlantic Marketplace must be viewed; not merely as financial entities, but as vehicles to expand US values and interests in the new geopolitical era. The implementation of these initiatives represented "unprecedented progress towards more open markets both at the regional and global levels."[112]

The Clinton administration was determined that its grand strategy should accurately reflect the varying challenges and opportunities presented by contemporary conditions. Clinton's team addressed each continent individually to determine how best to implement US strategy and whether one or more of the three components should be prioritized. Clearly, some regions posed more of a challenge than others in allocating resources and priorities. Clinton's Grand Strategy had an overriding goal in terms of implementation: how to integrate a "commitment to the promotion of democracy and the enhancement of American prosperity" with the "security requirements to produce a mutually reinforcing policy."[113] However, a quarter of the world's population was declining in growth, causing Alan Greenspan to observe that the United States "cannot forever be an oasis of prosperity." Indeed, 30 percent of US growth since Clinton became president had been due to expanding involvement in the global economy.[114] America's ability to offer aid and trade during the Cold War was a key facet in its arsenal of soft powers; however, its slide from being the world's greatest creditor to the world's greatest debtor nation had undermined this resource. Emerging democracies may have preferred greater financial assistance, but the US budget deficit tied Clinton's hands and the funds were simply not available to initiate a latter day Marshall Plan.

Western Europe

US Grand Strategy in Europe was primarily focused on building a continent that was "integrated, democratic, prosperous and at peace."[115] Having been a driving force for closer European integration since the Marshal Plan, the United States continued to promote closer political and economic ties on the European continent. The Clinton administration appreciated the importance of European stability to US national and economic security, since "vibrant European economies mean more jobs for Americans at home and investment opportunities abroad."[116] Economically, Europe was vital to the economic expansion element of US Grand Strategy, since what was good for Europe was seen to be good for the United States: "If Europe is at peace, America is more secure. If Europe prospers, America does as well."[117] Together the United States and Europe were responsible for the production of almost half of all global goods and services, while Transatlantic commerce employed 14 million on both sides of the Atlantic—with Europe accounting for more than 60 percent of US overseas investment.[118]

The administration sought to continue its work with the European Union in support of its economic goals and was also committed to "the encouragement of bilateral trade and investment in countries not part of the EU."[119] The Clinton administration recognized the opportunity for prosperity promotion in a developing European Union that was seeking to establish itself on the world stage. Just as US Grand Strategy sought to lock the US economy into an ever-increasing number of economic entities, so too was it designed to ensure closer economic cooperation with regional trading blocks and none loomed larger than the European Union. With the nations of Central and Eastern Europe free of Soviet domination, the European Union faced calls to expand, a move the Clinton administration openly supported, so long as it was "appropriate" and welcomed the European Union's Customs Union with Turkey.[120]

However, the recession that had contributed to Clinton's victory also impacted Europe, ensuring that economic conditions were far from ideal as the continent continued to integrate. Britain, France, and Germany were all undergoing economic difficulties, with almost 20 million unemployed across the continent. The price of peace was felt most clearly in Germany, which bore the financial burden of national unification. The Clinton administration recognized the economic plight of Western Europe and sought to reduce unemployment and promote long-term growth, holding a jobs conference in Detroit in March 1994 and a G7 summit in Naples in July 1994 to address the issue.[121]

The most significant manifestation of US–EU relations in the Clinton years was the December 1995 launch of the New Transatlantic Agenda, designed to enhance US–EU relations "from consultation to joint action on a range of shared interests, including promoting peace, stability, democracy and development; responding to global challenges; and contributing to the expansion of world trade and closer economic relations."[122] This led to the establishment of New Transatlantic Marketplace, designed to reduce barriers to trade and investment, as well as the establishment of the Transatlantic Business Dialogue, Transatlantic Consumer Dialogue, Transatlantic Environment Dialogue, and Transatlantic Labor Dialogue.[123] The US–EU Mutual Recognition Agreement eliminated "redundant testing and certification requirements covering $50 billion in two-way trade."[124] Such initiatives were designed to ensure continued dialogue aimed at lowering and eradicating barriers to increased US–EU trade and cooperation. Richard Holbrooke observed at the time that leaders had "to lead to break through the layers of ambivalence, confusion, complacence and history that inhibit reforms. As the great architect of European unity, Jean Monnet, observed, 'Nothing is possible without men, but nothing is lasting without institutions.'"[125]

On May 18, 1998, the Clinton administration launched the Transatlantic Economic Partnership, designed to strengthen economic and political relations, as well as diminish trade disagreements that had arisen in a number of bilateral relations with EU member states. The partnership addressed issues raised by US companies trading with the European Union, focusing on standards of manufacturing and regulatory issues for biotechnology while seeking to create opportunities for US service industries in Europe.[126] In January 1999, the Clinton administration welcomed the launch of the Euro currency, noting "the steady progress that Europe has demonstrated in taking the often difficult budget decisions that make this union possible" and insisting that "a successful economic union that contributes to a dynamic Europe" was in US interests.[127] More broadly, US Grand Strategy in Europe focused on working to meet a series of contemporary challenges, including ways to "build a more open world economy and without barriers to transatlantic trade and investment."[128] It was clear that the administration remained committed to "a very rich, active transatlantic agenda."[129]

Central, Eastern Europe, and Russia

The malaise that was felt in Western Europe could not dampen the euphoria that was evident in Central and Eastern Europe, where the end of the Cold War was most clearly felt. This region of the world presented perhaps the greatest opportunity for full implementation of the US Grand Strategy of Engagement and Enlargement. The Soviet withdrawal enhanced US national security; the end of command economies granted opportunities for prosperity promotion; while the collapse of communism presented opportunities for democracy promotion. This was identified as early as 1994 when the administration noted its "unparalleled opportunity to contribute toward a free and undivided Europe." Its goal was "an integrated democratic Europe co-operating with the United States to keep the peace and promote prosperity."[130] However, there was more to grand strategy than American largesse. Prosperity promotion, the most mercantile element of US Grand Strategy, continued to emphasize the pragmatic philosophy of the Clinton White House: "As we work to strengthen our own economies, we must know that we serve our own prosperity and our security by helping the new market reforms in the new democracies in Europe's East that will help to deflate the regions demagogues."[131]

The prosperity promotion aspect of US Grand Strategy was dedicated to ensuring that the economies of the Newly Independent States (NIS) were able to integrate into "international economic and other institutions and develop healthy business climates."[132] The administration declared that the "independence, sovereignty, territorial integrity and democratic and economic reform" of the NIS were important to US interests as it actively pursued bilateral relationships as well as the leadership of international institutions to mobilize resources.[133] Primary among these organizations was the WTO, which the administration worked with to ensure accession by Kyrgyzstan, Latvia, and Estonia, in addition to advocating membership for Georgia, Albania, Armenia, Croatia, Lithuania and Moldova, Russia, and Ukraine.

Among the former Soviet states, Ukraine was identified by the administration as being of specific importance. US Grand Strategy sought to rid the nation of a perceived lawlessness that threatened international principles of the marketplace and impeded efforts to implement democratic governance. The US–Ukraine Bi-National Commission was established to coordinate relations and encourage reform. The administration focused its energies on encouraging international support for Ukrainian efforts to reform its economy and energy sector, a move dominated by the closure of the Chernobyl nuclear facility. To succeed, Ukraine needed to attract foreign sources of investment to engender domestic growth and to integrate into the European, transatlantic, and global economic institutions.[134] To assist in this effort, the Clinton administration took the lead in "securing agreement by the G-7 to make available four billion dollars in grants and loans as Ukraine implemented economic reform."[135]

The evolving nature of US Grand Strategy was apparent in its focus on the Caspian Sea region. Stability in this part of the world was viewed as essential, delivering "security from the Mediterranean to China," as well as enabling the "rapid development and transport to international markets of the large Caspian oil and gas resources, with substantial US commercial participation."[136] On November 18, 1999, President Clinton attended the signing of the Baku-Tbilisi-Ceyhan pipeline agreement and the Trans-Caspian Gas Pipeline Declaration in Istanbul, both initiatives designed to bring oil and gas out of the Caspian region as environmentally as possible. US Grand Strategy in the Caspian was driven by economics but this move fully embraced the three-strand approach to foreign policy as espoused repeatedly by Governor Clinton since December 1991. In addition to the economic benefits that US companies would derive from the pipelines and energy supplies, the administration believed the process promised to draw together the Caspian nations of Azerbaijan, Turkey, Georgia, Kazakhstan, and Turkmenistan and encourage them to work together for the betterment of all, increase potential market penetration and opportunities for democracy promotion.

The administration sought to encourage US investment in the region's energy resources for "expanding and diversifying world energy supplies and promoting prosperity in the NIS."[137] The approach to the NIS continued the Clinton administration's three-pronged strategy: support for market reform in Central and Eastern Europe and the NIS promised to "help new democracies take root by avoiding conditions, such as corruption and poverty, that can weaken democratic governance and erode the appeal of democratic values."[138] The administration identified Poland as typifying the "new dynamism and rapid growth that extensive, democratic, free market reforms" that US Grand Strategy had made possible.[139] To this end, the White House sponsored a Trade and Investment Conference for Central and Eastern Europe in Cleveland in January 1995 and worked to encourage inward investment by private US organizations.[140] The administration recognized, however, that the fate of its grand strategy toward Europe would not be decided in Cleveland. Instead, "the circumstances affecting the smaller countries depend in significant measure on the fate of reform in the largest and most powerful—Russia."

Of all the individual nations in the world, none encompassed US hopes and fears more clearly than Russia and no other nation better epitomized the ambitions of US Grand Strategy and its three-strand approach of national security, prosperity promotion, and democracy promotion. Clinton had pledged to continue the emergency aid programs to Russia that President Bush had launched, including food for vast regions that were on the brink starvation, but realized this was not enough. The Russian people may have had political reform, but market reform was proving desperately hard to implement, ensuring that Russians were beginning to question the benefit of the entire reform movement; the ability to vote suddenly appeared less pressing compared to the ability to eat. Clinton saw the situation in Russia as a looming storm that threatened global economic and security assumptions. The end of the Cold War had already led to cuts in defense expenditures and a reduction in perceived threat levels; a potential collapse of the Yeltsin regime and a return to a hardline Russian government placed all such developments in doubt. However, given his domestic priorities and weak electoral mandate, President Clinton's ability to seek increased congressional funding for Russia was minimal.

The administration stressed that while it would "continue to promote Russian reform and international integration," US economic and political support depended on Russia's "commitment to internal reform and a responsible foreign policy."[141] To help engender economic relations, the Clinton administration liberalized controls on computer exports in September 1993 and eliminated controls on most civilian telecommunications equipment to Central and Eastern Europe, the NIS, and China in March 1994.[142] Reducing trade barriers was a tangible way in which Clinton's Grand Strategy could assist in the economic liberation of Russia and the NIS. With limited funds for an economic bailout, the administration recognized that "The success of market reforms in the countries recently emerged from communism will depend more on trade and investment than official aid."

Despite its fiscal restraints, the Clinton administration provided $4.3 billion in bilateral assistance to Russia during its first term. US Grand Strategy assisted in the rehabilitation of Russia by fighting inflation and stabilizing the ruble, ensuing that by 1997 over 70 percent of Russia's Gross Domestic Product was generated by the private sector.[143] Grand strategy ensured that the United States became Russia's largest foreign investor, with commercial transactions valued at more than $4 billion, as US–Russian trade rose 65 percent.[144] By the end of Clinton's first term in office, more than 120,000 Russian enterprises had been transferred to private hands as grand strategy committed the United States to assisting Yeltsin transform Russian society. The policy helped Russia to privatize more property in less time than any other foreign development venture in history and such developments, coupled with the 1996 elections, led the administration to believe that a new era may have arrived in Russia. The Clinton administration sought to ensure that Russia could not return to a command economy and perhaps nowhere better demonstrated what Leon Fuerth referred to as the Ratchet Principle of Clinton's Grand Strategy.[145]

The long-term logic of this approach was highlighted in 1998 as Russia faced an economic crisis. On August 17, Moscow announced that it was devaluing the ruble, imposing a moratorium on bank-held loans and defaulting on its short-term treasury bills. The stock market plummeted as the government struggled to pay its debts and salaries. Talk emerged of Russia having "abandoning the path of reform and returning to policies of the past, even policies that have already failed." Such prospects carried obvious threats to the West, since the situation threatened "not only the Russian economy and prospects for our economic cooperation—at worst, it could have an impact on our cooperation with Russia on nuclear disarmament, on fighting terrorism and the spread of weapons of mass destruction."[146] The circumstances caused the IMF and World Bank to shelve a $17 billion aid package, but the Clinton administration continued to work with the Kremlin "toward passage of key economic and commercial legislation," as it strove to promote "American investment and Russia's integration into various international economic institutions."[147] As the president observed, "never has there been a more important moment to set a clear direction for the future, to affirm the commitment of Russia to democracy and to free markets and to take decisive steps to stabilize the economy and restore investor confidence."[148]

Relations were conducted at the highest levels of government, with Presidents Clinton and Yeltsin developing a relationship based on mutual appreciation of the other's past and political predicament. In addition, the Gore-Chernomyrdin Commission ensured that the United States and Russia collaborated in the vital areas of defense, trade, and science and technology.[149] Despite the progress, the Clinton administration recognized that much remained to be done in order to build on the reform momentum of the Yeltsin years and ensure continued economic recovery coupled with enhanced democratic freedoms. Grand strategy committed the United States to continue to "promote political and economic reform in Russia, working to create a thriving market economy while guarding against corruption."[150] Clinton sought a strategy to help Russia become, "a going concern within ten years."[151] Such an exercise was more than the United States could achieve alone, however, and required sweeping internal reform and external assistance on an unprecedented scale, all at a time of widespread economic retraction. As on a range of issues, President Clinton discovered the limits of American power as his aspirations confronted political expediency and Russia became "a fifty-year problem, not a five-year problem," in which the administration could not have imagined "how much the kleptocracy would grab on as fast as it did."[152] As the Clinton administration prepared to leave office, it reminded the new occupants of the White House and the Kremlin that only "by supporting historic market reforms in these areas, we help new democracies take root by avoiding conditions, such as corruption and poverty, that can weaken democratic governance and erode the appeal of democratic values."[153]

China

The Clinton administration believed that China provided the perfect justification for its grand strategy of national security, prosperity promotion, and democracy promotion, since "the emergence of a politically stable, economically open and secure China is in America's interest."[154]

The administration's primary method for achieving its ambitions was economically driven as it sought to integrate China into the world economic system and gain access to its internal markets by lowering border barriers and removing restraints on economic activity.[155] The Clinton administration sought to use US capitol to leverage access and political reform in China: "America must look to the East no less than to the West. Our security demands it . . . Our prosperity requires it. More than 2 million American jobs depend upon trade with Asia. There, too, we are helping to shape an Asia–Pacific community of cooperation, not conflict."[156] The results, however, were decidedly mixed.

China had featured prominently during the 1992 campaign, as Governor Clinton lamented President Bush for "coddling dictators" and moving too quickly to stabilize relations after the Tiananmen Square protests. As John Brummett noted, Clinton "talked tough about removing China's MFN status if it did not change its ways in violating human rights and suppressing its people, but that was an irresponsible, self-penalising idea from which he not so subtly retreated once elected."[157] The Clinton campaign pledged to make China's continued MFN trading status dependent on changes to its human rights laws, an approach that continued in office until the White House recognized the futility of such a stance. The Chinese made it abundantly clear that they were not going to change their stance on the issue and so the administration capitulated, since it "could not get them to budge on human rights."[158] The White House presented the move as a victory that granted "American farmers, businesses and industries with market access to the world's most populous nation."[159] It was, however, a reversal of policy and a climb-down for the administration in the face of unwillingness by the Chinese to negotiate on the situation.

Announcing the shift in policy on May 28, 1993, the Clinton administration noted that China held an important place in US foreign policy: "Its future will do much to shape the future of Asia, our security and trade relations in the Pacific and a host of global issues from the environment to weapons proliferation. In short, our relationship with China is of very great importance." The White House insisted on its commitment "to supporting peaceful democratic and pro-market reform" in China and was "hopeful" that China's "process of development and economic reform will be accompanied by greater political freedom." The administration drew inspiration from the efforts of Governor Patten in Hong Kong, identified as "a catalyst of democratic values."[160] That view was reiterated a year later when the president stressed he was "supporting Governor Patten's efforts to have a genuine, long-term strategy for economic and political success in Hong Kong."[161] Such efforts reinforced President Clinton's assertion that "stability can no longer be bought at the expense of liberty . . . The more we bring China into the world, the more the world will bring change and freedom to China."[162] Finally, on May 24, 2000, the House of

Representatives voted 237 to 197 to approve normal trade relations with China. Only 73 of the 237 votes came from Democrats, so the bill passed due to the support of Republicans who only months before had sought to remove Clinton from office; "Clinton achieved a major victory, consistent with his tactic of using trade to promote political and economic ends."[163]

In keeping with overall grand strategy, the Clinton administration sought to develop an engagement with China that encompassed "economic and strategic interests." The administration recognized the economic benefits to be derived from China's development of "a more open market economy that accepts international trade practices."[164] Doing so, the administration maintained, was in the US national interest and, therefore, it pursued bilateral trade negotiations with China on a range of issues, relating to market access and intellectual property rights, which many in the United States believed were being widely abused. The challenge, as identified by Samuel Berger, was "to steer between the extremes of uncritical engagement and untenable confrontation."[165] The eventual bilateral agreement on intellectual property rights promised to save US companies billions of dollars in revenues lost because of piracy.

A key goal of US Grand Strategy in regard to China was its membership of the WTO on "commercial terms."[166] These terms were not for the benefit of China, but for nations such as the United States that wanted to do business there, since a " stable, open, prosperous China, shouldering its responsibilities for a safer world, is good for America."[167] In 1997, it was agreed that China's "full participation in the multilateral trading system" was in both county's interest.[168] When China's membership of the WTO was finally agreed upon, the administration hailed the decision as "a landmark accord."[169] Second-term National Security Adviser, Sandy Berger referred to the agreement as "the most constructive breakthrough in US–China relations since normalization in 1979."[170] Membership of the WTO promised to create opportunities as Chinese markets opened, encouraged economic reform, and enhanced "the understanding of the Chinese people of the rule of law in the development of their domestic civil society in compliance with international obligations."[171]

Clinton's Grand Strategy appreciated that China was a vital market for US goods and services and that exports would support hundreds of thousands of jobs across the United States. To ensure that the US domestic economy continued to thrive via exports to the burgeoning Chinese market, Clinton's Grand Strategy prioritized the removal of "distorting restraints on economic activity" and China's full integration into the market-based world economic system.[172] As with so many aspects of Clinton's Grand Strategy, there was a long-term goal involved in its approach to China. The administration was eager to determine "whether true economic growth will create a large middle class in China; whether the presence of a large middle class spurs democratic reforms because people who are educated want to be participants."[173] The success or failure of such an approach would necessarily be decades in the deciding. Undeniably, however, the US–Chinese relationship developed considerably during the Clinton years to one of "openness and candour." This is not to say that both sides were always in agreement, but it became possible to "speak openly and honestly in an effort to understand our differences and, if possible, to work toward a common approach to resolving them."[174]

The Western hemisphere

The passage of NAFTA, the completion of GATT, and the Summit of the Americas all represented "unprecedented progress toward more open markets both at the regional and global levels" in the Western hemisphere.[175] Progress in this area was a viable option due to the apparent end of armed conflicts, particularly in Central America, which the administration hoped was a turning point. Drawing a line between the various elements of its grand strategy, the Clinton administration observed that "sustained improvements in the security situation there . . . will be an essential underpinning of political and economic progress in the hemisphere."[176] The administration believed that many of the positive developments in the Western hemisphere were due to the economic and trade policies that had been initiated since the administration had come to power: by 1998, Latin America became the world's fastest growing economic region and the US's fastest growing export market, as exports to Latin America and the Caribbean were expected to exceed those to the European Union.[177]

The Clinton administration presented the NAFTA agreement as one of its most important foreign policy achievements—not merely an economic policy success—as it embraced all three components of US Grand Strategy: national security, prosperity promotion, and democracy promotion. Indeed, the administration believed that the growth of market economies in the region offered "an unparalleled opportunity to secure the benefits of peace and stability and to promote economic growth and trade."[178] As a result, the administration hosted the Summit of the Americas in Miami in December 1994, at which the hemisphere's 34 democratic nations pledged to negotiate the FTAA by 2005. President Clinton pledged "a more mature and cooperative relationship with the hemisphere" as the summit agreed on areas including counter-narcotics and anti-corruption, health, education, environmental protection, and the strengthening of democratic institutions. The ensuing Summit Action Plan resulted in increased activity between government agencies in the United States and in Central and Latin America on issues relating to finance and the environment.[179]

The biggest crisis the administration faced in the Western hemisphere was in regard to the Mexican Peso crisis of 1994/1995. Coming less than a year after NAFTA was implemented, the collapse of the Mexican economy confirmed the worst fears of those who had opposed the trade agreement and the policy implications that came with it. Fears grew that a contagion could be triggered, resulting in financial crisis in the Western hemisphere and possibly beyond. It was, perhaps, a stroke of good fortune that this crisis related to finance, allowing the president to act with a confidence that may have been lacking in a military operation. As their currency reserves fell to $3.5 billion, the Mexican government requested a loan of $40 billion from the United States, a figure that met with fierce opposition on Capitol Hill and among the general population, with 80 percent of Americans voicing their opposition to the bailout.[180]

The Clinton administration, however, supported the efforts of Mexican President Zedillo and the economic program he devised to rectify the situation, which gained the support of the IMF.[181] Speaking on January 18, 1995, President Clinton referred to the coalition of forces that initially supported a bipartisan agreement as being "significant; it may be historic," as he and the leaders of both parties in Congress and the Chairman of the Federal Reserve Board agreed to a rescue package. Such a deal, the president stressed, would be a guarantee, "not foreign aid . . . not a gift . . . not a bailout."[182] In his State of the Union address that month, President Clinton acknowledged the opposition to the deal, but insisted that action was required "not for the Mexican people but for the sake of the millions of Americans whose livelihoods are tied to Mexico's well-being."[183] American jobs, exports, and the safety of its borders were at risk. However, despite the support of the bipartisan leadership, members of Congress sought to attach a series of conditions to any bailout, including demands that Mexico increase border security, destroying any potential agreement.

Instead, on February 21, the White House released $20 billion from the Exchange Stabilization Fund to the Government of Mexico and the Bank of Mexico.[184] Revenues from crude oil exports and other petrol-based products were used to guarantee these loans. In addition, the United States required Mexico to maintain the value of peso deposits with the United States, ensuring that if the value of the peso dropped against the US dollar, Mexico would be required to further compensate the United States.[185] The IMF increased its contribution to $17.8 billion and several other central banks increased their participation to $10 billion.[186] Despite criticism from Rush Limbaugh for "giving away our money and taking away our rights," the deal turned out well for all involved.[187] By June 1996, Mexico had repaid three-quarters of its debt and US exports to Mexico had exceeded their 1994 postings by 11 percent.[188] Several months later, at his 1997 State of the Union, the newly reelected President Clinton was able to announce that Mexico had completed its loan repayment, 3 years ahead of schedule, with half-a-billion dollars profit to the United States.[189] Even Richard Haass, a noted critic of the Clinton White House, was forced to concede in his assessment of the administration that this constituted an "economic achievement" that had "rescued Mexico from an economic meltdown."[190]

While the administration secured a vital economic success, however, the congressional backlash contributed to the removal of the Presidential Fast Track negotiating authority with significant and far-reaching implications for US Grand Strategy.

Across the continent, the growing popularity and increasing availability of the internet, as championed by the Clinton administration, ensured that the peoples of the Western hemisphere could take increasing advantage of the opportunities created as markets became "connected through electronic commerce and as robust democracies allow individuals to more fully express their preferences."[191] The support for the internet revealed the grand strategy's interconnected nature as technology promoted trading opportunities for US companies in overseas markets and championed direct democratic participation by citizens in the hope of encouraging pro-Western governments and increased US national security. By 1998, President Clinton noted that the United States had been founded at a time of "enormous economic upheaval when the world was beginning to move from an agrarian to an industrial economy." He recognized that the world was "drawing up the blueprints for a new economic age," which could design "the architecture for a global economic marketplace, with stable laws, strong protections for consumers, serious incentives for competition, a marketplace to include all people and all nations."[192] It was clear how the Western hemisphere stood to benefit in such circumstances.

The Clinton administration's commitment to the region was personalized by the president, who invested time there in his second term to reinforce the aspirations of his grand strategy. He visited President Zedillo of Mexico in May 1997 and followed that with meetings with the leaders of Costa Rica and various Caribbean leaders in Barbados. In October 1997, President Clinton visited Venezuela, Brazil, and Argentina, on all occasions addressing the challenges that impacted all nations in the Americas: crime, immigration, drug manufacture, and distribution, as well as the potential benefits derived from a continent with a growing democratic base and more accessible markets.[193]

US Grand Strategy in the second term sought to aid nations in the Western hemisphere "translate economic growth into social progress," a move the administration felt was "critical for promoting sustainable growth and sustaining democracy," especially since, despite encouraging progress, nations in the Caribbean and Latin America had the greatest income disparities in the world "with the poorest 20% of individuals receiving just 4.5% of the total income within the region."[194] US Grand Strategy remained committed to prosperity promotion in the Western hemisphere: Canada was the United States's largest merchandise export market and trade partner in the world, as US exports grew rapidly under the US–Canada Free Trade Agreement. Grand strategy in the region continued to utilize the World Bank, the Inter-American Development Bank, and the IMF, in partnership with Latin American governments and private enterprise "to help the region's countries in their transition to integrated, mature market economies."[195] However, Argentina, which had openly embraced the Clinton administration's free market strategy, suffered its own economic collapse in 2001, but was denied an economic bailout by the newly installed George W. Bush administration. Washington's attempt to blame Argentina for the financial crisis set off a rise in Anti-Americanism that did much to end support for the proposed FTAA.[196]

The commitment to the Western hemisphere and the consistency of the grand strategy in the region were evident from a consideration of PDD-28. Prepared in 1994, it addressed US policy toward Latin America and the Caribbean and committed the administration to a hemisphere "of democratic nations with capable, efficient governments and vibrant civil societies and with open, dynamic economies providing rising living standards for their people and expanding export markets for US products and services."[197] PDD-28 encompassed the full range of US Grand Strategy initiatives, including national security, prosperity promotion, and democracy promotion. It was reinforced by the president's statement in his 1997 State of the Union Address that his grand strategy was "about more than economics: By expanding trade, we can advance the cause of freedom and democracy around the world. There is no better example of this truth than Latin America, where democracy and open markets are on the march together."[198]

Africa

Despite proclaiming that most parts of the world were natural locations for its grand strategy of Engagement and Enlargement, the Clinton administration conceded that Africa posed "one of our greatest challenges."[199] The administration acknowledged that the environmental, economic, social, ethnic, and political challenges associated with Africa contributed to a feeling of "Afro-pessimism."[200] The administration's ultimate ambition, "a stable, economically dynamic Africa," depended on the integration of African nations into the global economy. The prosperity promotion aspect of grand strategy, therefore, sought "to assist African nations to implement economic reforms, create favorable climates for trade and investment and achieve sustainable development." Grand strategy was not intended as an African panacea and the administration recognized that it would be unable to "address every challenge or reap every opportunity" available in Africa. Instead, in a continuation of the pragmatic approach that characterized much of the administration's approach to policy, the United States would "identify those issues where we can make a difference and which most directly affect our interests and target our resources efficiently."[201] The economic aspect of US Grand Strategy in Africa contained the dual caveat of seeking to aid continental development, while ensuring the United States benefited as a direct result.

As part of the administration's grand strategy in the region, the White House hosted the 1994 Conference on Africa. Attended by President Clinton, Vice President Gore, Secretary of State Christopher, National Security Adviser Lake and more than 200 members of the administration, members of Congress, human rights activists, business leaders, labor groups, religious organizations, development agencies, and academics, the conference addressed the role that the United States could play in the development of the continent. This was the first time the White House had sponsored an effort to bring together regional experts and the administration believed it "produced a wealth of new ideas and a new commitment to Africa."[202] The administration stressed that its grand strategy in relation to Africa sought to promote "democracy, respect for human rights, sustainable economic development and resolution of conflicts through negotiation, diplomacy and peacekeeping" and had deliberately supported efforts to increase an appreciation for the need for "budgetary and financial discipline."[203]

In the first years of the administration, the grand strategy spoke in broad, positive generalities about the desire to address challenges in Africa and "create a synergy that can stimulate development, resurrect societies and build hope." To do so, the administration sought to draw upon "the knowledge, experience and commitment of millions of Americans to enhance our nation's support for positive change in Africa" and in so doing, strengthen "the American constituency for Africa."[204] The administration established a series of initiatives to formalize relations between South Africa and the United States. One of the first was the US–South Africa Bi-National Commission, formed during the October 1994 state visit of President Mandela.[205] The commission was inaugurated on March 1, 1995 and was designed to strengthen the bilateral relationship and identify ways in which the United States could ensure South African Reconstruction and Development Program goals were met.[206]

Clinton's Grand Strategy sought to "spur economic growth and promote trade and investment by examining new ways to improve the economic policies of African nations and by sustaining critical bilateral and multilateral development assistance." Efforts to integrate African nations into the global economy presented political and economic benefits to all concerned, but particularly benefited US interests by opening previously untapped markets of more than 600 million people in sub-Saharan Africa to US goods and services. As of 1997 the United States exported more to this region than to all of the former Soviet states combined, but enjoyed only 7 percent market share in Africa.[207] Clinton's Grand Strategy sought to ensure that such moves led to an increase in the 100,000 American jobs that depended on exports to the continent.[208]

The administration's commitment to Africa was underscored by visits to the continent by senior personnel, as Vice President Gore and the First Lady represented the United States at Nelson Mandela's inauguration in May 1994. The vice president returned to South Africa in November 1995 where he and President Mandela held the first formal meeting of the US–South Africa Bi-National Commission. During his second term, President Clinton made a 12-day trip to Africa in March/April 1998, during which he co-hosted the Entebbe Summit for Peace and Prosperity, along with President Museveni of Uganda, to advance cooperation on conflict prevention, human rights, and economic integration. The trip afforded opportunities to announce "a number of new programs to support democracy, prosperity and opportunity, including initiatives on education, rule of law, food security, trade and investment, aviation and conflict resolution," as well as providing President Clinton with an opportunity to address "the violent conflicts that have threatened African democracy and prosperity."[209] A meeting of US and African officials followed the trip in March 1999, addressing "security, economic and political issues."[210]

On March 24, 1998, the administration announced the Education for Development and Democracy Initiative to improve access to technology at community resource centers and increase the quality of education in Africa. The administration planned to provide $120 million over 2 years to help fund the initiative, which focused on educating and empowering girls. The Africa Food Security Initiative was also introduced to improve African agriculture and food security. Budgeted at $61 million over 2 years, the program was designed to exacerbate similar efforts being enacted by the United States Agency for International Development (USAID). The focus of the project was to improve African agricultural practices, increase efficiencies, and encourage the use of technology to improve yields and distribution. Finally, the Multilateral Initiative on Malaria was launched to complement the Infectious Disease Initiative for Africa and support the Regional Malaria Lab in Mali.[211] By 2000, the initiative had expanded beyond its original focus on Ethiopia, Mali, Mozambique, Malawi, and Uganda into Tanzania, Zambia, Ghana, and Kenya. Notwithstanding natural disasters, productivity and agriculture incomes in these nations rose and as part of the initiative the countries either met or exceeded their performance targets in 1999 as food security improved.[212]

The Clinton administration acknowledged that developing countries faced "an array of challenges" as they sought "broad-based economic and social progress" to benefit from the opportunities afforded by the end of the Cold War and the onset of globalization.[213] In June 1997, the Clinton administration launched the Partnership for Economic Growth and Opportunity in Africa Initiative, designed to support economic reform in the continent. The plan was to help African countries to pursue "growth-oriented policies" and encourage them to "sustain growth and development."[214] While the plan sought to aid African development, it also fostered US investment and trade in the continent and, as a result, the initiative contained a variety of programs, including "greater market access, targeted technical assistance, enhanced bilateral and World Bank debt relief and increased bilateral trade ties."[215] With half the world's population existing on incomes of less than $2 a day, it was clear to see why US Grand Strategy took into account the threats posed by hunger, malnutrition, economic migration, and political unrest.[216] However, the administration only began to advocate the relief of unsustainable foreign debt obligations late into the second term. In June 1999, the administration adopted the Cologne Debt Initiative to reduce the debts of Heavily Indebted Poor Countries, in an effort to promote economic growth and poverty reduction.[217] The eventual enactment of the African Growth and Opportunity Act on May 18, 2000 marked the beginning of a new relationship between the United States and sub-Saharan Africa, just as the Clinton administration was coming to an end. The bill granted substantial preferential access to the US market for eligible sub-Saharan African countries "and benchmarks towards which current non-eligible countries could aspire and focus their development efforts."[218]

Reflections on prosperity promotion as grand strategy

The Clinton administration's decision to "tear down the wall in our thinking between domestic and foreign policy" ensured that this facet of US Grand Strategy bore political dividends.[219] The White House successfully blended the president's economic preferences into a grand strategy that promoted prosperity promotion abroad, resulting in economic renewal at home. The economic results of the era were remarkable, with the macroeconomic performance in particular being hailed as "exceptional" by the chairman of George W. Bush's Council of Economic Advisers, Gregory Mankiw.[220]

Clinton's Grand Strategy prioritized the revitalization of America's economy, which by 1996 was in a far better state than it had been 3 years earlier. The federal budget deficit had successfully been lowered as a percentage of the Gross Domestic Product from 4.9 percent in 1992 to 2.4 percent in 1995, the lowest since 1979.[221] Having campaigned in 1992 promising to focus on the economy, Clinton utilized US Grand Strategy during his first term to position himself for reelection in 1996. Indeed, US Grand Strategy, as espoused in the 1996 National Security Strategy Review, was specifically utilized as part of the administration's campaign for reelection. By combining economic initiatives with its foreign policy, the

Clinton administration was able to highlight how US Grand Strategy and specifically its trade initiatives, including NAFTA, the GATT agreement, and more than 80 other trade deals, had created more than 2 million American jobs.[222] The 1996 NSSR was determined to demonstrate that the events of the past 4 years had not been predetermined, but had been driven by the administration, often in the face of open hostility and criticism, from both sides of the political aisle.

Much of the prosperity promotion initiative was indicative of the evolving concept of globalization and the developing market-based economies, of which Bill Clinton was an early proponent, having alluded to them in his first Inaugural Address. As Robert Rubin observed, President Clinton was "the first American President with a deep understanding of how these issues were reshaping our economy, our country, and the world."[223] From its first days in office, the Clinton administration began "unabashedly using globalization to remake the world in its image."[224] This was a process the administration was determined to harness and manipulate, estimating that 2 million of the 7.5 million new jobs created since 1993 had been the result of efforts to expand market access for American products. In 2000, President Clinton insisted that globalization was "tearing down barriers and building new networks among nations, peoples and cultures at an astonishing and historically unprecedented rate."[225] The administration believed that its efforts had resulted in the creation of over 3 million new small businesses and the lowest combined rates of unemployment and inflation in 25 years.[226] The administration stressed that the prosperity promotion element of its grand strategy was good not only for US foreign policy, but also for the national economy and therefore for American voters. Globalization, however, like US Grand Strategy, was about more than economics. As President Clinton noted in his final State of the Union address in January 2000, "Our purpose must be to bring together the world around freedom and democracy and peace and to oppose those who would tear it apart."[227]

The prosperity promotion element of US Grand Strategy was perhaps the most successful element of Clinton's Grand Strategy, with much of its success being due to the administration's efforts to lock the American economy into the heart of the developing economic entities, including NAFTA, the WTO, and APEC. Each agreement represented a triumph for international free trade and for globalization. NAFTA established a free trade zone with the United States's closest trading partners; the WTO provided a mechanism to ensure US access to foreign markets; APEC granted the US access to the emerging markets of the Pacific Rim and "opened markets, expanded export and investment opportunities and protected intellectual property rights for American companies."[228] The Summit of the Americas provided an opening to the markets in the Western hemisphere, while the emerging Transatlantic Marketplace initiative allowed for even greater US penetration of the European Union. As declassified NSC memos from 1994 reveal, the administration believed that "with new nations interconnected economically and politically, it is foolhardy NOT to be looking to international bodies for solutions."[229] Clinton's success in placing the United States at the heart of these international institutions enabled the United States to lead and mold the bodies according to its own design. Indeed, it was noted that Clinton's ability to secure trade deals "was to economics what Richard Nixon's opening to China was to security."[230] By becoming the common denominator in all these financial entities, the United States was perfectly placed to benefit from and manipulate the direction of global economic policy.

As logical as this approach was, critics suggested that the administration had confused trade policy with foreign policy, with Leslie Gelb lamenting, "A foreign economic policy is not a foreign policy and it is not a national security strategy."[231] Gelb noted that international trade was the only area in which President Clinton had demonstrated conviction, but that despite its successes it failed to provide a framework with which to respond to the challenges that erupted in the 1990s and, was therefore, "a triumph of process over substance."[232] The promotion of free markets may have given direction to US Trade Representative Kantor and Commerce Secretary Brown, but critics remained unimpressed, viewing it as a policy with no connection to reality, as an aspiration rather than a strategy, "the predictable by-product of Lake, a former professor, pursuing arcane geopolitical textbooks."[233] Lake's time in academia hardly distinguished him from his predecessors at the NSC, including Kissinger and Brzezinski, and it is feasible to conclude that part of the criticism leveled at the administration stemmed in part from the administration's fundamental approach to grand strategy.[234] As Warren Christopher noted, "it used to be said that balance-of-power diplomacy and arms control were "high politics" and economics "low politics." The Clinton administration rejected such distinctions, believing instead, "that political and economic diplomacy are indivisible."[235]

The Clinton White House was adamant that it was more productive to assist American companies in the expanding markets of the world than to post the Marines "to quell unrest in economically inconsequential nations," as global organizations were utilized to aid the US recovery and ensure its continued dominance, through a process of globalization, if not outright Americanization.[236] Such a process was dependent on an engaged and internationalist approach to foreign affairs. As has been revealed throughout this book, and as acknowledged by Jeffrey Garten, "before he was elected, Clinton was promising to recast the entire intellectual basis of US trade policy . . . It was to be placed at the center of foreign policy, becoming at least as important as political and security questions."[237] Clinton was adamant that the United States must "remain actively engaged in global affairs," for while the Cold War may have ended, "the need for American leadership abroad" remained as strong as ever, with the president being personally "committed to building a new public consensus to sustain our active engagement abroad."[238]

However, due to US electoral timetables the policy needed to be results-driven to remain politically viable, ensuring that investments in foreign policy were "proximate and easily demonstrated in terms of job creation, growth, and export market shares."[239] Therefore, the grand strategy's prosperity promotion initiative was initially introduced in Central and Eastern Europe and the Asian Pacific region, where nations were in the advanced stages of becoming open-market democracies. There was little point in selecting China as a testing ground for the most sweeping sections of the policy, just as there was little point in selecting a nation in sub-Saharan Africa. Both locations presented near insurmountable obstacles to the speedy implementation of the policy. Rather, it was designed "to protect US strategic interests abroad and Clinton's personal popularity at home."[240] Accordingly, it was difficult to argue with the results of the initiative.

As the nation prepared to vote in 1996, a *New York Times/CBS News* poll revealed 55 percent approved of Clinton's handling of the economy, with 70 percent of respondents reporting that they felt the economy was very good or fairly good.[241] The domestic economic recovery was fueled in large part by the export market, which produced new jobs. The economy grew steadily and constantly throughout the administration's two terms. Unemployment fell, millions of new jobs were created, and the federal deficit was erased, so that by the election of 2000, debate focused on what to do with the vast and growing budget surplus that had been accumulated under Clinton's economic initiatives.[242]

Conclusion

The prosperity promotion element of grand strategy was central to President Clinton's endorsement of Engagement and Enlargement. It was as an economic variation of Rollback, based on the premise that in countries where command economies collapsed, free markets, teeming with American goods and services, may thrive. However, the Clinton administration ultimately failed to implement many of its policies, including the introduction of Chile into NAFTA in its second term, due to domestic political obstructions. Clinton may have sought to make the world safe for commerce, but like Wilson before him, he proved more adept at convincing the rest of the world to go along with his ideas than he was with members of the Congress, who spent much of his second term debating whether Clinton should be removed from office. Despite such domestic political issues, it was clear that by the end of the administration's time in office "the commercial side of it has more or less been a success."

As Charles Kupchan noted, the Uruguay Round was completed, "there hadn't been a return of protectionism . . . and that strategy of continued global liberalization is with us and it was born and pushed in the 1990s." The policy was predicated on the belief that once the newly democratic nations developed market economies, their citizens would seek US goods and services, strengthening ties between the nations and allowing for peace and prosperity to flourish. This was the fundamental aspiration of Clinton's Grand Strategy initiative and long after leaving office, in an age of ever-increasing Americanization of foreign markets, it is difficult to argue with its success.

The use of economics in US Grand Strategy was "a good way of bringing a president who had been a governor . . . to foreign policy through the back door" and enabled Clinton to marry his interests with the requirement to operate on a global basis. Clinton, like many of his predecessors, came into office with little foreign policy experience and "it took time for him to turn on." He was, however, "hardwired as a politician, so once you do the foreign policy thing and start talking about constituencies and votes, its like, 'Cool, I like this!'"[243] Accordingly, US Grand Strategy sought to ensure full US participation over an increasing array of international financial institutions and trade entities. Anthony Lake's position on this was clear: "If we can help lead the dozens of nations . . . who are trying to adapt to democracy and free markets, we help to create the conditions for the greatest expansion of prosperity and security the world has ever witnessed."[244] By the end of Clinton's second term in office, with the nation at peace and enjoying the longest economic boom in American history, few would have argued with such a forecast.

Notes

1   *Historical Statistics of the United States, Colonial Times to 1970* (US Department of Commerce, 1975); Joseph Freeman and Scott Nearing, *Dollar Diplomacy: A Study in American Imperialism* (New York: B. W. Huebsch and the Viking Press, 1928), p. 242.

2   James G. Blaine, quoted in Freeman and Nearing, *Dollar Diplomacy*, p. 243.

3   Achille Viallate, *Economic Imperialism and International Relations During the Last Fifty Years* (New York: Macmillan, 1923), p. 29.

4   Gresham quoted in Charles A. Beard, *Contemporary American History* (New York: Macmillan, 1914), p. 203.

5   Letter from Secretary of State Olney to Thomas F. Bayard, July 20, 1895, *Foreign Relations of the United States 1895 Part I: Great Britain* (Washington, DC: GPO, 1895), pp. 545–562, p. 558.

6   Albert Beveridge, quoted in Emily S. Rosenberg, *Spreading the American Dream: American Economic and Cultural Expansion 1980–1945* (New York: Hill & Wang, 1982), p. 22.

7 Rosenberg, *Spreading the American Dream*, p. 40.

8 Calvin Coolidge, "Address to the American Society of Newspaper Editors," Washington, DC, January 17, 1925; Henry F. Grady, "The New Trade Policy of the United States," *Foreign Affairs* 14, no. 2 (January 1936), pp. 283–296.

9 Charles Wilson, Testimony to the Senate Armed Services Committee, January 15, 1953.

10 Michael Mandelbaum, "The Bush Foreign Policy," *Foreign Affairs* 70, no. 1 (1990/1991), p. 21.

11 Dan B. Wood, *The Politics of Economic Leadership: The Causes and Consequences of Presidential Rhetoric* (Princeton, NJ: Princeton University Press, 2007), p. 4.

12 Warren Christopher, "Statement at Senate Confirmation Hearing," *US Department of State Dispatch* 4, Issue 4 (January 25, 1993), p. 45.

13 The administration's successful economic policies also contributed to President Clinton's consistently high approval ratings during his second term, which ensured that few Democrats were prepared to abandon the president during the impeachment hearings.

14 Mandelbaum, "The Bush Foreign Policy," p. 6.

15 Author's interview with Charles A. Kupchan.

16 Quoted in Erlanger and Sanger, "On Global Stage, Clinton's Pragmatic Turn," *New York Times* (July 29, 1996), p. A16. See also Alfred E. Eckes, Jr, *Opening America's Market: US Foreign Trade Policy Since 1776* (Chapel Hill, NC: University of North Carolina Press, 1995), p. 1.

17 Clinton and Gore, *Putting People First: How We Can All Change America*, pp. 131–132.

18 Memorandum to the President-Elect, quoted in Kenneth I. Juster and Simon Lazarus, *Making Economic Policy: An Assessment of the National Economic Council* (Washington, DC: Brookings Institution Press, 1997), p. 8.

19 Robert E. Rubin, *In An Uncertain World: Tough Choices from Wall Street to Washington* (New York: Random House, 2003), p. 114.

20 Ben Wildavsky, "Under the Gun," *National Journal* 26 (1996), p. 1417.

21 Clinton, *My Life*, p. 636.

22 Duffy and Goodgame, *Marching in Place*, p. 136.

23 Quoted in I. M. Destler, *The National Economic Council: A Work in Progress* (Washington, DC: Institute for International Economics, 1996), p. 8.

24 Robert Rubin, quoted in Gwen Ifill, "The Economic Czar Behind the Economic Czars," *New York Times* (March 22, 1993), p. A1.

25 For more information on the National Economic Council, see Jerel A. Rosati and James M. Scott, *The Politics of United States Foreign Policy*, Fifth Edition (Boston, MA: Wadsworth, Cengage Learning, 2011), pp. 231–258; Jonathan M. Orszag, Peter R. Orszag, and Laura D. Tyson, "The Role of Institutions in the White House: The Process of Economic Policy-Making During the Clinton Administration," in Jeffrey Frankel and Peter Orszag (eds),

American Economic Policy in the 1990s (Cambridge, MA: MIT Press, 2002), pp. 983–1005.

26   Brinkley, "Democratic Enlargement," p. 120.

27   *PPPWJC*, vol. 2 (1996), Remarks on the Resignation of Secretary of State Warren Christopher and an Exchange With Reporters, November 7, 1996, p. 2090.

28   Jeffrey Garten, "Clinton's Emerging Trade Policy: Act One, Scene One," *Foreign Affairs* 72, no. 3 (Summer 1993), p. 183.

29   Quoted in Martin Tolchin, "Mayors Press Clinton on Promise to Rebuild Nation," *New York Times* (January 25, 1993), p. A15.

30   Berman, *From the Center to the Edge*, p. 21.

31   *NSSR96*, p. 27.

32   Joseph E. Stiglitz, *Roaring Nineties: Why We're Paying the Price for the Greediest Decade in History* (London: Penguin, 2003), p. 4.

33   Berman, *From the Center to the Edge*, p. 25.

34   Bob Woodward, *The Agenda: Inside the Clinton White House* (New York: Simon & Schuster, 1994), p. 165.

35   Campbell and Rockman, "Introduction," p. 2.

36   Jeffrey E. Garten, "The Big Emerging Markets," *Columbia Journal of World Business* 31, no. 2 (Summer 1996), p. 9.

37   Michael Oppenheimer, "The New Mercantilism: Where is Business Leading Our Foreign Policy?" in Robert Hutchings (ed.), *At the End of the American Century: America's Role in the Post-Cold War World* (Washington, DC: Woodrow Wilson Center, 1998), pp. 162–166.

38   Christopher Andrew, *For the President's Eyes Only* (London: HarperCollins, 1995), pp. 540–541.

39   *NSSR94*, p. 14.

40   *NSSR96*, p. 24.

41   Loch K. Johnson, *Secret Agencies: US Intelligence in a Hostile World* (New Haven, CT: Yale University Press, 1998), p. 147.

42   Ibid., p. 54.

43   *NSSR94*, p. 14.

44   Tara Sonenshine to Bob Boorstin; re: Some Random Thoughts on the UNGA Speech, Clinton Presidential Records, National Security Council, Robert Boorstin (Speechwriting), OA/Box Number: 422, UNGA '94—NSC Memos, William J. Clinton Presidential Library.

45   Blumenthal, *The Clinton Wars*, p. 64.

46   Bob Boorstin et al. to Mack McLarty, George Stephanopoulos, David Gegen, and Mark Gearan; re: Fall Calendar, July 19, 1993, Clinton Presidential Records, National Security Council, Robert Boorstin (Speechwriting),

OA/Box Number: 413, Summer/Fall 1993 Calendar, William J. Clinton Presidential Library.

47 Michael Waldman et al. to Roy Neel and Circulation; re: Communications Strategy for Fall Issues, July 23, 1993, Clinton Presidential Records, National Security Council, Robert Boorstin (Speechwriting), OA/Box Number: 413, Summer/Fall 1993 Calendar, William J. Clinton Presidential Library.

48 *PPPWJC*, vol. 2 (1993), Message to the Congress Transmitting Proposed Legislation To Implement the North American Free Trade Agreement, November 3, pp. 1892–1893.

49 *PPPWJC*, vol. 2 (1993), The President's News Conference, November 10, 1993, pp. 1943–1946.

50 *NSSR94*, p. 25.

51 Author's interview with J. F. O. McAllister. For more on President's Clinton efforts to forge a bi-partisan coalition to ensure Congressional support for NAFTA, see David Cloud, "Clinton Forms New Coalition to win NAFTA's Approval," *Congressional Quarterly Weekly Report* 51 (October 16, 1993), p. 3181.

52 See *NSSR95*, p. 4; *NSSR96*, p. 28.

53 *NSSR97*, p. 16.

54 *NSSR99*, p. 40.

55 *NSSR2000*, p. 32.

56 *NSSR94*, p. 16.

57 Henry Kissinger, *Diplomacy*, p. 832.

58 Richard N. Haass, "The Squandered Presidency: Demanding More from the Commander-in-Chief," *Foreign Affairs* 79, no. 3 (May–June 2000), p. 137.

59 Wolfowitz, "Clinton's First Year," p. 29.

60 *NSSR95*, p. 20.

61 *NSSR97*, p. 16.

62 *NSSR96*, p. 7.

63 *NSSR95*, p. 20.

64 See *PPPWJC*, vol. 2 (1994), Remarks Welcoming Chile to the North American Free Trade Agreement Partnership in Miami, December 11, 1994, p. 2175.

65 Wolfowitz, "Clinton's First Year," p. 30.

66 James A. Baker III, *The Politics of Diplomacy: Revolution, War and Peace, 1989–1992* (New York: G.P. Putnam's Sons, 1995), p. 608.

67 *NSSR97*, p. 16.

68 Stephen D. Cohen, Robert A. Blecker, and Peter D. Whitney, *Fundamentals of US Foreign Trade Policy: Economics, Politics, Laws, and Issues*, Second Revised Edition (Boulder, CO: Westview Press, 2002), p. 329.

69 *NSSR97*, p. 15.

70   Martin Walker, "Home Alone: What Matters Now is Trade Not the Cold Not Tanks but Toyotas," *Guardian* (February 22, 1995), p. 12.

71   Martin Walker, "Major Asks Clinton to Consider Free Trade Area to Include Europe," *Guardian* (April 6, 1995), p. 13.

72   *PPPWJC*, vol. 1 (1998), Remarks to the People of Germany in Berlin, May 13, 1998, p. 752.

73   *NSSR94*, p. 24.

74   *NSSR94*, p. 16.

75   *NSSR95*, p. 29.

76   *NSSR97*, p. 16.

77   *NSSR98*, p. 45.

78   *NSSR94*, p. 24.

79   *NSSR99*, p. 34.

80   *NSSR95*, p. 20.

81   *NSSR99*, p. 37.

82   *NSSR98*, p. 45.

83   *NSSR2000*, p. 48.

84   Ikenberry, "American Grand Strategy in the Age of Terror," p. 21.

85   *NSSR94*, p. 6.

86   Tara Sonenshine to Bob Boorstin; re: Some Random Thoughts on the UNGA Speech, Clinton Presidential Records, National Security Council, Robert Boorstin (Speechwriting), OA/Box Number: 422, UNGA '94—NSC Memos, William J. Clinton Presidential Library.

87   *PPPWJC*, vol. 2 (1994), Remarks on the General Agreement on Tariffs and Trade, November 28, 1994, p. 2126.

88   *NSSR94*, p. 16.

89   *NSSR95*, p. 4, 21.

90   Author's interview with Charles A. Kupchan.

91   Haass, "The Squandered Presidency," p. 137.

92   *NSSR97*, p. 15.

93   *NSSR97*, p. 16.

94   *PPPWJC*, vol. 1 (1993), The President's News Conference With Prime Minister Kiichi Miyazawa of Japan, April 16, 1993, p. 439.

95   Ornstein, "Foreign Policy and the 1992 Election," pp. 5–6.

96   Jeffrey Garten, "Is America Abandoning Multilateral Trade?" *Foreign Affairs* 74, no. 6 (November–December 1995), pp. 50–62; Michael H. Armacost, *Friends or Rivals? The Insider's Account of US–Japanese Relations* (New York: Columbia University Press, 1996), p. 194.

97   *NSSR94*, pp. 16–17.

98   *NSSR96*, p. 29.

99   *NSSR98*, p. 46.

100 *NSSR99*, p. 38.

101 *NSSR98*, p. 47.

102 *PPPWJC*, vol. 1 (1993), Inaugural Address, January 20, p. 1.

103 Author's interview with Robert B. Reich (US Labor Secretary 1993–1997), Rothermere American Institute, Oxford, April 29, 2004.

104 *NSSR99*, pp. 23–24.

105 *NSSR94*, p. 17.

106 *PPPWJC*, vol. 2 (1998), Remarks to the 53rd Session of the United Nations General Assembly in New York City, September 21, 1998, p. 1630.

107 *PPPWJC*, vol. 2 (1998), Remarks to the Council on Foreign Relations in New York City, September 14, 1998, p. 1573.

108 Clinton, "Remarks to the Opening Ceremony of the 1998 International Monetary Fund/World Bank Annual Meeting," Washington, DC, October 6, 1998.

109 *NSSR2000*, p. 31.

110 *NSSR94*, p. 5.

111 William S. Cohen, "Remarks to International Institute for Strategic Studies," San Diego, September 9, 1999.

112 *NSSR96*, p. 28.

113 *NSSR94*, p. 21.

114 *PPPWJC*, vol. 2 (1998), p. 1573.

115 *NSSR98*, p. 37.

116 *NSSR94*, p. 21.

117 *PPPWJC*, vol. 1 (1998), Remarks to the People of Germany in Berlin, May 13, 1998, p. 751.

118 *NSSR99*, p. 33.

119 *NSSR94*, p. 22.

120 *NSSR96*, p. 38.

121 *NSSR94*, p. 22.

122 *NSSR96*, p. 38.

123 *NSSR99*, pp. 32–33.

124 *NSSR98*, p. 40.

125 Holbrooke, "America, A European Power," p. 51.

126 *NSSR98*, p. 40.

127 *PPPWJC*, vol. 1 (1999), Statement on the Launch of the New European Currency, January 4, 1999, p. 5.

128 *NSSR98*, p. 37.

129 Author's interview with Charles A. Kupchan.

130 *NSSR94*, p. 21.

131 *NSSR94*, p. 23.

132 *NSSR98*, p. 40.

133 *NSSR2000*, p. 47.

134 *NSSR97*, p. 23.

135 *NSSR95*, p. 27.

136 *NSSR97*, p. 23.

137 *NSSR98*, p. 40.

138 *NSSR99*, p. 33.

139 *NSSR97*, p. 22.

140 *NSSR99*, p. 33.

141 *NSSR2000*, p. 47.

142 *NSSR96*, p. 27.

143 *NSSR97*, p. 22.

144 Brinkley, "Democratic Enlargement," p. 126.

145 Author's interview with Leon Fuerth.

146 *PPPWJC*, vol. 2 (1998), p. 1574.

147 *NSSR97*, p. 22.

148 *PPPWJC*, vol. 2 (1998), p. 1574.

149 *NSSR96*, p. 39.

150 *NSSR99*, p. 33.

151 Talbot, *The Russia Hand*, p. 43.

152 Author's interview with J. F. O. McAllister.

153 *NSSR2000*, p. 47.

154 *NSSR97*, p. 16.

155 Ronald Steel, "The New Meaning of Security," in David Jablonsky et al. (eds), *US National Security: Beyond the Cold War*, pp. 40–51, p. 48.

156 *PPPWJC*, vol. 1 (1997), Address Before a Joint Session of the Congress on the State of the Union, February 4, 1997, p. 115.

157 Brummett, *High Wire*, p. 208.

158 Author's interview with Robert Reich.

159 *NSSR2000*, p. 32.

160 *PPPWJC*, vol. 1 (1993), Statement on Most-Favored-Nation Trade Status for China, May 28, 1993, pp. 770–771.

161 *PPPWJC*, vol. 1 (1994), The President's News Conference With Prime Minister John Major of the United Kingdom, March 1, 1994, p. 348.

162 *PPPWJC*, vol. 1 (1999), Address Before a Joint Session of the Congress on the State of the Union, January 19, 1999, p. 69.

163 Berman, *From the Center to the Edge*, pp. 111–112.

164 *NSSR94*, p. 24.

165 Samuel Berger, "A Foreign Policy for the Global Age," *Foreign Affairs* 79, no. 6 (November–December, 2000), p. 28.

166 *NSSR96*, p. 41.

167 *PPPWJC*, vol. 1 (1998), The President's News Conference With President Jiang Zemin of China in Beijing, June 27, 1998, p. 1070.

168 *NSSR98*, p. 46.

169 *NSSR99*, p. 38.

170 Berger, "A Foreign Policy for the Global Age," p. 28.

171 *NSSR2000*, p. 52.

172 *NSSR98*, p. 46.

173 Author's interview with Robert Reich.

174 *PPPWJC*, vol. 1 (1998), p. 1071.

175 *NSSR95*, p. 21.

176 *NSSR94*, p. 24.

177 *NSSR98*, p. 49.

178 *NSSR94*, p. 25.

179 *NSSR97*, p. 25.

180 John Greenwald and James Carney, "Don't Panic: Here Comes Bailout Bill," *Time* (February 13, 1995), p. 30.

181 *PPPWJC*, vol. 1 (1995), Statement on the Economic Situation in Mexico, January 11, 1995, pp. 38–39.

182 *PPPWJC*, vol. 1 (1995), Remarks on Loan Guarantees for Mexico, January 18, 1995, p. 61.

183 *PPPWJC*, vol. 1 (1995), Address Before a Joint Session of the Congress on the State of the Union, January 24, 1995, p. 83.

184 *PPPWJC*, vol. 1 (1995), Message to the Congress on the Financial Crisis in Mexico, March 9, 1995, p. 328.

185 Ibid., 329.

186 *PPPWJC*, vol. 1 (1995), Statement With Congressional Leaders on Financial Assistance to Mexico, January 31, 1995, p. 130.

187 Blumenthal, *The Clinton Wars*, p. 134.

188 Thomas Omestad, "Foreign Policy and Campaign '96," *Foreign Policy* 105 (Winter 1996–1997), p. 53.

189 *PPPWJC*, vol. 1 (1997), Address Before a Joint Session of the Congress on the State of the Union, February 4, 1997, p. 115.

190 Haass, "The Squandered Presidency," p. 137.

191 *NSSR98*, p. 48.

192 *PPPWJC*, vol. 2 (1998), Remarks on Electronic Commerce, November 30, 1998, p. 2097.

193 *NSSR98*, p. 48.

194 *NSSR2000*, p. 56.

195 *NSSR99*, p. 40.

196   Chris J. Dolan, John Frendreis, and Raymond Tatalovich, *The Presidency and Economic Policy* (Lanham, MD: Rowman & Littlefield Publishers, 2008), pp. 230–231.

197   PDD-28: US Policy Toward Latin America and the Caribbean, September 8, 1994, p. 2.

198   *PPPWJC*, vol. 1 (1997), Address Before a Joint Session of the Congress on the State of the Union, February 4, 1997, p. 115.

199   *NSSR95*, p. 31.

200   *NSSR94*, p. 26.

201   *NSSR97*, p. 28.

202   *NSSR94*, p. 27.

203   *NSSR96*, p. 43.

204   *NSSR94*, pp. 26–27.

205   Martha Bridgeman, "The US–South Africa Binational Commission," *South African Journal of International Affairs* 8, Issue 1 (2001), pp. 89–95.

206   *PPPWJC*, vol. 2 (1994), The President's News Conference With President Nelson Mandela of South Africa, October 5, 1994, p. 1699.

207   *NSSR97*, p. 28.

208   *NSSR98*, p. 56.

209   *NSSR98*, p. 54.

210   *NSSR99*, p. 47.

211   *NSSR98*, pp. 56–57.

212   *NSSR2000*, p. 64.

213   *NSSR99*, p. 25.

214   *NSSR97*, p. 28.

215   *NSSR98*, p. 56.

216   *NSSR99*, p. 25.

217   *NSSR2000*, p. 35.

218   *NSSR2000*, p. 63.

219   William J. Clinton, "A New Covenant for American Security," p. 113.

220   N. Gregory Mankiw, "U.S. Monetary Policy During the 1990s," in Frankel and Orszag (eds), *American Economic Policy in the 1990s*, p. 42.

221   *NSSR96*, p. 12.

222   *NSSR96*, p. 8.

223   Rubin, *In An Uncertain World: Tough Choices From Wall Street to Washington*, p. 121.

224   Kupchan, *The End of the American Era*, p. 111.

225   *PPPWJC*, vol. 3 (2000), Remarks at the University of Warwick in Coventry, United Kingdom, December 14, 2000, pp. 2697–2698.

226   *NSSR96*, p. 7.

227 *PPPWJC*, vol. 1 (2000), Address Before a Joint Session of the Congress on the State of the Union, January 27, 2000, p. 135.

228 Christopher, "America's Leadership, America's Opportunity," p. 17.

229 Sonenshine to Boorstin; re: Some Random Thoughts on the UNGA Speech, William J. Clinton Presidential Library.

230 Omestad, "Foreign Policy and Campaign '96," p. 53.

231 Dick Kirschten, "Martyr or Misfit?" *National Journal*, October 29, 1994, p. 2505.

232 Robert A. Manning and Patrick Clawson, "The Clinton Doctrine," *Wall Street Journal*, December 29, 1997, p. 6.

233 Brinkley, "Democratic Enlargement," p. 119.

234 For a broad critique of the economic policies of the Clinton administration, see Richard Lowry, *Legacy: Paying the Price for the Clinton Years* (Washington, DC: Regnery Publishing, 2003).

235 Christopher, "America's Leadership, America's Opportunity," p. 16.

236 Brinkley, "Democratic Enlargement," p. 125.

237 Garten, "Clinton's Emerging Trade Policy: Act One, Scene One," p. 183.

238 *NSSR94*, p. ii.

239 Oppenheimer, "The New Mercantilism: Where is Business Leading Our Foreign Policy?" p. 155.

240 Brinkley, "Democratic Enlargement," p. 113.

241 Omestad, "Foreign Policy and Campaign '96," p. 51.

242 Iwan W. Morgan, *The Age of Deficits: Presidents and Unbalanced Budgets from Jimmy Carter to George W. Bush* (Lawrence, KA: University Press of Kansas, 2009), pp. 158–205.

243 Author's interview with Charles A. Kupchan.

244 *NSSR96*, p. 9.

CHAPTER SIX

Democracy promotion

From the first days of his presidential campaign, Bill Clinton stressed the importance of democracy promotion as the third element of his grand strategy with which to address the post-Cold War world. This was the most ideological aspect of US Grand Strategy and the most challenging to implement, with its dedication to the spread of democracy, advocacy of human rights, and a commitment to humanitarian assistance. It remained consistent throughout the Clinton administration's time in office, with changes occurring to reflect ongoing operational developments and incidents. The passing of the Cold War enabled the White House to actively promote democracy, as it sought to reinforce the strategic gains made following the collapse of communism in Central and Eastern Europe. Where once a domino theory existed to explain the spread of communism, now such a process was attempted in reverse, as the Clinton administration sought to ensure that democracy flourished where it had once been forbidden.

Despite having been central to Bill Clinton's foreign policy from his December 1991 speech at Georgetown University until the publication of his administration's final National Security Strategy Review, the concept of democracy promotion become synonymous with his successor, President George W. Bush. Indeed, throughout Clinton's time in office, the concept received underwhelming public attention.[1] Despite this, democracy promotion was a central component of US Grand Strategy for the duration of the Clinton administration as the White House sought to advance the causes of freedom in the post-Cold War world.

Democracy promotion in US history

Just as historical tensions existed regarding the appropriate role for the United States to adopt on the world stage, between concepts of engagement and relative isolationism, so too has the United States engaged in an historical struggle over the appropriate manner in which to advance concepts of democracy. As a result, "the singularities that America has ascribed to itself throughout its history have produced two contradictory attitudes towards foreign policy."[2] One attitude maintains the United States should passively act as an example to the world; the other asserts that the nation has an obligation to actively advance the cause of democracy, believing that to do so increased US security.

For the first century of its existence, the United States largely embraced the former role, as advanced by George Washington and Thomas Jefferson, avoiding entangling alliances and acting as a global example to be emulated by others. The advice of the Founding Fathers echoed through successive generations, and on July 4, 1821, John Quincy Adams intoned, "wherever the standard of freedom and independence has been or shall be unfurled, there will [America's] heart, her benedictions and her prayers be." However, he insisted that the United States remain true to the intent of its founders, inasmuch as "she goes not abroad in search of monsters to destroy."[3] In this approach, he was emulating his father, the second president of the United States, who, along with Jefferson, believed that they were "lighting a beacon for mankind; theirs was a great creation, with government based on popular consent and limited under a written constitution."[4]

This passive approach to democratic advocacy encouraged a focus on the North American continent as the United States grew from a collection of 13 former colonies along the Eastern seaboard, to a vast continental power extending all the way to the Pacific. This Westward expansion, implemented in the name of Manifest Destiny, is all too often presented as a domestic excursion into the wilderness and as evidence of a desire to challenge frontiers, both old and new.[5] Often overlooked is the fact that the territories that were being peopled belonged to other nations: France, Spain, Mexico, not to mention the indigenous tribes of the North American people. The Westward expansion of the United States, taking with it a nascent form of liberal democracy, was arguably as dynamic as any subsequent overseas initiative the United States initiated. Although its foreign policy may have been passive in its first 100 years, American-style democracy was exported to a growing number of states and territories throughout the nineteenth century as the United States cemented its political, cultural, and social hold on the North American continent.

Despite the oft-stated belief that US efforts to export democracy began with President Wilson's intervention in First World War, the engagement in the Philippines during the presidency of William McKinley can perhaps be seen as a more definitive turning point, as the president announced that the nation had a duty to "uplift and civilize and Christianize."[6] Such a sentiment, with its inherent religious connotations, expressed a fundamental tenet of developing US foreign policy that reached global proportions in the twentieth century, as democracy itself came to be advocated with a missionary zeal and adopted a religious quality of its own. Where once Christianity was spread far and wide, now democracy was promoted on moral grounds as a tool to confront those nations that posed an existential challenge to the United States. Indeed, for some presidents the distinction between religion and democracy appeared to blur as "the justification of America's international role [became] messianic: America had an obligation, not to the balance of power, but to spread its principles throughout the world."[7] Theodore Roosevelt contributed to this developing approach to foreign intervention, announcing in 1904 that adherence to the Monroe Doctrine "may force the United States, however reluctantly, in flagrant cases of wrongdoing or impotence, to the exercise of an international police power."[8] However, once President Woodrow Wilson justified US intervention in the First World War on the grounds that "the world must be made safe for democracy," Republicans and Democrats embraced the approach, ensuring democracy promotion became the unifying principle at the heart of the Henry Luce's American Century.

In the 1940s, the Truman administration initiated a series of policy initiatives, including those espoused in NSC-68, to ensure the protection of democracy from those forces that threatened to subvert it. In the 1950s, the Eisenhower administration advocated a policy of Rollback to defend democracy and supported coups in Iran and Guatemala. In 1961, President Kennedy announced his intentions to defend freedom and democracy to the world in his inauguration as his administration committed itself to the "survival and the success of liberty."[9] In June 1982, President Reagan addressed the British Parliament and called for a "crusade for freedom," and a "campaign for democratic development."[10] Reagan became the first Republican president to "emphatically . . . embrace the essential tenets of liberal democratic internationalism, or what might be called Wilsonianism," as he sought to promote democracy in Nicaragua and Afghanistan.[11] In an intriguing development, it became apparent that "Wilson the idealist and Reagan the realist nonetheless shared a common interest in the promotion of global democracy."[12]

Reagan's successor, George H. W. Bush, not known for his embrace of "the vision thing," could still muster the rhetoric and the forces to continue this approach.[13] Addressing the UN General Assembly in October 1990, President Bush insisted that "calls for democracy and human rights are being reborn everywhere," which he felt promised hopes "for a more stable, more peaceful, more prosperous world."[14] Bush reiterated this in September 1991, as he insisted, "as democracy flourishes, so does the opportunity for a third historical breakthrough: international cooperation."[15] As the president who initiated a land war in the Persian Gulf to expel Saddam from Kuwait in the name of liberty, if not democracy, Bush noted that the United States was "a nation of rock-solid realism and clear-eyed idealism."[16]

The Bush administration's 1991 National Security Strategy concluded that a new era was evolving: "A truly global community is being formed, vindicating our democratic values." The administration insisted that it planned to "increase our efforts to clarify what America has to contribute to the solution of global problems—and to drive home democracy's place in this process."[17] The rhetorical promotion of democracy reached its apex in George W. Bush's second inaugural address, as the president announced, "It is the policy of the United States to seek and support the growth of democratic movements and institutions in every nation and culture with the ultimate goal of ending tyranny in the world."[18] The manner in which this was attempted, however, brought US intentions into question, as the initiation of what David C. Henrickson referred to as "Wilsonianism in boots," ensured that what the United States saw as benevolence was disputed far and wide.[19]

Defining democracy

In a political environment where bipartisanship is a rare commodity, the promotion of democracy has often been a rallying point for politicians of varying backgrounds, though disagreements have arisen over its implementation and ideological content. While the concept of promoting democratic values may be readily agreed upon, conceptions of what constitutes "democracy" differ widely, both in defining the term and in its implementation. Kissinger noted that the word "democracy" is often misapplied and is "often invoked to legitimise whoever is in power."[20] Clearly, the United States has identified its own brand of "liberal democracy" as a goal to be pursued, but this has also been poorly defined.[21] Michael Foley has suggested that American democracy is "a qualitatively exceptional form of democracy whose idiosyncratic nature is derived from the peculiarities of America itself."[22]

Democracy, as a political concept and a governing reality, has come a long way since 1776. As Michael Cox has noted, "one of the hidden and still understudied themes of nineteenth century politics is the extent to which negative images of American democracy were developed by elites across the European continent to try to justify their continued rule."[23] Far from being seen as an ideal, democracy was viewed as a threat to the status quo and dangerous to property rights. In 1861, the English educationalist Matthew Arnold posed the great, unanswerably question, "What influence may help us to prevent the English people from becoming, with the growth of democracy, Americanized?"[24]

The practicalities of democracy promotion

The American experience did much to alter perceptions of democracy and by the dawn of the twentieth century it was "taken for granted" that liberal democracies were "showing the way toward the good life in the good society." Indeed, it was suggested that "few had any doubts of the eventual, but certain, progress of all mankind toward more democracy and a wider freedom."[25] Having embraced, and as far as it was concerned, "perfected" democracy, the United States now felt that what worked at home could and perhaps should, be made to work elsewhere. Such an approach, however, presented several challenges. Firstly, as de Tocqville observed, "the great advantage of the Americans is that they have arrived at a state of democracy without having to endure a democratic revolution." Instead, they were "born equal instead of becoming so."[26] As Walter Lippmann noted several centuries later, "merely to enfranchise the voters, even to give them a true representation, will not in itself establish self government; it may just as well lead . . . to a new form of absolute state, a self-perpetuating oligarchy."[27]

Secondly, there was a hubristic quality to the assertion that a political system that had been embraced by a nation of immigrants, fleeing persecution, and oppression by vested interests would be embraced by the nations that had been left in the first place. There was, perhaps, a poetic quality to such thinking, but that was not going to make it any more palatable to rulers, despots, monarchs, and tyrants. Kennan critiqued such efforts to "transpose the Anglo-Saxon concept of individual law into the international field and to make it applicable to governments as it is applicable at home to individuals." This, he argued, smacked of naivety. "People are unable to understand that what might have been possible for the thirteen colonies in a given set of circumstances might not be possible in the wider international field."[28]

Thirdly, was the matter of timescales. As Lippmann noted, "democracy is not the creation of abstract theorists. It is the creation of men who step by step though centuries of disorder established a regime of order."[29] The constitutionally prescribed political timescales of American life, with elections every 2 years, do not reward careful, thought-out commitments to long-term initiatives. Instead, they reward short-term, easy fixes, designed to bring fast results with minimal expense and low casualties. Presidents, clearly, "do not pursue policy in a vacuum."[30] Their policies are in part dependent on election cycles, public support for the administration, and party control of Congress.

This has been exacerbated by the rise of 24-hour media and the explosion of social network platforms, all desperate for sensational stories and unlikely or unwilling to dwell on policy initiatives that are not high impact or dynamic in nature. Such a political and cultural environment appears ill-placed for long-term ideological projects designed to instill democracy in foreign lands. Brzezinski observed that "the spread of democracy is generally congenial to global peace"; however, the track record of American patience in regard to such overseas endeavors is not encouraging, as events in Somalia demonstrated.[31] Creating a political system that "protects freedom and sustains democracy . . . is hard work." It had not occurred overnight in the United States, but instead had taken 12 years, "from its Declaration of Independence in 1776 to ratification of its Constitution in 1788, to have a functional government."[32]

Finally, there remained the question over the rationale for such an enterprise. Was democracy promotion the benign act of a gentle, peace-loving superpower? Was it true, as Brzezinski insisted, that the United States merely "propagated a shared aspiration; it did not seek to impose its own political culture," or was this a naive interpretation of continuing efforts to remake the world in America's own self-image?[33] Was it "an unnecessary intrusion into the otherwise normal conduct of diplomatic relations," or instead "part of a practical strategy designed to advance American national interests?"[34]

All too often there appeared to be a stunning naivety to the concept of democracy promotion that emanated from Washington, as though having been the world's original constitutional democracy granted a sense of omnipotence or omniscience in regard to how best to govern far away lands. Despotism equated to evil in the minds of American policy makers and evil was portrayed as a threat to the American way of life that had to be extinguished. Such a concept was apparent in 1913 when the US Ambassador to London, Walter Page, advised the British Foreign Secretary Sir Edward Grey that the United States intended to "continue to shoot men . . . till they learn to vote and to rule themselves."[35] Such a stance reveals the contradiction in the American position, for "in a democracy the opposition not only is tolerated as constitutional but must be maintained because it is in fact indispensable. The democratic system cannot be operated without effective opposition."[36] Historically, therefore, the United States had not promoted nor exported democracy uniformly. With his victory in 1992, Bill Clinton had an opportunity to determine if the United States could extol the virtues of democracy any more equally and in a greater diversity of locations, in the new post-Cold War world.[37]

Promoting democracy in the Clinton administration

Bill Clinton identified the promotion of democracy as a key component of his grand strategy as early as December 1991. Speaking at Georgetown

University, Governor Clinton noted that "the defense of freedom and the promotion of democracy around the world aren't merely a reflection of our deepest values. They are vital to our national interests." Recognizing the calls to reduce defense spending, as well as the historic opportunity that existed to buttress the strategic gains made following the end of the Cold War, he insisted "as we restructure our military forces, we must reinforce the powerful global movement toward democracy."[38] Clinton's dedication to democracy promotion "stayed the course," during his 8 years in office, as the president "returned to the theme again and again."[39] As Clinton stated explicitly in 1997, democracy promotion was "one of the primary foreign policy objectives" of his administration, and remained so for the duration of his presidency.[40]

Anthony Lake was central to this effort and his philosophical approach to foreign policy was a strong influence on the president. Lake reiterated the administration's stance on democracy promotion in September 1993, insisting it was a policy that "protects our interests and security," and which "reflects values that are both American and universal." The opportunity existed, Lake observed, to "mobilize our nation in order to enlarge democracy, enlarge markets, and enlarge our future."[41] Lake heavily influenced the content and tone of US Grand Strategy in the first term and, while it may not have been everything he hoped for, he set the course for the administration's entire foreign policy.

Even Secretary of State Christopher, whose support for Lake's Democratic Enlargement policy was less than total, conceded in his appearance before Congress in March 1993 that the United States should "embrace and promote this process by sustained support for democratic institution-building in the former Soviet bloc and elsewhere. And we should by collective engagement, working in partnership with other great democracies, promote democracy around the globe."[42] Twelve days later, speaking in Chicago, he reiterated that "by helping promote democracy . . . we are also making a strategic investment in our nation's security."[43] Stuart Eizenstat, Under-Secretary of Commerce for International Trade noted in 1994, "Anthony Lake's enlargement strategy makes perfect sense. In the Cold War the concept was Containment, now it is to enlarge the scope of democracy. It's all about widening market access."[44] The combination of increasing access to markets and democracy promotion formed the basis of Lake's geostrategic outlook and was central to the Clinton administration's grand strategy.

Democracy promotion supported a key aspect of the entire grand strategy, which was to prevent a reversion to less open forms of government. Al Gore's national security adviser, Leon Fuerth, referred to the concept in terms of a Ratchet, designed to prevent reversals and ensure that, at the very least, democracy was maintained and expanded where possible. Democracy promotion provided the ideological rationale for this, as the administration observed that the number of states embracing democracy and rejecting authoritarian regimes was "one of the most gratifying and encouraging developments of the past fifteen years." In language that remained consistent throughout its first term, the administration conceded that while such advances were not guaranteed, grand strategy needed to address "the consolidation of those regimes and a broadening of their commitment to democracy." To achieve this, Clinton's Grand Strategy was committed to work "with new democratic states to help preserve them as democracies committed to free markets and respect for human rights."[45] The concept of democratic promotion bore the characteristics of American idealism, but the administration was eager to promote the policy as being more than just ideologically driven.

In this regard, democracy promotion, the final tenant of Clinton's Grand Strategy, complemented the emphasis on national security and prosperity promotion in content, intent, and tone. The Clinton administration presented Lake's Wilsonian-inspired concept as an indication of its commitment to democratic principles, but constantly stressed its real world, Realpolitik attributes. "In nearly every major foreign policy address they cite a host of ways that the spread of democracy abroad advances 'hard' U.S. security and economic interests, from reducing the chances of war to decreasing terrorism."[46] Clinton's Grand Strategy entailed a pragmatic embrace of democracy promotion, designed to ensure not only that democratic states survived and thrived, but also that they were accompanied by open markets, receptive to American goods and services.

Bureaucratic politics and democracy promotion

Although democracy promotion had been advocated, and in some cases actively pursued, by previous administrations, the Clinton White House sought to institutionalize the practice to an extent not previously attempted.[47] In an effort to avoid suggestions that the policy was beholden to any single individual or their department, the administration distributed responsibility for democracy promotion across the executive branch of government. At the State Department, the Clinton administration created the role of Under Secretary for Democracy and Global Affairs, a position initially held by Tim Wirth (1994–1997).[48] It also established the role of Assistant Secretary of State for Democracy, Human Rights, and Labor, in a role that built upon a position that President Carter had created in 1976, placing democracy promotion front and center.[49] The remit of the National Security Council was expanded to accommodate an office for democracy affairs and a new position of Assistant Secretary for Democracy and Peacekeeping was strongly considered over at the Pentagon.

In addition to the specific roles created at the NSC and the State Department, the Clinton administration also tasked the Assistant Secretary of State for Democracy, Human Rights, and Labor with overseeing an Inter-agency Working Group on Democracy, designed to coordinate programs and "reorganize the international affairs budget around strategic priorities."[50] This overarching, interagency approach reflected Secretary of State-designate Warren Christopher's announcement at his Senate confirmation hearings that "a strategic approach to promoting democracy requires that we coordinate all our leverage, including trade, economic and security assistance, and debt relief."[51] Having recognized the need for a coordinated effort, the administration's real challenge came in attempting to implement it within a federal bureaucracy that had historically proved notoriously change-averse.

The administration appointed USAID as the public face of its efforts to provide assistance to pro-democracy groups as part of its ongoing grand strategy initiatives. Since 1961, USAID had focused on issues of global economic and social development. During the Reagan administration, this role was expanded to incorporate a variety of roles, including the oversight of elections, particularly in the Western hemisphere.[52] With the end of the Cold War, USAID launched the Democracy Initiative in December 1990, placing the promotion of democracy at the forefront of its efforts. With the election of Bill Clinton, USAID became the logical agency to front the new attempt to promote democracy as an element of US Grand Strategy.

Democracy assistance programs benefited greatly as part of Clinton's Grand Strategy initiative, as spending increased from $100 million annually in 1990 to more than $700 million by 2000.[53] It was estimated that USAID spent $400 million on democracy assistance programs during FY 1994, as expenditure for USAID increased rapidly under the Clinton administration, rising from $5.3 million in 1990 to $119 million by 1994 for democratic governance programs in Africa.[54]

Democracy promotion, however, was not immune to domestic politics, especially following the 1994 mid-term elections. A key initiative of the administration was passage of the proposed the Peace, Prosperity and Democracy Act of 1994 (PPDA) to replace the Foreign Assistance Act of 1961. The initiative faltered however, as the new Chairman of the Senate Foreign Relations Committee, Jesse Helms, took offence at the levels of oversees aid: "The foreign aid program has spent an estimated $2 trillion of the American taxpayers' money, much of it going down foreign rat holes, to countries that constantly oppose the United States in the United Nations, and many reject concepts of freedom. We must stop this stupid business of giving away the taxpayers' money willy-nilly."[55] As the National Security Strategy of 1996 made clear, however, "Promoting democracy does more than foster our ideals. It advances our interests . . . Democracies create free markets that offer economic opportunity, make for more reliable trading partners and are far less likely to wage war on one another."[56] In such pronouncements, the Democratic Peace concept loomed large and demonstrated the inherent pragmatism that sat alongside idealism in the Clinton White House.

The Clinton administration's democracy promotion concept was imbued with national self-interest, concealed by a veneer of idealism, reflecting Anthony Lake's neo-Wilsonian approach to policy. "Democracy," insisted Lake, was "at once the foundation and the purpose of the international structures we must build."[57] The administration remained steadfast in its insistence that democracy promotion was vital not only to overseas recipients, but also to the United States as well, for despite the Wilsonian aspect to the principle, there was more than idealism at stake: "All of America's strategic interests—from promoting prosperity at home, to checking global threats abroad before they threaten our territory—are served by enlarging the community of democratic and free market nations."[58] The relationship between the three elements of the strategy was essential, not only to the program's success but also to any effort to comprehend the philosophical approach that led to its creation.

In 1991, Morton Halperin wrote in *Foreign Policy*, "When a people attempt to hold free elections and establish a constitutional democracy, the United States and the international community should not only assist but should guarantee the result."[59] Clinton's Grand Strategy incorporated Halperin's prescription, noting, "Domestic renewal will not succeed if we fail to engage abroad in foreign markets, to promote democracy in key countries and to counter and contain emerging threats."[60] However, those who believed that the United States would fight to ensure the survival and the success of liberty the world over had severely misread the document. This was a pragmatic policy for a pragmatic administration: "We must focus our efforts where we have the most leverage. And our efforts must be demanded driven—they must focus on nations where people are pushing for reform or have already secured it."[61]

Just as this was not an ideological struggle, neither was it unilateral, or designed to stand apart from the other components of grand strategy. It consistently recognized that the United States needed to aid "nations strengthen the pillars of civil society, improve their market institutions and fight corruption and political discontent through practices of good governance."[62] The policy recognized that "the first element of our democracy strategy is to work with the other democracies of the world and to improve our cooperation with them on security and economic issues. We also seek their support in enlarging the realm of democratic nations."[63] Clinton's strategy of democracy promotion, therefore, complemented the national security and prosperity promotion aspects of grand strategy and was a tool with which to cement US foreign initiatives into a growing number of multiregional institutions. Hence, throughout the administration, its policy spoke of helping to "staunch democratic reversals" in Haiti, Guatemala, and Nigeria and of providing democracies with "the fullest benefits of integration into foreign markets," which partly explained "why NAFTA and the GATT rank so high on our agenda."[64]

This may not have been a democratic crusade, but into the second term it remained expansive and idealist in nature, while acknowledging the need to adopt a tough stance when faced with political realities. The 1997 and 1998 grand strategy reports noted that the United States could not seek to export democracy unilaterally and sought "international support in helping strengthen democratic and free market institutions and norms in countries making the transition from closed to open societies." The administration continued to insist that "This commitment to see freedom and respect for human rights take hold is not only just, but pragmatic, for strengthened democratic institutions benefit the US and the world." The 1997 and 1998 reports emphasized US efforts to aid foreign nations "strengthen the pillars of civil society, supporting administration of justice and rule of law programs, assisting the development of democratic civil–military relations and providing human rights training to foreign police and security forces." The policy interaction that was central in the first term remained, as the second-term strategy insisted that the United States "must seek to improve their market institutions and fight corruption and political discontent by encouraging good governance practices."[65] Despite changes to the national security team, the goal of exporting democracy and open markets remained constant.

The Clinton administration sought to stress the success that democracy had enjoyed during its tenure in the White House, noting how the concept, "when allowed to be freely shared, can spread widely and rapidly, enhancing the security of all nations." However, the grand strategy stressed that moving forward, the United States "must focus on strengthening the commitment and capacity of nations to implement democratic reforms, protect human rights, fight corruption and increase transparency in government," an initiative exemplified by the Warsaw Declaration of June 2000 in which 106 countries embraced a criteria for democracy and pledged to help each other remain on the democratic path.[66] Clearly, therefore, this was to be a multilateral mission that, by its very nature, depended on the assistance of other nations and organizations for its success, including the United Nations. Despite congressional concerns over command and control during troop deployment, the United Nations remained the organization of choice for addressing a key aspect of democracy promotion: human rights.

Promoting human rights

The appointment of former Carter administration officials such as Anthony Lake, Warren Christopher, and Madeleine Albright guaranteed that an ethical dimension was intrinsic to Clinton's Grand Strategy, and this was most evident in its embrace of human rights. Grand strategy insisted the United States must "redouble" its efforts to guarantee basic human rights "on a global basis."[67] This aspect, as with all elements of the grand strategy, was designed to be mutually reinforcing, as the administration sought to "increase respect for fundamental human rights in all states and encourage an evolution to democracy," not universally, but "where that is possible."[68] The White House was adamant that "the more that democracy and political and economic liberalisation take hold in the world, particularly in countries of geo-strategic importance to us, the safer our nation is likely to be."[69] Markets and democracy formed the basis of Anthony Lake's geostrategic outlook and this was repeatedly exemplified in the administration's grand strategy.

Despite the idealistic nature of many aspects of the initiative, the administration was adamant that it not be misunderstood: "The core of our strategy is to help democracy and markets expand and survive," it reported. This would not occur everywhere, but where the United States had "the strongest security concerns and where we can make the greatest difference," as the administration attempted to blend idealism with a realist approach to policy implementation.[70] There were to be no flights of fancy, no efforts to liberate Cuba or Iran or sustained effort to hold China to account over its human rights abuses. The administration stressed that "the continued emergence of China as a great power that is stable politically and open economically, that respects human rights and the rule of law and that becomes a full partner in building a secure international order, is profoundly in America's interest and in the world's interest."[71] The White House was determined to clarify that "this is not a democratic crusade." It was, instead, "a pragmatic commitment to see freedom take hold where that will help us most."[72] In this regard, the administration drew a bold distinction between its efforts and the rhetorical high point of the Cold War when Clinton's political hero had asserted America's intention to "pay any price, bear any burden, meet any hardship, support any friend, oppose any foe to assure the survival and the success of liberty." Such pledges were now a thing of the past.

The Kennedy legend had served Clinton's purposes during the campaign, but in office, Clinton embraced Rooseveltian pragmatism over Kennedyesque romanticism. Gone was any pledge to "those people in the huts and villages of half the globe struggling to break the bonds of mass misery." No longer would the United States "pledge our best efforts to help them help themselves," despite Kennedy's promise to do so "for whatever period is required."[73] The Clinton administration was eager to champion its success in lobbying for the reaffirmation of the universality of human rights at a 1993 United Nations Conference and the establishment of a UN High Commissioner for Human Rights. However, US priorities had changed considerably since 1961 as the Clinton administration insisted, "we must focus our efforts where we have the most leverage."[74] Where this sentiment left Kennedy's assertion that "a free society [that] cannot help the many who are poor . . . [could not] save the few who are rich," remained unaddressed.[75]

Deep into the second term, Clinton's Grand Strategy continued "to press for political liberalization and respect for basic human rights worldwide, including in countries that continue to defy democratic advances."[76] Changes were apparent, however, as the administration advocated bilateral as well as multilateral action to ensure adherence to human rights and democratic principles.[77] The insertion of bilateral options was indicative of a sense of frustration within the administration in regard to the United Nations that had grown since the Somali operation and the difficulties in enacting policy in Bosnia due to Russia's veto on the Security Council. With a more robust second-term foreign policy team came a change in language and tone that was subtler than that of the George W. Bush administration in 2001, but which was determined not to be stymied by international prevarication in the face of US determination to act.

As the second term drew to a close, Clinton's Grand Strategy reiterated the need to work bilaterally and with international organizations, to promote "universal adherence to democratic principles and international standards of human rights." The policy noted the challenges posed by ethnic conflict, insisting that "innocent civilians should not be subject to forcible relocation or slaughter because of their religious, ethnic, racial, or tribal heritage," as such a situation constituted "a grave violation of universal human rights."[78] In 2000, US Grand Strategy went further, insisting that "when this occurs, the intersection of our values and national interests make it imperative," that the United States "work to strengthen the capacity of the international community to prevent and, whenever possible, stop outbreaks of mass killing and displacement."[79]

In the second term, US Grand Strategy reflected a traditional American philosophy in relation to democracy promotion and human rights advocacy. The administration continued to "encourage governments to not return people to countries where they face persecution—to provide asylum as appropriate, to offer temporary protection to persons fleeing situations of conflict or generalized human rights abuses."[80] In addition to previous years, the 2000 policy argued that by providing humanitarian assistance, US Grand Strategy was "in keeping with our values and objective of promoting democracy and human rights."[81]

Humanitarian assistance

Clinton's Grand Strategy was adamant that US global leadership had never been more important and insisted that the values that had previously been threatened by imperialism, fascism, and communism remained at risk in the post-Cold War world. As a result, its democracy promotion and human rights initiatives were complemented by humanitarian assistance programs, "designed to alleviate human suffering and to pave the way for progress towards establishing democratic regimes with a commitment to respect for human rights and appropriate strategies for economic development."[82] US Grand Strategy revealed the administration's priorities for the world at large: "to secure the peace won in the Cold War against those who would still deny people their human rights, terrorists who threaten innocents and pariah states who choose repression and extremism over openness and moderation."[83] The policy was primarily aimed at stemming the potential for international tensions that were the by-product of forced population migration and refugee flows. The dilemma for the Clinton White House was how to implement such policies and how much political capital to expend to ensure their success?

This was a dilemma for foreign policy in general, but particularly so with regard to humanitarian assistance, which in itself posed no direct challenge to US interests and so made justifying expenditure all the more difficult. It was also a policy that depended on long-term multilateral cooperation with a range of agencies including the International Red Cross and the UN High Commissioner for Refugees. Importantly, throughout the first term, the administration repeatedly committed to providing "appropriate financial support" to strengthen such entities and their missions, but stopped short of committing human resources in all instances. The administration sought to engage in "voluntary repatriation of refugees," in a way that took into account the "human rights concerns as well as the economic conditions that may have driven them out in the first place," ensuring that, once again, economic considerations found their way to the heart of grand strategy.

Espousing policy in this area was also problematic due to the track record of events during the first term. The administration could address humanitarian assistance in the abstract and insist that "helping refugees return to their homes in Mozambique, Afghanistan, Eritrea, Somalia and Guatemala" was a high priority, but its actions in Somalia, Haiti, Rwanda, and Bosnia called into question the commitment to the policy.[84] The unfortunate disconnect between policy development and its execution, therefore, raised ongoing questions about the implementation of Clinton's Grand Strategy as anything more than a philosophical exercise. Until the successful application of humanitarian policies in Haiti and Bosnia, grand strategy in this regard remained entirely theoretical, with sweeping assertions and promises of commitment, which appeared hollow in the face of hesitancy overseas. The administration's case was not aided by its glossing over of incidents that reflected poorly on the United States and its tendency to focus on areas where it could highlight relatively minor successes.

Having chosen initially not to intervene in Rwanda and Bosnia, US Grand Strategy sought to leverage credibility by highlighting the American lead "in assisting the UN to set up international tribunals to enforce accountability for the war crimes in the former Yugoslavia and in Rwanda."[85] Suffice to say, this appeared to many to be too little, too late for the people of the Balkans or Rwanda. However, to govern is to make choices and as defined by its grand strategy, Rwanda remained outside the US sphere of interest, since it had no strategic importance and appeared incapable of sustaining a viable middle class, necessary for the implementation of democracy promotion. The Clinton administration was also still in the process of withdrawing from Somalia, making another African deployment politically untenable. The administration had no interest or intention in intervening in Rwanda, despite Anthony Lake's personal interest in Africa.

However, the White House was torn on the issue, leading the NSC's legal adviser, Alan J. Kreczko, to advise the NSC's Senior Director for African Affairs that, "concluding that genocide has occurred/is occurring in Rwanda does not create a legal obligation to take particular action to stop it. (Human rights groups have argued to the contrary, saying failure to act makes one legally responsible as an accomplice. We would not agree.)" Kreczko conceded that "making such a determination will increase political pressure to do something about it."[86] Kreczko concluded that the drawdown of US forces in Rwanda had been a "very bad process, unnecessarily resorted to, with risk of embarrassing the POTUS if repeated."[87]

Despite the apparent disconnect between policy and practice, as its second term began, the Clinton administration continued to stress that its grand strategy was rooted in "efforts to promote democracy and human rights are complemented by our humanitarian assistance programs," which were "designed to alleviate human suffering, to help establish democratic regimes that respect human rights and to pursue appropriate strategies for economic development."[88] Not only was this seen as the morally correct course of action, but the most pragmatic, since it enabled the United States "to help prevent humanitarian disasters with far more significant resource implications." Pragmatism continued to define Clinton's Grand Strategy, a fact that the documentation makes explicit: "Supporting the global movement toward democracy requires a pragmatic and long-term effort focused on both values and institutions."[89] This policy required the United States to work in partnership with other nations, supranational entities, private firms, and nongovernmental organizations. This was a reflection of the administration's early embrace of globalization and its appreciation that the United States could not lead in all instances.

Clinton's Grand Strategy continued to stress a determination to work both multilaterally and bilaterally to protect vulnerable members of society. Where the first-term reports spoke in generalities, the strategy from 1998 was more direct and took issue with specific nations, such as Russia and China, which the administration pledged to "continue to work with" in an ongoing effort "to combat religious persecution."[90] From 1999, religious freedom was advanced as "one of the highest concerns in our foreign policy," since "freedom of thought, conscience and religion is a bedrock issue for the American people." The president signed the International Religious Freedom Act of 1998, to advance religious freedom and counter religious persecution. In September 1999, the administration released a 1,100-page document covering the status of religious freedom in 194 countries, as the first phase of the act. Finally, in October 2000, the administration "designated and sanctioned the Taliban regime in Afghanistan, Burma, China, Iran, Iraq, Sudan, and the Milosevic regime in Serbia as 'countries of particular concern' for having engaged in or tolerated particularly severe violations of religious freedom."[91] Such concerns were expressed directly to the Chinese leadership during Clinton's 1998 state visit when he rebuked President Jiang Zemin over the deaths in Tiananmen Square, insisting that "for all of our agreements, we still disagree about the meaning of what happened then. I believe and the American people believe that the use of force and the tragic loss of life was wrong."[92]

Pragmatism remained central to an appreciation of the administration's approach to democracy promotion and humanitarian assistance. The White House had a philosophical commitment to both, but in all cases it adopted a far more realist approach than its critics conceded or its supporters cared to admit. It was an approach that granted room to maneuver but which garnered few admirers due to its ideological flexibility. In a world in flux, however, such an approach appeared eminently logical, especially at a time when foreign affairs were far from the minds of the American electorate. Every potential intervention and every opportunity to offer humanitarian assistance was addressed on its merits, since "sometimes collective military action is both appropriate and feasible and necessary."[93] However, "sometimes concerted economic and political pressure, combined with diplomacy, is a better answer."[94] Joined up policy coordination was vital and "all public diplomacy and international information efforts [must] be coordinated and integrated into our foreign and national security policy-making process." As the administration prepared to leave the White House, it noted that at times "the imperative for action" would be "much less clear" and that "The United States and other countries cannot respond to every humanitarian crisis in the world."[95] Pragmatism, therefore, defined the administration until the very end.

The global implementation of democracy promotion

Clinton's Grand Strategy reflected the belief that security, economics, and democracy were "mutually supportive" and self-sustaining: an improving economic climate in newly democratic states may lead to improved international cooperation and create new markets for US exports. These policies were advocated on the principle that "secure nations are more likely to support free trade and maintain democratic structures . . . democratic states are less likely to threaten our interests and more likely to cooperate with the US to meet security threats and promote sustainable development."[96] They also aided in "protecting the lives and personal safety of Americans . . . and providing for the well-being and prosperity of our nation."[97] The pragmatism that defined Clinton's Grand Strategy was present in its global implementation of democracy promotion, as Lake insisted, "we are not starry eyed about the prospects for democracy—it will not take hold everywhere. But we know that the larger the pool of democracies, the better off we will be."[98] However, there remained the contentious question of how best to execute such policies.

In retrospect, the "uneven nature" of the administration's implementation of democracy promotion was "striking," as its focus ranged "from serious engagement to almost complete disinterest."[99] However, in language that remained consistent throughout its 8 years in office, the Clinton administration recognized as early as 1994 that attempts to consolidate democracy and markets must be "as varied as the nations involved." It was certain, however, that there were "common elements." The administration presented its grand strategy as a bespoke policy, reflecting the challenges and opportunities of the era: each region was assessed in terms of its needs, status, and capacity to implement the policy as the administration sought to ensure its approach was "tailored to their unique challenges and opportunities."[100]

The Pacific Rim/China

In its attempt to rationalize the global implementation of its grand strategy, the Clinton administration was loathed to accept that certain areas of the world were less receptive to democratic reform than others. However, throughout the first term, US Grand Strategy in China and the Pacific Rim remained consistent. "Nowhere," the administration insisted, were "the strands of our three-pronged strategy more intertwined, nor is the need for continued US engagement more evident." However, while the White House wished to support what it saw as "the wave of democratic reform sweeping the region," it found this difficult to implement during its time in office. The administration recognized that its grand strategy needed to be flexible to accommodate regional differences, acknowledging that Western concepts of democracy and social behavior differed greatly from those in Asia. This presented challenges not only in implementing political reform, but also in terms of the physiological barriers involved in changing attitudes:

> Some have argued that democracy is somehow unsuited for Asia or at least for some Asian nations—that human rights are relative and that they simply mask Western culturalism and imperialism. These voices are wrong. It is not Western imperialism, but the aspirations of Asian peoples themselves that explain the growing number of democracies and the growing strength of democracy movements everywhere in Asia. It is an insult to the spirit, the hopes, and the dreams of the people who live and struggle in those countries to assert otherwise.

In an effort to resolve the chasm between the policy of democracy promotion and its actual implementation, the administration stressed that "each nation must find its own form of democracy." This pragmatic approach, however, left the administration open to charges of double standards, but the alternative would have been an inflexible, seemingly intolerant foreign policy, offensive to many parts of the world and difficult, if not impossible, to implement. To many, however, this appeared to be an easy way out of an impossible dilemma and raised doubts over the administration's ability to face hard decisions and stand by them. The White House insisted, however, that there was "no cultural justification for torture or tyranny," and "refused to let repression cloak itself in moral relativism." Democracy and human rights, it stressed, were "universal yearnings and universal norms" and pledged to "continue to press respect for human rights in countries as diverse as China and Burma."[101]

The Clinton administration's decision to separate China's MFN status from its record on human rights was of vital significance in the region and reflected the financial motivations inherent in the grand strategy initiative. The administration presented this as an attempt to improve relations, but the decision proved to be one of the most significant of Clinton's time in office and revealed a move away from an initial idealism to a more pragmatic approach to world affairs. Whereas President Woodrow Wilson made the world safe for democracy, Clinton sought to make the world safe for commerce, as human rights took a secondary role to the promotion of trade.

The second-term grand strategy documentation was driven more by events than philosophy. In regard to East Asia and the Pacific, it focused heavily upon events that had transpired in Indonesia, East Timor, and Burma. It continued to argue against what it referred to as "cultural imperialism" by refusing to accept that "democracy is unsuited for Asia or at least for some Asian nations [and] that human rights are relative."[102] The democracy promotion aspect of US Grand Strategy in Asia during Clinton's second term sought to focus upon "cementing America's role as a stabilizing force in a more integrated Asia Pacific region"[103] by continuing to stress the inherent linkage between security, economics, and democracy, insisting that the United States "continue to support the democratic aspirations of Asian/Pacific peoples and to promote respect for human rights."[104] In its dealings with the Pacific Rim nations, the Clinton policy of Engagement and Enlargement can be seen to have combined the key tenets of democracy promotion, military preparedness, and prosperity promotion. However, such an approach was not tied to the Pacific Rim alone. The administration was at pains to define Engagement and Enlargement as a true global policy, one capable of replacing Containment for a new geopolitical age.

The Western hemisphere

If China and much of Asia presented a series of seemingly endless challenges, then the Western hemisphere appeared to be a very different proposition and was seen as "a fertile field for a strategy of Engagement and Enlargement."[105] Much had changed since the turbulent era of the 1960s–1980s, as the continent's rulers were turning increasingly democratic. The administration believed that what it defined as being "the unprecedented triumph of democracy," in the region presented "an unparalleled opportunity to secure the benefits of peace and stability" throughout the hemisphere.[106] The administration saw great hope in the fact that "the nations of the Western hemisphere have proclaimed their commitment to democratic regimes and the collective responsibility of the nations of the Organization of American States to respond to threats to democracy."[107]

However, Cuba remained a particular blot on the hemispheric landscape. The administration's efforts to support the restoration of democracy in Haiti enabled the White House to boast that, partly due to its action, Cuba remained the only nondemocratic state in the region. It acknowledged, however, that it remained "committed to extending democracy to the handful of remaining outposts where the region's people are not free. The Cuban Democracy Act remains the framework for our policy toward Cuba; our goal is the peaceful reestablishment of democratic governance for the people of Cuba."[108]

The Castro regime, like that of Saddam, was not prioritized. Successive American administration's had pledged to end Castro's time in power and had left office certain only in the knowledge that they had failed to do so. With the demise of the Soviet Union, Cuba had lost its international sponsor, as had the nations of Eastern Europe, and while the tide of democracy had not yet reached Cuban shores, it was deemed realistic to expect that it would ultimately do so. Until then, Cuba offered nothing in regard to the national security framework that Engagement and Enlargement was defining. It posed no threat to the United States; it was not initiating plans for democratic governance; and there were no signs of a market economy developing in the near future. US Grand Strategy was committed to the "peaceful establishment of democratic governance for the people of Cuba," a move that saw development in October 1995, when the United States took steps to "promote the cause of peaceful change in Cuba." These included tightening the economic embargo and "reaching out to nongovernmental organizations, churches, human rights groups and other elements of Cuba's civil society," in an attempt to "strengthen the agents of peaceful change."[109]

Having previously been a political victim of migration from Cuba while governor of Arkansas, Bill Clinton was determined that history not repeat itself and this was reflected in grand strategy that sought to prevent "a mass migration [from Cuba] that would endanger the lives of migrants and safety of our nation."[110] The administration sought to build upon the Papal visit of January 1998 by "expanding the role of the Catholic Church and other elements of civil society, and increase humanitarian assistance." It was anticipated that as Cubans felt an incentive to take charge of their own future, they were "more likely to stay at home and build the informal and formal structures that will make transition easier."[111] Castro's 33 year defiance of the United States continued unabated, and Clinton found that Dr Castro remained in office long after his own second term had expired. In the 1990s, however, the primary US objective was "to preserve and defend civilian elected governments and strengthen democratic practices respectful of human rights."[112]

Efforts to ensure free and fair elections in Peru were far from successful, but the White House's ability to leverage President Fujimori was reduced due to its dependency on his government in the continuing war on drugs. The most evident lack of progress in the hemisphere was in Haiti, where much was promised, but with disappointing results. The fiasco surrounding the reinstatement of ousted leader Jean-Bertrand Aristide encapsulated the well-intended but flawed efforts in the country, whose "catastrophic economic situation and ragged socio-political history" made it an unlikely location for a successful implementation of such a policy. Indeed, as Thomas Carothers has noted, "the fact that the administration chose one of the least promising countries in the world to be the leading edge of its democracy policy reflects a persistent unwillingness to think strategically rather than idealistically in this domain."[113]

Africa

Africa was a continent of special interest to Anthony Lake. His first public address as National Security Adviser had been on the subject, and he had a track record of publications dealing with the challenges faced by the continent. However, it was always going to be difficult to see how democracy promotion was to be implemented on the continent. Indeed the administration was stark, referring to Africa as "one of our greatest challenges for a strategy of Engagement and Enlargement." Specifically, there was little in the way of existing democracy to build on and, therefore, few opportunities to greatly enhance American interests on a continent that few believed posed a threat to America's national security.

However, the administration was eager to present a positive portrayal of its actions in Africa, especially in light of the Somali incident, which was now rendered in a new manner: "US forces in Somalia allowed us to break through the chaos that had prevented the introduction of relief supplies and UN peacekeepers. US forces prevented the deaths of hundreds of thousands of Somalis, established a logistics system and then turned over the mission to more than 25,000 UN peacekeepers." The report shied away from the events that led to the deaths of US servicemen in the operation. It was clear, however, as early as 1994, that despite the administration's good intentions, "the responsibility for the fate of a nation rests finally with its own people."[114]

Africa was recognized as being a particularly difficult region within which to enact a policy of Engagement and Enlargement, and the events in Mogadishu had done little to convince policy makers otherwise. The one great region of hope of course was South Africa, where Nelson Mandela had recently become president. The country's rejection of apartheid had now made possible what the administration referred to as "a bilateral commission to foster new cooperation between our nations."[115] The United States worked to assist the transition to democracy in South Africa, supporting the nation's first presidential election with $35 million in aid, followed quickly by a commitment of $600 million in trade and investment packages.[116]

While the historic developments in South Africa gave reason for rejoicing, however, the outlook in the rest of the continent remained grim. While USAID's Greater Horn of Africa program successfully prevented a famine that had threatened millions of lives, the administration's actions in Africa were constantly overshadowed by the Somali deployment.[117]

US Grand Strategy recognized its limitations and sought to find solace in "states whose entry into the camp of market democracies may influence the future direction of an entire region; South Africa now holds that potential with regard to sub-Saharan Africa."[118] US Grand Strategy noted that the "restoration of democracy and respect for human rights in Nigeria has long been one of our major objectives in Africa."[119] President Clinton met with Nigeria's President Obasanjo at the White House in October 1999 and reaffirmed the US commitment to assist him on "the challenges and security, economic, political and social issues." The administration noted the benefits derived from Nigeria's restoration of democracy and the hope that this may open the way for Nigeria to become a leader in Africa. Peaceful elections in 1999 and the inauguration of the new civilian government in May 1999 were seen as "important steps" in this process.

US Grand Strategy noted that in Africa, as elsewhere, "democracies have proved stronger partners for peace, stability and sustained prosperity," and pledged to work "to broaden the growing circle of African democracies."[120] Democracy promotion in Africa was attempted via a $30 million Great Lakes Justice Initiative, which committed the United States to working "with both the people and governments of the Democratic Republic of Congo, Rwanda and Burundi to support judicial systems which are impartial, credible, effective and inclusive." This initiative sought to strengthen Ministries of Justice and Interior, create civilian law enforcement, provide human rights training, and demobilize irregular elements of standing armies.[121]

US Grand Strategy in Africa continued to "support and promote . . . national reforms and the evolution of regional arrangements" that contributed to pan-African cooperation, but acknowledged that "the prosperity and security of Africa" depended on "African leadership, strong national institutions, and extensive political and economic reform."[122] It conceded, however, that it was "in the U.S. interest to support and promote such reforms,"[123] and in doing so defy what it acknowledged as a sense of "Afro-pessimism" that existed due to the "nexus of economic, political, social, ethnic and environmental challenges" that faced the continent.[124]

Europe

Despite the many challenges it faced in global regions, the Clinton administration had doubtless expected a far easier reception in Europe. Europe in general and the United Kingdom in particular greeted Clinton's election with caution. European leaders had developed strong working relations with the Bush administration and were wary of the New Democrat president, who appeared to view relations with Europe as passé and indicated that the White House prioritized dealings with the Pacific Rim nations. This sentiment echoed Secretary of State John Hay's statement in the early twentieth century that "the Mediterranean is the ocean of the past, the Atlantic the ocean of the present and the Pacific the ocean of the future."[125] Indeed, for the last 50 years "People have been speculating as to whether the United States is losing interest in Europe! Whether it's titling to Asia, whether the Special Relationship is no longer special, whether this particular president couldn't give a damn about it!"[126] These concerns were exacerbated when President Clinton failed to visit the continent during his first year in office, failing to do so until January 1994 when he addressed a NATO summit in Brussels.

The early detachment from Europe was reversed as President Clinton made four trips to the continent in 1994, a "commitment of presidential time and attention" that revealed what Richard Holbrooke referred to as "an inescapable but little-realized fact: The United States has become a European power in a sense that goes beyond traditional assertions of America's 'commitment' to Europe."[127] In addition to opening markets, the administration was eager to see democracy take hold in the former Warsaw Pact nations, believing that democratic and economic reform in former communist states were "the best measures to avert conditions which could foster aggressive nationalism and ethnic hatreds."[128] What was less self-evident was how the relationship might develop if and when true political and economic integration occurred in Europe, with the potential threats such an entity could pose for the United States. However, the Clinton administration was adamant that its goal remained "an integrated democratic Europe co-operating with the United States to keep the peace and promote prosperity."[129]

It was evident that elements of grand strategy were more applicable in certain regions than others and, while democracy promotion had little direct impact on Western Europe, the strategy was particularly relevant to Central and Eastern Europe. As President Clinton declared in Budapest, in December 1994, "The end of the Cold War presents us with the opportunity to fulfil the promise of democracy and freedom . . . we must not allow the Iron Curtain to be replaced by a veil of indifference."[130] Madeline Albright observed that in the early 1990s, Central Europe "was still seen by many Americans as a mysterious collective entity characterised by medieval castles, spicy sausages and an insufficient supply of vowels."[131] The view was not dissimilar in Western Europe, where members of the European Union were less than eager to incorporate the Central and Eastern European states. Various reasons existed for this reticence, not least of which was the recent recession, as well as political concerns over the potential eastward focus of the organization. These reasons contributed to the Clinton administration's embrace of NATO expansion "as a guarantor of European democracy and a force for European stability." The White House insisted that NATO must play the leading role in promoting "a more integrated, secure Europe prepared to respond to new challenges."[132]

Despite the organization's military focus, the administration recognized its capacity to advance political, social, and democratic reform by admitting former adversaries. There was also a logistical reason for adopting this approach: expanding NATO "was actually easier than the European Union, because NATO only involves a defense commitment, which they were very happy to give." Enlarging the European Union, however, involved "so many changes in your domestic legislation and so many transitional arrangements are required, that was always going to take a lot more time."[133] Suggestions made at the time that the nations of Eastern Europe may have been better integrated by expanding the European Union failed to account for the political realities of the era. This was not a viable option considering the nature of European relations at the time, for in addition to a continent-wide recession, there was the geopolitical reality to consider: coming so soon after the reunification of Germany, another seismic shift in the European Union was far from welcomed by France, which sought to ensure that the European Union remained focused on Western Europe.[134] This was recognized in Washington, as Holbrooke noted that expansion of NATO and the European Union would not be simultaneous and "their memberships will never be identical." They were, however, "clearly mutually supportive."[135]

By 1998, the Clinton administration could observe that "the prospect of joining or rejoining the Western democratic family through NATO, the EU and other institutions has strengthened the forces of democracy and reform in many countries of the region and encouraged them to settle long-standing disputes over borders and ethnic minorities."[136] This not only had security and economic implications, but also exemplified Leon Fuerth's Ratchet concept, of locking nations into new, democratically focused entities, in a deliberate attempt to prevent a reversion to Cold War alliances. The administration saw this move as a benefit to all and especially the United States: "Expanding the Alliance will promote our interests by reducing the risk of instability or conflict in Europe's eastern half. It will help assure that no part of Europe will revert to a zone of great power competition or a sphere of influence." Above all, it would "build confidence and give new democracies a powerful incentive to consolidate their reforms."[137]

The Clinton administration believed that NATO expansion was the first move in the process of integrating Central and Eastern Europe into the European Union, and therefore represented "another element of a policy aimed at 'locking in' democracy where it has been achieved in Eastern Europe."[138] This approach made great strides throughout the administration's time in office, ensuring that by 1997, the administration was already noting that its ambition was to "complete" the construction of a truly democratic Europe.[139] Although the concept of nation building may have been off the table, the administration was insistent that in Central and Eastern Europe, it was determined to work "with our West European partners [to help] these nations build civil societies."[140] To this end, the administration worked actively with varying groups to ensure that "throughout the region, targeted exchange programs have familiarized key decision-makers and opinion-moulders with the workings of American democracy."[141] Grand strategy focused on support for increased integration and the utilization of supranational organizations to cement democratic and market reforms. These varied from state to state and from region to region, depending on which approach was the most practical. By January 2001, the Clinton administration highlighted elections in Croatia, Montenegro, and Kosovo as evidence of its successful advocacy of democracy in the region. Such initiatives had been possible due to "the UN, EU, and NATO operations in the area focused on developing professional civil and military institutions that are respectful and promote human rights and respect for civil authority." Efforts to implement democracy in this region served to deepen "support for those civil efforts that promote democracy, the rule of law and respect for human rights."[142]

These moves were complemented by the administration's support of the International Criminal Tribunal for the former Yugoslavia, which it heralded as a direct result of its efforts at Dayton in 1995. It was clear from the administration's consideration of grand strategy on the European continent that this work would not be completed during its time in office. This was to be "the work of generations." Setbacks would occur and the process would be complex. However, "as long as these states continue their progress towards democracy and respect the rights of their own and other people, that they understand the rights of their minorities and their neighbours," the administration planned to "support their progress with a steady patience."[143] This element of grand strategy with regard to democracy promotion in Europe remained constant during the Clinton years. It sought "to build a Europe that is truly integrated, democratic, prosperous and at peace" and in doing so, "complete the mission the United States launched fifty years ago with the Marshall Plan and the North Atlantic Treaty Organization."[144]

Russia and the newly independent states

From the beginning of the Clinton administration's time in office, the most ideological aspect of its grand strategy was designed to "to support the growth of democracy and individual freedoms" that had begun in Russia. The White House believed that such reforms enhanced US security and provided a solution to "the aggressive nationalism and ethnic hatreds unleashed by the end of the Cold War."[145] Success was far from certain, however, as Strobe Talbott warned, "among the contingencies for which [we] must be prepared is that Russia will abandon democracy and return to threatening patterns of international behaviour that have sometimes characterized its history."[146]

From their first meeting in April 1993, however, President Clinton and Boris Yeltsin developed a strong working relationship that set the tone for US–Russian relations in the 1990s. Clinton recognized the scale of the task ahead: "The Russians are trying to undertake three fundamental changes at once: moving from a Communist to a market economy; moving from a tyrannical dictatorship to a democracy; and moving to an independent nation state away from having a great empire. And these are very difficult and unsettling times."[147] Therefore, support for Russia was designed to be "tangible to the Russian people . . . our challenge is to provide some tools to help the Russians do things that work for themselves."

In its priorities, it is possible to see Clinton's philosophy of foreign and domestic linkage in contrast to the policies of the past. Present were the New Democrat notions of providing opportunity while demanding greater responsibility in return, the idea that foreign investment should be promoted as a means to enhance American security and the realization that such programs would not result in immediate success and needed to be viewed as long-term initiatives.[148] The Clinton administration presented its initiatives as an extension of its domestic agenda, since a resurgent Russia would cause America "to restructure our defenses to meet a whole different set of threats than those we now think will occur . . . Therefore, our ability to put people first at home requires that we put Russia and its neighbours first on our agenda abroad."[149]

President Clinton saw his relationship with Russia as fulfilling two criteria. First, it was portrayed as an extension of efforts to enhance the US economy and, secondly, it granted him a specific role to play on the world stage—a role he turned to with increasing regularity as his domestic programs floundered in Congress. However, given the political climate during the 1990s, grand strategy did not escape partisan criticism, especially on Capitol Hill, where not everyone endorsed this relationship, or Clinton's approach to Russia. Senate Majority Leader Bob Dole insisted that it was wrong to ignore Yeltsin's "serious errors," his "move toward authoritarian rule," or the fact that he had "lost the political support of virtually all reform-minded Russians."[150] Dole insisted that US policy toward Russia should be based on an acceptance that the nations were rivals with conflicting national interests. The Clinton administration, he insisted, had a "misguided devotion" to a "Yeltsin first policy," which caused the loss of "a tremendous opportunity to state American concerns forcefully before thousands were slaughtered in Chechnya."[151]

Not surprisingly the administration did not concur with Dole's sentiment. Anthony Lake stressed, "To state that this is a Russia-first policy or that we have somehow failed to make known our concerns on Chechnya is simply wrong."[152] However, maintaining a working relationship with Yeltsin was essential for Clinton's Grand Strategy which sought to maintain peace with the former Cold War rival, while simultaneously supporting the spread of democracy in the former Soviet satellite states. In spite of criticism, the administration took comfort from the fact that Russians were now capable of electing their leaders "for the first time in 1,000 years" and presented this as a reason why the United States "should support those Russians who are struggling for a democratic, prosperous future."[153]

As Walter Russell Mead noted, "Russians must choose their future for themselves and in their own way. But with the help of Japan and our allies in Europe, we can create the conditions that give the Russian people a real chance to build prosperity and democracy." However, the Clinton administration's support for Yeltsin ensured that the White House was forced to overlook the Russian military engagement in Chechnya and was unable to adequately engender a true sense of democracy. So long as Boris Yeltsin remained in power, "there was also a tendency to underestimate the strength of the dark forces in Russia and to overestimate the ability of the Russian government to create and maintain the conditions for Polish style economic reforms."[154] Too much, it appeared, was dependent on the personal relationship between Clinton and Yeltsin, a fact that became all too apparent when the Russian leader suddenly left office, replaced by the former KGB colonel, Vladimir Putin. Despite the peaceful transfer of power from Yeltsin to Putin, doubts were now raised as to the viability of democracy under the former KGB chief.[155]

On June 3, 2000, Clinton held his first formal meeting with Putin. A memo from Sandy Berger stressed the importance of visuals as well as content: "On Saturday evening, you will have a meeting/working dinner with President Putin. The pictures of your first encounter will be important, and we recommend business attire. We want to convey 'getting down to business' and avoid the inaccurate charge that we're embracing Putin without question." Gone were the bear-hugs and laughter associated with the Yeltsin era as both sides recognized the beginning of a new stage in US–Russian relations. Berger stressed "this is a working visit with a broad agenda of establishing a relationship with the newly elected government," in which "the importance of continued engagement with Russia and the Newly Independent States" was to be prioritized.[156] As President Clinton became the first American president to address the Russian Duma, he sought to use the opportunity to press for continued Russian progress on economic reform, arms control, and encouraging Putin to preserve Russia's democratic gains. Whatever progress was made with Russia, however, US efforts at rapprochement with the Kremlin and its efforts to utilize the United Nations as a vehicle of choice for foreign policy initiatives were both hindered by developments in the Balkans, where US Grand Strategy initiatives were put to the test.

Democracy promotion in the Balkans

The Balkan crisis evolved during the end of the Cold War when the world's attention was diverted away from the region. By the time focus had been brought to bear on the situation, European insistence on taking the lead initially enabled the United States to avoid the issue. However, a degree of paranoia affected both parties: the United States refused to send observers to European-sponsored peace talks for fear of implying

US involvement, while European determination to pursue a diplomatic solution led them to preclude the use of NATO, which was dependent on American hardware. As early as May 1991, the *International Herald Tribune* carried the headline: "NATO's Bosnia Dithering: Waiting for the US to Lead."[157]

Critics of US inaction in the region overlook the assertion of Luxembourg's Foreign Minister Jacques Poos that "this is the hour of Europe, not of America," a sentiment echoed by the President of the European Community, Jacques Delors, who declared, "we do not interfere in American affairs; we trust America will not interfere in European affairs."[158] These statements highlighted European impotence and were used by Washington as a rationale for avoiding military intervention. They were, in the words of Sir Malcolm Rifkind, "simply foolish."[159] However, the United States decided to take the Europeans at their word. "They will screw it up," Secretary of State Eagleburger argued, "and this will teach them a lesson."[160] Eagleburger's comments proved to be prophetic, with disastrous implications for European aspirations of military and diplomatic self-sufficiency and far worse implications for those living in the Balkans.

During the 1992 campaign, Clinton had promised a "forward leaning position" and refused to rule out air strikes against Serb positions or the lifting of the arms embargo on the Bosnians.[161] During his confirmation hearings, Warren Christopher said that the world "must bring real pressures, economic and military, to bear on the Serbian leadership" and that unilateral American action was not impossible.[162] Once in office, however, Clinton was faced with the practical realities of such a policy and began to prevaricate on potential deployments, an approach that did little to inspire confidence in the administration or the president.

Clinton initially asked Colin Powell about the prospect of using airpower, but without being "too punitive." Powell mocked this request in his memoir, noting, "there it was again, the ever-popular solution from the skies, with a good humanist twist; let's not hurt anybody."[163] This was indicative of the relationship between the White House and the Pentagon in the first 18 months of the administration, as the "deep division" over the "merits of intervention" contributed to a sense of a lack of direction. The Bosnian situation may have been "the most urgent foreign policy issue facing the Clinton administration" but it faced "a lot of pushback" from the Pentagon, in the days before the United States "had sort of grown comfortable again with limited war." Time and again, Powell reported, "we don't do this stuff, we don't do mountains and valleys and weird ethnic guerrilla groups."[164]

On its second full day in office, the Clinton administration produced PRD-1 to address US policy in the former Yugoslavia. Signed by Anthony Lake on January 22, 1993, the document raised the possibility of a full NSC meeting on the situation, with a view to deciding "broad strategic goals and strategies that will guide [US] policies toward the Former Yugoslavia." Lake suggested that the administration needed to decide "what it wants to achieve and what price it is prepared to pay to get it." Ahead of any meeting, Lake urged his staff that "no presumptions should be made about limitations on policy" but they were only given 4 days to respond to a range of questions regarding potential US involvement in the Balkans—a timescale that Lake conceded "may make a coordinated product impossible." However, if coordination was possible within such a timescale, agencies were advised that "any differences of opinion should be clearly stated rather than compromised for the sake of an agreed product."[165]

Accordingly, the administration held a series of NSC meetings in its first months to understand what had been done so far in the Balkans and what its new strategy should be. Defined by Madeleine Albright as being "numerous, rambling and inconclusive," they singularly failed to achieve a consensus.[166] President Clinton pledged to provide 25,000 troops to a multilateral peacekeeping operation, but only after a comprehensive peace settlement was reached.[167] There was a feeling at the NSC that "the situation in Bosnia could not wait for a year's study since the situation was not theoretical."[168] The White House discovered that neutralizing President Bush's foreign affairs experience on the campaign was far easier than conducting a coherent foreign policy once in office.

One of the biggest challenges Clinton faced was from critics who suggested he had no foreign policy to speak of. Dan Rather asked the president, "you seem to have been all over the place in terms of policy toward Bosnia. One, tell us exactly what US policy toward Bosnia is at the moment and what we can expect in the future." Clinton insisted that he was "appalled by what [had] happened there," but added that his "ability to do anything about it is somewhat limited." Clinton was "convinced that anything we do would have to be done through the United Nations or through NATO or through some other collective action of nations."[169] This response was indicative of two elements within the Clinton White House; first, the faith in multilateralism as endorsed by the president and his national security adviser, and secondly the belief that the United States should work with its allies in consultation, rather than be seen to be dictating solutions across the Atlantic.

Unlike many of his predecessors, Bill Clinton prioritized negotiation, conciliation, and empathizing with his friends and adversaries; his natural inclination was to confer, not to instruct or to seek military engagement. This reflected the view of many within the administration, including Nancy Soderberg, who acknowledged, "we were unwilling to use force to try to solve Bosnia and it took us two years to figure out that we'd have to use force to do that." This was a generation to whom "the use of force was reserved for World War One, or the World War Three syndrome and containing the Soviet Union, not these smaller 'Teacup Wars' as Leslie Gelb called them."[170]

This, however, led to misunderstandings about America's intentions in the post-Cold War world—Clinton was reacting to America's changed position in the world while other nations lagged behind. Nowhere was this more evident than in the administration's dealings with its European allies over Bosnia. Clinton's approach took the rest of the world time to adjust to and, in the meantime, European leaders continued to look to the White House to solve what many in the United States believed to be a European problem.

The American press were fundamentally opposed to any deployment in the region, with *The Wall Street Journal* fearing that sending US ground troops to enforce any settlement could lead to "another Beirut, or even to Vietnam if larger powers begin to side with the Serbs."[171] Charles Krauthammer noted that US troops could be sent to "a swamp of historical grievances."[172] Even the *New York Times* feared that Clinton was on the "slippery slope of military engagement" that could put 15,000 American servicemen into a "cauldron of violence that our European allies have refused to take on themselves."[173] Recognizing the historic parallels, President Clinton steadfastly refused to be drawn into the conflict.

Former Secretary of State Cyrus Vance and former British Foreign Secretary Lord Owen had searched for an acceptable peace initiative throughout 1992. However, when their plan was revealed, many believed it legitimized the Serb seizure of territory. The plan recommended dividing Bosnia into ten provinces, made up of distinct ethnic communities, a move dependent on Serb forces returning conquered lands to non-Serbs. Beyond the practical flaws, there were serious moral issues with the plan, which contravened the UN Charter that outlawed the acquisition of territory by force. Acceptance of the Vance-Owen plan, therefore, necessitated defying the charter of the United Nations, "accepting territorial conquest . . . accepting genocide as a way of acquiring territory" and most troubling, "accepting the destruction of a UN member state."[174] The plan also violated the Wilsonian concept of self-determination—a vital tenet to members of Clinton's foreign policy team. Such philosophical niceties were lost on David Owen, who accused Clinton of "scuttling the chances of ending the war."[175]

There were other sensibilities to consider beyond David Owen's ego, however, not least of which were Russia's historic ties to Serbia and the risks posed by intervening in a civil war that had the potential to renew Cold War enmities. To avoid rejecting the Vance-Owen plan outright and damaging Russian sensibilities, the administration pressed for stronger sanctions, the enforcement of a no-fly zone, and the creation of an international war crimes tribunal to punish those who had violated human rights. While many welcomed the president's proposals as a viable alternative to the Vance-Owen plan, others were more sceptical; former UN Ambassador Jeane Kirkpatrick claimed that the plan was inadequate and called for unilateral American military intervention.[176] The *New*

York Times warned of the dangers in becoming embroiled in the Balkans and asked "Is anyone around the Oval Office reading history books?"[177] Anthony Lake admitted the lessons being learned were from Vietnam: "Don't make commitments that you can't meet. And just don't wander into something."[178]

The Clinton administration made it clear that the United States would not act unilaterally, as Warren Christopher urged "the entire international community [to] do its utmost to provide economic aid and reconstruction assistance to the Bosnian state."[179] Madeleine Albright compounded this statement by stressing that the United States "will not act unilaterally when a multilateral presence is clearly needed and available."[180] Accordingly, the approach to Bosnia was viewed as a policy of "creeping US disengagement" devised with the aim of "educating America's allies into their new responsibilities in a post-Cold War world, in which US leadership will no longer be automatic."[181] The Clinton administration concluded that the United States had not gone through the Cold War merely to emerge as the world's policeman and that from now on the United States would adopt a pragmatic approach to foreign policy. On some issues, it planned to work with Russia, on others with NATO allies, sometimes with the United Nations, and sometimes would not get involved at all.

Time White House correspondent Jef McAllister noted that the administration "blundered all over the place," in regard to Bosnia during its initial months.[182] However, Europe and the United States did not fundamentally disagree on their goals in Bosnia. Both sought the end of bloodshed, the return of confiscated land to the country's Muslims and Croats and feared that Western inaction risked widening the conflict. The disagreements arose over tactics, with European governments dismissing Clinton's initial plan to arm the Bosnian Muslims and conduct air raids against Serb targets as short-sighted and ill-conceived, especially considering the presence of European peacekeeping troops working under a UN flag who would have been in the target zones. Only once a grand strategy had been decided upon and a major reorganization of the White House completed, could the Balkan crisis finally be addressed.

By April 1993, Warren Christopher was forced to concede, "The United States simply doesn't have the means to make people in that region of the world like each other."[183] The Balkan situation was defined not as "a moral outrage necessitating outside military action," but as "a quagmire embodying ancient feuds that defied imposed resolutions."[184] Despite the outrage espoused on the campaign trail, the Clinton White House was intent on focusing on health care reform, the North American Free Trade Agreement, budget reduction, and reinventing government and did not intend "to get distracted with bombing raids against the Bosnian Serbs."[185] Even Clinton's supporters, however, worried that the situation made the president appear "irresolute" and "unsure about the use of force, whether in deploying it or refusing to deploy it."[186] However, unilateral US action in the Balkans was not an option, regardless of whatever may have been gleaned from prior remarks.

Clinton felt that "America's allies had to be encouraged to emerge from the shadow of Washington's tutelage and take the lead in solving regional problems."[187] This was a position supported by Colin Powell who opposed using limited American military force in Bosnia, arguing against air strikes and stressing that any intervention would need 300,000 American troops, which was "sufficient to kill off the whole idea."[188] Powell maintained that no US forces should be deployed in the absence of a political goal and the conditions he set for the use of force were such that they effectively ruled out a Balkan intervention, revealing time and again how he was "the most dominant voice of caution" with respect to the Balkans.[189] He also stressed that "No matter what we did, it would be easy for the Serbs to respond by seizing UN humanitarian personnel as hostages."[190] Not for the first time, it appeared that the Tarnoff Doctrine, unveiled in an off-the-record briefing, was guiding US Grand Strategy.

As concerns grew over the potential international ramifications of military intervention, a clash of opinion erupted over how best to utilize US forces. Defense Secretary Aspin was divided between a personal desire to deploy forces and Powell's hesitancy to do so; Anthony Lake had no interest in entering an un-winnable war, but shared Albright's view that Bosnia affected European security and therefore America's interests. Leon Fuerth and Al Gore favored air power to slow Serb advances. George Stephanopoulos warned that military intervention could divert attention from the domestic agenda, while Warren Christopher "had trouble identifying any option he could recommend."[191] In keeping with his diplomatic approach, the secretary of state "laid down four strict conditions for military intervention, which would render it almost impossible in the conditions prevailing in Bosnia."[192] The advisers were not aided by the president, who lamented, "I don't want to have to spend any more time on [Bosnia] than is absolutely necessary, because what I got elected to do was to let America look at our own problems."[193]

On Capitol Hill, Senator Sam Nun raised the specter of Somalia as a rationale for avoiding a deployment: "My big question will be not how do we go about it . . . but how do we get out if the parties begin fighting again?"[194] This contrasted with those who felt that national power should be used to promote national objectives, as Madeleine Albright asked, "What's the point of having this superb military if we can't use it?"[195] This clash of opinion, over which Colin Powell believed he may "have an aneurysm," ensured that consensus was a rarity.[196] Albright's remarks revealed the "sense of frustration that was palpable about the fact that more was not happening" in the Balkans.[197] The crisis was seen as "very personal and visceral" by Albright and led her to contrast the situation with events in her native Czechoslovakia in 1938. She "could not stand doing nothing on Bosnia," said Toby Gati, Chief of Intelligence at the State Department; "She kept on saying, 'We have to do more, why aren't we doing more?'" In a memo to the president dated August 1993, Albright argued that Bosnia would taint the administration's foreign policy objectives and urged that military pressure should be applied to bring the Serbs to the negotiating table.[198] Albright was particularly cutting regarding the Powell Doctrine, which she suggested only applied when "dealing with a crazy dictator with six months to prepare and the earth was flat and you'd use overwhelming force and somebody else would pay. But those circumstances don't come along very often."[199] Albright conceded that two trains of thought were prevalent at the time: the "Vietnam Syndrome" that dictated absolute noninvolvement, and the "Gulf War Syndrome," which she defined as "Don't do it unless you can deploy 500,000 marines."[200]

In contrast to Somalia, Bosnia was routinely considered by the Principals Committee of the National Security Council, in meetings chaired by Anthony Lake. However, this body proved to be as divided as any other on the issue and its meetings often displayed a "dispirited, inconclusive quality," with "little enthusiasm for any proposal for action."[201] Madeleine Albright conceded, America "couldn't hope to persuade others if we had not least persuaded ourselves . . . with a new president, a wary secretary of state, a negative Pentagon, nervous allies and crises in Somalia, then Rwanda and Haiti blowing up, we weren't prepared to run the risks of leadership in Bosnia."[202] The administration faced a serious dilemma in dealing with the Balkan crisis: the United States did not have the votes on the Security Council to end the arms embargo; a cease-fire would reward ethnic cleansing, while the use of significant force to punish the Serbs could have led to UN peacekeepers being taken hostage and jeopardizing the humanitarian mission.

It was clear that action was needed and what consensus there was, eventually focused on the concept of Lift and Strike: the end of the Bosnian arms embargo with threats of NATO air strikes against Serb military units. Vitally, there would be no threat to American ground troops, as none would be provided: "This option seemed appealing when compared to doing nothing or joining the fighting."[203] Yet Lift and Strike would have been a more palatable choice if the crisis had only recently begun. If the United States were to Lift and Strike, allied troops serving under the United Nations would be caught in the front line, as potential hostages or targets for retaliation. If the United Nations withdrew, the humanitarian effort would falter, perhaps irrevocably. British Defence Secretary at the time, Malcolm Rifkind, felt "the Americans were trying to eat their cake and have it too. They consistently refused to offer any manpower in Bosnia. They were trying, as it were, to lead on the policy, but without accepting the need for their own contribution other than up in the sky, and that was utterly unacceptable given the function of the UN."[204] When Lift and Strike emerged as the US policy, British Foreign Secretary Douglas Hurd was forced to admit his "deep reservations" in the House of Commons, as "privately, both British and US officials [admitted] that differences over Bosnia brought US–British relations to their lowest point since the 1956 Suez crisis."[205]

The Clinton administration deployed the secretary of state to Europe to address this situation. Importantly, the White House announced that the final decision would be made once Christopher returned from Europe, forcing him to adopt a "listening mode," rather than being able to inform European leaders of the White House plans.[206] In London, Christopher was received at Chevening, the Foreign Secretary's official residence, by Prime Minster John Major, Foreign Secretary Douglas Hurd, and Defence Secretary Malcolm Rifkind. As Sir Malcolm later reflected, "We just went through the whole American proposal and we were pretty sceptical because we didn't believe it had been properly thought through and it became manifestly clear that it hadn't been properly thought through." Basic questions regarding the physical implementation of Lift and Strike went unanswered, as Christopher "didn't have any answers to offer at that stage on how they would have managed that."[207]

Christopher had been appointed secretary of state because he conveyed the impression of being "a safe pair of hands," whom Clinton found "reassuring."[208] However, his European visit singularly failed to help Clinton's international standing. His attempts to promote the Lift and Strike policy were met with derision: "It was largely a plan designed to satisfy the cantankerous Congress and it meant that America would step in to change the Bosnian situation without exposing itself to any of the consequences if things went wrong." The US Ambassador to London noted that it was "a cockamamie idea."[209] Essentially, there would be no American ground troops, which appalled European leaders. "Frankly, he didn't do a very good job of presenting his case," said one British official. The Europeans were expecting a plan, but Christopher thought he had come to listen, not to lead. The comparison with Bush's secretary of state was damning: "I knew Jim Baker," said a senior European diplomat; "Jim Baker was a friend of mine. Believe me, Warren Christopher is no Jim Baker."[210] Following "a perfectly friendly discussion" with the British government, Christopher "was left in no doubt that [they] were profoundly unimpressed and un-attracted by what he was proposing." Upon his return to Washington, the Clinton administration "just dropped the idea, they said there's just not the support." Sir Malcolm Rifkind reflected "We took from that, that that meant actually that they were doing this in order to keep their critics in Congress happy, rather than that they passionately believed this was the way to go and what flows from that its that they might not have been too upset by our pretty negative reaction."[211]

Christopher's European trip had dreadful ramifications and left the White House open to attack from all quarters. "For an American Secretary of State to go and see the allies about a matter on which the president campaigned and about a matter on which the administration was said to have strong feelings and then come back and say, 'They won't go along with it, so we're going to change our policy,' well, that was without precedent," declared Richard Perle, former Assistant Secretary of Defense.[212] The trip "was not consistent with global leadership," Christopher later admitted, as the European mission became a profound lesson in how not to exercise American leadership. Fears grew that the administration did not understand foreign policy and the use of power, for it appeared that while the president and his administration talked about multilateralism, neither he nor his advisers knew quite how to achieve it.[213]

By October 1993, it was suggested that the administration had placed the Balkan crisis "on the back burner, desperately hoping the issue will go away."[214] Despite European misgivings, however, the president was not about to buckle: "I do not believe the United States needs to send a lot of troops there which might get involved in a civil war on the ground when we had a plan which would have led to a settlement," he told Larry King.[215] The administration blamed the failure of its Bosnian policy on the Europeans, who were understandably furious.[216] Britain in particular had been prepared to accede to air strikes if Clinton had insisted, but no formal request had been made. However, the president understood the futility of endorsing a policy in the Balkans when faced by an intransient Boris Yeltsin who refused to permit UN action against the Serbs. This was not a point that could be made public, as the idea of US foreign policy being dictated by a neutered Russian state was not something that would have made positive headlines in the *New York Times*. Regardless of the bloodshed in the Balkans, Clinton's decision to maintain the relationship with the Kremlin and ensure Yeltsin's political survival was simply too important to risk over the land Bismarck once claimed was "not worth the bones of a single Pomeranian grenadier."[217]

The Balkan crisis revealed the uncertainty at the heart of the administration over US national interests. International ramifications appeared to be secondary to domestic implications, as time and again grand strategy was hampered by regional crises. An ambivalent electorate greatly impacted President Clinton's international standing, since his "affinity for appeasing opinion at home made it difficult for his allies to predict how his administration would behave, though it kept him well ahead in the domestic opinion polls."[218] Yet public ambivalence also came to Clinton's aid as the White House avoided the backlash it received following the Somali imbroglio, since there was never a popular consensus in favor of intervention in the Balkans: "As awareness of ethnic cleansing spread, the proportion of those who wanted the United States to 'do something' increased, but they probably never constituted a majority."[219] Even the *National Review* conceded only "modest risks" were justified, as the United States had no vital interests at stake.[220] Americans may have been appalled at the Balkan atrocities, but their horror never amounted to a resolve to commit ground troops, as opinion polls constantly recorded a two-to-one majority against intervention in Bosnia.[221] However, neither Lake nor Clinton made a serious attempt to build public support for ground troops or for any forceful use of American power in the Balkans.

Other issues influenced the Clinton administration's Balkan policy, or lack thereof. The deaths of US servicemen in Somalia and the ensuring political fallout had implications not only in Rwanda, but also "delayed aggressive engagement in Bosnia." Somalia and the ensuing debacle initiated a policy debate over the future of multilateral peacekeeping operations that Nancy Sodeberg conceded, "took us two years. It took us two years to figure out the new balance of force and diplomacy in the post-Cold War era."[222] It was a 2-year period, however, in which lives were lost as the result of political and bureaucratic resistance on both sides of the Atlantic. During that time, Madeleine Albright conceded "our goal was a negotiated solution, but we never applied the credible threat of force necessary to achieve it. Instead we employed a combination of half-measures and bluster that didn't work."[223]

By the mid-1990s, as the Balkan crisis deepened, the Clinton administration took comfort from the knowledge that they were not responsible for the outbreak of hostilities, that the European powers were in disarray over the issue, and that "little support existed," for the deployment of American troops into "the new world disorder."[224] The Clinton administration was in the awkward position of benefiting from public apathy and hence not under pressure to intervene militarily overseas, while still having to attempt to build a new world "in the domestic circumstances not of the 1940s but of the 1920s, when there was no single, foreign threat against which to rally public opinion."[225] Despite President Bush's assertion that the Vietnam Syndrome had been buried in the sands of the Persian Peninsula, many in Washington feared being sucked into another civil war. An article by Arthur Schlesinger Jr in the *Wall Street Journal*, warning that Clinton's domestic strategies could wither in the Balkans as Lyndon Johnson's had in Vietnam, confirmed the president's worst fears.[226]

Yet despite the lack of public or editorial support, the Balkan crisis was inflicting serious damage on the Atlantic relationship, in spite of what the administration saw as its record of progressive reform: "It had built a new relationship with Russia and the other former Soviet republics; started to enlarge NATO; tackled the Irish problem; strengthened American ties with the Baltic nations and Central Europe; and gained congressional approval for the NAFTA and GATT trade agreements."[227] However, as long as the belief persisted that America was failing to act over the worst atrocity to impact the continent since 1945, such achievements would be negated. Accordingly, the administration was caught between its assertions and its aspirations, with senior members expressing fears for the future of the transatlantic partnerships that had sustained Europe and the United States during the Cold War.

By 1995, events were moving in a direction that threatened not only the credibility of US foreign policy, but also the president's prospects for reelection, as Britain and France considered a withdrawal of forces that would have required US assistance. These aspects, coupled with the slaughter of 6,000 Muslims at Srebrenica, proved to be the catalyst for a reversal of attitudes. Having defined the new geopolitical era as "a contest that pits nations and individuals guided by openness, responsive government and moderation against those animated by isolation, repression and extremism," Anthony Lake subsequently advised Clinton that the debacle over Bosnia threatened to impact his reelection hopes.[228]

A series of memoranda were put to the president for his consideration, including several from Madeleine Albright who urged US engagement was in keeping with its interests, while continued disengagement would destroy American credibility. Albright feared that Clinton's "entire first term [was] going to be judged by how you deal with Bosnia."[229] Albright's forthright manner came to the fore, as she noted at a meeting of the foreign policy team in late June: "When US leadership is weak in one area, it affects leadership in others." She lamented that "the strategy we have now makes the president look weak" and that to survive politically, the administration needed "to get ahead of the game."[230]

With the State Department unable to initiate a viable option, Anthony Lake introduced a shift in policy: "The choice was no longer between staying out and going in. It was between going in to get the allies out or going in to impose a peace. As the crisis deepened, a *Pax Americana* came to be seen as the least unpalatable option."[231] NATO unity was prioritized over issues such as bombing Serb forces, or lifting the arms embargo. The policy of deferring to the Europeans was at an end. No longer would President Clinton place his fortunes in the hands of foreign leaders, as he led for both international and domestic reasons. French President Jacques Chirac had suggested that the post of Leader of the Free World was "vacant."[232] Clinton needed to demonstrate otherwise to survive politically.

In August 1995, Lake met with European leaders to inform them that the UN mission in Bosnia should be allowed to collapse, so their troops would no longer find themselves hostages on the ground. This was not a consultation; the administration's philosophy had changed to an approach they termed "Tell, don't ask."[233] Lake's presentation was a reverse of Christopher's previous efforts, telling the Europeans, "If you won't act with us, we're going to have to adapt this new strategy."[234] Unsurprisingly perhaps, Lake's move revealed the true nature of government bureaucracy as it was suggested he "was pulling an end run around the State Department."[235] Regardless of departmental in-fighting, the president announced, "We have obligations to our NATO allies and I do not believe we can leave them in the lurch." The administration's appeal to NATO and cooperation with European allies was a sound political strategy. Many members of Congress, including senior Republicans, urged Clinton to define a new strategy for NATO in the post-Cold War era.[236] Clinton responded by authorizing substantial air strikes against the Bosnian Serbs, ensuring that NATO conducted military air strikes for the first time in its history, with US bombers completing 2,318 of the 3,500 sorties flown in the operation. As Clinton led NATO in a new direction that was backed by the allies, it became much more difficult to criticize the policy.[237]

In its dealings with Bosnia, the administration tested the boundaries of a new and improved relationship with NATO. Since the US relationship with the United Nations had been strained during the Somali crisis, the concept of identifying a new international body with which to address the problems of the world was not surprising. The Clinton team remained pragmatic and retained the right to use the United Nations when needed, but would not become part of the United Nations task force already deployed to the Balkans. Instead, "Should large-scale fighting resume and UN troops need to be withdrawn, the President has agreed . . . to provide US support, including the use of ground forces, to a NATO-led operation to help assure a safe withdrawal."[238] The assertion of NATO airpower, the unity of Europe and America, and the intense efforts of Richard Holbrooke resulted in the peace talks at a US Air Force base in Dayton, Ohio. There, Holbrooke arranged a power-sharing agreement with the warring parties, resulting in "the first, most intricate and, arguably, the most significant foreign policy success of the Clinton administration."[239] A NATO-dominated International Protection Force (IFOR) of 60,000 heavily armed troops, including 20,000 Americans, was dispatched to enforce the agreement, replacing the lightly armed United Nations contingent of peacekeepers. The Dayton Accords altered the perception and the practices of the Clinton administration. The White House recognized that it had succeeded in halting the bloodshed and "Criticism of President Clinton as a weak leader ended abruptly, especially in Europe and among Muslim nations."[240]

The crisis in the Balkans began before the Clinton administration came to power, but neither President Bush nor the Europeans had developed a viable plan to end the war. With many Americans questioning US interests in the Balkans and with European leaders insisting that America stay out of its affairs, it was little surprise that the administration failed to prioritize the conflict. However, its location and potential made it a prime candidate for its grand strategy of Engagement and Enlargement and, as a result, intervention should have come much sooner. Yet the ramifications of the Somali operation cannot be denied. The early idealism that had defined that administration in 1993 had been tested to a point that Lake was forced to concede: "You don't solve foreign societies. You plant, you plough, you seed, you water, you weed and then you harvest. You just have to keep working." Ultimately, however, "If you don't learn from experience, you're not concentrating."[241]

The decision to intervene in Bosnia was a vital one for the administration. Not to have done so would have seriously undermined its future role in Europe, but the ramifications of a flawed engagement could have been equally calamitous and risked drawing the United States into a civil war that could have undermined the administration's domestic agenda. By risking the possible rather than the inevitable, the administration had an opportunity to build on the success of Bosnia to espouse a new direction for international relations. From 1996, US Grand Strategy envisioned a continent at peace and sought "to ensure that the hard-won peace . . . will survive and flourish after four years of war." Yet while it is clear to see the development of a more assertive US foreign policy, the Clinton administration was unable to build upon its success at Dayton to implement sweeping change.

While few doubted the importance of the Dayton peace deal, the time taken to arrive at its conception was hardly a matter of pride for any concerned. The language used to define the ensuing peace mission was also revealing: in light of the Somali mission, the United States deployed troops in Bosnia as part of a NATO-led initiative, not under a UN banner and the mission was a peace implementation force not a peacekeeping operation. There would be no ideological mission and no nation-building exercises, despite the need to reestablish order in the ravaged land. Rather, the coalition of 25 nations limited their ambitions to "assisting the parties in implementing the military aspects of the peace agreement, including monitoring the cease-fire, monitoring and enforcing the withdrawal of forces and establishing and manning the zone of separation."[242] It appeared that the Clinton administration had heeded the words of Lord Salisbury; "It's difficult enough to go around doing what is right without going around trying to do good."[243]

The Bosnia mission revealed the lessons learned from Somalia: never lose command of the mission and plan for an exit before the troops arrive. In this case, the Clinton administration agreed that "We anticipate a one-year mission . . . in Bosnia. We believe that by the end of the first year, we will have helped create a secure environment so that the people of Bosnia can travel freely throughout the country, vote in free elections and begin to rebuild their lives." There would necessarily be a relief effort launched in Bosnia, but the administration was aware of the need to separate it from the military exercise in light of the Somali mission: "This broad civilian effort is helping the people of Bosnia to rebuild, reuniting children with their parents and families with their homes and will allow the Bosnian people to choose freely their own leaders." Nation building would occur, but not under the guidance of the US military. Neither would the American taxpayer be expected to bankroll the operation:

"In view of the large role that US forces are playing in implementing the military aspects of the agreement, we believe it is appropriate for Europe to contribute the largest share of the funds for reconstruction." No doubt remembering the initial declaration that the Bosnia crisis was a European dilemma, not an American one, the administration was keen to see such a belief acknowledged financially. "The European Union has taken the lead in these efforts in tandem with the international financial institutions, in particular the World Bank."[244]

With the peace deal at Dayton closely identified with Richard Holbrooke, the State Department emerged victorious from the encounter, despite the initiative having been launched by Anthony Lake, whose successful 1995 mission to inform the European allies of Clinton's plan sat in stark contrast to Warren Christopher's efforts in 1993. Despite his widely acknowledged triumph, however, Richard Holbrooke's ultimate prize eluded him. When the second-term foreign policy team was announced, he found himself passed over for secretary of state once again, on the basis that he was "a pain in the ass and he never got the top job because he remained a pain in the ass his whole life."[245] It was exactly due to Holbrooke's directness and stubbornness, however, that peace had been secured at Dayton, leading to the most successful diplomatic engagement of the entire Clinton presidency.

Reflections on democracy promotion

The democracy promotion aspect of US Grand Strategy committed the United States to the defense of principles, peoples, and liberties. Anthony Lake was adamant that American leadership in the world was a prerequisite, since "it can mean more democracies and fewer dictatorships." Lake invited Congress to "join with the president in helping shape a second American Century of security and prosperity."[246] Lake's ideological philosophy was clear: "If we can help lead the dozens of nations . . . who are trying to adapt to democracy and free markets, we help to create the conditions for the greatest expansion of prosperity and security the world has ever witnessed."[247] Despite this optimistic aspiration, the Clinton administration drew criticism for the democracy promotion element of its grand strategy initiative, ensuring that what the strategy lacked in quantifiable success was made up for in its ability to rally opposition.

Gaddis suggested that Clinton's Grand Strategy amounted to "foreign policy by autopilot, a grand strategy of laissez-faire" that "never specified who or what was to be engaged or enlarged," while Kissinger noted that the strategy was lacking in "operational terms."[248] Others insisted that the suggestion that democracies did not fight each other ignored tensions between India and Pakistan, Greece and Turkey, "not to mention nineteen democracies demolishing much of Serbia." Critics lamented that the democracy promotion aspect of grand strategy offered "little guidance when national interests among democracies don't coincide and [there is] no framework for dealing with non-democratic states."[249] As the administration prepared to leave office, Thomas Carothers reflected that democracy promotion had "not lived up to the expansive rhetoric," but conceded that "policy so rarely does."[250]

The White House did not need to rely on Republicans for criticism of its democracy promotion efforts, as it was clear that not everybody in the administration embraced the concept. In a resignation letter that was written but never accepted, Anthony Lake conveyed his misgivings about the levels of support for his policies at the White House. "What concerns me," Lake wrote, "is a growing sense that your and my own priorities and philosophies may not be the same." Lake knew the president found his Democratic Enlargement speech to be "aesthetically displeasing," but insisted that "there was little in the rhetoric that could not have been redeemed by vigorous, determined pursuit of our goals." He continued:

> While I have no doubt we agree on the importance of open markets to American workers and reshaping our military forces, I do not sense the same depth of commitment on issues involving the spread of democracy and human rights or the carnage of foreign civil wars. These last are messy issues that require painful choices. But once involved, we can only resolve them though pragmatic but persistent and, when necessary, forceful action.[251]

In the autumn of 1993, Lake was not alone in his doubts concerning President Clinton's capacity to exert such assertive action.

Democracy promotion was advanced as a global strategy, but was clearly targeted in Europe and parts of Asia where success was most likely. These areas had benefited previously from America largesse and as such had an existing foundation of freedom upon which to build. The administration's efforts in Europe culminated in June 2000, with the awarding of the Charlemagne Prize to President Clinton in recognition of his leadership on European integration.[252] US interests in these regions had "evolved from compulsory and coercive, to cooperative and collegial, the result was the same: stable countries supporting American interests and sharing American values and perspectives." Colonel M. Thomas Davis of the Brookings Institution captured the policy most succinctly when he suggested that the actual US objective was simply one of stability, since "history is loaded with examples indicating that where stability is threatened, American interests are as well."[253]

The initial incarnation of Clinton's Grand Strategy recognized that what it proposed was "the work of generations. There will be wrong turns and even reversals, as there have been in all countries throughout history."[254] The administration, however, did not have an infinite timescale within which to work. With electoral timescales set in stone, it recognized that advances were necessary to prevent foreign policy becoming another tool at the disposal of political opponents. As a result, grand strategy was tasked with assisting states that directly affected US strategic interests; "those with large economies, critical locations, nuclear weapons, or a potential to generate refugee flows into our own nation or into key friends and allies." Above all, the administration consistently noted that it must focus its efforts "where we have the most leverage."[255] Pragmatism, along with domestic political realities, was a vital component of US Grand Strategy in the post-Cold War World.

Conclusion

Democracy promotion was the most ideological component of US Grand Strategy during the Clinton administration. As with national security and prosperity promotion, it had been at the heart of Bill Clinton's foreign policy initiative since the start of his presidential campaign and remained central to his grand strategy throughout his two terms in the White House. The administration wished to support the spread of democracy, but sought to do so using market forces, not military might. Under Clinton, democracy would be encouraged and nurtured, but not imposed, in a classic example of the United States seeking to act as an example to others, rather than actively seeking to impose its values abroad. Democracy promotion required international support; however, events in Somalia and Rwanda, along with the election of less-internationally focused Republicans in Congress ensured that multilateral operations were no longer *en vogue*.

Critics accused the Clinton administration of blind engagement, but this was a pragmatic policy from the start, which insisted US involvement "must be carefully tailored to serve [its] interests and priorities."[256] This was vital to understanding US Grand Strategy in the 1990s: idealism when possible, realism when necessary; the prioritizing of human rights where feasible, the elevation of the national interest at all times; multilateralism when possible, unilateralism when necessary. Indeed, the administration was forthright in its language, insisting that "in this time of global change, it is clear we cannot police the world, but is it equally clear we must exercise global leadership."[257]

In retrospect, it could be claimed that the best the policy achieved was to maintain the equilibrium. During the Clinton years, democracy thrived and grand strategy actively supported this. The enlargement of the NATO military alliance encouraged the spread of democratic principles to Central and Eastern Europe in a process described later as "brilliantly successful."[258] Democracy was sustained and supported by the United States during these years, ensuring that where it was existed, it was aided to ensure its continued success. However, where democracy was challenged, suppressed, or forbidden, US Grand Strategy proved ineffectual. Democracy was promoted but not imposed; encouraged but not exported. However, the wording of US Grand Strategy explicitly stated that this would not be an ideological crusade; it was pragmatic and aimed at supporting US national interests. The Clinton administration had no ideological intent or desire to initiate overseas adventures in the name of liberty, freedom, or democracy. Its focus was on domestic affairs and addressed foreign policy when necessary, but all too often through a domestic prism.

The democracy promotion element of US Grand Strategy was a product of its time, instigated by an administration that chose not to seek unnecessary foreign intervention. It was designed to be initiated along with market reform and, as such, was inseparable from the second component of the grand strategy, prosperity promotion. It was specifically not designed to be enacted using military power, which became policy under the George W. Bush administration. The two administrations, therefore, perfectly encapsulated the continuing historical struggle in US political life in regard to democracy promotion.

Notes

1 There were exceptions to this. See Thomas Carothers, *The Clinton Record on Democracy Promotion* (Washington, DC: Carnegie Endowment for International Peace, 2000); Mark Peceny, *Democracy at the Point of Bayonets* (Pennsylvania: The Pennsylvania State University Press, 1999); Joanne Gowa, *Building Bridges or Democracies Abroad? US Foreign Policy after the Cold War* (Princeton, NJ: Princeton University Press, 2000).

2 For more on this, see Walter Russell Mead, *Special Providence: American Foreign Policy and How It Changed the World* (New York: Knopf, 2003) and Kissinger, *Diplomacy*, p. 18.

3 John Quincey Adams, Speech to the US House of Representatives on Foreign Policy, July 4, 1821. Available at http://millercenter.org/president/speeches/detail/3484.

4 Robert G. Wesson, *Foreign Policy for a New Age* (Boston, MA: Houghton Mifflin Company, 1977), p. 154. See also Henry Steele Commager, "The Revolution as a World Ideal," *Saturday Review* (December 13, 1975), pp. 13–14.

5 Manifest Destiny carried American democracy across the continent. Newspaper editor John L. O'Sullivan insisted in 1845 that it was the birthright of pioneers "to overspread and to posses the whole of the continent which Providence has given us." Quoted in Richard N. Current, Alexander

DeConde, and Harris L. Dante, *United States History* (New York: Scott, Foresman, 1967), p. 234.

6   Quoted in Frances FitzGerald, "Reflections: Foreign Policy," *New Yorker* (November 11, 1985), p. 112.

7   Kissinger, *Diplomacy*, p. 30.

8   Theodore Roosevelt, Message of the President (annual), December 6, 1904, *Foreign Relations of the United States 1904* (Washington, DC: GPO, 1905), pp. ix–xlvii, p. xli.

9   *PPPJFK*, vol. 1 (1961), Inaugural Address, January 20, 1961, p. 1.

10 *PPPRR* (1982), "Address to Members of the British Parliament," June 8, 1982.

11 Smith, *America's Mission*, p. xv.

12 Loch K. Johnson, *Seven Sins of American Foreign Policy* (New York: Pearson Longman, 2007), p. 44.

13 Quoted in Robert Ajemian, "Where Is The Real George Bush?" *Time* (January 26, 1987).

14 *PPPGB*, vol. 2 (1991), Address to the UN General Assembly, October 1, 1990.

15 *PPPGB*, vol. 2 (1991), "Pax Universalis," address to the United Nations, September 23, 1991. The first two movements that Bush referred to were individual enterprise and international trade.

16 *PPPGB*, vol. 1 (1991), Address Before a Joint Session of the Congress on the State of the Union, January 29, 1991, p. 75.

17 *NSSUS91*, p. 14.

18 *PPPGWB*, vol. 1 (2005), Inaugural Address, January 20, 2005, p. 66.

19 David C. Henrickson, "The Lion and the Lamb: Realism and Liberalism Reconsidered," *World Policy Journal* 20 (Spring 2003), p. 97; Johnson, *Seven Sins of American Foreign Policy*, p. 22. See also Thomas Carothers, "The Backlash against Democracy Promotion," *Foreign Affairs* 85, no. 2 (March/April 2006), pp. 56–68.

20 Kissinger, *Does America Need a Foreign Policy?* p. 32.

21 For more on this, see Barry Holden, *Understanding Liberal Democracy*, Second Edition (Hemel Hempstead: Harvester Wheatsheaf, 1993) and K. Graham, *The Battle of Democracy* (Brighton, Sussex: Wheatsheaf, 1986)

22 Michael Foley, "The Democratic Imperative," in Tony McGrew (ed.), *The United States in the Twentieth Century: Empire* (London: Hodder & Stoughton, 1994), p. 171.

23 Cox, Ikenberry, and Inoguchi (eds), *American Democratic Promotion: Impulses, Strategies and Impacts*, pp. 1–2.

24 W. H. G. Armytage, *Four Hundred Years of English Education* (Cambridge: Cambridge University Press, 1964), p. 137.

25 Walter Lippmann, "The Shortage of Education," in *The Atlantic Monthly* CXCIII (May 1954), p. 35, from an address delivered at the fifth annual dinner of the National Citizens' Commission for the Public Schools in San Francisco on March 19, 1954. Reprinted in Clinton Rossiter and James

Lare (eds), *The Essential Lippmann: A Political Philosophy for Liberal Democracy* (New York: Vintage Books, 1965), pp. 29–32.

26 Alexis de Tocqueville, *Democracy in America*, Reprint Edition, Volume II (New York: Alfred A. Knopf, 1994), p. 100.

27 Walter Lippmann, "How Can the People Rule?" in *The Good Society* (Boston, MA: Little, Brown & Company, 1937). Reprinted in Rossiter and Lare (eds), *The Essential Lippmann*, pp. 14–20, 18–19.

28 George F. Kennan, "Diplomacy in the Modern World," *American Diplomacy*, pp. 95–96.

29 Walter Lippmann, "The Vindication of Democracy," Today and Tomorrow Column, *New York Herald Tribune*, July 5, 1934. Reprinted in Rossiter and Lare (eds), *The Essential Lippmann*, p. 228.

30 Adam L. Warber, *Executive Orders and the Modern Presidency: Legislation from the Oval Office* (Boulder, CO: Lynne Reinner Publishers, Inc., 2006), p. 16.

31 Zbigniew Brzezinski, *The Choice: Global Domination or Global Leadership* (New York: Basic Books, 2004), p. 224.

32 Lawrence J. Haas, *Sound the Trumpet: The United States and Human Rights Promotion* (Lanham, MD: Rowman & Littlefield Publishers, 2012), p. 141. See also Johnson, *Seven Sins of American Foreign Policy*, p. 173.

33 Brzezinski, *The Choice*, p. 224.

34 Cox, Ikenberry, and Inoguchi, *American Democratic Promotion: Impulses, Strategies and Impacts*, p. 7. For material relating to these three perspectives, see Henry Kissinger, "Reality and Illusion about the Chinese," *Independent* (October 18, 1999); Strobe Talbott, "Democracy and the National Interest," *Foreign Affairs* 74, no. 6 (1996), pp. 47–63; Gorm Rye Olsen, "Europe and the Promotion of Democracy in Post-Cold War Africa: How Serious is Europe and for What Reason?" *African Affairs* 9 (1998), pp. 343–368.

35 Desmond C. M. Platt, *Finance, Trade and British Foreign Policy 1815–1914* (Oxford: Clarendon Press, 1968), p. 326.

36 Walter Lippmann, "The Indispensable Opposition," *Atlantic Monthly* CLXIV (1939), p. 186. Reprinted in Rossiter and Lare (eds), *The Essential Lippmann*, p. 233.

37 See Graham T. Allison, Jr and Robert P. Beschel, Jr, "Can the United States Promote Democracy?" *Political Science Quarterly* 107, no. 1 (Spring 1992), pp. 81–98.

38 Clinton, "A New Covenant for American Security," p. 113, 118.

39 Carothers, *The Clinton Record on Democracy Promotion*, p. 1.

40 *PPPWJC*, vol. 1 (1997), Preface to the Report Entitled "Support for a Democratic Transition in Cuba," January 28, 1997, p. 88.

41 Lake, "From Containment to Enlargement," p. 658.

42 Warren Christopher, Statement before the Subcommittee on Commerce, Justice, State, and Judiciary, House Appropriations Committee, Washington, DC, March 10, 1993.

43 Warren Christopher, "The Three Pillars of US Foreign Policy and Support for Reform in Russia," Address before the Chicago Council on Foreign Relations, the Executive's Club of Chicago and the Mid-American Committee, Chicago, IL, March 22, 1993, in Christopher, *In The Stream of History*, p. 44.

44 Brinkley, "Democratic Enlargement," p. 127.

45 As restated in *NSSR94*, p. 19; *NSSR95*, p. 22; *NSSR96*, p. 32.

46 Carothers, *The Clinton Record on Democracy Promotion*, p. 1.

47 In doing so, the Clinton administration built upon tentative steps taken by both the Reagan and George H. W. Bush administrations.

48 This position remained intact throughout the George W. Bush administration before being re-titled as the Under Secretary of State for Civilian Security, Democracy, and Human Rights by the Obama administration in 2012.

49 From 1976 to 1993, this post had been the Assistant Secretary of State for Human Rights and Humanitarian Affairs. Between 1981 and 1985 this role was held by Elliot Abrams, who was later named as Special Assistant to the President and Senior Director for Democracy, Human Rights, and International Operations at the National Security Council under President George W. Bush.

50 Carothers, *The Clinton Record on Democracy Promotion*, p. 4.

51 Warren Christopher, Statement Before the Senate Foreign Relations Committee, Washington, DC, January 13, 1993, in Christopher, *In The Stream of History*, p. 28.

52 Thomas Carothers, *In the Name of Democracy: U.S. Policy Toward Latin America in the Reagan Years* (Berkeley, CA: University of California Press, 1991), pp. 206–226; Larry Diamond, *Promoting Democracy in the 1990s: Actors and Instruments, Issues and Imperatives* (Washington, DC: Carnegie Commission on Preventing Deadly Conflict, 1995).

53 Carothers, *The Clinton Record on Democracy Promotion*, p. 4.

54 Thomas Carothers, "The NED at Ten," *Foreign Policy* 95 (Summer 1994), p. 124.

55 Jesse Helms, quoted in Jan Nijman, "United States Foreign Aid: Crisis? What Crisis?" in Richard Grant and Jan Nijman (eds), *The Global Crisis in Foreign Aid* (Syracuse, NY: Syracuse University Press, 1998), p. 36.

56 *NSSR96*, p. 2.

57 Address by Anthony Lake, National Security Advisor—The Council on Foreign Relations (Rob edits—new version—extensive comments), September 12, 1994, Clinton Presidential Records, National Security Council, Robert Boorstin (Speechwriting), OA/Box Number: 420, [Anthony] Lake—Council on Foreign Relations—9/12/94 [1], William J. Clinton Presidential Library.

58 As restated in *NSSR94*, pp. 18–19, *NSSR95*, p. 22, *NSSR96*, p. 32.

59 Morton Halperin, "Guaranteeing Democracy," *Foreign Policy* 91 (Summer 1993), p. 105.

60 *NSSR94*, p. 29.

61 *NSSR94*, p. 19.

62 *NSSR95*, p. 23.

63 *NSSR94*, p. 19.

64 *NSSR96*, p. 33.

65 *NSSR98*, pp. 33–34.

66 *NSSR2000*, pp. 35–36.

67 *NSSR94*, p. 20.

68 *NSSR95*, p. 22.

69 *NSSR94*, p. 2.

70 *NSSR94*, p. 19.

71 *PPPWJC*, vol. 1 (1997), Statement on the Death of Deng Xiaoping, February 19, 1997, p. 179.

72 *NSSR94*, p. 19.

73 *PPPJFK*, vol. 1 (1961), Inaugural Address, January 20, 1961, p. 1.

74 *NSSR94*, p. 19.

75 *PPPJFK*, vol. 1 (1961), Inaugural Address, January 20, 1961, p. 1.

76 *NSSR97*, p. 20.

77 See *NSSR98*, p. 34 and how this deviates from language in *NSSR97*, p. 20.

78 *NSSR99*, p. 26.

79 *NSSR2000*, p. 37.

80 *NSSR97*, p. 20.

81 *NSSR2000*, p. 38.

82 *NSSR96*, p. 33.

83 *NSSR95*, p. 2.

84 *NSSR95*, p. 24.

85 *NSSR95*, p. 24.

86 Alan Kreczko to Donald Steinberg, re: Genocid, May 25, 1994, National Security Council, Multilateral and Humanitarian Affairs-Eric Schwartz, OA/Box Number: 4016: Rwanda II, 1994 [2], William J. Clinton Presidential Library.

87 Alan J. Kreczko to Anthony Lake; re: Rwanda Drawdown, July 28, 1994, Clinton Presidential Records, NSC Emails A1-Record (January 93–September 94), (Rwanda and Lake), OA/Box Number: 570000, William J. Clinton Presidential Library.

88 *NSSR97*, p. 20.

89 *NSSR98*, p. 35.

90 *NSSR98*, p. 34.

91 *NSSR2000*, pp. 37–38.

92 *PPPWJC*, vol. 1 (1998), The President's News Conference With President Jiang Zemin of China in Beijing, June 27, 1998, p. 1071.

93 *NSSR2000*, p. 37.

94 *NSSR99*, p. 26.

95 *NSSR2000*, p. 37.

96 *NSSR94*, pp. i–ii.

97 *NSSR94*, p. 6.

98 Address by Anthony Lake, National Security Advisor—The Council on Foreign Relations.

99 Carothers, *The Clinton Record on Democracy Promotion*, p. 2.

100 *NSSR95*, pp. 21–23.

101 *NSSR94*, p. 24.

102 *NSSR98*, p. 47.

103 *NSSR98*, p. 41.

104 *NSSR2000*, p. 54.

105 *NSSR94*, p. 24.

106 *NSSR94*, p. 25.

107 *NSSR94*, p. 19.

108 *NSSR94*, p. 25.

109 *NSSR96*, p. 42.

110 *NSSR97*, p. 26.

111 *NSSR95*, p. 51.

112 *NSSR94*, p. 130.

113 Carothers, *The Clinton Record on Democracy Promotion*, p. 8.

114 *NSSR94*, p. 26.

115 *NSSR95*, p. 31.

116 *PPPWJC*, vol. 2 (1994), The President's News Conference With President Nelson Mandela of South Africa, October 5, 1994, p. 1699.

117 *NSSR95*, p. 32.

118 *NSSR97*, p. 19.

119 *NSSR98*, p. 57.

120 *NSSR99*, p. 47

121 *NSSR98*, p. 57.

122 *NSSR99*, p. 47.

123 *NSSR98*, p. 57.

124 *NSSR94*, p. 26.

125 Quoted in Baker, *The Politics of Diplomacy*, p. 609.

126 Author's interview with Sir Malcolm Rifkind.

127 Holbrooke, "America, A European Power," p. 38.

128 *NSSR98*, p. 41.

129 *NSSR94*, p. 21.

130 *PPPWJC*, vol. 2 (1994), Remarks to the Conference on Security and Cooperation in Europe in Budapest, Hungary, December 5, 1994, p. 2144.

131 Albright, *Madam Secretary*, p. 166.

132 *NSSR97*, p. 21.

133 Author's interview with Sir Malcolm Rifkind.

134 Mark Danner, "Marooned in the Cold War: America, the Alliance, and the Quest for a Vanished World," *World Policy Journal* 14, no. 3 (Fall 1997), pp. 1–23.

135 Holbrooke, "America, A European Power," p. 47.

136 *NSSR2000*, p. 47.

137 *NSSR95*, p. 27.

138 Carothers, *The Clinton Record on Democracy Promotion*, p. 2.

139 *NSSR97*, p. 21.

140 *NSSR2000*, p. 47.

141 *NSSR99*, p. 34.

142 *NSSR99*, p. 48.

143 *NSSR94*, p. 23.

144 *NSSR98*, p. 37.

145 *NSSR94*, p. 23.

146 Talbott, "Why NATO Should Grow," p. 29.

147 *PPPWJC*, vol. 1 (1993), Remarks and an Exchange With Reporters in Vancouver, Canada, April 3, p. 392.

148 See John Dumbrell, "Lessons from Russia: Clinton and US Democracy Promotion," *The Slavonic and East European Review* 86, no. 1 (January 2008), pp. 185–186.

149 *PPPWJC*, vol. 1 (1993), Remarks to the American Society of Newspaper Editors in Annapolis, pp. 376–377.

150 Elaine Sciolino, "Dole Hammers on Yeltsin As US Frustration Grows," *New York Times* (March 2, 1995), p. A10.

151 Sciolino, "Dole Hammers on Yeltsin As US Frustration Grows," p. A10.

152 Anthony Lake, *Press Briefing*, The White House Briefing Room, March 1, 1995.

153 *PPPWJC*, vol. 1 (2000), Address Before a Joint Session of the Congress on the State of the Union, January 27, 2000, p. 136.

154 Walter Russell Mead to President Clinton, re: Foreign Policy and the State of the Union Address, December 30, 1993, Clinton Presidential Records, Speechwriting, Carter Wilkie, OA/Box Number: 4273 State of the Union 1994 [I], William J. Clinton Presidential Library.

155 David W. Rivera and Sharon Werning Rivera, "Yeltsin, Putin, and Clinton: Presidential Leadership and Russian Democratization in Comparative Perspective," *Perspectives on Politics* 7, no. 3 (September 2009), pp. 591–610.

156 To President Clinton from Samuel Berger and Stephanie Streett. Subject: Communications plan for your trip to Portugal, Germany, Russia, and Ukraine, Clinton Presidential Records National Security Council,

Speechwriting (Thomas Rosshirt) OA/Box Number: 4020: [Memorial Day] (3), William J. Clinton Presidential Library.

157 "NATO's Bosnia Dithering: Waiting for the US to Lead," *International Herald Tribune* (March 29–30, 1991), p. 1.

158 Poos, quoted in John Dickie, *Special No More: Anglo-American Relations, Rhetoric and Reality* (London: Weidenfeld & Nicolson, 1994), p. 248; Delors, quoted in Richard Holbrooke, *To End A War*, Modern Library Paperback Revised Edition (New York: Modern Library, 1999), p. 21.

159 Author's interview with Sir Malcolm Rifkind.

160 Brendan Simms, *Un-Finest Hour: Britain and the Destruction of Bosnia* (London: Penguin, 2001), p. 54.

161 Author's interview with Charles A. Kupchan.

162 Warren Christopher, "Statement at Senate Confirmation Hearing," *US Department of State Dispatch* 4, Issue 4 (January 25, 1993) p. 45.

163 Powell, *My American Journey*, p. 562.

164 Author's interview with Charles A. Kupchan.

165 PRD-1: US Policy Regarding the Situation in the Former Yugoslavia, January 22, 1993, pp. 1–2.

166 Albright, *Madam Secretary*, p. 180.

167 *PPPWJC*, vol. 1 (1993), The President's News Conference with President Francois Mitterrand of France, March 9, p. 259.

168 Author's interview with Leon Fuerth.

169 *PPPWJC*, vol. 1 (1993), Interview with Dan Rather of CBS News, March 24, 1993, pp. 350–351.

170 Author's interview with Nancy Soderberg. See Leslie H. Gelb, "Quelling the Teacup Wars: The New World's Constant Challenge," *Foreign Affairs* 73, no. 6 (November–December 1994), pp. 2–6.

171 Quoted in Martin Fletcher, "Clinton Line Raises Fears of a Vietnam," *The Times* (February 13, 1993), p. 10.

172 Charles Krauthammer, "The Bosnia Trap; We Are Now Responsible for a Balkan Peace," *Washington Post* (February 12, 1993), p. A27.

173 "Marching Blind Into Bosnia," *New York Times* (February 11, 1993), p. A30.

174 Anthony Lewis, "The Price of Surrender," *New York Times* (October 1, 1993), p. A31.

175 R. W. Apple, Jr, "Mediator Is Upset at US Reluctance Over Bosnia Talks," *New York Times* (February 3, 1993), p. A1; David Owen, *Balkan Odyssey* (New York: Harcourt Brace, 1995), pp. 116–117.

176 Steven A. Holmes, "Ex-Officials Urge US to Act to End Serbian Siege," *New York Times* (February 19, 1993), p. A3.

177 "Marching Blind Into Bosnia."

178 De Parle, "The Man Inside Bill Clinton's Foreign Policy," p. 33.

179 Warren Christopher and Edward Walker, "Bosnia-Herzegovina," *US Department of State Dispatch* 4, no. 14 (April 5, 1993), p. 200.

180 Madeleine Albright, "Current Status of US Policy on Bosnia, Somalia, and UN Reform," *US Department of State Dispatch* 4, no. 14 (April 5, 1993), p. 207.

181 Martin Walker, "America is Coming Home," *The Guardian* (May 25, 1993), p. 20.

182 Author's interview with J. F. O. McAllister.

183 Thomas L. Friedman, "Bosnia Reconsidered," *New York Times* (April 8, 1993), p. A5.

184 Henriksen, *Clinton's Foreign Policy in Somalia, Bosnia, Haiti and North Korea*, p. 14.

185 Thomas L. Friedman, "Clinton Rebuffs Bosnian Leader In Plea for Help," *New York Times* (September 9, 1993), p. A1.

186 Blumenthal, *The Clinton Wars*, p. 63.

187 Walker, "America is Coming Home," p. 20.

188 Steven Erlanger and David E. Sanger, "On World Stage, Many Lessons for Clinton," *New York Times* (July 29, 1996), p. A1.

189 Author's interview with Charles A. Kupchan.

190 Powell, *My American Journey*, p. 576.

191 Albright, *Madam Secretary*, p. 180.

192 Walker, *Clinton: The President They Deserve*, p. 263.

193 Quoted in McAllister and Mader, "Secretary Of Shhhhh!" pp. 32–34.

194 Elaine Sciolino, "Nunn Says He Wants Exit Strategy Before US Troops Go to Bosnia," *New York Times* (September 24, 1993), p. A1.

195 Dobbs, *Madeleine Albright*, p. 360.

196 Powell, *My American Journey*, p. 576.

197 Author's interview with Charles A. Kupchan.

198 Dobbs, *Madeleine Albright*, pp. 358–359.

199 Erlanger and Sanger "On World Stage, Many Lessons for Clinton," p. A1.

200 Dobbs, *Madeleine Albright*, p. 359.

201 Holbrooke, *To End A War*, p. 81.

202 Albright, *Madam Secretary*, p. 181.

203 Hyland, *Clinton's World*, p. 34.

204 Author's interview with Sir Malcolm Rifkind.

205 Dickie, *Special No More*, p. 250; Posen and Ross, "Competing Visions for US Grand Strategy," p. 47.

206 Walker, *Clinton: The President They Deserve*, p. 265.

207 Author's interview with Sir Malcolm Rifkind.

208 Author's interview with J. F. O. McAllister.

209 Seitz, *Over Here*, p. 329.

210 Walker, "America is Coming Home," p. 20.

211 Author's interview with Sir Malcolm Rifkind.

212 Walker, *Clinton: The President They Deserve*, p. 266.

213 Erlanger and Sanger, "On World Stage, Many Lessons for Clinton," p. A1.

214 Anthony Lewis, "The Siege Is Over," *New York Times* (October 18, 1993), p. A17.

215 *PPPWJC*, vol. 1 (1993), Interview with Larry King, July 20, 1993, p. 1145.

216 This debacle continued after Clinton left office, with Hillary Clinton recording in her memoirs that, "Bill was frustrated by Europe's failure to act after it had insisted that Bosnia was in its own backyard and was its problem to solve." Hillary Rodham Clinton, *Living History* (New York: Simon & Schuster, 2003), p. 170.

217 Quoted in Walker, *Clinton: The President They Deserve*, p. 264.

218 John Major, *The Autobiography* (London: HarperCollins, 1999), p. 499.

219 Holbrooke, *To End A War*, p. 360.

220 "Requiem for a Policy," *National Review* (June 7, 1993).

221 Patrick Cockburn, "Clinton Concentrates on the Home Front," *Independent* (September 28, 1993), p. 10.

222 Author's interview with Nancy Soderberg.

223 Albright, *Madam Secretary*, p. 181.

224 Soderberg, *The Superpower Myth*, p. 4.

225 Address by Anthony Lake, National Security Advisor—The Council on Foreign Relations.

226 Walker, *Clinton: The President They Deserve*, p. 266.

227 Holbrooke, *To End A War*, p. 361.

228 Address by Anthony Lake, National Security Advisor—The Council on Foreign Relations.

229 Blumenthal, *The Clinton Wars*, p. 153.

230 Albright, *Madam Secretary*, p. 186.

231 Dobbs, *Madeleine Albright*, p. 363.

232 Elaine Sciolino, "Bosnia Policy Shaped by US Military Role," *New York Times* (July 29, 1996).

233 Soderberg, *The Superpower Myth*, p. 81.

234 Author's interview with Anthony Lake.

235 De Parle, "The Man Inside Bill Clinton's Foreign Policy," p. 33.

236 Goldgeier, *Not Whether But When: The Decision to Enlarge*, p. 35. See also Gerald B. Solomon, *The NATO Enlargement Debate, 1990–1997* (Westport, CT: Praeger, 1998).

237 See Ivo H. Daalder, *Getting to Dayton: The Making of America's Bosnia Policy* (Washington, DC: Brookings Institution Press, 2000).

238 *NSSR95*, p. 26.

239 Klein, *The Natural*, p. 74.

240 Holbrooke, *To End A War*, p. 361.

241 Erlanger and Sanger, "On World Stage, Many Lessons for Clinton," p. A1.

242 *NSSR96*, pp. 35–36.

243 Lord Salisbury quoted in Chris Patten, *East and West* (London: Macmillan Publishers, 1998), p. 294.

244 *NSSR96*, p. 36.

245 Author's interview with J. F. O. McAllister.

246 Lake, "A Second American Century," A21.

247 *NSSR96*, p. 9.

248 Gaddis, "Foreign Policy by Autopilot"; "Calling Dr. Kissinger," *The Economist* (January 14, 1995), p. 23.

249 Robert Manning, "Overall Spin Masking Clinton's Failures," *San Jose Mercury News* (June 6, 1999).

250 Carothers, *The Clinton Record on Democracy Promotion*, p. 1.

251 Resignation Letter, Anthony Lake Papers, Manuscript Division, Library of Congress, Washington, DC, Box 48, Folder 2.

252 Memo To President Clinton from Samuel Berger and Stephanie Streett. Subject: Communications plan for your trip to Portugal, Germany, Russia, and Ukraine, Clinton Presidential Records National Security Council, Speechwriting (Thomas Rosshirt) OA/Box Number: 4020: [Memorial Day] (3), William J. Clinton Presidential Library.

253 Davis, "Goodwill Is the Mission, Too."

254 *NSSR94*, p. 97.

255 *NSSR96*, pp. 32–33.

256 *NSSR94*, p. i.

257 *NSSR94*, p. 5.

258 Author's interview with Sir Malcolm Rifkind.

CHAPTER SEVEN

Reflections on Clinton's Grand Strategy

Bill Clinton was not the first American president who came to power hoping to concentrate on domestic affairs, only to have foreign crises thrust upon him to the detriment of his original aspirations; nor was he the first president to take office following a US victory in a tumultuous conflict with an apparent mandate to steer a new course in policy. Clearly, however, the Clinton team faced anything but a clean slate when they first arrived in the White House, finding themselves hindered by the remnants of President Bush's ongoing policy directives and enactments: crises in the Caribbean, Africa, and the Balkans, unrest in Russia, major decisions to be made regarding China, the future of global and regional trade, and defense alliances all required presidential attention. Although President Bush had claimed that only the United States could "provide the kind of leadership necessary" for his New World Order, "no Bush doctrine or grand design existed for meeting the collective security needs of the new world order."[1] Accordingly, the Clinton administration inherited a rapidly transforming international environment that demanded constant fire fighting.

Rather than providing the necessary attention, however, the administration in general and the president in particular initially appeared content to let issues drift. The president was not disinterested in foreign policy as has often been suggested, but Bill Clinton's priority upon assuming the presidency was a domestic renewal. Where issues of foreign trade impacted his plans for the American economy, he was engaged, but this was not a president that intended to dwell on foreign affairs for their own sake. Foreign policy was utilized to further the goals of the administration, but it did not become a goal in and of itself. As a result, many have questioned the enduring nature of Clinton's Grand Strategy and have rejected the idea that a coherent plan even existed. This, however, is an injustice to those who contributed to the formulation of foreign policy during the time period. The Clinton administration produced a coherent vision that it updated in accordance with legislation every calendar year. An examination of speeches and documents clearly reveal specific positions that Bill Clinton adopted on the campaign and which later formed the core elements of his administration's grand strategy. Such policies remained consistent from the time of Governor Clinton's Georgetown Address of December 1991 through the duration of his two terms as president of the United States.

Clinton's Grand Strategy was based on American ideals and geopolitical realities and reflected a concerted effort to define an innovative approach to foreign policy in a new era, based on the reinforcing principles of national security, prosperity promotion, and democratic promotion. As Warren Christopher announced, "a vibrant economy will strengthen America's hand abroad, while permitting us to maintain a strong military without sacrificing domestic needs. And by helping others to forge democracy out of the ruins of dictatorship, we can pacify old threats, prevent new ones, and create new markets for US trade and investment."[2] The strategy was designed to ensure America's continued interaction with the world through trade and open markets and rejected the principle of universality; simply because an approach was right for the United States, this did not mean it would be right for all people. Instead, the administration sought to bestow a bespoke approach to regions of the world. This was a very American concept, defined by Walter Russell Mead as being "uniquely far-reaching and systemic," with a deep-rooted belief in human rights, values, and trade, but which recognized that America must remain strong militarily.[3]

Clinton's Grand Strategy was a break from the past for it recognized the limits of American power, but sought to overcome them by adopting a multilateral approach to foreign policy. This belief resulted in the early embrace of the United Nations as the organization of choice to execute US foreign policy in the 1990s. While this enthusiasm was tempered by the events in Somalia, the administration remained committed to the concept of multilateralism, no matter how much it felt the need to advocate unilateralism in the face of congressional hostility. However, for those who placed their faith in a preponderance of power, the idea that a change in the form of other countries' governments could increase US national security appeared tenuous, "especially coming from someone so inexperienced in the ways of the world as Bill Clinton."[4] However, the president's "ability was not as limited and his performance in foreign policy [was not] as bad as many critics charged."[5] President Clinton's contribution to strategic thinking was to link economic security formally with national security in a pragmatic policy for an evolving international environment.

Clinton's Grand Strategy advanced the belief that democracies were unlikely to threaten American interests and would support free trade, as international stability became the ambitious by-product of globalization. The policy ensured that the United States remained "the world's indispensable nation" by embedding itself at the center of all major international organizations and structures: GATT, NATO, WTO, NAFTA, and APEC. The policy resulted in the expansion of NATO without causing irreparable damage to US–Russian relations; allowed for the removal of nuclear weapons and materials from Ukraine, Kazakhstan, and Belarus; contributed to the Balkan peace deal; expanded trade throughout North America as a result of NAFTA; helped rescue the Mexican economy; and moved Haiti toward democracy.[6] The policy combined Wilsonian principles with the financially motivated notion of opening foreign markets to US exports. Under President Clinton, therefore, US Grand Strategy encompassed prudent realism and moral idealism, to protect the nation from external threats and to stand for ideals worthy of emulation.

Grand strategy as presidential doctrine

A major reason that the US Grand Strategy of Engagement and Enlargement is not universally accepted as The Clinton Doctrine is because President Clinton did not deliver the speech that introduced its key concepts. The president may have been content to allow his advisers to announce major policy initiatives, but this greatly reduced their impact. Having Anthony Lake declare that "the successor to a doctrine of Containment must be a strategy of enlargement" ensured that the national and international attention that a similar presidential announcement would have received was missing.[7] Similarly, a high profile unveiling of the annual grand strategy documents by the president alongside his national security team would have increased the policy's standing.

The Clinton White House appeared content to allow vital foreign policy initiatives to be unveiled by lower ranking members of the administration in a move that undermined the policies by raising doubts about the level of commitment to them within the Oval Office. While President Clinton did make foreign policy addresses, they were few and far between, and often failed to inspire confidence in his ability to convey strong leadership in matters of military planning or international relations. Anthony Lake commented that "a lot of the strategy comes more through presidential speeches than through the documents" and while this is undoubtedly true, the key foreign policy addresses of the Clinton administration, particularly in the first term, were delivered by officials and not by the president.[8] Of course the processes involved in presidential speechmaking are not straightforward, as interested parties from the State Department to the Congress seek to influence tone and content. This can mean that presidents are "reluctant to articulate foreign policy in detail and with precision," as the process "can be extremely time consuming and contentious. But a reluctance to articulate policy with precision is usually a mistake."[9] Such was the case with the Clinton administration, as its willingness to delegate the pronouncement of grand strategy did much to undermine confidence in the eventual policy.

There was also tension within the administration over the need for a Clinton Doctrine or even the existence of a grand strategy: Tara Sonenshine of the NSC wrote in 1994, "I keep hoping that someone will pull together a Clinton Doctrine description which explains that Clinton's foreign policy is based on a careful calibration of force and diplomacy in which we use these dual levers to bring about the resolution of conflicts."[10] However, within days Sonenshine's NSC colleague, Bob Borrstin, advised Anthony Lake that the president "should not introduce any new all-encompassing term or phrase to describe our foreign policy," when he addressed the UN General Assembly, "nor should it explicitly go back to engagement, enlargement and three pillars," because "the press doesn't buy them."[11] Lake had previously attempted to coordinate a series of speeches in September 1993 around the concept of Democratic Enlargement, which had backfired when the four speeches failed to convey a single, simple message. However, it had also been undermined by Lake himself, who had told the *New Republic* the day beforehand that he was "sceptical about doctrines on immensely complicated and difficult issues [that] have all the answers before you ask the questions."[12] Policy divisions were present, therefore, not only between departments, but within them as well, ensuring that tension was never far from the surface.

While consultation is a prerequisite in any government bureaucracy, the Clinton administration appeared to take such a process to extremes, as its initial grand strategy document went through 21 drafts and 2 authors before finally appearing in the summer of 1994. Such hesitancy did little to inspire confidence either in personnel or in the direction of policy, since it appeared that the document was a compromise solution, reached after endless wrangling between the State Department and the National Security Council in particular. Despite the compromise, the State Department harbored a growing concern over the emphasis on trade policy, while the apparent refusal of the secretary of state to give his full support to the eventual strategy did much to undermine faith in it, revealing the "typical" and "cautious" approach of the department.[13]

Warren Christopher reportedly wanted nothing to do with Anthony Lake's Democratic Enlargement policy, which he viewed as "a trade policy masquerading as foreign policy."[14] Lake, in contrast, felt that Engagement was "rather wimpy, because of course we were going to be engaged" and believed that this was included "just to make everyone happy." Lake conceded that Christopher "didn't use it, he didn't like it, it went, in his view, too far . . . but not in the view of Madeleine or me or most of the people."[15] As Carl Bildt observed, "A great deal of blood can be spilt in the course of inter-agency debates in Washington" and the struggle to define foreign policy in the Clinton administration was a prime example of such wrangling.[16] Reflecting on the situation, Charles A. Kupchan observed, "I don't think that there really was a grand strategy. I think that there were ideas floating around and that there were guiding presumptions about America and its role in the world. The administration was more characterized by pragmatism and problem solving." This is not to suggest that this was a flawed approach: "I think in general in foreign policy, it was a successful presidency and America ended up stronger, ended up respected, more prosperous."[17] Perhaps, therefore, doctrinal constructs are of less importance than results?

Clinton's Grand Strategy was a fine concept, but providing demonstrable results proved difficult as the crises that confronted the administration came not from interstate activity but predominantly from internal disputes within Backlash States. Therefore, while the policy succeeded in providing direction in Central and Eastern Europe and, along with Dual Containment, gave direction to policy regarding Iraq and Iran, where there was no democratic development—and in the face of genocide—the policy offered little strategic value. While the promotion of free markets was a priority for the administration, its grand strategy did not provide an adequate guide for how to promote democracy. The policy served as a general rationale for promoting political liberalization and challenging Backlash States, but it did not provide specifics about what actions should be taken prior to democratic development in these regions. However, as Leon Fuerth noted,

> There is always a gap between philosophy and events. You need to judge an administration on its actions, not its doctrines. Should we have had a doctrine on the use of force that would have bound us to implement it everywhere and in all situations? Can a statement explain what we should do or whom we should support in all circumstances? Should we always adhere to a doctrine? The NSSR was designed to explain the general logic, the processes and impressions of the individuals involved in policy formulation.[18]

The grand strategy of Engagement and Enlargement succeeded despite the best efforts of the foreign policy intelligentsia to write it off and in spite of limited public knowledge or interest. As Kupchan noted, the administration could rightly claim to have "brought peace to the Balkans . . . expanded trade and presided over the greatest expansion in the American economy."[19] In the administration's policies toward Russia, its approach to NATO expansion, its endorsement of European enlargement, and normalization of trade with the Pacific Rim nations, one can see the tangible results of a policy of Engagement and Enlargement that aided not only the US economy, but also the global economy during the 1990s.

The evolution of grand strategy

Anthony Lake observed that "there's a tendency for all of us, when we're going back and analysing things, to impute more order to processes than in fact there is and to give more weight to strategy papers than they deserve."[20] However, the official grand strategy documents of the Clinton administration are revealing for the manner in which they evolved over 8 years. As a candidate in 1992, Bill Clinton stressed the desire to offer more opportunity in return for an assumption of greater responsibility on behalf of the American people. In 1995, he turned this ethos to the area of foreign policy, recognizing that "we have a special responsibility that goes along with being a great power." This was not a traditional liberal approach to grand strategy, however, for it was tempered by a steely realism, born of tragic circumstances in Somalia. The Clinton administration was determined to stress the lessons it had learned from the events in Mogadishu and expressed them at length: "When our national security interests are threatened, we will, as America always has, use diplomacy when we can, but force if we must. We will act with others when we can, but alone when we must."[21] This was, and had been, the guiding principle of Clinton's foreign policy, but it went largely unrecognized throughout his time in office.

Following criticism over Somalia and the Republican takeover of Congress in 1994, the administration stressed a more defined concept of the use of force, as specific criteria were applied prior to troop deployment and military intervention. This did not signify a withdrawal from the world, but was a sign that the United States was determined to prioritize its own interests. This was done in part to refute Jeane Kirkpatrick's claim that "the Clinton administration offers us a vision of foreign policy from which national self-interest is purged."[22] From 1995, "although the United States would not wholly eschew multilateral actions in global affairs, the administration would be more amenable to utilising unilateral actions— and would undertake them only if necessary."[23] Grand strategy became tempered by a greater degree of realism, as the administration conceded "democracy and economic prosperity can take root in a struggling society only through local solutions carried out by the society itself." The administration pledged to deploy troops overseas "only when our interests and our values are sufficiently at stake," a position stressed in repeated national security documentation and as devised in PDD-25.[24] However, despite alterations to the philosophy, the basic tenants of Clinton's Grand Strategy remained the desire to free both peoples and markets and to bind them together in a world of growing interdependency and increasing globalization. The strategy was guided by a commitment to freedom, equality, and human dignity, but this idealism became increasingly tempered as time progressed.

While the first administration had to establish policy, by the time of the second Clinton administration, "the broad policy framework had been set."[25] The second term grand strategy placed prominence on negotiation and engagement, particularly with regard to China and Russia. However, Engagement was a procedure, a tool of diplomacy, whereas Democratic Enlargement was an aim, albeit one that lacked a method. As was noted, "engagement is just a fancy word for diplomacy. That's what the State Department does . . . having engagement as the goal means that, by definition, a meeting is a success if you simply show up."[26] The policy could, therefore, be seen as far more cautious than in the first term, in which great strides were sought if not necessarily achieved.

Anthony Lake's philosophy was apparent throughout: "This is not a crusade, but a genuine and responsible effort, over time, to protect American strategic interests, stabilise the international system and enlarge the community of nations committed to democracy, free markets and peace."[27] Such a declaration was indicative of the philosophy and expectation that the Clinton administration started out with. However, it was the dynamic reach of US Grand Strategy that proved to be its downfall, as the inability to enact the policy within a 4-year time frame, and thereby demonstrate tangible results proved to be its undoing.[28] There was also a question about the wisdom of pursuing both Democratic Enlargement and NATO Enlargement simultaneously, since "democratic enlargement was difficult and other foreign policy issues that did not fit neatly under the rubric needed attention."[29]

Clinton's Grand Strategy necessarily took time to implement in key geostrategic locations. Indeed the concept of open markets leading to free and fair societies seemingly backfired in Russia where "the power of the oligarchs increased, government legitimacy fell and the needs of the Russian people were ignored."[30] The second Clinton administration chose to concentrate on more traditional concepts such as reducing nuclear weapons and increasing aid to Russia. In China, the administration continued its free trade policy "in the hope that an expanding free market would create a more assertive Chinese middle class."[31] Clinton's second term cabinet were also somewhat more robust than the first, a situation personified by Madeleine Albright, who feared that "the lessons of Vietnam could be learned too well" and lead to a paralysis of American leadership.[32]

Policy evolution was a visible process during the Clinton years and by 1998 the emphasis had moved toward Homeland Defense. This did not mean an embrace of NMD or the establishment of a Department of Homeland Security, but rather an acknowledgement of the threats posed by terrorism, international crime, drug trafficking, and WMD. However, much of the philosophy remained consistent, as the 1998 grand strategy document contained the three familiar pillars upon which US Grand Strategy continued to be based: National security, democracy promotion, and prosperity promotion. However, while democracy promotion had not been erased, it was now below the horizon, as it was felt that "by the start of the second term attempts at Democratic Enlargement had reached an equilibrium."[33]

Time also saw alterations to the policy of Dual Containment. Martin Indyk observed that "over time the nature of the threats changed. The Iraqis became more of a problem, more difficult to contain." By November 1998, the Clinton administration changed its policy from Dual Containment to Containment Plus Regime Change and declared that its objective was "not only to contain Saddam as long as he was around, but also to help the Iraqi people remove him and set up a different kind of government." However, the administration took the opposite approach to Iran following the election of Khatami and was prepared to move from containment to engagement if they were prepared to meet halfway. Regretfully, the Tehran regime failed to respond, ensuring that the containment policy remained in place.

By December 2000, US Grand Strategy was defined as "A National Security Strategy for a Global Age," though the goals remained familiar: "enhancing security at home and abroad, promoting prosperity and promoting democracy and human rights."[34] The document had a tougher edge to it, but it remained at heart, an internationalist policy that warned against a "retreat into a policy of Fortress America." To do so, the document warned, risked "a global loss of our authority and with it ultimately our power. A strategy of engagement, however, is the surest way to enhance not only our power but also our authority and thus our leadership, into the twenty-first century."[35] This was the final grand strategy document released by the Clinton White House and the last such report prior to the attacks of September 2001, an event that refocused attention on foreign policy after a decade of ambivalence. Despite having updated US Grand Strategy on an annual basis, Leon Fuerth insisted that "events were more influential than documents" and that "ultimately, consistency can be over-rated."[36] The Clinton administration's grand strategy documents, therefore, were "more a statement of strategy and intent than a guide to action."[37] As a result, it is important to "consider reality more than theoretical concepts within a doctrine" when judging the success or failure of the administration.[38]

The evolution of personnel

Just as doubts remain over the veracity of Clinton's Grand Strategy, so too do they loom large in any consideration of his national security team.

The group that Clinton initially assembled to devise grand strategy was drawn from the upper echelons of the Democratic Party, but many failed to measure up. Clinton's plan had been simple: "It was going to be a well-organized administration, the president was going to be the boss and Lake and Berger . . . would be the intellectual cranks, Christopher would go around the world and be the guy who shows up at the press conferences and does the right kind of thing."[39] Instead, his first term team was quickly tainted by events in Somalia and the president's perceived lack of faith in them proved to be contagious, with regular reports of imminent departures and impending resignations.

This was reflected in how the administration was perceived, as the National Security Council in particular became concerned at the administration's inability to convey its message. In June 1994, Tara Sonenshine and Tom Ross noted that the administration was suffering from "major weaknesses in the current foreign policy communications apparatus" and devised a 6-month strategy to reengage the public and the foreign policy elite. Sonenshine was forthright in her concerns over interdepartmental intransigence, insisting that "too much happens at State and Defense without White House knowledge." As a result, she noted, "too many journalists now find they can play one agency off another." Instead of the efficient media operation that had defined the Clinton campaign in 1992, a dysfunctional approach blighted the administration once in office, ensuring that "neither those who make foreign policy nor those whose responsibility it is to articulate the policy are consistently doing so in a way that communicates strength, clarity and decisiveness." As a result, "too much of that reporting and analysis takes places without an administration point of view. We are, therefore, constantly on the defensive."[40]

There was a constant evolution of personnel within the national security structure, with individuals moving in, up or out of the administration, in part as a reflection of President Clinton's growing confidence in foreign affairs. The president grew into the role and this was reflected in his choice of advisers and the way his administration operated. The initial 18 months was defined by an "open access, user friendly" style at the National Security Council. However, the departure of Thomas "Mack" McLarty as Chief of Staff and the arrival of Leon Panetta "led to a tighter ship" and ended the sense of "a certain lack of discipline."[41] This shake up that occurred within the White House staff following the 1994 midterms, however, should have been accompanied by changes in the foreign policy team. Warren Christopher singularly failed to provide the sense of purpose required of a Secretary of State in the modern era, as Shimon Peres' observation that he was "very finely made . . . like an English suit" perfectly encapsulated the rather effete quality Christopher brought to the role.[42] Tony Lake was "soft-spoken, unassuming, and bookish" and appeared more concerned with preserving the harmony among key players and overcompensated for the internal division of the Carter years, while Les Aspin's failing health was a metaphor for a man running out of time in every sense.[43]

Despite the best attempt at achieving cordial relations, it was acknowledged that the relationship between Christopher and Lake "was still not a good one, replete as it was with mistrust and unilateral manoeuvring," a situation that had "substantial effects on US policy making."[44] Throughout the first term, Lake was the key advocate of Democratic Enlargement, had overseen its development, and ensured its place within US Grand Strategy. He was "a very cerebral person, a nice by Washington standards person . . . not a back stabber, or an elbow thrower . . . he's on the nice end of that spectrum in that regard . . . a thinking man's NSC adviser."[45] He was the driving force behind foreign policy in the first term, leading Leon Panetta to concede that there were "very few times [that Lake's position was] reversed or changed or modified."[46] However, despite having been vital to the campaign and to the development of policy, Lake failed to develop a warm relationship with the president. He had wanted to resign in the autumn of 1993, partly due to "a series of constant and growing frustrations—partly at the interagency difficulties in pushing though new approaches as hard times bring out new hesitancies and partly also with a White House that . . . still treats foreign policy as [a] wholly owned subsidiary."[47] He remained distant from a chief executive known for his touchy–feely approach to interpersonal relationships and as a result, the bond that had developed between previous presidents and their national security advisers failed to materialize.

This lack of empathy compounded a sense that the first term team had somehow failed to come together as expected. Kupchan noted that "If there were a criticism that I would level at the group, it was that they were too nice and they were not sufficiently hard headed enough in resolving differences of opinion and bringing the policy debate to a sharp conclusion."[48] Despite their shared experience in the Carter administration and apparent public displays of harmony, tensions existed that refused to dissipate. Madeleine Albright noted changes in Lake's demeanor: "I was unnerved by the manner of Tony Lake. The pressures of the job had made Tony less easygoing and patient than the clever friend whom I had long known."[49]

Lake "stayed on through the entire first tem, driven in part by the need to resolve the festering problem in Bosnia, somewhat to the frustration of Berger, who had gotten him the job and had thought that he might take over a year or two earlier."[50] Indeed, it was understood that Lake had advised his family that he would only serve for 2 years.[51] Lake had sought to act as a "behind-the-scenes consensus builder" who presented the varying views of senior advisers to the president. He later lamented adopting this "discreet posture," since "in the post-Cold War world, the president needs all the help he can get in explaining his policies to the nation."[52]

Despite finding him "not entirely simpatico," President Clinton intended to move Lake to Langley at the start of his second term, where he would remain within the administration as Director of Central Intelligence (DCI).[53] President Clinton announced that Lake's role at the NSC had given him "a unique understanding of the strengths and weaknesses of our intelligence operations."[54] The president referred to Lake as "one of my closest advisers and one of my most trusted ones. He was an integral part of every foreign policy decision we made and his legacy can be seen around the world."[55] Writing in *Foreign Policy*, Melvin Goodman noted that Lake was an ideal candidate to "restore the integrity and credibility of the CIA and to confront its Cold War legacy."[56] However, Lake became the most high profile victim of the increasing partisanship that swept Washington. His posting as national security adviser had not required congressional approval, but the bid to become DCI was derailed in hearings before the Senate Select Committee on Intelligence. In Lake's place, Clinton selected George Tenet as the DCI, who continued to serve into the following administration.[57]

With Lake no longer at the NSC, Clinton finally nominated his friend of 30 years, Samuel Berger, who had been offered the role 4 years earlier. Berger "was not someone you would necessarily think of as a foreign policy thinker, but he was a good nuts and bolts guy who knew everyone and made sure you didn't screw up, which was Clinton's instinct."[58] The changes from Lake to Berger were not major ensuring that policy positions that had been initiated by Lake were credited to Berger toward the end of the administration's time in office. Writing in the *Washington Post*, Sebastian Mallaby suggested that Berger had brought a much needed balance between realism and idealism since "he had declined to be a Wilsonian idealist or a Henry Kissinger realist. He has refused to chose between a go-it-alone conservatism and liberal internationalism," a stance that perfectly described Anthony Lake's approach since he joined the Clinton campaign in 1991 at Berger's invitation.[59]

The appointment of William Perry as Defense Secretary helped to improve interdepartmental relations. Similar moves at State and the NSC in 1994/1995 could have greatly aided the administration, and enabled members of the second term to be promoted sooner, or empowered others, such as Richard Holbrooke, with greater responsibility. However, along with the obvious problems of replacing the entire foreign policy team was the challenge of getting candidates confirmed in the new 105th Congress—a fact that undoubtedly tempered the temptation to clean house in 1995, especially since "there were concerns that replacing Christopher would have been a bloodbath."[60]

Clinton's second-term foreign policy team of Secretary of State Madeleine Albright, National Security Advisor Samuel Berger, and Secretary of Defense William Cohen were "less talented than their predecessors, but also less restrained" and better reflected the president's evolving aspirations.[61] Clinton's selection of Albright was not guaranteed, indeed "it was surprising, Clinton ambled into it, wasn't sure he wanted her." Eventually, President Clinton "warmed to her story and to her as more than a figurehead, an embodiment of American values that would work well aboard, but he was worried about her ability to make the trains run on time." Richard Holbrook was considered "and would have gotten the job, but Clinton didn't trust him as a team player."[62] As a team, they were far more prepared to endorse unilateral action than their predecessors. Despite this, during Clinton's time in office, "the chances of an American serviceman being killed by hostile action while on active duty were less than 1 in 160,000. He was six time more likely to be murdered by one of his comrades, nineteen times more likely to kill himself, and fifty times more likely to die in an accident," odds that changed considerably following Clinton's departure from office.[63]

Considering the critiques of grand strategy

The Clinton administration envisioned its replacement of Containment to be the quintessential foreign policy initiative for addressing the final decade of the twentieth century. However, its reception was less than glorious: Republicans were damning; foreign policy analysts were scathing; the press was unimpressed; and former members of Clinton's campaign team were dismissive. Before the administration had left office, its grand strategy was damned for being "indecisive, incoherent, contradictory, confused, lacking in vision and purpose."[64] Clearly, this was not the reception that the Clinton administration had hoped for. However, this was the good news, for at least the aforementioned groups noticed that a strategy had been designed. The vast majority of Americans remained blissfully unaware that a new global strategy had been devised, as polls repeated revealed Americans to be "uninformed, confused, or apathetic."[65] With the end of the Cold War, foreign policy ceased to be a daily concern for most Americans and, as a result, Clinton's Grand Strategy initiative was "a public relations dud; few liked it or even took a passing interest."[66]

The Clinton administration sought to convey the "new dangers, opportunities, and responsibilities" that had arisen at a time when Americans were "preoccupied with domestic concerns."[67] However, having campaigned on a domestic agenda, critiquing President Bush for his emphasis on foreign affairs, President Clinton was ill-placed to complain when much of the country ignored issues relating to foreign policy, while those who did express an opinion were unimpressed when the administration singularly failed "to build a domestic political consensus in support of its strategic vision."[68] In a survey of public opinion on foreign policy conducted in late 1994, only 31 percent of the public judged the Clinton administration's handling of foreign policy as "good" or "excellent."[69]

The administration did not need to look far for critics of its grand strategy, for what its policy lacked in overall success, it made up for in an ability to rally opposition. Senator John McCain accused Clinton of having "pursued a feckless, photo-op foreign policy" during which there had been "little or no effort to define a coherent plan for United States engagement in the world."[70] The editor of *Foreign Affairs*, William G. Hyland, suggested that Clinton's foreign policy amounted to little more than one of "selective engagement" and alleged that a "magnificent historical opportunity to shape the international system had been missed."[71] Richard Haass turned criticism of US Grand Strategy in the 1990s into an art-form, declaring that Clinton "inherited a world of unprecedented American advantage and opportunity," and presided over an age of "underachievement and squandered potential."[72] Henry Kissinger went further, as he dismissed not only the president, but also his entire generation, as one dedicated to the "self-indulgence or self-righteousness of the protest period." Clinton's generation, Kissinger lamented, had "not yet raised leaders capable of evoking a commitment to a consistent and long-range foreign policy."[73]

Former Clinton campaign adviser Michael Mandelbaum berated the administration for its efforts, declaring that, "the seminal events of the foreign policy of the Clinton administration were three failed military interventions in its first nine months in office."[74] Mandelbaum, passed over for a high-ranking position in the White House, lamented that "after three years the Clinton administration had not articulated a clear foreign policy doctrine for the post-Cold War world."[75] However, by the time this had been published, the Clinton administration had produced two national security strategy reports and was preparing a third. The issues that Mandelbaum referenced had also been inherited from "a supposed master of foreign policy, George Bush" and Clinton "essentially tried to maintain the policies he inherited in those trouble spots."[76] Mandelbaum had also previously written that "whoever won the election in 1992 would have had to face a tough choice in 1993 regarding Somalia . . . The Bush people might have made a different choice than Clinton and just pulled out, but they can't now say that they could have avoided that choice."[77] As Jacob Heilbrunn noted, "US foreign policy has been increasingly successful precisely because Bill Clinton has refused to embrace chimerical visions. As a result, he has skilfully piloted the US through a sea of New World disorder."[78]

Jacques Attali, former adviser to François Mitterrand, expressed concerns that the Clinton administration had failed to provide "long-term vision. Leadership becomes an empty concept when day-to-day actions do not occur within a broader context."[79] However, a broader context had been espoused, though roundly ignored, something that did not prevent

Richard Haass from writing in *Foreign Affairs* that Clinton had failed to establish "an overarching intellectual framework" for foreign policy and that as a result, "few relationships or institutions bear his imprint."[80] Yet the decision to expand NATO, the alterations to APEC, and the moves to enact NAFTA and the WTO were all decisions made by the Clinton White House that had major, long-term implications for the United States and the world well into the twenty-first century. As the great architect of European unity, Jean Monnet, observed, "Nothing is possible without men, but nothing is lasting without institutions."[81]

Not all criticism was unfounded. John Lewis Gaddis suggested that that US Grand Strategy amounted to little more than "foreign policy by autopilot," that "never specified who or what was to be engaged or enlarged."[82] This was perhaps a fair critique of the policy; it presented admirable concepts, but little to help with implementation. Clearly, aspirations were set, but the policy lacked a methodology. Clinton's Grand Strategy contained the goal of aiding nations in their efforts to attain democracy, but offered little by way of a strategy, which required more than the prioritizing of goals. As George Kennan explained, in foreign policy, the "what" cannot be separated from the "how."[83] However, Gaddis later observed that the administration "assumed the continued primacy of states within the international system" and that it needed only to "engage" with them in order to "enlarge" the processes of self-determination and economic integration. Gaddis suggested that the administration's view of states was that "if you could bind them together by removing restrictions on trade and investment as well as on the movement of peoples and ideas, then the causes of violence and the insecurity it breeds would drop away." Such efforts were deemed to be "well intentioned but shallow."[84] Gaddis, however, failed to address the focus on Backlash States that Anthony Lake raised or efforts to combating international terrorism.

Accordingly, Clinton's critics often revealed their own ignorance of the policy-making process and the track record of debate on the subject. Writing in *Foreign Affairs*, Jonathan Clarke complained that "all too often the slogan comes first, the substance second," using as evidence of this, the president's lament that his administration had failed to design a "bumper sticker" that encapsulated its foreign policy. Clarke complained that under Clinton, "policymakers reach first for the sound bite tested in focus groups . . . and then try to construct a policy that fits it."[85] Such an assault on the manner in which foreign policy was devised revealed a lack of insight into the evolution of policy and totally misconstrued the president's remarks, which had conceded not that there was no policy, but rather that the White House had failed to reduce its policy to a simple expression, necessary to engage the general public. In every sense, Clarke failed to appreciate the manner in which policy had been devised and the importance of conveying a message to the media and the world at large. Robert Kagan critiqued the administration for failing to contain China, remove Saddam Hussein, maintain US military strength, or deploy NMD.[86] However, as Stephen Walt noted, the administration's foreign policy was "well suited to an era where there [was] little to gain in foreign policy and much to lose. The American people recognise this and have made it clear that they want neither isolationism nor costly international crusades."[87]

President Clinton recognized that due to America's electoral timescales he had a finite period in which to enact his domestic program and, therefore, prioritized his deficit reduction plan and efforts to introduce universal health-care coverage to the detriment of other considerations. For much of President Clinton's first year in office, "there was no pressure . . . to focus on foreign policy. He was content to focus on his domestic agenda . . . There was a preference to deal with events rather than formulate doctrines."[88] By doing so, the president remained true to his goal of focusing on America's economy, but this helped to formulate a belief that he was disengaged from the foreign policy decision-making process. This reduced the authority of the White House and of America's officials around the globe, leading to claims that the Clinton administration "almost turned foreign policy into a vaudeville act."[89] The repercussions demonstrated that Bill Clinton could not afford to abdicate interest over one area of government merely for the benefit of another. As President of the United States, Bill Clinton needed to demonstrate mastery of his entire White House, not merely those areas of policy that interested him. His failure to do so sufficiently in this first year in office was something his critics never forgave him for.

Perhaps the most remarkable critique of the administration, however, came not from opponents, but from its former members. Michael Mandelbaum's devastating broadside, "Foreign Policy as Social Work," has been well documented, but Kupchan's comments in *The End of the American Era* warrant consideration. He noted that, "although members of the Clinton team effectively blended realism and liberalism in practice, they never did so self-consciously—that is, they never articulated a set of guiding principles that could serve as the conceptual foundation for their actions." This is a remarkable declaration from a former member of the NSC that raises questions about the impact, even internally, of the annual National Security Strategy Review, which laid out, year by year, precisely the "guiding principles" that Kupchan refers to. He remarked that as Clinton "failed to arm himself with a clear set of guiding strategic principles that he could impart to the electorate, he was not even able to begin the task of laying the foundation for a new American internationalism." Yet time and again, throughout the administration, Clinton and his officials sought to do so, detailing the three central elements to policy that had been present since the Georgetown University speech of December 1991. Kupchan concludes that "without such conceptual coherence, the whole of Clinton's foreign policy ended up being much less than the sum of its parts. The administration may have gotten right many specific policies, but those policies did not add up to a coherent grand strategy."[90] This reinforced the fears of the NSC's Tara Sonenshine that the administration's message was simply not being conveyed adequately, either internally or externally.

Certainly, the administration's shortcomings were recognized by its own officials. Members of the NSC noted that the president needed "to speak with the confident voice of the captain and navigator of our ship of state" because the American people "crave a sense of national direction."[91] This, alas, was not always forthcoming, enabling Richard Haass to conclude that Clinton "gave the American people the foreign policy that polls suggested they wanted—unlike a truly great president, who would have tried to lead them toward the foreign policy they needed."[92] Yet during the 1990s the American people were content to focus on a domestic agenda and were not seeking foreign wars. Indeed, there is little to suggest that things would be any different had it not been for the terrorist attacks of 2001. Despite setbacks, the moves made with both Russia and China were examples of the policy being utilized to improve both American exports and the safety of the world. These successes were compounded by the successful expansion of NATO, done without drawing the Russians into either a conflict or alienation. It was also a policy that was palatable to the rest of the world and did not produce the vitriolic backlash that marked the administration of Clinton's successor.

The significance of Clinton's Grand Strategy

Whatever their policy successes and despite their best efforts, the Clinton administration was unable to define the era through which it governed and remained exposed to criticism that it failed to define US foreign policy, as the end of the Cold War "meant the loss of a single enemy . . . around which to rally a national and international consensus."[93] In this regard, little had changed since Al Gore wrote in 1992, "our geo-politics are labelled post-Cold War. We know what we are not, but we don't seem to know what we are."[94] Fundamentally, an administration must define "what constitutes a vital interest—a change in the international environment so likely to undermine the national security that it must be resisted no matter what form the threat takes or how ostensibly legitimate it appears."[95] This was perhaps the greatest failure of Clinton's Grand Strategy, as it failed to engage either the public or foreign policy experts. Wolfowitz noted that the administration had "failed to explain what American interests are worth defending and to justify the actions that it has taken in relation to those interests."[96] This was compounded by the fact that so few in the administration appeared interested in promoting the concept to the American public, who in turn were not very interested in hearing about it. Therefore, the only people to comment were those who feared the policy threatened to surrender

America's primacy in the world. Eventually the White House realized that in an age when the United States lacked both a defined enemy and a defined role, it was no longer advisable to develop narrow concepts and attempt to manipulate foreign policy to match.

This had been the view of Warren Christopher all along and his stance had supporters. John Lewis Gaddis called it "a defensible position," adding that "there is something to be said for staying flexible . . . One of the distinct advantages of a world without clear and present dangers is that it allows such improvisation."[97] Gaddis was far from endorsing the administration, however, and lamented "the absence of any grand design," believing that "there's a kind of incrementalism and *ad-hocism* to things."[98] Gaddis was echoed by Condoleezza Rice, writing in *Foreign Affairs*: "The absence of an articulated 'national interest' either produces a fertile ground for those wishing to withdraw from the world or creates a vacuum to be filled by parochial groups and transitory pressures." Despite Dr Rice's concerns, the Clinton administration's National Security Strategy Reviews were hardly "hijacked by isolationist tendencies" and were not prey to "parochial groups and transitory pressures."[99] Indeed, the central themes of the annual reports remained consistent with Clinton's December 1991 address at Georgetown University.

Clinton openly advocated making economic security a central element of grand strategy. His agenda was the foundation for a new, post-Containment American mission in the world, as Clinton positioned the United States as "a power for free markets, democracy and development."[100] Yet the belief that foreign and domestic agendas could be combined for the good of the nation was a revolutionary concept and one that appalled those who maintained their faith in classic power politics. However, the Clinton administration was governing the nation through a new age that called for new concepts. The guiding mantra had been Franklin Roosevelt's desire for "bold, persistent experimentation" and in its grand strategy, Clinton's team believed it had found a way to engage in such an activist approach to policy, coupled with a much needed pragmatic stance.[101]

For all of the interdepartmental compromises, even critics conceded that no policy "set forth to address the disorder and chance of a rapidly evolving world order can be frozen in rigid application"; attempting to do so would have been futile and potentially disastrous.[102] As Lake acknowledged, "Nobody in any government I am aware of except perhaps in the Soviet Union, or in Mao's China, says at a meting, 'OK, what did we say in the strategy document, therefore, here's what our policy is.'"[103] Neither the policy of Containment that preceded Engagement and Enlargement nor that of Pre-Emption that followed it tied the United States to specific unyielding action regardless of the ramifications. Indeed, the Containment doctrine, "so celebrated in hindsight . . . saw inconsistent implementation."[104] As Anthony Lake observed in his 1994 speech to the Council on Foreign Relations, "while the policy of Containment looks obvious to us in retrospect, we should remember that it took . . . several years to define their way and build a policy consensus . . . And they had the advantage of an ideologically and geographically defined adversary with whom to contend."[105] This did not prevent Richard Haass from observing in *Foreign Policy* that, "the one attempt to articulate an overall construct was embodied in then national security advisor Anthony Lake's September 1993 address . . . but this neo-Wilsonian vision has had a negligible impact on day-to-day affairs."[106] Policy documents can only ever exist as a guideline and in many cases "there is no relationship between the document and policy."[107] Within the Clinton White House, the grand strategy documents "were designed to provide guidance for overall policy. However, the responses to ongoing issues should be given more attention than theoretical documents. The Clinton worldview was not driven by a doctrinal situation."[108]

Official US foreign policy, as printed, can only ever be theoretical, designed to indicate direction and principles. "Nobody looks at them to clear up issues. Any concept that the policy influences events or people's reaction to them is just wrong."[109] To presume that such documents are consulted in time of crisis is to misunderstand both the rationale for such documentation and also the nature of government and emergency responses. "For all administrations they are more a statement of strategy and intent than a guide to action."[110] This was recognized by those covering the administration, as Jef McAllister of *Time* observed, such documents "might be good for imposing discipline on the machine, but its probably not the place where real creative thinking gets done . . . When the president wants to come up with a new foreign policy its usually done with him, the secretary of state and the national security adviser and a speech writer or two."[111] Such documents exist for two reasons: to provide public reassurance about the overall strategy of the administration and to fulfill a legal requirement to report such a strategy to Congress. For critics to lament that the Clinton administration's "early experiments" with its ambition of Democratic Enlargement and tactic of Assertive Multilateralism "were quickly abandoned, with *ad hoc* decision-making becoming the norm" fails to convey the realities of the administration or the manner in which all foreign crises are addressed as they occur.[112]

In 2010, Krasner noted that "most foreign policies most of the time have not been guided by grand strategy," and that most efforts to articulate a holistic vision have failed. Rather than attempting to initiate grand strategy, Krasner suggests, states should base their foreign policy around Orienting Principles, an approach that warrants consideration in light of the critiques leveled at the Clinton administration's foreign policy initiatives. Such an approach, Krasner believes, "is distinct from pure *ad hocery*. It aspires to something beyond specific short- or medium-term material interests."

The Clinton administration was repeatedly accused of adopting an *ad hoc* approach to foreign policy, a claim this book has sought to refute, but does this necessarily mean that it was inadvertently adopting Krasner's model? Clinton's initiatives were certainly more far reaching in their ambitions than mere short- or medium-term goals, indeed, this may have served to undermine their viability due to the need to produce results in a finite political timeframe. Krasner concludes that "coherence is more likely to be achieved by aiming at something more modest, a principle around which foreign policy might be oriented."[113] This perhaps is the clearest point of departure from the aspirations of the Clinton administration; while the Clinton approach was based on three key principles around which it oriented its foreign policy, these elements were far from modest. Indeed, it was their broad aspirations that proved more complex to deliver upon than to articulate, that contributed to doubts about their viability.

It is clear that while grand strategy documents are important for discerning aspirations and intentions, they can only ever be seen as the beginning of policy development. Nancy Soderberg suggested "basically it's an internal document that was largely ignored. A lot of work went into it but it was pretty much ignored . . . Rob Bell slaved away on these things year after year and most people never read them."[114] Accordingly, "the Clinton administration's presentation of its strategy was been more consistent than its actions."[115] Changes in policy during the course of an administration are far from unusual and are indeed quite normal, since the alternative is stagnation. A consideration of the Reagan White House, for an example, reveals an administration that went from decrying the Soviet Union as an evil empire in 1981, to the signing of nuclear reduction treaties in 1987. It should be no surprise, therefore, to view changes in foreign policy during the Clinton administration—as its natural inclination for multilateralism morphed into a grudging recognition that American unilateralism was required in the face of perceived UN timidity—as being quite normal. Considering the rapidly changing environment Clinton's team found itself addressing, evolution was expected. Indeed, to adhere rigidly to a policy in an environment where change was the only constant, would itself have been a mistake.

Clinton's Grand Strategy attempted to walk a fine line between defending the administration's inclination toward multilateralism, which it referred to as "an important component of our strategy" and the fact that world events predicated the need to espouse a more robust unilateral approach to foreign policy.[116] The documents were adamant that America's "security preparedness depends on durable relationships with allies and other friendly nations. Accordingly, a central thrust of our strategy of engagement is to sustain and adapt the security relationships we have with key nations around the world."[117] This continued interaction with loyal allies proved essential to the United States during the 1990s and beyond, as the nation sought to define itself in an age free of communism, but not yet defined by attacks on the American homeland.

The continued relevance of Clinton's Grand Strategy

The Clinton administration left the White House on January 20, 2001. Since then, tumultuous events have occurred that have raised questions about the continued relevance of its time in office. However, the issues that have defined the Bush and Obama presidencies: terrorism, health care reform, economic boom and bust, globalization, and financial reform can be traced back to Clinton's time in office. As such, Clinton's grand strategy looms over his successors, creating a continuity of both personality and policy. Since January 1993, the same issues have dominated; the same regions have tested; and a surprisingly small number of individuals have led US Grand Strategy. Time and again, the same names, faces, and places have appeared to lead, challenge, taunt, and defend US interests around the world, in a pattern that reveals the continued relevance of Clinton's Grand Strategy.

Due to the relative calm of President George W. Bush's first 8 months in office, the events of September 2001 are often viewed as the start of a new era, signifying the end of the post-Cold War period and the start of the War on Terror. However, as this book has revealed, international terrorism was a major challenge to the Clinton administration during its 8 years in power. Within weeks of taking office, Clinton was faced with the first effort to destroy the World Trade Center in Manhattan. This was followed by the 1995 bombing of the Alfred P. Murrah Federal Building in Oklahoma City, the attack on the 1996 Olympic Games in Atlanta and attempts to bring down airlines and attack the infrastructure around Manhattan on Millennium Eve. Suggestions that the United States was not engaged in an ongoing struggle with the forces of political violence during the 1990s fail to appreciate the rising tide of anti-American sentiment that the Clinton administration sought to quell during its time in office.

Throughout the Clinton presidency, Osama bin Laden remained a target for US intelligence services as he established his position alongside Ayman al Zawarhi, striking at targets in Egypt, Tanzania, and Albania in a struggle against the central tenants of Western civilization. The Clinton administration's attempt to destroy terrorist training camps in Afghanistan was overshadowed by the president's impeachment hearings, causing political opponents to suggest that the administration was "wagging the dog," a charge latter exacerbated by claims that Bill Clinton bore personal responsibility for the 2001 attacks.[118] On closer inspection, however, a far more complex tale emerges, of an administration focused on removing this threat to the American homeland and of stubborn resistance from the military and Capitol Hill—in stark contrast to the robust authority granted to President George W. Bush. As President Clinton lamented in a private meeting with President-Elect Bush as they prepared for the transfer of power, "One of the great regrets of my presidency is that I didn't get [bin Laden] for you, because I tried to."[119]

If the attacks of September 2001 narrowed the world's attention on Osama bin Laden and al Qaeda, there remained those in the Bush administration who never wavered from their focus on Saddam Hussein. As the twin towers burnt, efforts were made to link the Iraqi leader to the attacks, with or without evidence of such a conspiracy.[120] Clinton's Grand Strategy adopted a variety of policy approaches intended to reduce Saddam's capacity to threaten the United States and its neighbors. The fundamental approach was to keep Saddam "in his box" and isolated from world affairs. This took the form of policies designed to reduce international access to Iraq in the form of Dual Containment; inclusion of Iraq on a list of pariah nations, referred to as Backlash States that proceeded the Axis of Evil by almost a decade; the continuation of air patrols and efforts to ensure compliance with UN resolutions from the end of the 1991 Gulf War; and finally the adoption of regime change as official US foreign policy in 1998, 3 years prior to the presidency of George W. Bush. Vitally, however, the Clinton White House refused to prioritize the threat posed by Saddam and viewed him as an irritant as opposed to a serious threat to regional or global harmony.

The Iraqi leader's stubborn refusal to placate Western concerns with regard to potential violations of UN resolutions ensured that Iraq was never far from the minds of Clinton's national security team. The Iraqi leader was not, however, a priority for the president who had no intention of entering into a personal battle of wits that had occurred between Saddam and his predecessor and which defined his successor's time in office. The Clinton administration believed that it had an appropriate approach to Saddam that kept him isolated and unable to initiate military action, but without the need to engage in a costly land war, while remaining hopeful of his eventual overthrow by Iraqi nationals. This ambition was one that Clinton's successor was not prepared to delay, with devastating consequences for America's global standing and economic well-being that continued to impact the administration of Barack Obama.

Clinton's Grand Strategy initiatives in African set a precedent for future missions in Liberia, Sudan, Uganda, Libya, Egypt, and Tunisia. While the action of a small group of Somali's meant they had "effectively written themselves off the map," the importance of the continent could not be ignored during Obama's time in office.[121] Events in Somalia continued to haunt US decision making, however, ensuring a hesitancy to deploy ground forces even at the height of the Arab Spring, resulting in the Obama policy of "leading from behind."[122] The lack of direct US action in the uprisings and the hesitation to place ground troops on the African continent can be attributed, in part, to events that occurred under the auspices of Clinton's Grand Strategy and the administration's response to them is vital for appreciating subsequent US reluctance to engage in the region.[123]

Africa may not have become a continent that the United States was eager to deploy troops to, but it became a strategic staging post for a new generation of un-manned aerial aircraft that had first come to prominence during the Clinton years.[124] Drones had been a developing technology during the Clinton administration, used mainly as a surveillance platform. They had, however, become integral to the search for bin Laden and, as described by Richard Clarke, were hunting for the elusive terrorist in the hope of relaying his whereabouts to a nearby Los Angeles class attack submarine, waiting to guide a missile to his location.[125] While no sightings proved verifiable, the development of drone technology and their deployment against international terrorists were a key component in Clinton's Grand Strategy that continues to influence policy.

The Clinton administration reformulated concepts of foreign affairs to incorporate prosperity promotion as a central component of grand strategy and strove to reduce the budget deficit so that by the time it left office, debate centered on what to do with the vast government surplus that had been amassed. During the 1990s, Bill Clinton "restored the Democrat's reputation for economic competence that had been established by Franklin D. Roosevelt, consolidated by Harry Truman, John F. Kennedy and Lyndon B. Johnson and surrendered by Jimmy Carter."[126] As a result, both Democrats and Republicans sought to lay claim to Clinton's economic record in a bid to out-promise one another during the 2012 election. In a remarkable turn of events, even Bill Clinton's former critics conceded that the 1990s were the most affluent decade in American history with unemployment and inflation under control, government spending reduced, new approaches to welfare introduced (with the help of Republicans in Congress), and a stock market that rose to record highs. Breaking down the wall between foreign and domestic economic policy as an aspect of grand strategy ensured that President Clinton's economic policies not only reversed the financial woes of the United States, but also did much to alter the perception of the Democratic Party standing for higher taxes and increased government expenditure, creating a formidable precedent for his successors to meet.

However, the economic repercussions of the Clinton years continue to be of direct relevance for altogether less favorable reasons, as the deregulation policies of that era, which enabled such rampant growth, gave way to the eventual collapse of the very institutions that thrived in the 1990s. Indeed, it appears possible to track the end of the boom almost precisely to the end of the Clinton presidency, as the dot.com bubble burst in his final months in office. The market stalled during the drawn out election of 2000 and collapsed after the attacks of 9/11. The aftermath saw slow and hesitant growth throughout the decade, but the confidence of the 1990s was clearly lacking and was removed entirely in the aftermath of the collapse of Lehman Brothers in 2008. It is possible, therefore, to see the origins of the age of austerity in the boom days of the Clinton years, a time that witnessed a transition from recession to boom and eventual bust, with damning implications.

Just as the economic implications of Clinton's Grand Strategy continue to resonate, so too do members of his administration. Hillary Clinton is merely the most prominent of a series of political figures from the era that ensure the continued relevance of Clinton's Grand Strategy.[127] Others include Leon Panetta, Dennis Ross, Rahm Emanuel, George Mitchell, Eric Holder, Susan Rice, and John Podesta. This "revolving door" approach to political appointments is based on a desire to retain institutional memory and draw on those with executive department experience. With the same small group of individuals rotating in and out of power, however, campaigns based on a platform of "change" appear at odds with the reality of inherent continuity at an institutional and personnel level.[128]

The strategies and approaches to grand strategy that evolved throughout the Clinton administration had a direct bearing on its interaction with the world, on the way in which the United States was perceived and on the legacy that was bequeathed to future occupants of the White House. Issues of globalization, international trade, the rise of China, and the emergence of the European Union were all addressed as part of an evolving grand strategy. All had consequences for Clinton and his successors as the United States sought to recalibrate America's global focus in the aftermath of the Cold War.

Conclusion: A strategy grand enough for the times

As the first administration to come to power following the end of the Cold War, the Clinton team was required to devise a new approach with which to address the world and the rapidly changing geopolitical environment. Its efforts to devise a grand strategy where endangered by bureaucratic sensibilities, personal rivalries, and the rapidly changing environment through which it sought to govern. Despite such difficulties, the Clinton administration successfully produced a series of strategy documents in line with the 1986 Goldwater-Nichols Act designed to demonstrate the direction and intent behind US Grand Strategy.

However, with no external threat to motivate public opinion, the Clinton years quickly become viewed as the age between eras: between the end of the Cold War and before the War on Terror. Indeed, it is looking increasingly likely that Bill Clinton was elected at the only time in his life when it was theoretically possible. Before 1992, the ongoing Cold War dictated that foreign policy experience was essential for the presidency and, that once in office, foreign policy would dominate the administration. Clearly, Clinton would have failed on both criteria, with no foreign policy experience gained during his time as governor and with no particular predilection in that direction to guide him even if he had been elected. A decade later, the events of September 2001 dictated that foreign policy initiatives and the War on Terror dominated administrations to the detriment of domestic affairs. Perhaps, therefore, "Bill Clinton was lucky to serve as president in such quiet times, times he palpably made better through his economic and domestic policy actions."[129]

As he prepared to leave office, President Clinton raised Thomas Jefferson's warning of entangling alliances. He insisted, however, that despite the eminent wisdom of his predecessor, "America cannot and must not disentangle itself from the world. If we want the world to embody our shared values, then we must assume a shared responsibility." Rather than withdrawing from the world, Clinton insisted, the United States "must embrace boldly and resolutely that duty to lead—to stand with our allies in word and deed and to put a human face on the global economy, so that expanded trade benefits all peoples in all nations, lifting lives and hopes all across the world."[130]

Foreign policy may not have driven Bill Clinton's presidential odyssey, but despite this, his administration achieved notable successes, including the passage of NAFTA, expansion of NATA, the normalization of relations with China, conclusion of the GATT negotiations that led to the formation of the WTO, protection of the Mexican peso, the Dayton Peace Accords, and the securing of nuclear materials in the former Soviet Union. The administration made strides toward peace in the Middle East and Northern Ireland and stood by Russia as it struggled to embrace democracy. The administration bequeathed its successor a foreign policy legacy that included "a commitment to a sustained role for the United States in global affairs after the Cold War, an enhanced position for economic issues on the foreign-policy agenda and a redefinition of the global threat environment that the United States faces."[131] It failed, however, to secure backing for the Comprehensive Test Ban Treaty, chose not to embrace NMD, and was unable to expand NAFTA to include Chile. It also failed in its efforts to develop agreement over the circumstances in which America should engage in regional conflicts and "the question of how values and interests should shape American foreign policy remained unresolved."[132]

During its time in office, the Clinton administration underwent a severe learning curve. The president entered office critiquing President Bush for being "the foreign policy president," yet "travelled abroad more than any other US president, making almost as many overseas trips as Ronald Regan and George Bush combined."[133] Just as the president grew into his role, so too did his administration, a point conceded by Anthony Lake: "In Somalia we tried to do too much. In Rwanda we did too little. In Haiti and Bosnia, after false starts, we eventually got it right."[134] Yet the Clinton administration kept America out of foreign wars, arranged the expansion of NATO, ended the genocide in the Balkans, and made valiant efforts to progress the peace process in the Middle East. As David Gergen observed, "one could say of his foreign policy what Twain said of Wagner: 'His music is better than it sounds.'"[135]

Warren Christopher noted that foreign policy "is always a work in progress" and this was never more accurate than under President Clinton, who inherited a dangerous international situation with massive nuclear proliferation in the former Soviet republics, tensions in the Middle East, and massive deficits at home.[136] "Did they succeed in making the world anew? Probably not. Did they succeed in something that would rival Acheson's *Present at the Creation*? No. Probably not."[137] However, while Engagement and Enlargement was an imperfect policy, in an age when the old rules did not apply and no New World Order had emerged, Clinton's Grand Strategy provided a flexible and pragmatic response to an evolving world order.

Notes

1 Larry Berman and Bruce W. Jentleson, "Bush and the Post-Cold-War World: New Challenges for American Leadership," in Campbell and Rockman (eds), *The Bush Presidency: First Appraisals*, pp. 93–94.

2 Warren Christopher, "Statement at Senate Confirmation Hearing," *US Department of State Dispatch* 4, Issue 4 (January 25, 1993), p. 45.

3 Mead, *Special Providence: American Foreign Policy and How it Changed the World*, p. 285.

4 For a summary of the arguments for and against Democratic Promotion see Christopher Layne and Sean M. Lynn-Jones (eds), *Should America Promote Democracy?* (Boston, MA: MIT Press, 1998).

5 John Brummett, *High Wire*, p. 209.

6 *PPPWJC*, vol. 1 (1997), Inaugural Address, January 20, 1997, p. 44.

7 Anthony Lake, "From Containment to Enlargement," p. 658.

8 Author's interview with Anthony Lake.

9 Hamilton, *A Creative Tension*, pp. 44–45.

10 Tara Sonenshine to Bob Boorstin; re: Some Random Thoughts on the UNGA Speech, n.d., Clinton Presidential Records, National Security Council, Robert Boorstin (Speechwriting), OA/Box Number: 422, UNGA '94—NSC Memos, William J. Clinton Presidential Library.

11 Bob Boorstin to Anthony Lake; re: Preliminary UNGA Thoughts, Clinton Presidential Records, National Security Council, Robert Boorstin (Speechwriting), OA/Box Number: 422, UNGA '94—Outline, William J. Clinton Presidential Library.

12 Heilbrunn, "Lake Inferior," pp. 29–35.

13 Author's interview with Morton Halperin.

14 Brinkley, "Democratic Enlargement," p. 121.

15 Author's interview with Anthony Lake.

16 Holbrooke, *To End A War*, p. 369.

17 Author's interview with Charles A. Kupchan.

18 Author's interview with Leon Fuerth.

19 Author's interview with Charles A. Kupchan.

20 Author's interview with Anthony Lake.

21 *NSSR95*, p. ii.

22 Quoted in Walker, "Home Alone: What Matters Now is Trade Not the Cold Not Tanks But Toyotas," p. 12.

23 James M. McCormick, *American Foreign Policy and Process*, Fourth Edition (Belmont, CA: Thomson Wadsworth, 2005), p. 189.

24 *NSSR95*, p. ii.

25 Lael Brainard (Special Assistant to the President for International Economic Policy, 1995–97) quoted in *The National Security Council Project Oral History Roundtables: The Clinton Administration National Security Council*, moderated by Ivo H. Daalder and I. M. Destler Center for International and Security Studies, University of Maryland, September 27, 2000.

26 Manning, "Orwellian Spin Masking Clinton's Failures."

27 Lake, "Confronting Backlash States," p. 55.

28 Richard Haass wrote in 1997 that the neo-Wilsonian vision represented by a strategy of enlargement "has had a negligible impact on day-to-day affairs. Enlarging the community of market democracies might look good on paper, but it has provided few policy-relevant guidelines for pressing foreign policy problems such as those presented by Bosnia, Iraq, North Korea, Rwanda, or Somalia." See Richard N. Haass, "Fatal Distraction: Bill Clinton's Foreign Policy," *Foreign Policy* 108 (Autumn 1997), pp. 112–123.

29 Goldman and Berman, "Engaging the World," p. 236.

30 Ibid., p. 245.

31 Klein, *The Natural*, p. 76.

32 Albright, *Madam Secretary*, p. 182.

33 Author's interview with Leon Fuerth.

34 *NSSR2000*, p. 1.

35 *NSSR2000*, p. 67.

36 Author's interview with Leon Fuerth.

37 Author's interview with Anthony Lake.

38 Author's interview with Leon Fuerth.

39 Author's interview with J. F. O. McAllister.

40 Tara Sonenshine and Tom Ross to Mark Gearan; re: Six-Month Public Affairs Strategy, June 10, 1994, Clinton Presidential Records, National Security

Council, Robert Boors tin (Speechwriting), OA/Box Number: 420, NSC—Public Affairs Strategy, William J. Clinton Presidential Library.

41 Author's interview with Charles A. Kupchan.

42 Author's interview with J. F. O. McAllister.

43 Chollet and Goldgeiger, *America Between The Wars*, p. 29.

44 Elizabeth Drew, *Showdown: The Struggle Between the Gingrich Congress and the Clinton White House* (New York: Simon & Schuster, 1996), p. 243.

45 Author's interview with Charles A. Kupchan.

46 Brinkley, "Democratic Enlargement," p. 127.

47 Resignation Letter, Anthony Lake Papers, Manuscript Division, Library of Congress, Washington, DC, Box 48, Folder 2.

48 Author's interview with Charles A. Kupchan.

49 Albright, *Madam Secretary*, p. 166.

50 Daalder and Destler, *In the Shadow of the Oval Office*, p. 208.

51 DeParle, "The Man Inside Bill Clinton's Foreign Policy," p. 33.

52 Lake, *Six Nightmares*, p. 131, 262.

53 Author's interview with J. F. O. McAllister.

54 Clinton, *My Life*, p. 737.

55 *PPPWJC*, vol. 1 (1997), Remarks on Withdrawal of the Nomination of Anthony Lake To Be Director of Central Intelligence and an Exchange With Reporters, March 18, 1997, p. 319.

56 Goodman, "Ending the CIA's Cold War Legacy," p. 143.

57 *PPPWJC*, vol. 1 (1997), Remarks Announcing the Nomination of George J. Tenet To Be Director of Central Intelligence and an Exchange With Reporters, March 19, 1997, p. 324.

58 Author's interview with J. F. O. McAllister.

59 Sebastian Mallaby, "The Man Without a Bumper Sticker," *Washington Post* (January 15, 2001), p. A21.

60 Author's interview with J. F. O. McAllister.

61 Joe Klein, *The Natural*, p. 75.

62 Author's interview with J. F. O. McAllister.

63 Niall Ferguson, *Colossus: The Rise and Fall of the American Empire* (London: Penguin Books, 2004), p. 140.

64 Emily O. Goldman and Larry Berman, "Engaging the World: First Impressions of the Clinton Foreign Policy Legacy," in Colin Campbell and Bert A. Rockman (eds), *The Clinton Legacy* (New York: Chatham House, 2000), p. 226.

65 Brummett, *High Wire*, p. 209.

66 Brinkley, "Democratic Enlargement," p. 119.

67 *NSSR95*, p. 33.

68 Posen and Ross, "Competing Visions for US Grand Strategy," p. 7.

69 John E. Rielly (ed.), *American Public Opinion and US Foreign Policy 1995* (Chicago: The Chicago Council on Foreign Relations, 1995), p. 16.

70 Quoted in Jane Perlez, "For 8 Years, A Strained Relationship With the Military," *New York Times* (December 28, 2000), p. A13.

71 Hyland, *Clinton's World*, p. 204.

72 Haass, "The Squandered Presidency," p. 136.

73 Kissinger, *Does American Need A Foreign Policy?* pp. 29–30.

74 Mandelbaum, "Foreign Policy As Social Work," p. 16.

75 Ibid., p. 30.

76 Brummett, *Highwire*, p. 209.

77 Friedman, "A Broken Truce," p. A1.

78 Quoted in Brinkley, "Democratic Enlargement," pp. 124–125.

79 Quoted in "Foreign Policy Dreaming," *Washington Times* (January 12, 1998).

80 Haass, "The Squandered Presidency," pp. 139, 136.

81 Holbrooke, "America, A European Power," p. 51.

82 Gaddis, "Foreign Policy by Autopilot."

83 George F. Kennan, "The Failure in Our Success," *New York Times* (May 17, 1994), p. A17.

84 John Lewis Gaddis, *Surprise, Security and the American Experience* (Cambridge, MA: Harvard University Press, 2004), pp. 77–78.

85 Jonathan Clarke, "Rhetoric Before Reality; Loose Lips Sink Ships," *Foreign Affairs* 74, no. 5 (September–October 1995), p. 4.

86 Robert Kagan, "The Clinton Legacy Aboard: His Sins of Omission in Foreign and Defense Policy," *Weekly Standard* (January 15, 2001).

87 Stephen Walt, "Two Cheers for Clinton's Foreign Policy," *Foreign Affairs* 79, no. 2 (March–April 2000), p. 79.

88 Author's interview with Morton Halperin.

89 Seitz, *Over Here*, p. 332.

90 Kupchan, *The End of the American Era*, p. 233.

91 Carter Wilkie to Don Baer; re: Major Speeches in September, August 17, 1994, Clinton Presidential Records, National Security Council, Robert Boorstin (Speechwriting), OA/Box Number: 420, NSC—Public Affairs Strategy, William J. Clinton Presidential Library.

92 Haass, "The Squandered Presidency," p. 140.

93 Ambrose and Brinkley, *Rise to Globalism*, p. 403.

94 Gore, *Earth in the Balance*, p. 239.

95 Kissinger, *Diplomacy*, p. 812.

96 Wolfowitz, "Clinton's First Year," p. 32.

97 Gaddis, "Where Do We Go From Here?"

98 Quoted in John F. Harris, "Despite 'Lessons,' Clinton Still Seen Lacking Strategy," *Washington Post* (March 27, 1999), p. A15.

99   Condoleezza Rice, "Promoting the National Interest," *Foreign Affairs* 79, no. 1 (January–February 2000), pp. 45–62.

100   Blumenthal, *The Clinton Wars*, p. 155.

101   *PPPWJC*, vol. 1 (1993), Inaugural Address, January 20, 1993, p. 2.

102   Henriksen, *Clinton's Foreign Policy in Somalia, Bosnia, Haiti and North Korea*, p. 39.

103   Author's interview with Anthony Lake.

104   Author's interview with Morton Halperin.

105   Address by Anthony Lake, National Security Advisor—The Council on Foreign Relations.

106   Haass, "Fatal Distraction," p. 113.

107   Henriksen, *Clinton's Foreign Policy in Somalia, Bosnia, Haiti and North Korea*, p. 39.

108   Author's interview with Leon Fuerth.

109   Author's interview with Morton Halperin.

110   Author's interview with Anthony Lake.

111   Author's interview with J. F. O. McAllister.

112   Haass, "The Squandered Presidency," p. 139.

113   Krasner, "An Orienting Principle for Foreign Policy," pp. 3–5.

114   Author's interview with Nancy Soderberg.

115   Posen and Ross, "Competing Visions for US Grand Strategy," p. 42.

116   *NSSR94*, p. 13.

117   *NSSR94*, p. 6.

118   John Harris, "Conservatives Sound Refrain: It's Clinton's Fault," *Washington Post* (October 7, 2001), p. A15.

119   Chollet and Goldgeiger, p. 306; Clinton, *My Life*, p. 935.

120   Clarke, *Against All Enemies*, pp. 30–33.

121   Bowden, *Black Hawk Down*, p. 485.

122   Robert Singh, *Barack Obama's Post-American Foreign Policy: The Limits of Engagement* (London: Bloomsbury, 2012), p. 41.

123   James D. Boys, "Exploiting Inherited Wars of Choice: Obama's Use of Nixonian Methods to Secure the Presidency," *American Politics Research* 42, no. 5 (September 2014), pp. 815–840.

124   See Daniel Klaidman, *Kill or Capture: The War on Terror and the Soul of the Obama Presidency* (New York: Houghton Mifflin Harcourt, 2012) and David E. Sanger, *Confront and Conceal: Obama's Secret Wars and Surprising Use of American Power* (New York: Crown, 2012).

125   Clarke, *Against All Enemies*, p. 199.

126   Iwan Morgan, "A New Democrat's New Economics," in Mark White (ed.), *The Presidency of Bill Clinton: The Legacy of a New Domestic and Foreign Policy* (London and New York: I.B. Taurus, 2012), p. 65.

127 Jonathan Allen and Amie Parnes, *HRC: State Secrets and the Rebirth of Hillary Clinton* (New York: Crown, 2014).

128 For more on Obama's appointees see James Mann, *The Obamians: The Struggle Inside the White House to Redefine American Power* (New York: Viking 2012).

129 Klein, *The Natural*, p. 21.

130 *PPPWJC*, vol. 3 (2000), Farewell Address to the Nation, January 18, 2001, p. 2953.

131 James J. McCormick, "Clinton and Foreign Policy: Some Legacies for a New Century," in Steven E. Schier (ed.), *The Post-Modern Presidency: Bill Clinton's Legacy in US Politics* (Pittsburgh, PA: University of Pittsburgh Press, 2000), p. 82.

132 McCormick, "Clinton and Foreign Policy," p. 82.

133 Kupchan, *The End of the American Era*, p. 17.

134 Albright, *Madam Secretary*, p. 141.

135 Gergen, *Eyewitness to Power*, p. 340.

136 Berman and Goldman, "Clinton's Foreign Policy at Midterm," p. 291.

137 Author's interview with Charles A. Kupchan.

BIBLIOGRAPHY

Documents/speeches

A National Security Strategy of Engagement and Enlargement. Washington, DC: US Government Printing Office, July 1994.

A National Security Strategy of Engagement and Enlargement. Washington, DC: US Government Printing Office, February 1995.

A National Security Strategy of Engagement and Enlargement. Washington, DC: US Government Printing Office, February 1996.

A National Security Strategy For A New Century. Washington, DC: US Government Printing Office, May 1997.

A National Security Strategy For A New Century. Washington, DC: US Government Printing Office, October 1998.

A National Security Strategy For A New Century. Washington, DC: US Government Printing Office, December 1999.

A National Security Strategy For A Global Age. Washington, DC: US Government Printing Office, December 2000.

A wide range of Governor Clinton's campaign speeches and statements are available at: ftp://ftp.ibiblio.org/pub/academic/political-science/speeches/clinton.dir/

A wide range of presidential materials are available at the Clinton Presidential Library website: http://www.clintonlibrary.gov/

Anthony Lake's papers, covering 1916-2003 may be accessed via the Manuscript Division of the Library of Congress.

Clinton era National Security Strategy Review documents were published by the US GPO and are available online at http://nssarchive.us/

Clinton era PDD and PRD documents are being declassified on a rolling basis. They can be accessed in hard copy at the Clinton Presidential Library at Stack V, Row 44, Section 1, Shelf 2, or online at http://www.clintonlibrary.gov/pdd.html

Materials released by the Defense Department during the Clinton years are available at the DoD archive: http://www.defense.gov/speeches/secdefarchive.aspx

National Security Strategy of the United States. Washington, DC: US Government Printing Office, August 1991.

Previously declassified materials from the Clinton administration are being released on a rolling basis and can be accessed via the Clinton Library website: http://www.clintonlibrary.gov/declassified.html; http://www.clintonlibrary.gov/formerlywithhelddocuments.html

State Department materials from the Clinton era may be accessed at the
Electronic Resource Collection (ERC) run by the State Department and the
University of Illinois at Chicago (UIC): http://dosfan.lib.uic.edu/ERC/index.
html

The Presidential Papers of US administrations can be accessed via the University
of Michigan Digital Library: http://quod.lib.umich.edu/p/ppotpus/

The Public Presidential Papers of George H. W. Bush and Bill Clinton are
available as part of the Presidential Papers series, maintained by the US
Government Printing Service: http://www.gpo.gov/fdsys/browse/collection.
action?collectionCode=PPP

The State Department Dispatch for the Clinton years (1993–1999) can also be
accessed via the ERC site: http://dosfan.lib.uic.edu/ERC/briefing/dispatch/

Books/reports

Acheson, Dean. *Present at the Creation: My Years at the State Department.* New
York: W.W. Norton, 1969.

Albright, Madeleine. *Madam Secretary: A Memoir.* London: Macmillan,
2003.

Allen, Jonathan and Amie Parnes. *HRC: State Secrets and the Rebirth of Hillary
Clinton.* New York: Crown, 2014.

Ambrose, Stephen E. *Eisenhower Volume Two: The President.* New York:
Simon & Schuster, 1984.

Ambrose, Stephen E. and Douglas Brinkley. *Rise to Globalism*, Eighth Revised
Edition. New York: Penguin, 1997.

Andrew, Christopher. *For the President's Eyes Only.* London: HarperCollins,
1995.

Armacost, Michael H. *Friends or Rivals? The Insider's Account of US–Japanese
Relations.* New York: Columbia University Press, 1996.

Armytage, W. H. G. *Four Hundred Years of English Education.* Cambridge:
Cambridge University Press, 1964.

Art, Robert. *A Grand Strategy for America.* Ithaca, NY: Cornell University Press,
2003.

Bacevich, Andrew. *American Empire: The Realities and Consequences of US
Diplomacy.* Cambridge, MA: Harvard University Press, 2002.

Baker, James A. III. *The Politics of Diplomacy: Revolution, War and Peace,
1989–1992.* New York: G.P. Putnam's Sons, 1995.

Beard, Charles A. *Contemporary American History.* New York: Macmillan, 1914.

Bell, Sidney. *Righteous Conquest: Woodrow Wilson and the Evolution of the
New Diplomacy.* Port Washington, NY: Kennikast Press, 1972.

Berman, William C. *From the Centre to the Edge: The Politics and Policies of
the Clinton Presidency.* Lanham, MD: Rowman & Littlefield Publishers, Inc.,
2001.

Beschloss, Michael and Strobe Talbott. *At the Highest Levels: The Inside Story of
the End of the Cold War.* Boston, MA: Little, Brown, 1993.

Best, Richard A., Jr and Herbert Andrew Boerstling. "Proposals for Intelligence
Reorganization, 1949–1996." A Report Prepared for the Permanent Select

Committee on Intelligence, House of Representatives, Washington, DC: Congressional Research Service, February 28, 1996.

Betts, Richard K. *US National Security Strategy: Lenses and Landmarks.* Princeton Project on National Security, Princeton, NJ: Woodrow Wilson School of Public and International Affairs, 2004.

Blumenthal, Sidney. *Pledging Allegiance: The Last Campaign of the Cold War.* New York: HarperCollins, 1991.

— *The Clinton Wars: An Insider's Account of the White House Years.* London: Penguin Books, 2003.

Bowden, Mark. *Black Hawk Down.* London: Bantam Press, 1999.

Brands, Hal. *What Good is Grand Strategy? Power and Purpose in American Statecraft from Harry S. Truman to George W. Bush.* Ithaca, NY: Cornell University Press, 2014.

Brummett, John. *Highwire: From The Backwoods to the Beltway—The Education of Bill Clinton.* New York: Hyperion, 1994.

Brzezinski, Zbigniew. *Out of Control: Global Turmoil on the Eve of the Twenty-First Century.* New York: Collier, 1993.

— *The Choice: Global Domination or Global Leadership.* New York: Basic Books, 2004.

Burke, Jason. *Al-Qaeda.* London: Penguin Books, 2007.

Bush, George. *All the Best, George Bush: My Life in Letters and Other Writings.* New York: Scribner, 1999.

Bush, George and Brent Scowcroft. *A World Transformed.* New York: Alfred A. Knopf, 1998.

Campbell, Colin and Bert A. Rockman (eds) *The Bush Presidency: First Appraisals.* Chatham, NJ: Chatham House, 1991.

— (eds) *The Clinton Presidency: First Appraisals.* Chatham, NJ: Chatham House, 1995.

— (eds) *The Clinton Legacy.* New York: Chatham House, 2000.

Campbell, Kurt M. and James B. Steinberg. *Difficult Transitions: Foreign Policy Troubles at the Outset of Presidential Power.* Washington, DC: Brookings Institution Press, 2008.

Carothers, Thomas. *In the Name of Democracy: U.S. Policy Toward Latin America in the Reagan Years.* Berkeley, CA: University of California Press, 1991.

— *Aiding Democracy Abroad: The Learning Curve.* Washington, DC: Carnegie Endowment for International Peace, 1999.

— *The Clinton Record on Democracy Promotion.* Washington, DC: Carnegie Endowment for International Peace, 2000.

Carter, Ashton B., William J. Perry, and John D. Steinbruner. *A New Concept of Cooperative Security.* Washington, DC: Brookings Institution, 1992.

Cerami, Joseph R. and James F. Holcomb, Jr (eds) *US Army War College Guide to Strategy.* Carlisle Barracks, PA: Strategic Studies Institute, US Army War College, 2001.

Chollet, Derek and James Goldgeiger. *America Between The Wars: From 11/9 to 9/11 The Misunderstood Years Between the Fall of the Berlin Wall and the Start of the War on Terror.* New York: Public Affairs Books, 2008.

Christopher, Warren. *In The Stream of History: Shaping Foreign Policy for a New Era.* Stanford, CA: Stanford University Press, 1998.

— *Chances of a Lifetime.* New York: Scribner Books, 2001.

Clarke, Richard A. *Against All Enemies: Inside America's War on Terror.* London: Simon & Schuster, 2004.

Clausewitz, Carl Von. *On War*, Edited and translated by Michael Howard and Peter Paret. Princeton, NJ: Princeton University Press, 1989.

Clinton, Hillary Rodham. *Living History.* New York: Simon & Schuster, 2003.

Clinton, William J. *Between Hope and History: Meeting America's Challenges for the 21st Century.* New York: Random House, 1996.

— *My Life.* London: Hutchinson, 2004.

Clinton, William J. and Al Gore. *Putting People First: How We Can All Change America.* New York: Random House, Times Books, 1992.

Cohen, Stephen D., Robert A. Blecker, and Peter D. Whitney. *Fundamentals of US Foreign Trade Policy: Economics, Politics, Laws, and Issues*, Second Revised Edition. Boulder, CO: Westview Press, 2002.

Coll, Steve. *Ghost Wars.* New York: Penguin, 2004.

Collins, John M. *Grand Strategy: Principles and Practices.* Annapolis, MD: Naval Institute Press, 1973.

Cox, Michael G., John Ikenberry, and Takashi Inoguchi (eds) *American Democracy Promotion: Impulses, Strategies, and Impacts.* Oxford: Oxford University Press, 2000.

Cox, Michael, Timothy J. Lynch, and Nicolas Bouchet (eds) *US Foreign Policy and Democracy Promotion.* Abingdon, Oxon: Routledge, 2013.

Crabb, Cecil V., Leila S. Sarieddine, and Glenn J. Antizzo, *Charting a New Diplomatic Course: Alternative Approaches to America's Post-Cold War Foreign Policy.* Baton Rouge, LA: Louisiana State University Press, 2001.

Current, Richard N., Alexander DeConde, and Harris L. Dante. *United States History.* New York: Scott, Foresman, 1967.

Daalder, Ivo H. *Getting to Dayton: The Making of America's Bosnia Policy.* Washington, DC: Brookings Institution Press, 1999.

Daalder, Ivo H. and I. M. Destler. *In the Shadow of the Oval Office: Profiles of the National Security Advisers and the Presidents they Served—From JFK to George W. Bush.* New York: Simon & Schuster, 2009.

Destler, I. M. *The National Economic Council: A Work in Progress.* Washington, DC: Institute for International Economics, 1996.

de Tocqueville, Alexis. *Democracy in America*, Reprint Edition, Volume II. New York: Alfred A. Knopf, 1994.

Diamond, Larry. *Promoting Democracy in the 1990s: Actors and Instruments, Issues and Imperatives.* Washington, DC: Carnegie Commission on Preventing Deadly Conflict, 1995.

Dickie, John. *'Special' No More: Anglo-American Relations, Rhetoric And Reality.* London: Weidenfeld & Nicolson, 1994.

Dobbs, Michael. *Madeleine Albright: A Twentieth-Century Odyssey.* New York: Henry Holt & Company, 1999.

Dolan, Chris J., John Frendreis, and Raymond Tatalovich. *The Presidency and Economic Policy.* Lanham, MD: Rowman & Littlefield Publishers, 2008.

Drew, Elizabeth. *On the Edge: The Clinton Presidency.* New York: Simon & Schuster, 1994.

— *Showdown: The Struggle Between the Gingrich Congress and the Clinton White House.* New York: Simon & Schuster, 1996.

Dueck, Colin. *Reluctant Crusader: Power, Culture and Change in American Grand Strategy*. Princeton, NJ: Princeton University Press, 2008.

Duffy, Michael and Dan Goodgame. *Marching in Place: The Status Quo Presidency of George Bush*. New York: Simon & Schuster, 1992.

Dumbrell, John. *Clinton's Foreign Policy: Between the Bushes, 1992–2000*. Abingdon, Oxon: Routledge, 2009.

Drezner. Daniel W. (ed.) *Avoiding Trivia: The Role of Strategic Planning in American Foreign Policy*. Washington, DC: Brookings Institution Press, 2009.

Earle, Edward Mead (ed.) *Makers of Modern Strategy: Military Thought from Hitler to Machiavelli*. Princeton, NJ: Princeton University Press, 1943.

Eckes, Alfred E., Jr. *Opening America's Market: US Foreign Trade Policy Since 1776*. Chapel Hill, NC: University of North Carolina Press, 1995.

Ellis, Joseph J. *American Sphinx: The Character of Thomas Jefferson*. New York: Vintage Books, 1996.

Esler, Gavin. *The United States of Anger: The People and the American Dream*. London: Michael Joseph Ltd., 1997.

Ferguson, Niall. *Colossus: The Rise and Fall of the American Empire*. London: Penguin Books, 2004.

Fierlbeck, Katherine. *Globalizing Democracy: Power, Legitimacy and the Interpretation of Democratic Ideas*. Manchester: Manchester University Press, 1998.

Frankel, Jeffrey and Peter Orszag (eds) *American Economic Policy in the 1990s*. Cambridge, MA: MIT Press, 2002.

Freedman, Lawrence. *The Evolution of Nuclear Strategy*. New York: St. Martin's Press, 1981.

Freeman, Douglas Southall. *Washington*. New York: Collier Books, 1992.

Freeman, Joseph and Scott Nearing. *Dollar Diplomacy: A Study in American Imperialism*. New York: B. W. Huebsch and the Viking Press, 1928.

Fuller, John Frederick Charles. *The Generalship of Ulysses S. Grant*. New York: Dodd, Mead & Co., 1929.

Gaddis, John Lewis. *Strategies of Containment: A Critical Appraisal of American National Security Policy During the Cold War*, Revised and Expanded Edition. New York: Oxford University Press, 2005.

— *Surprise, Security and the American Experience*. Cambridge, MA: Harvard University Press, 2004.

Gardner, Lloyd. *Safe for Democracy: The Anglo-American Response to Revolution, 1913–1923*. New York, Oxford University Press, 1984.

Gelb, Leslie H. *Power Rules: How Common Sense Can Rescue American Foreign Policy*. New York: HarperCollins, 2009.

Gergen, David. *Eyewitness to Power: The Essence of Leadership, Nixon to Clinton*. New York: Simon & Schuster, 2000.

Goldgeier, James M. *Not Whether But When: The US Decision to Enlarge NATO*. Washington, DC: Brookings Institution Press, 1999.

Goldman, Peter, Thomas M. DeFrank, Mark Miller, Andrew Murr, and Tom Matthews. *Quest For The Presidency 1992*. College Station, TX: A & M Press, 1994.

Gore, Al. *Earth in the Balance: Ecology and the Human Spirit*. New York: Houghton Mifflin, 1992.

Gowa, Joanne. *Building Bridges or Democracies Abroad? U.S. Foreign Policy after the Cold War.* Princeton, NJ: Princeton University Press, 2000.

Graham, K. *The Battle of Democracy.* Brighton, Sussex: Wheatsheaf, 1986.

Grant, Richard and Jan Nijman (eds) *The Global Crisis in Foreign Aid.* Syracuse, NY: Syracuse University Press, 1998.

Greene, John Robert. *The Presidency of George Bush.* Lawrence, KS: University Press of Kansas, 2000.

Haas, Lawrence J. *Sound the Trumpet: The United States and Human Rights Promotion.* Lanham, MD: Rowman & Littlefield Publishers, 2012.

Halberstam, David. *War in a Time of Peace: Bush, Clinton and the Generals.* New York: Random House, 2001.

Halperin, Morton B. *Bureaucratic Politics and Foreign Policy.* Washington, DC: The Brookings Institution, 1974.

Hamilton, Lee. *A Creative Tension: The Foreign Policy Roles of the President and Congress.* Washington, DC: Woodrow Wilson Center Press, 2002.

Hamilton, Nigel. *Bill Clinton: An American Journey: Great Expectations.* London: Century Books, 2003.

Harris, John F. *The Survivor: Bill Clinton in the White House.* New York: Random House, 2005.

Hart, Gary. *The Fourth Power: A Grand Strategy for the United States in the Twenty-First Century.* New York: Oxford University Press, 2004.

Helgerson, John L. *Getting To Know the President: CIA Briefings of Presidential Candidates, 1952–1992.* Washington, DC: The Center for the Study of Intelligence, Central Intelligence Agency, 1996.

Hendrickson, Ryan C. *The Clinton Wars: The Constitution, Congress and War Powers.* Nashville, TN: Vanderbilt University Press, 2002.

Henriksen, Thomas H. *Clinton's Foreign Policy in Somalia, Bosnia, Haiti and North Korea.* Stanford, CA: Stanford University Press, 1996.

Hermann, Charles E. (ed.) *American Defense Annual: 1994.* New York: Lexington Books 1994.

Herrnson, Paul S. and Dilys M. Hill (eds) *The Clinton Presidency: The First Term, 1992–96.* New York: St. Martin's Press, 1999.

Hill, Matthew Alan, *Democracy Promotion and Conflict-Based Reconstruction: The United States and Democratic Consolidation in Bosnia, Afghanistan and Iraq.* Abingdon, Oxon: Routledge, 2011.

Hoffman, Bruce. *Inside Terrorism*, Revised and Expanded Edition. New York: Columbia University Press, 2006.

Hoffman, Stanley. *Primacy or World Order: American Foreign Policy Since The Cold War.* New York: McGraw-Hill Book Company, 1978.

Holbrooke, Richard C. *To End a War.* New York: Modern Library, 1999.

Holden, Barry. *Understanding Liberal Democracy*, Second Edition. Hemel Hempstead: Harvester Wheatsheaf, 1993.

Hutchings, Robert (ed.) *At the End of the American Century: America's Role in the Post-Cold War World.* Washington, DC: Woodrow Wilson Center Press, 1998.

Hyland, William G. *Clinton's World: Remaking American Foreign Policy.* Westport, CT: Praeger Publishers, 1999.

Indyk, Martin. *Special Report: Clinton Administration Policy toward the Middle East*, Washington Institute for Near East Policy, May 1993.

Indyk, Martin, Kenneth G. Lieberthal, and Michael E. O'Hanlon. *Bending History: Barack Obama's Foreign Policy*. Washington, DC: Brookings Institution, 2012.

Jablonsky, David Ronald Steel, Lawrence Korb, Morton H. Halperin, and Robert Ellsworth. *US National Security: Beyond the Cold War*. Carlisle, PA: Strategic Studies Institute, U.S. Army War College, 1997.

Johnson, Loch K. *Secret Agencies: U.S. Intelligence in a Hostile World*. New Haven, CT and London: Yale University Press, 1996.

— *Seven Sins of American Foreign Policy*. New York: Pearson Longman, 2007.

Juster, Kenneth I. and Simon Lazarus. *Making Economic Policy: An Assessment of the National Economic Council*. Washington, DC: Brookings Institution Press, 1997.

Kennan, George F. *Memoirs 1925–1950*. New York: Pantheon Books, 1967.

— *American Diplomacy*, Expanded Edition. Chicago: University of Chicago Press, 1985.

Kennedy, Paul (ed.) *Grand Strategies in War and Peace*. New Haven, CT: Yale University Press, 1991.

Kissinger, Henry. *White House Years*. Boston, MA: Little, Brown, 1979.

— *Diplomacy*. New York: Touchstone Books, 1994.

— *Does American Need A Foreign Policy? Towards A Diplomacy for the Twenty-First Century*. New York: Simon & Schuster, 2001.

Klaidman, Daniel. *Kill or Capture: The War on Terror and the Soul of the Obama Presidency*. New York: Houghton Mifflin Harcourt, 2012.

Klein, Joe. *The Natural: The Misunderstood Presidency of Bill Clinton*. New York: Doubleday, 2002.

Kupchan, Charles A. *The End of the American Era*. New York: Random House, 2002.

Lake, Anthony. *Six Nightmares: Real Threats in a Dangerous World and How America Can Meet Them*. Boston, MA: Little, Brown, 2000.

Layne, Christopher and Sean M. Lynn-Jones (eds) *Should America Promote Democracy?* Boston, MA: MIT Press, 1998.

Leffler, Melvyn. *A Preponderance of Power: National Security, the Truman Administration, and the Cold War*. Stanford, CA: Stanford University Press, 1992.

Liddell Hart, Basil Henry. *Strategy*, Second Revised Edition. New York: Meridian Books, 1991.

Lind, Michael. *The American Way of Strategy: U.S. Foreign Policy and the American Way of Life*. Oxford: Oxford University Press, 2008.

Lowry, Richard. *Legacy: Paying the Price for the Clinton Years*. Washington, DC: Regnery Publishing, 2003.

Machiavelli, Niccolò. *The Prince and The Discourses*. New York: Random House, 1950.

Major, John. *The Autobiography*. London: HarperCollins, 1999.

Mann, James. *The Obamians: The Struggle Inside the White House to Redefine American Power*. New York: Viking, 2012.

Maraniss, David. *First In His Class: The Biography of Bill Clinton*. New York: Simon & Schuster, 1996.

Matalin, Mary and James Carville. *All's Fair: Love, War and Running for President*. New York: Random House, 1994.

McCormick, James M. *American Foreign Policy and Process*, Fourth Edition. Belmont, CA: Thomson Wadsworth, 2005.

McGrew, Tony. *The United States in the Twentieth Century: Empire*. London: Hodder & Stoughton, 1994.

MacKinnon, Michael G. *The Evolution of US Peacekeeping Policy Under Clinton: A Fairweather Friend?* London: Frank Cass, 2000.

Mead, Walter Russell. *Special Providence: American Foreign Policy and How It Changed the World*. New York: Alfred A. Knopf, 2001.

Miles, Alex. *US Foreign Policy and the Rogue State Doctrine*. Abingdon, Oxon: Routledge, 2013.

Morgan, Iwan W. *The Age of Deficits: Presidents and Unbalanced Budgets from Jimmy Carter to George W. Bush*. Lawrence, KS: University Press of Kansas, 2009.

Murray, Williamson, Richard Hart Sinnreich, and James Lacey (eds) *The Shaping of Grand Strategy: Policy, Diplomacy, and War*. New York: Cambridge University Press, 2011.

Nordlinger, Eric A. *Isolationism Reconfigured: American Foreign Policy for a New Century*. Princeton, NJ: Princeton University Press, 1996.

Nye, Joseph S. *The Paradox of American Power: Why the World's Only Superpower Can't Go It Alone*. Oxford: Oxford University Press, 2002.

O'Clery, Conor. *The Greening of the White House*. Dublin: Gill & Macmillan, 1997.

Oakley, Meredith L. *On the Make: The Rise of Bill Clinton*. Washington, DC: Regnery Publishing, 1994.

Owen, David. *Balkan Odyssey*. New York: Harcourt Brace, 1995.

Paine, Thomas. "Common Sense," in Nina Baym, Ronald Gottesman, Laurence B. Holland, David Kalstone, Francis Murphy, Hershel Parker, William H. Pritchard, and Patricia B. Wallace (eds), *The Norton Anthology of American Literature*, Third Edition, Volume 1. New York: W.W. Norton, 1989, 617–635.

Parmet, Herbert S. *George Bush: The Life of a Lone Star Yankee*. New York: Scribner, 1997.

Patten, Chris. *East and West: The Last Governor of Hong Kong on Power, Freedom and the Future*. London: Macmillan, 1998.

Peceny, Mark. *Democracy at the Point of Bayonets*. Pennsylvania: Pennsylvania State University Press, 1999.

Platt, Desmond C. M. *Finance, Trade and British Foreign Policy 1815–1914*. Oxford; Clarendon Press, 1968.

Pomper, Gerald (ed.) *The Election of 1992*. Chatham, NJ: Chatham House, 1993.

Powell, Colin. *My American Journey*. New York: Random House, 1995.

Prados, John. *Keepers of the Keys: A History of the National Security Council from Truman to Bush*. New York: William Morrow, 1991.

Preston, Thomas. *The President and His Inner Circle: Leadership Style and the Advisory Process in Foreign Affairs*. New York: Columbia University Press, 2001.

Reich, Robert B. *Locked In The Cabinet*. New York: Alfred A. Knopf, 1997.

Renshon, Stanley A. *High Hopes. The Clinton Presidency and the Politics of Ambition*. New York and London: Routledge Books, 1998.

Rielly, John F. (ed.) *American Public Opinion and U.S. Foreign Policy 1995*. Chicago: The Chicago Council on Foreign Relations, 1995.

Rosati, Jerel A. and James M. Scott. *The Politics of United States Foreign Policy*, Fifth Edition. Boston, MA: Wadsworth, Cengage Learning, 2011.

Rosenberg, Emily S. *Spreading the American Dream: American Economic and Cultural Expansion 1980–1945*. New York: Hill & Wang, 1982.

Rossiter, Clinton and James Lare (eds) *The Essential Lippmann: A Political Philosophy for Liberal Democracy*. New York: Vintage Books, 1965.

Rothkopf, David. *Running the World: The Inside Story of the National Security Council and the Architects of American Power*. New York: Public Affairs, 2004.

Rubin, Robert E. *In An Uncertain World: Tough Choices From Wall Street to Washington*. New York: Random House, 2003.

Rubinstein, Alvin, Albina Shayevich, and Boris Zlotnikov (eds) *The Clinton Foreign Policy Reader: Presidential Speeches With Commentary*. New York: M.E. Sharpe, 2000.

Russett, Bruce. *Grasping the Democratic Peace: Principles for a Democratic World*. Princeton, NJ: Princeton University Press, 1993.

Russett, Bruce and John O'Neil. *Triangulating Peace: Democracy, Interdependence and International Organisations*. New York: Norton, 2001.

Sale, Richard. *Clinton's Secret Wars: The Evolution of a Commander in Chief*. New York: St. Martin's Press, 2009.

Sanger, David E. *Confront and Conceal: Obama's Secret Wars and Surprising Use of American Power*. New York: Crown, 2012.

Schier, Steven (ed.) *The Post-Modern Presidency: Bill Clinton's Legacy in US Politics*. Pittsburgh, PA: University of Pittsburgh Press, 2000.

Schlesinger, Arthur M., Jr. *The Cycles of American History*. London: Andre Deutsch, 1986.

Schlesinger, Robert. *White House Ghosts: Presidents and their Speechwriters*. New York: Simon & Schuster, 2008.

Schneider, Barry R. and Jim A. Davis (eds) *Avoiding the Abyss: Progress, Shortfalls and the Way Ahead in Combating the WMD Threat*. Westport, CT: Praeger Security International, 2006.

Seitz, Raymond. *Over Here*. London: Weidenfeld & Nicolson, 1998.

Simms, Brendan. *Un-Finest Hour: Britain and the Destruction of Bosnia*. London: Penguin, 2001.

Singh, Robert. *Barack Obama's Post-American Foreign Policy: The Limits of Engagement*. London: Bloomsbury, 2012.

Smith, Curt. *George H. W. Bush: Character at the Core*. Washington, DC: Potomac Books, 2014.

Smith, Stephen A. (ed.) *Bill Clinton on Stump, State and Stage: The Rhetorical Road to the White House*. Fayetteville, AR: The University of Arkansas Press, 1994.

— *Preface to the Presidency: Selected Speeches of Bill Clinton 1974–1992*. Fayetteville, AR: University of Arkansas Press, 1996.

Smith, Tony. *America's Mission: The United States and the Worldwide Struggle for Democracy in the Twentieth Century*. Princeton, NJ: Princeton University Press, 1994.

Snider, Don M. *The National Security Strategy: Documenting Strategic Vision*, Second Edition. US Army War College, Carlisle, PA: Strategic Studies Institute, 1995.

Soderberg, Nancy. *The Superpower Myth: The Use and Misuse of American Might*. Hoboken, NJ: John Wiley & Sons, 2005.

Solomon, Gerald B. *The NATO Enlargement Debate, 1990–1997*. Westport, CT: Praeger, 1998.

Sorensen, Theodore C. *Kennedy*. New York: Konecky & Konecky, 1965.

Stephanopoulos, George. *All Too Human: A Political Education*. London: Hutchinson, 1999.

Stiglitz, Joseph E. *Roaring Nineties: Why We're Paying the Price for the Greediest Decade in History*. London: Penguin, 2003.

Talbott, Strobe. *The Russia Hand: A Memoir of Presidential Diplomacy*. New York: Random House, 2002.

Tsongas, Paul. *A Call to Economic Arms*. Boston, MA: Foley, Hoag, & Eliot, 1991.

Turque, Bill. *Inventing Al Gore: A Biography*. Boston, MA and New York: Houghton Mifflin Books, 2000.

Tzu, Sun. *The Art of War*, Translated by Samuel B. Griffith. New York: Oxford University Press, 1971.

Viallate, Achille. *Economic Imperialism and International Relations During the Last Fifty Years*. New York: Macmillan, 1923.

Waldman, Michael. *POTUS Speaks: Finding The Words That Defined The Clinton Presidency*. New York: Simon & Schuster, 2000.

Walker, Martin. *The Cold War and the Making of the Modern World*. London: Forth Estate, 1993.

— *Clinton: The President They Deserve*. London: Forth Estate, 1996.

Warber, Adam L. *Executive Orders and the Modern Presidency: Legislation from the Oval Office*. Boulder, CO: Lynne Reinner Publishers, Inc., 2006.

Wesson, Robert G. *Foreign Policy for a New Age*. Boston, MA: Houghton Mifflin Company, 1977.

White, Mark (ed.) *The Presidency of Bill Clinton: The Legacy of a New Domestic and Foreign Policy*. London and New York: I.B. Taurus, 2012.

Wood, Dan B. *The Politics of Economic Leadership: The Causes and Consequences of Presidential Rhetoric*. Princeton, NJ: Princeton University Press, 2007.

Woodward, Bob. *The Commanders*. New York: Simon & Schuster, 1991.

— *The Agenda: Inside the Clinton White House*. New York: Simon & Schuster, 1994.

— *Maestro*. New York: Simon & Schuster, 2000.

News magazines and journal articles

Albright, Madeleine. "Enlarging NATO: Why Bigger Is Better," *The Economist* (February 15, 1997), 23.

— "United Nations," *Foreign Policy* 138 (September–October 2003), 16–18, 20, 22, 24.

Allison, Graham T. Jr and Robert P. Beschel, Jr "Can the United States Promote Democracy?" *Political Science Quarterly* 107, 1 (Spring 1992), 81–98.

Anderson, Bruce. "An Admiral at the Court of St. James's," *Stanford Magazine* (July/August 1997), 7.

Anderson, Jim. "The Tarnoff Affair," *American Journalism Review* 16 (March 1994), 40–44.

Barnes, Fred. "Neoconned," *New Republic* (January 25, 1993), 14–15.

Berger, Samuel. "A Foreign Policy for the Global Age," *Foreign Affairs* 79, 6 (November–December 2000), 22–39.

Bergsten, Fred C. "Globalizing Free Trade," *Foreign Affairs* 75, 3 (May–June 1996), 105–120.

Boren, David L. "The Intelligence Community: How Crucial?" *Foreign Affairs* 71, 3 (Summer 1992), 52–62.

Boys, James D. "What's So Extraordinary About Rendition?" *The International Journal of Human Rights* 15, 4 (May 2011), 589–604.

— "A Lost Opportunity: The Flawed Implementation of Assertive Multilateralism (1991–1993)," *European Journal of American Studies* 7, 1 (December 2012), 2–14.

— "Exploiting Inherited Wars of Choice: Obama's Use of Nixonian Methods to Secure the Presidency," *American Politics Research* 42, 5 (September 2014), 815–840.

Bridgeman, Martha. "The US–South Africa Binational Commission," *South African Journal of International Affairs* 8, 1 (2001), 89–95.

Brinkley, Douglas. "Democratic Enlargement: The Clinton Doctrine," *Foreign Policy* 106 (Spring 1997), 111–127.

Brzezinski, Zbigniew, Brent Scowcroft, and Richard Murphy. "Differentiated Containment," *Foreign Affairs* 76, 3 (May–June 1997), 20–30.

"Calling Dr. Kissinger." *The Economist* (January 14, 1995), 23.

Carothers, Thomas. "The NED at Ten," *Foreign Policy* 95 (Summer 1994), 123–138.

— "Democracy Promotion Under Clinton," *The Washington Quarterly* 18, 4 (Autumn 1995), 13–28.

— "The Backlash against Democracy Promotion," *Foreign Affairs* 85, 2 (March/April 2006), 56–68.

Christopher, Warren. "America's Leadership, America's Opportunity," *Foreign Policy* 98 (Spring 1995), 6–27.

Church, George J. and Dan Goodgame. "His Seven Most Urgent Decisions," *Time* 141, 4 (January 25, 1993), 30–33.

Clarke, Jonathan. "The Conceptual Poverty of US Foreign Policy," *The Atlantic Monthly* 272, 3 (September 1993), 54–66.

— "Rhetoric Before Reality: Loose Lips Sink Ships," *Foreign Affairs* 74, 5 (September–October 1995), 2–7.

Clarke, Walter and Jeffrey Herbst. "Somalia and the Future of Humanitarian Intervention," *Foreign Affairs* 75, 2 (March–April 1996), 70–85.

De La Billiere, General Sir Peter. "Choosing Our Next Target," *Newsweek* 121, 4 (January 25, 1993), 46.

Danner, Mark. "Marooned in the Cold War: America, the Alliance, and the Quest for a Vanished World," *World Policy Journal* 14, 3 (Fall 1997), 1–23.

Dumbrell, John. "Lessons from Russia: Clinton and US Democracy Promotion," *The Slavonic and East European Review* 86, 1 (January 2008), 185–186.

Gaddis, John Lewis. "Foreign Policy by Autopilot," *Hoover Digest* no. 3 (July 30, 2000).

— "Where Do We Go From Here?" *Hoover Digest* no. 4 (October 30, 2000).

— "A Grand Strategy of Transformation," *Foreign Policy* 133 (November–December 2002), 50–57.

Garten, Jeffrey E. "Clinton's Emerging Trade Policy: Act One, Scene One," *Foreign Affairs* 72, 3 (Summer 1993), 182–189.

— "Is America Abandoning Multilateral Trade?" *Foreign Affairs* 74, 6 (November–December 1995), 50–62.

— "The Big Emerging Markets," *Columbia Journal of World Business* 31, 2 (Summer 1996), 6–31.

Gause, F. Gregory III. "The Illogic of Dual Containment," *Foreign Affairs* 73, 2 (March–April 1994), 56–66.

Gelb, Leslie H. "Quelling the Teacup Wars: The New World's Constant Challenge," *Foreign Affairs* 73, 6 (November–December 1994), 2–6.

Goldgeiger, James M. and Michael MacFaul. "A Tale of Two Worlds: Core and Periphery in the Post-Cold War Era," *International Organizations* 46, 2 (Spring 1992), 467–491.

Goodgame, Dan and Michael Duffy. "Clinton On His Foreign Policy Gains: Blending Force With Diplomacy," *Time* 144, 18 (October 31, 1994), 35–37.

Goodman, Melvin A. "Ending the CIA's Cold War Legacy," *Foreign Policy* 106 (Spring 1997), 128–143.

Grady, Henry F. "The New Trade Policy of the United States," *Foreign Affairs* 14, 2 (January 1936), 283–296.

Greenwald, John and James Carney. "Don't Panic: Here Comes Bailout Bill," *Time* 145, 6, (February 13, 1995), 34–37.

Haass, Richard N. "Paradigm Lost," *Foreign Affairs* 74, 1 (January–February 1995), 43–58.

— "Fatal Distraction: Bill Clinton's Foreign Policy," *Foreign Policy* 108 (Autumn 1997), 112–123.

— "The Squandered Presidency: Demanding More from the Commander in Chief," *Foreign Affairs* 79, 3 (May–June 2000), 136–140.

Halperin, Morton. "Guaranteeing Democracy," *Foreign Policy* 91 (Summer 1993), 105–122.

Hames, Tim. "Foreign Policy and the American Elections of 1992," *International Relations* 11 (April 1993), 3315–3330.

Hamilton, Lee. "A Democrat Looks at Foreign Policy," *Foreign Affairs* 71, 3 (Summer 1992), 32–51.

Heilbrunn, Jacob. "Lake Inferior: The Pedigree of Anthony Lake," *New Republic* 27 (September 1993), 29–35.

Hendrickson, David C. "The Recovery of Internationalism," *Foreign Affairs* 73, 5 (September–October 1994), 26–43.

— "The Lion and the Lamb: Realism and Liberalism Reconsidered," *World Policy Journal* 20, 1 (Spring 2003), 93–102.

Hoffman, Stanley. "A New World and Its Troubles," *Foreign Affairs* 69, 4 (Fall 1990), 115–122.

Holbrooke, Richard. "America, A European Power," *Foreign Affairs* 74, 2 (March–April 1995), 38–51.

Hyland, William G. "A Mediocre Record," *Foreign Policy* 101 (Winter 1995–1996), 69–74.

Ikenberry, G. John. "American Grand Strategy in the Age of Terror," *Survival* 43, 4 (Winter 2001–2002), 19–34.

Indyk, Martin. Interview, *Al-Qabas* (January 31, 1999).

Kagan, Robert. "The Clinton Legacy Aboard: His Sins of Omission in Foreign and Defence Policy," *Weekly Standard* (January 15, 2001).

Kaplan, Lawrence J. "Dollar Diplomacy Returns," *Commentary* 105, 2 (February 1998), 52–54.

Kern, Heinz A. J. "The Clinton Doctrine: A New Foreign Policy," *Christian Science Monitor* (June 18, 1993).

Kirschten, Dick. "Martyr or Misfit?" *National Journal* (October 29, 1994).

Kissinger, Henry. "Clinton and the World," *Newsweek* 121, 5, 1 (February 1993), 45–47.

Klein, Joe. "Hoping for Passion," *Newsweek* (February 1, 1993).

— "A High Risk Presidency," *Newsweek* (May 3, 1993), 32–34.

Kramer, Michael. "Moving In," *Time* 141, 1 (January 4, 1993), 28–32.

— "The Cost of Removing Saddam," *Time* 144, 17 (October 24, 1994), 39.

Krasner, Stephen D. "An Orienting Principle for Foreign Policy," *Policy Review* no. 163 (October 2010), 3–12.

Lake, Anthony. "Confronting Backlash States," *Foreign Affairs* 73, 2 (March–April 1994), 45–55.

Layne, Christopher. "Kant or Cant: Myths of the Democratic Peace," *International Security* 19, 2 (Fall 1994), 5–49.

Mandelbaum, Michael. "The Bush Foreign Policy," *Foreign Affairs* 70, 1 (1990–1991), 5–22.

— "Foreign Policy As Social Work," *Foreign Affairs* 75, 1 (January–February 1996), 16–32.

McAllister, J. F. O. and William Mader. "Secretary Of Shhhhh!" *Time* 141, 23 (June 7, 1993), 32–34.

McAllister, J. F. O. and James L. Graff. "When to Go, When to Stay," *Time* 142, 14 (October 4, 1993), 40–42.

McDougall, Walter. "Can the United States Do Grand Strategy?" *Orbis* 54, 2 (Spring 2010), 165–184.

Mead, Walter Russell. "An American Grand Strategy: The Quest for Order in a Disordered World," *World Policy Journal* 10, 1 (Spring 1993), 9–37.

Miller, Linda B. "The Clinton Years: Reinventing Foreign Policy," *International Affairs* 70, 4 (October 1994), 621–634.

Moran, Theodore H. "International Economics and National Security," *Foreign Affairs* 69, 5 (Winter 1990/1991), 74–90.

Morrow, Lance. "Man of the Year: The Torch is Passed," *Time* 141, 1 (January 4, 1993), 20–26.

Muller, Henry and John F. Stacks. "First, We Have to Roll Up Our Sleeves," *Time* 141, 1 (January 4, 1993), 34–38.

Muravchik, Joshua. "Carrying a Small Stick," *National Review* (September 2, 1996), 57–62.

Nye, Joseph S., Jr. "Peering into the Future," *Foreign Affairs* 73, 4 (July–August 1994), 82–93.

O'Grady, Joseph. "An Irish Policy Born in the USA: Clinton's Break With The Past," *Foreign Affairs* 75, 3 (May–June 1996), 2–7.

Olsen, Gorm Rye. "Europe and the Promotion of Democracy in Post-Cold War Africa: How Serious is Europe and for What Reason?" *African Affairs* 97, 388 (July 1998), 343–367.

Omestad, Thomas. "Foreign Policy and Campaign '96," *Foreign Policy* 105 (Winter 1996–1997), 36–54.

Oren, Ido. "The Subjectivity of the 'Democratic Peace': Changing US Perceptions of Imperial Germany," *International Security* 20, 2 (Fall 1995), 147–184.

Ornstein, Norman J. "Foreign Policy and the 1992 Election," *Foreign Affairs* 71, 3 (Summer 1992), 1–16.

Pederson, Daniel. "The World Crowds In: An Interview with Douglas Hurd," *Newsweek,* 25 (January 1993), 48.

Posen, Barry R. and Andrew L. Ross. "Competing Visions for US Grand Strategy," *International Security* 21, 3 (Winter 1996/1997), 5–53.

Remnick, David. "A Very Big Delusion," *New Yorker* (November 2, 1992), 4.

"Requiem for a Policy," *National Review* (June 7, 1993).

Rice, Condoleezza. "Promoting the National Interest, *Foreign Affairs* 79, 1 (January–February 2000), 45–62.

Rivera, David W. and Sharon Werning Rivera, "Yeltsin, Putin, and Clinton: Presidential Leadership and Russian Democratization in Comparative Perspective," *Perspectives on Politics* 7, 3 (September 2009), 591–610.

Solomon, Burt. "Vulnerable to Events," *National Journal* (January 6, 1990).

Special Report: Policymaking For A New Era, *Foreign Affairs* 71, 5 (Winter 1992), 175–189.

Spiro, David. "The Insignificance of the Liberal Peace," *International Security* 19, 2 (Fall 1994), 50–86.

Talbott, Strobe. "Why NATO Should Grow," *New York Review of Books* 42, 13 (August 10, 1995), 27–30.

— "Democracy and the National Interest," *Foreign Affairs* 75, 6 (November–December 1996), 47–63.

Thompson, Scott and Edward Spannaus. "Is the 'Tarnoff Doctrine' Now US Strategic Policy?" *Executive Intelligence Review* 20, 23 (June 11, 1993), 50–51.

Tucker, Robert W. "The Triumph of Wilsonianism," *World Policy Journal* 10, 4 (Winter 1993–1994), 83–99.

Ullman, Richard H. "A Late Recovery," *Foreign Policy* 101 (Winter 1995–1996), 75–79.

Walt, Stephen. "Two Cheers for Clinton's Foreign Policy," *Foreign Affairs* 79, 2 (March–April 2000), 63–79.

Watson, Russell with John Barry and Douglas Waller. "A New Kind of Containment," *Newsweek* (July 12, 1993), 30.

"What Foreign Policy?" *New Republic* (September 20, 1991).

Wildavsky, Ben. "Under the Gun," *National Journal* 26 (1996).

Wolfowitz, Paul D. "Clinton's First Year," *Foreign Affairs* 73, 1 (January–February 1994), 28–43.

Zakaria, Fareed. "The Rise of Illiberal Democracy," *Foreign Affairs* 76, 6 (November/December 1997), 22–43.

Zegart, Amy. "A Foreign Policy for the Future," *Defining Ideas*. Stanford, CA: The Hoover Institute (November 20, 2013).

INDEX

Page numbers in *italic* refer to notes.